Civil Rights Rhetoric
and the American Presidency

Number Twelve
Presidential Rhetoric Series

Martin J. Medhurst, General Editor

Civil Rights Rhetoric
and the American Presidency

Edited by

James Arnt Aune and Enrique D. Rigsby

TEXAS A&M UNIVERSITY PRESS
COLLEGE STATION

The paper used in this book
meets the minimum requirements
of the American National Standard for Permanence
of Paper for Printed Library Materials, Z39.48-1984.
Binding materials have been chosen for durability.

Library of Congress Cataloging-in-Publication Data

Civil rights rhetoric and the American presidency / edited by James Arnt
Aune and Enrique D. Rigsby— 1st ed.
    p. cm. — (Presidential rhetoric series ; no. 12)
 Includes bibliographical references and index.
 ISBN 1-58544-440-5 (cloth : alk. paper)
 1. Presidents—United States—Racial attitudes. 2. African
Americans—Civil rights—History. 3. Civil rights—Government
policy—United States—History. 4. Rhetoric—Political aspects—United
States—History. 5. Presidents—United States—Biography—Miscellanea.
I. Aune, James Arnt. II. Rigsby, Enrique D. III. Series.
 E176.1.C57 2005
 323.1196′073′009--dc22
                        2005004681

To Nick, Daniel, Jeremiah, Andrew, Zachary, and Joshua

May you know a world of true equality for all

Contents

Acknowledgements   ix

Introduction   3
Rhetorical Constitutions and Reconstitutions
of the Meaning of Civil Rights
James Arnt Aune and Enrique D. Rigsby

CHAPTER 1   16
The Politics of Place and Presidential Rhetoric
in the United States, 1875–1901
Kirt H. Wilson

CHAPTER 2   41
Calvin Coolidge and the Rhetoric of "Race" in
the 1920s
Marouf Hasian Jr.

CHAPTER 3   62
"We Go Ahead Together or We Go Down Together":
The Civil Rights Rhetoric of Eleanor Roosevelt
Diane M. Blair

CHAPTER 4   83
Inaugurating the Second Reconstruction: President
Truman's Committee on Civil Rights
Steven R. Goldzwig

CHAPTER 5   114
JFK and Civil Rights: Sooner or Later
E. Culpepper Clark

CHAPTER 6   134
    Calling Washington Collect: Robert Parris Moses and
    the Kennedy Administration
    Richard J. Jensen and John C. Hammerback

CHAPTER 7   155
    The Genesis of a Rhetorical Commitment: Lyndon B.
    Johnson, Civil Rights, and the Vice Presidency
    Garth Pauley

CHAPTER 8   198
    Reagan on Civil Rights: Returning to Strict Construction
    of the Constitution
    Craig R. Smith

CHAPTER 9   231
    George Bush and the Transformation of Civil Rights
    Discourse, 1965–1990
    David Zarefsky

CHAPTER 10   268
    Celebritized Justice, Civil Rights, and the Clarence
    Thomas Nomination
    Trevor Parry-Giles

CHAPTER 11   301
    The Promise and Failure of President Clinton's Race
    Initiative of 1997–1998: A Rhetorical Perspective
    Martín Carcasson and Mitchell Rice

Index   339

Acknowledgments

The chapters appearing in this volume were first presented at the sixth annual conference on presidential rhetoric, called "The White House and Civil Rights Policy," which was held at the Presidential Conference Center on March 2–5, 2000, at Texas A&M University, College Station, Texas. These conferences are sponsored by the Program in Presidential Rhetoric, a research unit of the Center for Presidential Studies in the George Bush School of Government and Public Service.

The editors wish to acknowledge the assistance of the Center for Presidential Studies and its former director, George C. Edwards III; the Department of Speech Communication under the leadership of Richard L. Street Jr.; the College of Liberal Arts and its former dean Woodrow Jones; and the Office of the Vice President for Research and Associate Provost for Graduate Studies. They also wish to recognize the support of Linda Giesen and Herman Giesen of Dallas, Texas, and Emil Ogden and Clementine Ogden of College Station, Texas.

A very special thanks is extended to the members of the Program in Presidential Rhetoric who, under the leadership of Martin J. Medhurst, coordinated this conference: Vanessa B. Beasley, Leroy G. Dorsey, Tarla R. Peterson, and Kurt Ritter. We also offer thanks to our graduate and undergraduate students who served in a number of key roles and helped to facilitate the successful administration of the conference. We especially wish to thank Rachel Martin, our graduate student and conference intern, for assisting Martin Medhurst. The committee members are indebted to the many scholars who chaired panels or served as paper respondents. Their contributions added greatly to the intellectual conversations. Gillian Teubner and Paul Stob helped the editors prepare the final manuscript for publication. Mary Lenn Dixon and the staff of Texas A&M University Press have been a model of professional competence and enthusiastic supporters of the Program in Presidential Rhetoric.

Finally, we wish to acknowledge the contributing scholars who make this volume possible. Their presentations resulted in a delightfully engaging conference marked by excitement and spirited discussion. Their scholarship contributes greatly to furthering our understanding of the rhetorical dimensions of presidential discourse.

*Civil Rights Rhetoric
and the American Presidency*

INTRODUCTION

Rhetorical Constitutions and Reconstitutions of the Meaning of Civil Rights

James Arnt Aune and Enrique D. Rigsby

In *When Words Lose Their Meanings: Constitutions and Reconstitutions of Language, Character, and Community,* James Boyd White's ground-breaking book, the author contends that our public language is constantly changing—it is "perpetually remade by its speakers, who are themselves remade, both as individuals and communities, in what they say." He defines the subject of rhetoric as "the study of the ways in which character and community—and motive, value, reason, social structure, everything, in short, that makes a culture—are defined and made real in performances of language."[1]

The present volume examines the way in which American presidents and their administrations have constituted and reconstituted the meaning of civil rights from Rutherford B. Hayes to William Jefferson Clinton. As White reminds us, if the end of art is beauty and if the end of philosophy is truth, then the end of rhetoric is *justice.*[2] Perhaps more than in any other policy arena, presidential discourse on civil rights and justice toward African Americans illustrates both the highest level of eloquence and the lowest level of rhetorical self-deception possible in a representative democracy.

All of the chapters in this volume are written by scholars of rhetoric and public affairs. Despite some differences in focus and method, all of them share the assumption that presidential rhetorical performances *matter*. Presidents and their audiences are not merely passive "subject positions" of an all-constraining ideology, and their communicative acts are not simply an outer shell covering the "real" processes of politics (whether the real is defined in terms of economic forces, partisan bargaining, or utility-maximizing "rational actors").

Fortunately, recent work in political science and history has cleared the way for a richer understanding of presidential rhetoric, leaving the rhetorical scholar less defensive than in earlier times. Jeffrey Tulis, for example, has defined the twentieth-century "rhetorical presidency" as a fundamental departure from the intent of the framers of the Constitution, who endeavored to prevent demagoguery and preserve republican government through the separation of powers. Nineteenth-century presidential rhetoric reflects this conception in two ways. The president was to communicate with Congress about questions of policy, while rhetoric directed primarily to the people, as in inaugural addresses and proclamations, was to emphasize general constitutional principles and avoid specific policy proposals.[3]

Although Tulis is highly critical of the rhetorical presidency, the chapters in this volume illustrate what might be the rhetorical presidency's finest hour, when Eleanor Roosevelt (as surrogate for FDR), Harry Truman, John F. Kennedy, Lyndon Johnson, and Bill Clinton addressed the American people directly on civil rights, perhaps the fundamental (and unresolved) constitutional question in the American polity. Although Tulis is highly critical of and incessantly persistent about his claim that the rhetorical presidency is a twentieth-century phenomenon, there is growing evidence to the contrary. Melvin C. Laracey, for example, contends that Tulis is incorrect and notes that presidents prior to the twentieth century were rhetorical in public appearances—an act Laracey refers to as "going public."[4] Laracey argues that the work of both Tulis and Samuel Kernell is flawed due to a Federalist perception of the presidency that constructs a constitutional conception of the office disallowing any deviation from outdated Federalist mandates—such as going public.[5] In an effort to expose the flaws constructed by both Tulis and Kernell, Laracey reminds the reader that going public is neither a departure from constitutional order nor a political tool devised solely for twentieth-century politics. Laracey insists that presidents have been appealing directly to constituents—thus functioning rhetorically—from the beginning of our democracy: "In sum, going public is a more complex, less constitutionally suspect practice than it has been given credit for by many scholars. Contrary to many of those pronouncements, going public has been a legitimate potential tool for presidents since essentially the beginning of our constitutional republic. Like the use of other presidential tools such as the veto, its use has waxed and waned depending on strategic circumstances and the proclivities of individual presidents. That presidents have employed this tool off and on for most of our history means that, while we have unquestionably become more democratized, whether we are any less constitutional depends, in the final analysis, on [the person] with whom you are talking."[6] Despite criticisms aimed at what constitutes a rhetorical presidency, the chapters in the present volume illustrate what might be the rhetorical presidency's finest hour.

Other historians and political scientists continue to debate the relative importance of presidential action on civil rights. Russell Riley, for example, contends that presidents have not been primarily leaders in civil rights policies but have been more concerned with what he calls "nation-keeping."[7] In contrast, Steven Shull places the presidency at the center of the civil rights policy arena, as demonstrated through case studies of school desegregation, equal employment, and fair housing.[8]

Perhaps the most enduring insight of political-communication researchers of the presidency and civil rights is the concept of agenda setting. Jeffrey E. Cohen, for example, did a content analysis of presidential State of the Union addresses from 1953 to 1989. He found that, although civil rights sentences never account for more than 20 percent of any address, in 1968, 1976, and 1989, civil rights discourse was a significant portion of the president's agenda. In 1959, 1977, 1980, and 1981, civil rights did not appear at all. He then compared the agenda percentages with the percentage of Gallup Poll respondents immediately before the address who cited civil rights as "the most important problem." He concludes that deteriorating economic or international conditions tend to reduce the likelihood that presidents will respond to civil rights concerns. However, "the more emphasis the president gives to civil rights, the more important that policy area becomes to the public."[9]

Agenda setting, the rhetorical presidency, and the constraints of electoral politics are all important dimensions of the presidency and civil rights. However, the focus of the chapters in this volume is less on a general theory of the presidency and civil rights and more on an understanding of the unique rhetorical performances of American presidents as they constitute and reconstitute the nature of the American community.

The first two chapters examine the intersection between rhetorical practices and "ideology," in the Marxian sense of a collective system of beliefs and values that simultaneously tries to resolve certain deeply felt social problems and exhibits severe cognitive distortions. For both Kirt H. Wilson and Marouf Hasian Jr., the role of the rhetorical critic lies not only in unmasking the contradictions inherent in ideology but also in using rhetorical concepts to identify the specific argumentative and figurative mechanisms by which an ideology does its work.

Kirt H. Wilson tells the depressing tale of how presidents Hayes, Garfield, Arthur, Cleveland, Harrison, and McKinley abandoned the promise of civil rights. The rhetorical and ideological mechanism by which the Southern "Redeemers" reestablished the racial caste system is what Wilson calls the "politics of place." In the mythology of an "organic" slave society, "place" was a central condensation symbol. Everyone via their race, social position, and geographic location had a distinct place in the social and, indeed, natural hierarchy. The symbol of place did important ideological work for the Redeemers because it demonstrated how Americans could retain the notion of "equality" while preserving a caste system. Everyone has equal rights, but those rights are determined by the needs of their place. Whites have those rights needed to lead society, while African Americans have those rights needed to form a prosperous laboring population. President Hayes's rhetoric reflects this ideological transformation, as does the silence of his successors while black civil rights were dismantled by the courts, Congress, and the state legislatures. As Wilson demonstrates, the rhetoric of Booker T. Washington was the culmination of the politics of place, as President McKinley traveled to Tuskegee in 1898 to anoint him as "one of the great leaders of his race."

Marouf Hasian Jr. examines the presidential rhetoric of Calvin Coolidge on race and immigration as a complex interaction of eugenic ideology, foreign-policy concerns, and domestic racism. He juxtaposes the debate over the 1924 Immigration Act with Coolidge's civil rights rhetoric to illustrate how essentialist notions of race and ethnicity, supported by the "scientific" theory of eugenics, worked as a problem-solving device for avoiding the problems of the "Old World," as manifested in the tragedy of World War I.

Chapters three and four, by Diane Blair and Steven Goldzwig respectively, illustrate how creative rhetorical invention can lay the foundation for a positive reconstitution of the American community. Blair gives us what amounts to a rhetorical biography of Eleanor Roosevelt, demonstrating how her "performance" of the role of first lady enabled her to articulate what Blair calls her "four equalities": equality before the law, equality of education, equality to hold a job appropriate to one's ability, and equality of participation through the political ballot. These four equalities prefigured and then echoed FDR's more famous "four freedoms." ER's focus on equality enabled her to speak out on the issue of race discrimination without appearing dangerously radical. Her strategy also represented a new, international dimension of civil rights argument: what we might call "the whole world is watching" topos, which later became very important during the Cold War.[10]

Steven Goldzwig draws our attention to President Truman's appointment of the President's Committee on Civil Rights (PCCR), perhaps the most significant presidential action on civil rights since Reconstruction. Through a careful analysis of archival materials, Goldzwig makes a persuasive case not only for Truman's "good intentions" with regard to civil rights, but also for his design of the commission as an effective model for federal action. The PCCR "opened up a national dialogue on race that set a social, legal, and moral agenda for the next 50 years." Goldzwig provides a cogent alternative account of other historical assessments of Truman that emphasize either his partisan goals in the 1948 election or the larger imperatives of the Cold War, reminding the often-cynical academic reader that not only do public figures occasionally act on their ideals but also that such action may indeed work.

Chapters five, six, and seven examine the much-debated, civil rights legacy of John F. Kennedy's administration. The first, by E. Culpepper Clark, examines the question from "the top down," making a compelling argument that JFK, in however flawed a way, did in fact move the nation further on the issue of civil rights than any other imaginable figure could have. Clark creatively integrates his archival work as a historian with his own memories as a white Southerner during the civil rights movement, reminding us of the central place both JFK and Martin Luther King Jr. have in the political iconography of ordinary Americans committed to racial equality. His essay originally was the keynote address at the 2000 Texas A&M University Presidential Rhetoric Conference, on which this book is based.

Richard Jensen and John C. Hammerback paint a slightly different portrait of Kennedy by juxtaposing his public rhetoric with his interaction with Robert Moses, a voting-rights activist in Mississippi who became progressively disillusioned with the high "eloquence" of King and Kennedy as he faced racist violence. Kennedy was constrained by his belief that the executive needed to work in harmony with Congress, while Moses insisted on concrete results at the local level. Jensen and Hammerback develop their highly useful notion of the contrasting rhetorics of mobilizing and organizing to assess the relative success of both Moses and Kennedy.

In his chapter on the Kennedy administration, Garth Pauley examines a now little-known but exceptionally eloquent speech given by Vice Pres. Lyndon Johnson at Gettysburg, Pennsylvania, on May 30, 1963. The speech reflects both Johnson's own commitment to civil rights and the Kennedy administration's efforts to cultivate support for Kennedy's civil rights bill. Pauley not only examines the role of the speech in reflecting and shaping Johnson's own civil rights policies later on but also uses the case study to examine perhaps the least understood aspect of executive-branch rhetoric: the limitations and possibilities of vice-presidential speech making.

Once the Civil Rights Act of 1964 and the Voting Rights Act of 1965 were passed, the nature of civil rights rhetoric and policy inevitably required a "reconstitution," in James Boyd White's terms. Before Martin Luther King Jr.'s martyrdom in Memphis in April, 1968, he had begun an uneasy, only partially successful, reconstitution of civil rights rhetoric by focusing more and more on economic inequality. Conservatives increasingly made their peace with new civil rights legislation and, by the 1980s, even began depicting King as an ally in their fight for conserving the Western and American cultural heritage. Crime, however, ever coded in the American imagination in racial terms, and affirmative action remained—and remain to this day—cultural sites of ideological struggle over the nature and limits of racial equality.

Chapters eight, nine, and ten in the volume examine efforts by conservative presidents to reconstitute the American civil rights legacy in their own terms. Ronald Reagan's attempts to control an "activist" judiciary, the Bush administration's fight over "quotas" in the Civil Rights Act of 1990, and Bush's appointment of Clarence Thomas to the Supreme Court in 1991 represent—depending on one's point of view—either an effort to reemphasize individual liberty and initiative against the egalitarian social engineering of the 1960s or an attempt to construct a new partisan majority by appealing to the racial anxieties of blue-collar whites. Key to all three cases is the fact, as David Zarefsky puts it, that the rhetorical force of the god term "civil rights" had been blunted by the devil term "quotas."

Craig R. Smith's chapter examines the Reagan administration's civil rights policy through a constitutional lens. He begins by making a persuasive case for Reagan's own personal commitment to racial equality. He then examines the fight over the reconstitution of the Civil Rights Commission, the initiatives of William Bradford Reynolds in reforming affirmative-action policy, the influence of Edwin Meese and the rise of a new conservative "brains trust" in Washington, and the controversy over the *Grove City* Supreme Court case. In the long run, Smith argues, the Reagan administration successfully raised philosophical questions about original intent, states' rights, and sovereign immunity that most people believed had been laid to rest in the 1960s. Reagan's true civil rights legacy is the conservative Supreme Court majority, which continues to this day.

David Zarefsky examines George H. W. Bush's major statements on civil rights and affirmative action, especially his veto of the 1990 Civil Rights Act as a "quota" bill. Zarefsky deftly illustrates a set of rhetorical dissociations in the meanings of "affirmative action," "quotas," and "civil rights" that gave Bush room to maneuver in eventually signing a 1991 bill essentially similar to that of 1990. Unfortunately, as Zarefsky carefully proves, President Bush failed to advance the national debate on affirmative action because he never really defined "quotas" or specified what was objectionable about the 1990 bill.

In his chapter, Trevor Parry-Giles turns our attention again to perhaps the single most-studied event of the Bush presidency: the nomination of Clarence Thomas to the Supreme Court. Parry-Giles contends that the entire Thomas controversy needs to be understood in light of the Bush administration's effort to "celebritize" Clarence

Thomas as a way of circumventing rational deliberation over his legal philosophy and personal character. Paradoxically, the confrontation between Thomas and the Judiciary Committee over Anita Hill's charges only expanded the highly affective, nondeliberative aspects of the nomination process. The celebritization of Clarence Thomas, Parry-Giles concludes, is but part of a larger and disturbing trend away from rational deliberation in American political culture.

In the final chapter of the volume, Martín Carcasson and Mitchell Rice examine President Clinton's 1997–1998 race initiative. They consider a large sample of presidential remarks connected to the initiative and argue that it failed for a number of internal reasons (as opposed to the external constraint of the Lewinsky scandal), particularly Clinton's assumption that avoiding difficult issues would somehow decrease their salience and his inadequate justification of his continued support for affirmative action. He had some limited success with his promotion of "promising practices" at the local level, but perhaps his greatest legacy will simply be the reintroduction of race into the national conversation at a time when no racial "crisis" was evident. As Carcasson and Rice conclude—an observation that could apply to all of the case studies in this volume—"one positive aspect of Clinton's efforts may be that his failures will be taken into account and perhaps even avoided by the next major effort at understanding and improving racial equality in America."

Civil rights has been and continues to be a pervasive theme in American political culture. Arguably, the fifties and sixties alone represent two of the most important decades in U.S. history.[11] Any effort to capture its protean dimensions of civil rights in a single volume is bound to include major omissions and blind spots. Perhaps the most obvious one, from a glance at the table of contents, is the lack of a chapter on Richard Nixon. Nixon's legacy (to steal an image from Oliver Wendell Holmes Jr.) is a "brooding omnipresence" hanging over the American presidency. Hugh Davis Graham has done more than any other scholar to assess the meaning of Nixon's legacy for civil rights.[12] Nixon, Graham writes, remains an enigmatic figure. Reflecting his 1968 campaign's "Southern strategy," Nixon attempted to slow down school desegregation and nominate Southern conservatives to judgeships, although with limited success. He has probably, as Joan Hoff argues, been given insufficient credit for advances in political rights for women and minorities.[13] However, despite efforts to depict him as a Tory radical (beginning with Daniel Patrick Moynihan's hopes for the Family Assistance Plan—an episode that cries out for more careful historical and rhetorical analysis), Nixon was largely uninterested in domestic politics and used issues such as affirmative action and welfare reform to attempt to play on political divisions within the dominant coalition.[14] Nixon promoted the Labor Department's plan for minority hiring in federal contracts, as well as affirmative action generally, in the hopes that it would "drive a wedge between two traditional Democratic constituencies, organized labor and black civil rights groups."[15] Graham's conclusion seems persuasive: "A supreme irony of Nixon's long and convoluted career was his ability, playing the risky, high-stakes game of political preemption, to win reelection for himself, and arguably national realignment under a Republican majority, by opposing the consequences of his own handiwork (affirmative action)."[16]

In addition to further study of Nixon and other presidents, there are additional broad questions implicit in this volume for further research by rhetorical scholars interested in civil rights and the presidency:

1. What is the nature of the interaction between the judicial constitutional rhetoric of the Supreme Court and other appellate courts and the executive branch? What are the relative weights that may be assigned to the influence of legal, presidential, legislative, and social-movement rhetoric in civil rights successes from 1948 to 1970?

2. What role has civil rights played in the continuing dynamic identified by Jeffrey Tulis and others as the shift to a rhetorical presidency? On a related, but little-studied, issue, how has the legacy of segregation and the civil rights movement contributed to the meaning of federalism in the United States? Critical legal-studies theorist Mark Tushnet, for example, argues that a paradoxical effect of the civil rights movement has been a disempowering of local communities. Since only strong Washington, D.C.–based law and policy could overcome the legacy of Jim Crow, liberals became perhaps overly enamored of the Supreme Court and the presidency as agents of social change, thus damaging the positive benefits that states' rights in a federal system have on political participation.[17]

3. In the long run, how has presidential civil rights rhetoric helped constitute and reconstitute the American community, in James Boyd White's terms? Is that community based on the general "American creed" of equal opportunity formulated by Gunnar Myrdal in *An American Dilemma*? What have been the strengths and weaknesses of the heavy dependence of the civil rights movement (and its presidential supporters) on an essentially Christian religious rhetoric? Does that dependence, as Adolph Reed Jr. has persuasively argued, handicap public deliberation in the long run because of the inherently authoritarian nature of religious appeals?[18] Is it time for liberals and progressives to abandon a race-based public language for a more class-based one, as figures as diverse as William Julius Wilson, Adolph Reed, and Cornel West have argued?

4. And what of presidential appeals to what, following Philip Wander, we might call the "third persona" of civil rights rhetoric—the "middle American," the "silent majority," the "blue-collar white ethnic," and the "angry white male," to name but a few of that persona's incarnations since 1968? What sort of creative rhetorical strategies might overcome the alienation—real or imagined—of these citizens?

Anyone who studies civil rights in American politics hopes for a point at which the topic will seem as quaint as the debate over the National Bank or the free coinage of silver. We are reminded of the story of the two Jewish men who are conversing about their children. One man says that, after much searching, his son finally found a job as a watchman at the city gates, assigned to announce when the Messiah comes. The other man says, "Well, at least it's steady work."[19]

Despite signs of hope during the 1990s—the continuing growth of the black middle class, the decline in the crime rate, the defusing of welfare as a partisan issue by the 1996 reforms, and, perhaps, President Clinton's National Conversation on Race—the year 2001 revealed an electorate as much divided by race as before. African American support for the Democrats was decisive in the popular vote, and allegations of race-based voting irregularities continue to dog the legitimacy of the George W. Bush administration. Tensions between African Americans and Hispanics appear to be increasing, if the 2001 mayoral election in Los Angeles is any indication.

Some right-wing commentators are using the 2001 election results to proclaim that the GOP's efforts to reach out to Hispanics and African Americans is a complete failure and call for a reracializing of Republican politics.[20] Tensions related to race and immigration continue to increase in Western Europe as well. Jacques Le Pen and Jörg Haider remain uncomfortable reminders of the darker days of the twentieth century. In the spring of 2001, Italy elected militantly anti-immigrant Prime Minister Silvio Berlusconi, whose governing coalition includes the openly fascist National Alliance. The effort to bridge our racial and ethnic divides through creative political and scholarly activity remains, alas, steady work.

Notes

1. James Boyd White, *When Words Lose Their Meaning: Constitutions and Reconstitutions of Language, Character, and Community* (Chicago: University of Chicago Press, 1984), pp. x–xi.
2. Ibid., p. xi.
3. Jeffrey K. Tulis, *The Rhetorical Presidency* (Princeton, N.J.: Princeton University Press, 1987); Richard J. Ellis, ed., *Speaking to the People: The Rhetorical Presidency in Historical Perspective* (Amherst: University of Massachusetts Press, 1998); Martin J. Medhurst, ed., *Beyond the Rhetorical Presidency* (College Station: Texas A&M University Press, 1996).
4. Melvin C. Laracey, *Presidents and the People: The Partisan Story of Going Public* (College Station: Texas A&M University Press, 2002).
5. Samuel Kernell, *Going Public: New Strategies of Presidential Leadership*, 3rd ed. (Washington, D.C.: Congressional Quarterly Press, 1997).
6. Laracey, *Presidents and the People*, p. 171.
7. Russell L. Riley, *The Presidency and the Politics of Racial Inequality: Nation-Keeping from 1831 to 1965* (New York: Columbia University Press, 1999). For a similar argument, see Ronald D. Sylvia, "Presidential Decision Making and Leadership in the Civil Rights Era," *Presidential Studies Quarterly* 25(3) (1995): 391–412.
8. Steven Shull, *American Civil Rights Policy from Truman to Clinton: The Role of Presidential Leadership* (New York: M. E. Sharpe, 1999). Shull performs an extensive content analysis of presidential messages on civil rights. For an institutional perspective on the executive branch's implementation of civil rights laws, see Allan Wolk, *The Presidency and Black Civil Rights* (Rutherford, N.J.: Fairleigh Dickinson University Press, 1971). Executive-branch decision making represents one important area of research where scholars of organi-

zational and group communication might contribute to the study of rhetoric and public affairs.

9. Jeffrey E. Cohen, "The Dynamics and Interactions between the President's and the Public's Civil Rights Agendas: A Study in Presidential Leadership and Representation," *Policy Studies Journal* 21(3) (1993): 519. In the same issue of the journal, Shull and Ringelstein examine the public papers of the presidents to assess presidential support for, attention to, and symbolism of civil rights; Steven A. Shull and Albert C. Ringelstein, "Assessing Presidential Communications in Civil Rights Policymaking," *Policy Studies Journal* 21(3) (1993): 522–34. They find that the issue of civil rights was especially salient to Reagan, Bush, Johnson, and Carter. Reagan had the fewest policy statements of the four. Bush's policy statements were more frequent and longer than those of any other president. Democratic presidents paid more attention to civil rights all the way around.

10. See Mary L. Dudziak, *Cold War Civil Rights* (Princeton, N.J.: Princeton University Press, 2000).

11. For a treatment of the civil rights movement in the fifties and sixties, consider the following works: Taylor Branch, *Parting the Waters: America in the King Years 1954–1963* (New York: Simon and Schuster, 1988), and David J. Garrow, *Bearing the Cross: Martin Luther King Jr. and the Southern Christian Leadership Conference.* Each book was awarded a Pulitzer Prize and received critical acclaim. The works provide a thorough chronicle of the fragile coalition of civil rights agents who remained together from the Montgomery bus boycott (1955–1956) to the death of Martin Luther King Jr. (Apr. 4, 1968). Richard Kluger, *Simple Justice: The History of the Brown v. Board of Education and Black America's Struggle for Equality* (New York: Vintage, 1975). Kluger presents the constitutional underpinnings of the *Brown* case and addresses the way in which the United States Supreme Court systematically and strategically worked to overturn the *Plessy v. Ferguson* decision of 1896. To gain a universal sense of the activism of the sixties, consider Terry Anderson, *The Movement and the Sixties: Protests in America from Greensboro to Wounded Knee* (New York: Oxford University Press, 1996), and Todd Gitlin, *Years of Hope, Days of Rage* (New York: Bantam, 1987).

12. Hugh Davis Graham, "Richard Nixon and Civil Rights: Explaining an Enigma," *Presidential Studies Quarterly* 26(1) (1996): 93–107. See also his *Civil Rights and the Presidency: Race and Gender in American Politics, 1960–1972* (New York: Oxford University Press, 1992).

13. Joan Hoff, *Nixon Reconsidered* (New York: Basic, 1994).

14. Graham, "Richard Nixon and Civil Rights," p. 102.

15. Ibid., p. 95.

16. Ibid., p. 104.

17. Mark Tushnet, *Red, White, and Blue: A Critical Analysis of Constitutional Law* (Cambridge: Harvard University Press, 1988).

18. Adolph L. Reed Jr., *The Jesse Jackson Phenomenon: The Crisis of Purpose in African-American Politics* (New Haven: Yale University Press, 1986), p. 60.
19. We borrow the Yiddish folktale from Irving Howe, *Steady Work: Essays in the Politics of Democratic Radicalism, 1953–1966* (New York: Harcourt, Brace, and World, 1966).
20. See, for example, Paul Gottfried, "Q: Should the GOP Do More to Reach Out to Black Voters?" *Insight on the News,* Jan. 8, 2001, p. 41.

CHAPTER I

The Politics of Place
and Presidential Rhetoric
in the United States,
1875–1901

Kirt H. Wilson

D avid Brion Davis writes that emancipations are deceptive, even paradoxical, phenomena. Western cultures celebrate emancipations as defining moments when freedom triumphs over greed and slavery, yet they rarely eliminate the systems of domination that characterize the past.[1] Frederick Douglass appreciated this problem only too well when he spoke before an audience gathered to celebrate the freeing of the District of Columbia's slaves. On April 16, 1888, he explained: "I admit that the Negro, and especially the plantation Negro, the tiller of the soil, has made little progress from barbarism to civilization, and that he is in a deplorable condition since his emancipation. That he is worse off, in many respects, than when he was a slave, I am compelled to admit, but I contend that the fault is not his, but that of his heartless accusers. He is the victim of a cunningly devised swindle, which paralyzes his energies, suppresses his ambition, and blasts all his hopes; and though he is nominally free he is actually a slave. I here and now denounce this so-called emancipation as a stupendous fraud—a fraud upon him, a fraud upon the world."[2]

Several events had led Douglass to his conclusion. The Thirteenth Amendment gave black tenant farmers a share in agricultural profits, but those earnings were in a sharp decline. As the crop-lien system became common throughout the South, farmers entered a downward spiral of debt. Poor production, climate irregularities, pests, fraud, and coercion made their situation worse. Segregation, first as a matter of custom and eventually as legal prescription, descended across the South. The Supreme Court's decision in the 1883 *Civil Rights Cases* guaranteed Jim Crow's role as the de facto arbiter of public accommodations. The violence of the Reconstruction era developed into a cultural ritual. Urban riots and rural lynchings became the ultimate means of controlling black communities. Amid all this, the most depressing fact for many African Americans was that the federal government seemed unwilling to protect the rights of its newest citizens.[3]

This history is dimly familiar to many of us because of the histories of C. Vann Woodward, John Hope Franklin, and Lerone Bennett Jr. Indeed, it is not news that the return of "home rule" also brought segregation and violence. Less clear, however, are the details of the decline of civil rights and the role of the presidency in that process. This chapter examines the last quarter of the nineteenth century to understand how presidents Hayes, Garfield, Arthur, Cleveland, Harrison, and McKinley influenced the evolution of black civil rights. I argue that although Jim Crow and lynch law are crucial elements in this history, they are the surface manifestations of a deeper shift in the culture of the United States. When the Southern Redeemers came to power in the 1870s, they articulated a social and political ideology that I term the "politics of place." Through rhetoric, legislation, and coercion, Southern conservatives tried to reestablish the caste system of the antebellum era. African Americans resisted that process, yet the politics of place invaded almost every aspect of U.S. life. It affected the constitutional interpretations of the Supreme Court and influenced the political judgments of Congress. It even defined specific limits on the authority of the president. From 1875 to 1901, U.S. presidents engaged in the culture of place to various degrees. By the turn of the century, their participation had severely constrained the presidency's authority to protect black rights, and it virtually guaranteed the continuation of slavery's class system.

Reconstruction and Redemption:
A Return to the Organic Culture?

Scholars attribute the end of Reconstruction to the Compromise of 1877 and the subsequent inauguration of Rutherford B. Hayes. An able politician, Hayes had been elected governor of Ohio three times. More important, his nomination did not divide a besieged Republican party. He had "no bitter opponents and no questionable record, being, above all, a man with unique strategic advantages" as a compromise candidate with widespread appeal. Despite Hayes's moderation, the 1876 election was close and controversial. Both Tilden and Hayes claimed victory in South Carolina, Florida, and Louisiana. The Republicans' scorecard made Hayes the new president, winning 185 electoral votes to Tilden's 184. Democrats argued that the Republicans had invalidated the legitimate results of disputed Southern counties. Tilden had won the popular vote; therefore, he was the winner. In Louisiana and South Carolina, rival state governments assembled and demanded that Congress recognize their candidate. After more than a month of turmoil, a committee of ten congressmen and five Supreme Court justices decided in Hayes's favor, eight to seven. Tilden's supporters would not accept defeat, and they threatened to obstruct the committee's decision. Then, in private negotiations, Democrats promised to end their filibuster if Hayes agreed to end Reconstruction. Regardless of whether an agreement transpired between Hayes's representatives and the Democrats, Stanley Matthews, an advisor to the president-elect, announced that Hayes would not interfere in Southern politics. The Democrats halted their dilatory tactics, and Hayes was inaugurated.[4]

Although the centennial election and its subsequent crisis are a useful point at which to fix the end of Reconstruction, the study of nineteenth-century civil rights requires that one consider the continuity between 1875 and 1877. President Hayes's election led to the removal of federal troops, but the process of redemption had been under way for ten years. Democrats had regained control of Maryland and West Virginia as early as 1867 and 1870. Georgia conservatives wrested control of the legislature and the governor's office in 1870 and 1871. In fact, by 1876, only South Carolina and Florida remained in Republican hands.[5] The politicians who redeemed the South accomplished their task in part by articulating a rhetoric that combined aspects of the antebellum rhetorical culture with the themes of the industrial revolution.[6] The discourse of Southern conservatives was attractive to Northern politicians, and its romantic paternalism was instrumental in helping the South regain local control. In the hands of Alexander Stephens and Sen. Lucius Q. C. Lamar, this rhetoric reassured Northern Republicans that they could put aside the problems of African Americans because the South would protect black rights.

The persuasiveness of this discourse is evident in Hayes's speeches. Touring the South in the fall of 1877, he proclaimed that most Southern whites had "no desire to invade the rights of the colored people." To a biracial gathering in Atlanta, he articulated this rather tortured statement:

> What troubles our people at the North, what has troubled them, was that they feared that these colored people, who had been made freemen by the war, would not be safe in their rights and interests in the South unless it was by the interference of the general Government. Many good people had that idea. I had given that matter some consideration, and now, my colored friends, who have thought, or who have been told, that I was turning my back upon the men whom I fought for, now, listen! After thinking over it, I believed that your rights and interests would be safer if this great mass of intelligent white men were let alone by the general Government. [Immense enthusiasm and cheering for several minutes.] And now, my colored friends, let me say another thing. We have been trying it for these six months, and, in my opinion in no six months since the war have there been so few outrages and invasions of your rights, nor you so secure in your rights, persons, and homes, as in the last six months.[7]

Hayes believed that his "let-alone" policy would reconcile the races and the nation.[8] Southern conservatives were only too pleased to hear their own arguments coming from a Republican president. With the knowledge that they had persuaded Hayes of their good will, they began to reestablish the social system of the antebellum era.

In recent years, space and place have become important concepts among theorists and critics.[9] One should remember, however, that the nineteenth-century South understood these notions with an unrivaled complexity.[10] Space and place were concepts that regulated the most intimate aspects of their daily lives. Joel Williamson writes that Southern culture prior to the Civil War had more in common with the feudal system of medieval Europe than with the industrial society of the Northern United States. The South, reacting to the threat of slave insurrections, created a strict caste system in which every member of society occupied a very specific position, both socially and geographically. Plantation owner, local merchant, free black artisan, and field slave were constrained by norms that determined exactly how they lived and moved in relation to one another. The glue that held this system together was the concept of place. Place existed as a condensation symbol in Southern culture. It signified a person's identity and one's location within the organic communities of Southern culture. Individual and social, place determined the spaces that a person could occupy, how one interacted privately or publicly with others, and even a person's rights. As the Southern conservatives restored home rule, they returned to a concept of place as a means to limit black civil rights.[11]

Conservatives molded the concept of place into a specific set of ideological principles sustained by the following arguments. First, they argued that physical racial differences signified deeper psychological and spiritual differences that kept the races forever separate. Second, they affirmed that God had established a natural order in which each person, as well as each race, occupied a specific position that humans could neither deny nor change. Each position implied a social role, and each role entailed distinct responsibilities. Everyone, whites and blacks, were subject to this order and the implications of its class hierarchy. Third, opponents of desegregation argued that their ideology did not nullify the general idea of equality; rather, place refined the abstract idea so that equality better reflected nature. Alexander Stephens, an architect of this rhetoric, illustrates this idea well. He explains: "While I do not hold to the doctrine of the equality of races of men, yet I do maintain the great truth, however paradoxical it may appear to some, that all men are created equal. . . . This truth was never meant, however, in my opinion, to convey the idea that men were created equal in all respects. . . . [It] requires no leveling of the population of a State, either upward or downward—no equality and fraternity, as announced by the Jacobins of France—but that every one should act toward another as that other ought, in turn, to act upon *a reversal of their positions in the different and various relations of life,* either socially, politically, or otherwise."[12]

According to Stephens, the Declaration of Independence was the political application of the Golden Rule. It established a principle of reciprocity that made society both compassionate and just. Fourth and finally, good race relations, argued desegregation's opponents, were possible only when every member of a community respected the social order. If either individual citizens or government agencies disrupted the positions established by God and nature, chaos would ensue. Taken together, these four assumptions made up the political and social ideology of place.

To understand the practical implementation of this ideology—the politics of place—one need only consider an 1879 debate sponsored by the *North American Review.* Among the speakers that attended the symposium were James Blaine, James Garfield, Wendell Phillips, and Lucius Q. C. Lamar. Each was asked to respond to two questions: Ought the negro to be disfranchised? Ought he to have been enfranchised? Lamar, a prominent senator from Mississippi, offered a carefully worded answer to the first question. Ignoring the issue of whether African Americans should have received suffrage, he said, "In all my experience of Southern opinion I know no Southern man of influence or consideration who believes that the disfranchise-ment of the negro, on account of race, color, or former condition of servitude, is a political possibility."[13] Lamar preferred to argue on pragmatic rather than principled grounds.

Next, he denied the accusation that Southern conservatives had used force to limit black suffrage and reestablish white control of Southern politics. Then, in a revealing moment, Lamar backed away from his denials and asked his audience whether it would have been wrong if whites had manipulated Southern politics to regain control. He answered his rhetorical question with a no. The hegemony of Southern whites did not undermine Reconstruction's constitutional amendments because these amendments were meant only as a shield to protect a free *laboring class,* Lamar explained. Southern whites had a divine responsibility to lead society, and it made no sense to interpret the Constitution as a restriction of their duties. Besides, he asked, "is free labor anywhere on earth more firmly established, more fully developed, or more absolute in its demands . . . than in the South? In all respects, negro freedom and negro equality before the law, security of person and property, are ample and complete."[14]

Lamar's comments are revealing because they demonstrate how the politics of place constrained African Americans' civil rights. Before the Civil War, Republicans had based their antislavery policies on the notion of "limited absolute equality." The central tenet of this position was that material equality was impossible; therefore, the government's responsibility to people of color ended when their economic viability was secured.[15] As the New South developed, its adherents used the ideology of place to refine the concept of limited absolute equality. According to the Southern conservatives, a person's rights were determined by the needs of that person's place. Whites possessed those rights that were necessary to lead society. African Americans were a "prosperous laboring population," an extensive working class for industry and agriculture; therefore, they were entitled to a different set of rights.[16] Explained with the body metaphors that were popular during this period, blacks were the hands and feet of society. They were not and should not attempt to become its head. Therefore, according to Lamar, the Constitution guaranteed them only those rights that were necessary to fulfill their role as an economic resource. Lamar concluded that since African Americans possessed economic freedom, they also possessed all of their constitutional rights.

Regardless of whether President Hayes was aware of the full consequences of his hands-off policy, his administration's agenda favored the conservatives. In his Atlanta address of 1877, he had said, "Here we are, Republicans, Democrats, colored people, white people, Confederate soldiers, and Union soldiers, all of one mind and one heart today! [Immense cheering] And why should we not be? What is there to separate us longer? "[17] Ironically, separation was something that blacks desired in 1877. So long as the federal government chose not to intervene in Southern politics, integration would bring exploitation, not equality. Integration without federal control meant that African Americans would be forced into their proper place. Integration would return a caste system that determined the physical, intellectual, and political spaces available to people of color. As Woodward notes, "Redemption was not a return of an old system nor the restoration of an old ruling class. It was rather a new phase of the revolutionary process begun in 1865."[18] If the races came together according to the terms of the New South, African Americans would experience a new form of degradation never before realized in the United States.

Equal Citizenship or Separate but Equal?

Between 1877 and 1892, one finds scattered presidential statements that affirm African Americans' rights to equal citizenship. In the speech in which Hayes declared his intent to leave black rights in the hands of the South's "intelligent" white population, he also acknowledged the following: "I believe it is the duty of the general Government to regard equally and alike the interests and rights of all sections of this country. [Cheers] I am glad that you agree with me about that. I believe, further, that it is the duty of the Government to regard alike and equally the rights and interests of all classes of citizens. [Cheers] That covers the whole matter. That wipes out in the future in our politics the section line forever. [Cheers] Let us wipe out in our politics the color line forever. [Cheers]"[19]

Although Hayes's successor, Pres. James Garfield, did not proclaim a desire to rid America of the color line, many of his comments also encouraged African Americans. For example, almost half of his inaugural address was devoted to the problems the black voters encountered. He declared, "The elevation of the negro race from slavery to the full rights of citizenship is the most important political change we have known since the adoption of the Constitution of 1787." To Southern whites, he added that "under our institutions, there was no middle ground for the negro race between slavery and equal citizenship. There can be no permanent disfranchised peasantry in the United States." Then he declared: "The free enjoyment of equal suffrage is still in question, and a frank statement of the issue may aid its solution. It is alleged that in many communities negro citizens are practically denied the freedom of the ballot. In so far as the truth of this allegation is admitted, it is answered that in many places honest local government is impossible if the mass of uneducated negroes are [sic] allowed to vote. These are grave allegations. So far as the latter is true, it is the only palliation that can be offered for opposing the freedom of the ballot. Bad local government is certainly a great evil, which ought to be prevented; but to violate the freedom and sanctity of the suffrage is more than an evil—it is a crime which, if persisted in, will destroy the government itself."[20]

Garfield's long-term solution to the Southern problem was better education for blacks. He explained to a delegation of African Americans from South Carolina that "a trained man is two or three men in one in comparison with an untrained man . . . [and] the way to make the majority always powerful over the minority is to make its members as trained and intelligent as the minority itself. That brings the equality of citizenship."[21] Notably, Garfield's educational agenda was not limited to vocational schooling. Sinkler writes that the president did not believe that creating a perpetual labor class was the answer to the Southern problem. The real issue was "how best to lead [blacks] from the plane of drudgery to one of some culture and finally of high culture."[22]

Even Grover Cleveland, the nation's first Democratic president since the war, affirmed black civil rights. In his inaugural Cleveland declared, "In the administration of a government pledged to do equal and exact justice to all men there should be no pretext for anxiety touching the protection of the freedmen in their rights or their security in the enjoyment of their privileges under the Constitution and its amendments." He then proceeded to repudiate the notion that African Americans occupied a lesser place in America's social system. He said, "All discussion as to their fitness for the place accorded to them as American citizens is idle and unprofitable except as it suggests the necessity for their improvement. The fact that they are citizens entitles them to all the rights due to that relation and charges them with all its duties, obligations, and responsibilities."[23]

The comments of Hayes, Garfield, and Cleveland present the critic or historian of civil rights policy with a problem. Were the presidents' affirmations of black equality accurate reflections of their racial attitudes? As Edwin Black reminds us when speaking to the relationship between rhetoric and psychology, "The possibilities of deception, deliberate or unconscious, seem endless, and consequently the problems presented [to] the psychological critic seem insoluble."[24] Do we have reason to suspect the public statements of Hayes and Garfield? George Sinkler and Kenneth O'Reilly make a persuasive affirmative case.[25] Too often, the public talk of post-Reconstruction presidents conflicted with their private comments. O'Reilly notes that in Garfield's diary the president wrote that Washington, D.C., "was too 'infested' " with African Americans for his liking. President Harrison went out of his way to assure Southern whites that he would appoint blacks only to minor positions where they would have no "personal contact with and official authority over white citizens."[26] President Cleveland, responding to the allegation that he had dined with Frederick Douglass, wrote to Charles Bartlett that he had never, while sleeping or waking, alive or dead, dined, lunched, or supped, with any colored man, woman, or child.[27]

One can explain this incongruity by arguing that the presidents used their public statements to hide a gradual but certain betrayal of African Americans. According to this narrative, Hayes, Garfield, Arthur, Harrison, and McKinley shared the prejudice and racism of other European Americans; consequently, they abandoned black equality at the first convenient opportunity.[28] Although there is an element of truth in this claim, I argue that the situation was more complex than this. Indeed, a narrow historical focus on the racial attitudes of individual presidents misses the cultural, political, and discursive aspects of civil rights history during this period.

Historians acknowledge that the Southern conservatives of the post-Reconstruction era attempted to circumscribe the civil rights of African Americans, but they have failed to consider how the politics of place limited the presidency's authority to effect black civil rights. I posit that the personal feelings of late-nineteenth-century presidents were not a decisive influence on civil rights policy. Sinkler's *Racial Attitudes of American Presidents* and O'Reilly's *Nixon's Piano* shed some light on the relationship between the presidency and black rights, but their focus on attitude is limiting. Rather, I approach the presidents' rhetoric as a temporal series of institutional utterances in negotiation with the increasingly powerful discourse of place. President Hayes set a precedent by collaborating with the politics of place. By 1883, the Supreme Court had accepted the conservative ideology, adding constitutional legitimacy to the idea that one's place could determine one's civil rights. By 1891, Congress was committed to the industrial benefits that came with the politics of place; consequently, it ignored President Harrison's request for legislation to protect blacks' voting rights. With the second term of President Cleveland and the administration of William McKinley, the presidency also had a vested interest in the politics of place, and it advanced the culture of place as the only solution to the "Southern problem."

The Presidency and the Politics of Place

Place is evident in presidential discourse as early as 1880. On May 20, Hayes gave a speech at the anniversary of the Hampton Institute, a black vocational school, where he made the following pronouncement: "We would not undertake to violate the laws of nature, we do not wish to change the purpose of God in making these differences of nature. We are willing to have these elements of our population separate as the fingers are, but we require to see them united for every good work, for national defense, one, as the hand. And that good work Hampton is doing."[29]

Many may find the hand metaphor in this passage familiar. Fifteen years later, Booker T. Washington would popularize this metaphor in his famous Atlanta Exposition Address.[30] Whether Washington heard President Hayes's speech is not clear, but it is probable. He was working at Hampton at the time, and it seems likely that he attended the address.

More to the point, the metaphor signals an initial engagement with—and perhaps even an element of self-persuasion of—the conservatives' ideology. Specifically, it demonstrates Hayes's acceptance of inherited difference and distinct social roles. Just as each finger is separate, each "element of our population" is discrete, according to the metaphor. No two fingers have the same length, and each one serves a distinctive purpose. Furthermore, the passage suggests that divine law, not human institutions, created these differences. Individual citizens, regardless of race, could cooperate for "every good work," but that association did not undermine distinctions of person or position. Hayes argued for a functional association, not an ontological one.

This passage is revealing as well because it adopts a limited role for the presidency. It reads, "We are willing to have these elements of our population separate as the fingers are, but we require to see them united for every good work." These connected, yet independent, clauses establish a passive persona for the executive branch. The phrases "we are willing" and "we require to see" imply that others will act while the president watches from the outside. When linked to Hayes's hands-off policy, it seems clear that the president envisioned the role of the institution as one of indirect leadership. I would argue that the way that Hayes positions himself signals an additional acceptance of the politics of place. Recall that the concept of place stemmed from the antebellum organic social structure. According to Southern politicians, the president could not and should not attempt to direct race relations because he was not a part of the complex Southern culture. He did not have a direct knowledge of the Southern body and its inner workings. Perhaps more to the point, there could be only one head, and Southern conservatives claimed that position for themselves. The executive branch might recommend general goals, but the actual work of policing civil rights had to be left to those who understood the South's unique social system.

Of course, neither this passage nor Hayes's policy determined his successors' actions. He simply established a trajectory that others could follow or abandon. As the 1880s progressed, however, presidents departed from the margins of civil rights issues with decreasing regularity. The strategic use of silence in the face of civil rights' decline demonstrates this passivity well.

The Presidents' Rhetoric of Silence

The rhetoric of silence is not unknown to communication scholars, although the literature is not extensive. According to Robert Scott, voice and silence exist in dialectical tension; the presence of one suggests the absence and potential of the other. For that reason, silence can speak. Given the structure of its context, silence communicates specific meanings to an audience. Barry Brummett adds that silence often functions strategically in politics "when someone has pressing reason to speak, but does not." One of the meanings often communicated by silence is that of intentional passivity. Silence, according to Brummett, encourages the public to assume that politicians will not act because they do not wish to act. With the exception of Benjamin Harrison, the silence coming from the White House grew more pronounced as each year passed.[31]

On October 15, 1883, the Supreme Court declared that the 1875 Civil Rights Act was unconstitutional. According to the *Civil Rights Cases,* the denial of equal accommodations in inns, public conveyances, and places of public amusement was not a badge of slavery; therefore, the Thirteenth Amendment did not authorize federally mandated desegregation. Furthermore, the Court argued that the Fourteenth Amendment existed only as a prohibition against state activity. Justice Joseph Bradley, writing for the majority, explains: "Individual invasion of individual rights is not the subject-matter of the [Fourteenth] amendment. . . . It nullifies and makes void all State legislation, and State action of every kind, which impairs the privileges and immunities of citizens of the United States. . . . It does not invest Congress with power to legislate upon subjects which are within the domain of State legislation; but to provide modes of relief against State legislation, or State action, of the kind referred to. It does not authorize Congress to create a code of municipal law for the regulation of private rights; but to provide modes of redress against the operation of State laws."[32]

With few exceptions, white citizens, the press, and most business leaders applauded the decision.[33] African Americans and leaders within the Republican party expressed their disapproval. A crowd gathered in Washington, D.C., on October 22 to listen to the protest speeches of Robert G. Ingersoll and Frederick Douglass. In his address, Douglass said, "We have been, as a class, grievously wounded, wounded in the house of our friends, and this wound is too deep and too painful for ordinary and measured speech. . . . When a deed is done for slavery, caste and oppression, and a blow is struck at human progress, whether so intended or not, the heart of humanity sickens in sorrow and writhes in pain."[34]

Douglass was distressed by the Court's decision because it represented a constitutional interpretation grounded in the ideology of place. In the 1873 *Slaughter-House* decision, the Court had ruled that Reconstruction's constitutional amendments had not abolished the system of American Federalism.[35] State governments still possessed the authority to determine the civil rights of their citizens. At the same time, the Court had declared that the amendments were intended to abolish slavery. Accordingly, the federal government had a responsibility to protect the freedom of its newest citizens. Prominent black leaders interpreted the *Slaughter-House* decision to mean that Congress and the president could and should protect those of color from any social system akin to slavery. This would include the practices of the politics of place. Now, with the 1883 decision, the Court denied this interpretation. Douglass knew what this meant, and he put it in stark terms: "When a colored man is in the same room or in the same carriage with white people, as a servant, there is no talk of social equality, but if he is there as a man and a gentleman, he is an offense. What makes the difference? It is not color, for his color is unchanged. The whole essence of the thing is a studied purpose to degrade and stamp out the liberties of a race. It is the old spirit of slavery, and nothing else."[36] In a very real sense, the 1883 *Civil Rights Cases* made the *Plessy v. Ferguson* decision inevitable. The first was a negative injunction on federal power; the second was a positive affirmation of state authority. Both inscribed the politics of place into the hermeneutic practices of the nation's judicial system.

If Douglass hoped that the federal government would enact legislation to overcome the Court's decision, he would be disappointed, but not because Congress was unwilling. Sen. John Sherman said the justices had undermined the "cornerstone of Republican principles." The former secretary of the interior, Samuel J. Kirkwood, called the decision a terrible mistake. Louis T. Michener of Indiana expressed the hope that President Arthur would recommend a constitutional amendment that contained the language of the Civil Rights Act. Sen. Benjamin Harrison, soon to be president himself, promised blacks that something would be done.

This talk went well beyond posturing. Five bills, including a constitutional amendment, were introduced to replace the 1875 act, but amid all of this noise and clamor, President Arthur remained silent. The meaning of his silence was obvious, especially as his first message to Congress was the first since the Civil War to avoid any reference to African Americans. For a month and a half, Arthur demurred, and his silence reinforced the passive stance established by Hayes. Finally, in his second annual message, he informed Congress that any legislation that it could pass to "lawfully" protect the "equal enjoyment" of civil rights by every U.S. citizen would receive his "unhesitating approval." Without Arthur's active leadership, however, none of the new civil rights initiatives made it out of Congress. Douglass commented later that there was nothing in Arthur's tenure to suggest that he had any sympathy with the oppressed race in the South.[37] Arthur's tepid reaction to the *Civil Rights Cases* discouraged African Americans, but blacks were far more unnerved by the silence of later presidents when racial violence exploded across the South.

Violence against blacks has a long history in the United States, but in the final decade of the nineteenth century, "lynching became a special Southern occurrence in which black men were the special victims." "There was," writes Williamson, "something new and horribly palpable on the earth." The explosion of white-on-black violence began in 1889 and peaked in 1892. From 1889 to 1899 an average of one person was lynched every other day, and two-thirds of these were African American. Even as incidents of lynching declined, urban race riots increased, with major incidents in 1898, 1900, and 1905.[38]

U.S. presidents said little and did even less in response to this terror. President Cleveland failed to make even one public statement about lynching during his second term in office (1893–1896). President McKinley offered a single brief comment in his inaugural address. "Lynchings," he said, "must not be tolerated in a great and civilized country like the United States." When eleven African Americans were murdered in a riot in Wilmington, North Carolina, the black community expected McKinley's support, but he said nothing.[39] On March 21, 1898, Ida Wells-Barnett went directly to the president to protest the murder of a black postmaster and his family in South Carolina. Part of her statement reads as follows: "For nearly twenty years lynching crimes, which stand side by side with Armenian and Cuban outrages, have been committed and permitted by this Christian nation. . . . To our appeals for justice the stereotyped reply has been that the government could not interfere in a state matter. . . . [Yet] Italy and China have been indemnified by this government for the lynching of their citizens. We ask that the government do as much for its own." McKinley assured Wells-Barnett of his personal sympathy but then did nothing.[40]

President Harrison fares a little better. In his 1892 message to Congress, he declared that "the frequent lynching of colored people accused of crime is without the excuse . . . that the accused have an undue influence over courts and juries." Yet Harrison argued that there was nothing that he could do. To a black delegation he wrote that the Constitution gave him no authority to act against such outrages. Harrison was correct, at least in part. Compared to the twentieth century, nineteenth-century presidents had little power. As the weakest division of the national government, the executive branch found it almost impossible to act independently of Congress. This was particularly true during the post-Reconstruction era. Congress had the authority to make appropriations, set salaries for federal employees, and prepare the budget. Woodrow Wilson remarked at the time that the legislative branch had all of the substantial powers of government.

Despite this situation, it is crucial to remember that the legal and political constraints on President Harrison were neither predestined nor omnipotent. Like all such forces, they were the creation of human agents, agents who participated in the politics of place. The Supreme Court, for example, chose to interpret the Constitution in a manner that favored the legitimacy of segregation. Kaczorowski argues that the Court's increasingly narrow interpretation of the Thirteenth and Fourteenth amendments was at odds with the opinions of lower circuit courts.[41]

Although the nineteenth century entailed a tradition of limited executive power, presidents had found creative ways to expand their authority. The period from 1875 to 1901 was no different. President Hayes mobilized federal troops to protect the railroad industry against striking workers. In 1893, President Cleveland used soldiers to disburse "Coxey's Army," and, in 1894, he used the army to break up another national railroad strike. Even if one accepts the argument that late-nineteenth-century presidents were powerless to end racial violence, this does not explain their silence. Justus Doenecke writes that the presidents' best chance to influence policy was to play the role of a symbolic moral leader.[42] When it came to race, most presidents avoided this option. For example, in his 1899 annual message, McKinley spoke against lynching, but only as it pertained to the deaths of Italian citizens in Louisiana. The absence of any reference to African Americans seemed like a calculated decision to maintain distance between the institution of the presidency and racial violence.[43]

The presidents' silence and inaction are significant because lynch law was the physical manifestation of the politics of place. Lynchings were ritualized events in the South. The black victim was taken forcibly by a small group of men. As they reached a predetermined location, a crowd would gather. Often this spot had been used repeatedly. Usually the accuser, a white woman, would be brought forward to confront the victim and demand justice. Depending on the alleged crime, torture would follow along with an attempt to gain the victim's confession. The mode of execution varied in relation to the allegations. Mobs used hanging, shooting, burning, dragging, cutting, or some combination of these actions to kill their black victim. Regardless of the means, every aspect of this practice involved a symbolic as well as a literal violation of the victim's person and space. Lynching was designed to reinforce the message that African Americans did not control their persons or their position in society. Moreover, the practice told the black community that no one was safe. With a word or even a rumor, any black person could be next. Lynchings communicated the proper place of blacks through the systematic invasion of their most private space, their bodies. Harrison, Cleveland, and McKinley did not approve of this activity, but, constrained by forces that past presidents had helped to establish, they did nothing to prevent them.[44]

The Limiting Effects of the Politics of Place

Because the executive's authority was limited by the politics of place, individual presidents found it more difficult to depart from institutional precedents. Pres. Benjamin Harrison is a case in point. When he succeeded Grover Cleveland in 1889, blacks were hopeful that the tide had finally turned in their favor. Harrison had been a "bloody shirt" Republican. In 1876, he had repudiated the conservative forces of the Southern Redeemers. He had condemned the Supreme Court in 1883, and he had affirmed his support for federal control of elections in 1885. During the presidential election, he abandoned his earlier sectionalism but not black rights.[45] In a speech commemorating George Washington's birthday, he said that the South must stop oppressing those "who equally with themselves under the Constitution are entitled to vote."[46] That summer he spoke to several gatherings of African Americans, and in Indianapolis he offered an emotional description of his childhood experiences with slavery.[47]

After his inaugural address, Harrison continued to make strong statements compared to other post-Reconstruction presidents. In his first annual message, he wrote: "The colored people did not intrude themselves on us. They were brought here in chains and held in communities where they are now chiefly found, by a cruel slave code. . . . If it be said that these [Southern] communities must work out this problem for themselves we have a right to ask whether they are at work upon it. Do they suggest any solution? When and under what conditions is the black man to have a free ballot? When is he in fact to have those full civil rights which have so long been his in law? When is that equality of influence which our form of government was intended to secure to the electors to be restored? This generation should courageously face these grave questions, and not leave them as a heritage of woe to the next."[48] Harrison went further and encouraged Congress to pass specific legislation.[49]

In December, 1889, separate bills to protect black voting rights appeared in the House and the Senate. One was drafted by Henry Cabot Lodge and nicknamed the "Force Bill" by its opponents. It gave federal circuit-court judges supervision of all congressional races. Since most of these judges were Republican, both parties assumed that Lodge's measure would be used to protect black voters. The House debate over the bill was acrimonious; the extreme language used by both sides had not been heard since the debate over the 1875 Civil Rights Act. Nevertheless, on July 2, 1890, the bill passed by a vote of 155 to 149. It never went any further. A Democratic filibuster prevented its consideration in the Senate. Republicans were worried about the Sherman Antitrust Act and the Sherman Silver Purchase Act, so they put the measure aside, promising to return to it. President Harrison agitated for the bill in private conversations with senators and in successive annual messages. Nevertheless, as he returned to the issue each year, his comments became less thoughtful and more general, less passionate and more pro forma. Taking his statements as a whole, one cannot help but notice Harrison's retreat until, by his fourth message, he avoided any direct reference to black voters, stating that election reform was necessary to end the "mutual charges of unfairness and fraud between the great parties."[50]

Harrison's retreat is explained in part by Congress's unwillingness to act. Republicans could not overcome Democratic filibusters because many in the party agreed with the Democrats that people of color did not need suffrage to fulfill their social (i.e., economic) responsibilities. Indeed, historians often cite the defeat of the federal elections bill as the moment when congressional Republicans abandoned African Americans for good. Whatever personal convictions Harrison possessed were simply no match for the politics of place that now seemed to control both the Supreme Court and Congress. Congress would not consider a new civil rights bill for African Americans until the 1930s.[51]

Conclusion

Few histories have caused more research and controversy than *The Strange Career of Jim Crow* by C. Vann Woodward. Over the years the debate over his work has centered on what is termed the Woodward thesis: Segregation grew slowly during the post-Reconstruction era, and it did not take its final shape until after the turn of the century. Woodward's critics disagree, arguing that segregation was the cultural norm at least by 1865 if not before the war. Within this sometimes contentious historiography, there is a point of consensus that often goes unnoticed. Both Woodward and his critics agree that the last decade of the nineteenth century witnessed a sharp radicalism in Southern politics. The need for legally sanctioned segregation moved from a general concern to a preoccupation to an obsession among European Americans.[52]

The Triumph of the Politics of Place

Historians offer various explanations for this shift. Some argue that a new breed of politician, the radical, overthrew the Southern conservative. These people believed that freedom had caused African Americans to retrograde to barbarism. Radicals spoke openly of white supremacy and denied any responsibility toward people of color. Other historians suggest that the industrial revolution destroyed any real hope that whites and blacks could return to the familial relationships of the antebellum period. As black workers came into contact with the white laboring class, whites demanded legal segregation to assert their superiority over the competition.[53] As I conclude this chapter, I would like to forward a third hypothesis.

The 1890s witnessed the triumph of the politics of place, brought about in part by presidents Cleveland and McKinley, who became active supporters of the conservative ideology. Indeed, it seems plausible that the presidents began to use the politics of place as a means to obtain the South's cooperation in the complex process of building the modern nation-state. Anthony Marx argues that the United States, like South Africa, used race as a tool to unite European Americans.[54] Identification by antithesis provided a coalition between the white North and South, which was further strengthened by systemic practices of segregation. This coalition allowed industrial capitalism to expand without Southern interference. By becoming a voice for the ideology of place, presidents found that they could pursue a variety of agendas at home and abroad. The South never capitulated completely to the interests of the federal government, but its resistance lessened once the presidents fell into line on the race issue.

The association between the presidency and the politics of place is well illustrated by the astounding rise of Booker T. Washington. It is easy to forget that when Washington burst onto the national scene in 1895, he was not the only prominent black leader in the United States. Alexander Crummell, Bishop Henry McNeal Turner, Mary Church Terrell, and even the young W. E. B. Du Bois were influential figures in the black community, yet they were ignored by the presidents, perhaps because they were voices of resistance. Washington quickly became the black voice for place. We do not know whether the hand metaphor originated with him or with President Hayes, but we do know that whites across the North and the South reacted warmly when he said, "In all things that are purely social we can be as separate as the fingers, yet one as the hand in all things essential to mutual progress."[55] President Cleveland read the Atlanta speech with "great enthusiasm." On October 9, 1895, Cleveland wrote Washington to thank him for the copy of the speech that he had received. He said, "Your words cannot fail to delight and encourage all who wish well for the race; and if your colored fellow citizens do not from your utterances gather new hope and form new determinations to gain every valuable advantage offered them by their citizenship, it will be strange indeed."[56] The relationship between the two men grew, and soon the former president was raising funds for the Tuskegee Institute. In 1899, Cleveland secured a check for $25,000 from one female patron.[57]

The McKinley administration matched Cleveland's enthusiasm. The president ignored most black leaders, but he traveled to Tuskegee in December, 1898, to lavish praise on Booker T. Washington. According to McKinley, Washington "has won a worthy reputation as one of the great leaders of his race, widely known and much respected at home and abroad as an accomplished educator, a great orator, and a true philanthropist." McKinley explained further, "Patience, moderation, self-control, knowledge, character will surely win you victories and realize the best aspirations of your people. An evidence of the soundness of the purposes of this institution is that those in charge of its management evidently do not believe in attempting the unattainable, and their instruction in self-reliance and practical industry is most valuable."[58]

Thus, through the conscious promotion of Cleveland, McKinley, and eventually Theodore Roosevelt, Booker T. Washington was transformed from a small-time president of a black vocational school to the most powerful black man in the nation. In return, Washington became a staunch supporter of these administrations and a sharp critic of those who resisted the now institutionalized culture of place.[59]

By the turn of the century, blacks could no longer withstand the legal and physical manifestations of place politics. Blacks continued to resist, but the philosophy of Booker T. Washington discouraged political agitation. I do not believe that Washington intended to capitulate to racism; evidence suggests that he worked behind the scenes to further black civil rights. Yet, as Woodward writes, "in proposing [publicly] the virtual retirement of the mass of Negroes from the political life of the South and in stressing the humble and menial role that the race was to play, [Washington] would seem unwittingly to have smoothed the path to proscription."[60] If the consequences of Washington's public discourse were unintended, the behavior of the presidents was not. By 1901, the executive branch had a vested interest in the politics of place, and it used Washington to further those interests. Blacks made good laborers for the manufacturing centers of the nation. They made good soldiers in Cuba and the Philippines. They made especially good scapegoats to mitigate the problems of industrialization. All that was necessary to avail oneself of this resource was to keep African Americans in their proper place.

Notes

1. David Brion Davis, "The Emancipation Moment," in *Lincoln, the War President: The Gettysburg Lectures,* ed. Gabor S. Boritt (New York: Oxford University Press, 1992), pp. 63–88.
2. Frederick Douglass, "I Denounce the So-Called Emancipation as a Stupendous Fraud," in *Lift Every Voice: African American Oratory, 1787–1900,* ed. Philip S. Foner and Robert James Branham (Tuscaloosa: University of Alabama Press, 1998), p. 698.
3. Roger L. Ransom and Richard Sutch, "Debt Peonage in the Cotton South after the Civil War," *Journal of Economic History* 32 (1972): 641–69; C. Vann Woodward, *The Strange Career of Jim Crow,* 3rd ed. (New York: Oxford University Press, 1974); Howard N. Rabinowitz, *Race Relations in the Urban South, 1865–1890* (New York: Oxford University Press, 1978); *Civil Rights Cases,* 109 U.S. 3 (1883); Stanley P. Hirshson, *Farewell to the Bloody Shirt: Northern Republicans and the Southern Negro, 1877–1893* (Bloomington: Indiana University Press,

1966); Lerone Bennett Jr., *Before the Mayflower: A History of Black America,* 6th ed. (New York: Penguin, 1993); John Hope Franklin, *From Slavery to Freedom: A History of Negro Americans,* 5th ed. (New York: Knopf, 1980).

4. Eric Foner, *Reconstruction: America's Unfinished Revolution, 1863–1877* (New York: Harper and Row, 1988), pp. 564–87; Brooks D. Simpson, *The Reconstruction Presidents* (Lawrence: University Press of Kansas, 1998), pp. 191–96; William Gillette, *Retreat from Reconstruction, 1869–1879* (Baton Rouge: Louisiana State University Press, 1979), chap. 13.

5. Foner, *Reconstruction,* pp. 421–25; C. Vann Woodward, *Origins of the New South* (Baton Rouge: Louisiana State University Press, 1951), chap. 1.

6. See Celeste Michelle Condit and John Louis Lucaites, *Crafting Equality: America's Anglo African Word* (Chicago: Chicago University Press, 1993), pp. 116–19; Waldo W. Braden, ed., *Oratory in the New South* (Baton Rouge: Louisiana State University Press, 1979).

7. Rutherford B. Hayes, "Atlanta Speech," Sept., 1877, in *The Life of Rutherford Birchard Hayes,* ed. Charles R. Williams (Boston: Houghton Mifflin, 1914), 2:252.

8. See Simpson, *The Reconstruction Presidents,* chap. 7.

9. See Raymie E. McKerrow, "Space and Time in the Postmodern Polity," *Western Journal of Communication* 63 (1999): 271–90; Michel deCerteau, *The Practice of Everyday Life,* trans. Steven Rendall (Berkeley: University of California Press, 1984).

10. See G. P. Mohrmann, "Place and Space: Calhoun's Fatal Security," *Western Journal of Speech Communication* 51 (1987): 143–58.

11. Joel Williamson, *The Crucible of Race* (New York: Oxford University Press, 1984); Woodward, *Origins of the New South,* pp. 208–210.

12. *Congressional Record,* 43rd Cong., 1st sess., Jan. 5, 1874, p. 379; emphasis added.

13. Lucius Q. C. Lamar, "Ought the Negro to Be Disfranchised? Ought He to Have Been Enfranchised?" In *Lucius Q. C. Lamar: His Life, Times, and Speeches,* ed. Edward Mayers (Nashville: Publishing House of the Methodist Episcopal Church, South, 1896), p. 719.

14. Ibid., p. 722.

15. Earl Maltz, "Reconstruction without Revolution," *Houston Law Review* 24 (1987): 222–26.

16. See, for example, Henry Grady, "The New South," in *American Political Discourse,* ed. Ronald F. Reid (Prospect Heights, Ill.: Waveland, 1995), pp. 556–57.

17. Hayes, "Atlanta Speech," p. 251.

18. Woodward, *Origins of the New South,* pp. 21–22.

19. Hayes, "Atlanta Speech," p. 252.

20. James Abram Garfield, "Inaugural Address," Mar. 4, 1881, in *The*

Works of James Abram Garfield, ed. Burke A. Hinsdale (Boston: Osgood, 1882–1883), p. 790.

21. Hirshson, *Farewell to the Bloody Shirt,* pp. 91–92; Justus D. Doenecke, *The Presidencies of James A. Garfield and Chester A. Arthur* (Lawrence: Regents Press of Kansas, 1981), pp. 48–49.

22. Garfield quoted in Sinkler, *The Racial Attitudes of American Presidents* (Garden City, N.Y.: Doubleday, 1971), p. 209.

23. Grover Cleveland, "First Inaugural Address," in *Grover Cleveland, 1837–1908,* ed. Robert I. Vexler (Dobbs Ferry, N.Y.: Oceana, 1968).

24. Edwin Black, *Rhetorical Criticism: A Study in Method* (Madison: University of Wisconsin Press, 1965), p. 27.

25. George Sinkler, *The Racial Attitudes of American Presidents;* Kenneth O'Reilly, *Nixon's Piano* (New York: Free Press, 1995).

26. O'Reilly, *Nixon's Piano,* pp. 56, 59.

27. See Sinkler, *The Racial Attitudes of American Presidents,* p. 227.

28. Rayford Logan, *The Betrayal of the Negro, from Rutherford B. Hayes to Woodrow Wilson* (New York: Collier, 1965).

29. Quoted by Sinkler, *The Racial Attitudes of American Presidents,* p. 168. The original appears in the unpublished papers of Rutherford B. Hayes.

30. Booker T. Washington, "Atlanta Exposition Address," in *Lift Every Voice,* pp. 800–845.

31. Robert L. Scott, "Rhetoric and Silence," *Western Communications Journal* 36 (1972): 146–58; Keith V. Erickson and Wallace V. Schmidt, "Presidential Political Silence: Rhetoric and the Rose Garden Strategy," *Southern Journal of Communication* 47 (1982): 402–421; Barry Brummett, "Towards a Theory of Silence as a Political Strategy," *Quarterly Journal of Speech* 66 (1980): 289–303; Robert L. Scott, "Dialectical Tensions of Speaking and Silence," *Quarterly Journal of Speech* 79 (1993): 1–18.

32. *Civil Rights Cases,* 109 U.S. 11 (1983). Justice John Harlan dissented, arguing that his colleagues had sacrificed the substance and spirit of the Fourteenth and Fifteenth amendments.

33. Valeria W. Weaver, "The Failure of the Civil Rights of 1875 and Its Repercussions," *Journal of Negro History* 54 (1969): 370.

34. Frederick Douglass, "Speech at Lincoln Hall, October 22, 1883," *Proceedings of the Civil Rights Mass Meeting* (Washington, D.C.: C. P. Farrell, 1883), p. 4.

35. *The Slaughter-House Cases,* 16 Wallace 36 (1872).

36. Douglass, "Speech at Lincoln Hall," p. 13.

37. Chester A. Arthur, "Third Annual Message," Dec. 4, 1883, in *Messages and Papers of the Presidents,* ed. James D. Richardson (1897; reprint; New York: Bureau of National Literature, 1917), 10:4775 [hereafter *Messages*]. See also Hirshson, *Farewell to the Bloody Shirt,* pp. 104–105; Doenecke, *Presidencies,* pp. 112–13, 124–25; and O'Reilly, *Nixon's Piano,* pp. 56–57.

38. Williamson, *The Crucible of Race,* p. 117; see also Gunnar Myrdal, *An American Dilemma: The Negro Problem and Modern Democracy* (New York: Harper and Brothers, 1944), pp. 560–64.

39. William McKinley, "Inaugural Address," Mar. 4, 1897, *Messages,* 13:6240; Lewis L. Gould, *The Presidency of William McKinley* (Lawrence, Kans.: Regents, 1980), pp. 28–29, 156–58.

40. Ida B. Wells-Barnett, "Remarks to President McKinley," in *Lift Every Voice,* pp. 861–62. See also Ida B. Wells-Barnett, "Southern Horrors: Lynch Law in All Its Phases," in *Man Cannot Speak for Her,* comp. Karlyn Kohrs Campbell (New York: Praeger, 1989), 2:385–419.

41. Robert J. Kaczorowski, "The Enforcement Provisions of the Civil Rights Act of 1866: A Legislative History in Light of *Runyon v. McCrary,*" *Yale Law Journal* 98 (1989): 574; Kaczorowski, *The Politics of Judicial Interpretation: The Federal Courts, Department of Justice, and Civil Rights, 1866–1876* (New York: Oceana, 1985).

42. Doenecke, *Presidencies,* p. 16.

43. Benjamin Harrison, "Annual Message," Dec. 4, 1892, in *Messages,* 12:5767; Sinkler, *The Racial Attitudes of American Presidents,* pp. 277–78; Homer E. Socolofsky and Allan B. Spetter, *The Presidency of Benjamin Harrison* (Lawrence: University Press of Kansas, 1989).

44. Williamson, *The Crucible of Race,* pp. 183–89.

45. Harry J. Sievers, S.J., ed., *Benjamin Harrison, 1833–1901* (Dobbs Ferry, N.Y.: Oceana, 1969); Sinkler, *The Racial Attitudes of American Presidents,* pp. 242–88; Hirshson, *Farewell to the Bloody Shirt,* pp. 164–72.

46. Benjamin Harrison, "Michigan Club Banquet," Feb. 22, 1888, *Speeches of Benjamin Harrison: Twenty-Third President of the United States* (New York: United States Book, 1892), p. 13.

47. See his speech before the Harrison League of Indianapolis, June 30, 1888, *Speeches of Benjamin Harrison,* pp. 33–35. See also Harrison's speeches in Sievers, *Benjamin Harrison.*

48. Benjamin Harrison, "First Annual Message," Dec. 3, 1889, in *Messages* (1897, reprint; New York: Bureau of National Literature, 1920), 11:5491.

49. Hirshson, *Farewell to the Bloody Shirt,* pp. 164–72; Sinkler, *The Racial Attitudes of American Presidents,* pp. 225–56.

50. Quotation from Benjamin Harrison, "Fourth Annual Message," Dec. 6, 1892, in *Messages,* 12:5766–67. See also Benjamin Harrison, "Second Annual Message," Dec. 1, 1890, in *Messages,* 11:5563–64; Benjamin Harrison, "Third Annual Message," Dec. 9, 1891, in *Messages,* 12:5643–45.

51. Socolofsky and Spetter, *Presidency of Benjamin Harrison,* pp. 62–66; Hirshson, *Farewell to the Bloody Shirt,* pp. 200–235; Sinkler, *The Racial Attitudes of American Presidents,* pp. 260–63.

52. See the special "Perspectives" section that appears in the *Journal of American History* 75 (1998): 841–68.

53. These narratives are evident in many of the sources listed earlier.

Williamson's *The Crucible of Race,* Woodward's *Origins of the New South,* and Rabinowitz's *Race Relations in the Urban South* are particularly insightful.

54. Anthony W. Marx, "Race-Making and the Nation State," *World Politics* 48 (1996): 180–208.

55. Washington, "Atlanta Exposition Address," p. 804.

56. Grover Cleveland to Booker T. Washington, Dec. 3, 1899, in *Letters of Grover Cleveland,* ed. Allan Nevins (Boston: Houghton Mifflin, 1933), p. 413.

57. Ibid., pp. 521–22; See also Grover Cleveland, "Address to Southern Educational Association," Apr. 14, 1903, in *Grover Cleveland: Addresses, State Papers, and Letters,* ed. Albert Ellery Bergh (New York: Sun Dial Classics, 1908), pp. 423–24.

58. William McKinley, "Speech at Tuskegee Normal and Industrial Institute," Dec. 16, 1898, in *Speeches and Addresses of William McKinley* (New York: DoubleDay and McClure, 1900), p. 168.

59. For a discussion about Washington's power and his relationships to several presidents, see Bennett Jr., *Before the Mayflower,* pp. 263–74.

60. Woodward, *The Strange Career of Jim Crow,* p. 82.

CHAPTER 2

Calvin Coolidge
and the Rhetoric of
"Race" in the 1920s

—

Marouf Hasian Jr.

There are racial considerations too grave to be brushed aside for any sentimental reasons. Biological laws tell us that certain divergent people will not mix or blend.
—Calvin Coolidge, "Whose Country Is This?"

alvin Coolidge is often remembered as an enigmatic chief executive, a civic leader who had his share of both detractors and supporters. Although he was president for only a little more than five years, it is clear that he was a very popular leader who could have held office longer if he had so wished.[1] His critics complained about his regimentation, his lack of activism, and his abandonment of the progressive policies that had marked a part of his earlier political career. Edward Ellis characterizes him as the "high priest of the cult of big business" and a supporter of those who believed that success "justified everything."[2]

Yet Coolidge's aloofness and quiet demeanor resonated with many Americans who lived during the 1920s. For example, M. E. Hennessy would make these observations in 1924: "His taciturnity and self-repression are characteristic of the stock from which he sprang—a people noted for self-reliance, independence, simplicity and plain living. Men born and bred as he, on a mountain top, are likely to be reserved and slow to speak. The stillness of the hills is reflected in their manners. All of the Republic Presidents, not excepting even Theodore Roosevelt, have come from the race of frontier pioneers or were their near descendants. . . . [F]ive generations of Coolidges have cultivated the stony hillsides and managed affairs in their own democratic ways."[3]

Another of Coolidge's contemporaries, William Allen White, noticed that Coolidge "took color from his times. He felt that he was the head of the part of talent and wealth and that talent meant, of course, acquisitive talent which produced and owned the wealth of the land—the Hamiltonian idea made perfect."[4] Living in the "Age of Normalcy," his minimalist views of government meshed perfectly with those of many of his constituents, who were more interested in the automobile, Prohibition, and the Ku Klux Klan than they were in foreign wars or intrigues. The horrors of the fields of Flanders and the dangers of Bolshevism were still fresh in the minds of many Americans.

Although there are many fascinating dimensions of the Coolidge years that are still in need of critical investigation, I am primarily interested in describing and evaluating the "racial" dimensions of this politician's domestic and foreign policies.[5] More specifically, I would like to unpack some of the rhetorical aspects of Coolidge's discourse in order that we might gain a better appreciation of this politician's arguments and the ideologies of some of his contemporaries. Sobel has recently averred that "few presidents were as outspoken on the need to protect the civil rights" of black Americans as Calvin Coolidge, but in his cursory discussion of the racial debates of the times, he provides little evidence of any substantive changes beyond calling for more money for select black colleges or crop-support programs.[6] To be sure, these are important topics, but we need a much deeper and broader understanding of the role that race played in the 1920s.[7]

In order to accomplish this task, I have divided this chapter into three major sections. In the first segment I look at how Coolidge and his contemporaries wrote about the American "race" by decoding some of the rhetoric that surrounded the immigration-restriction battles of the 1920s.[8] The second part analyzes some of the ambiguities that existed in the Coolidge administration's treatment of African Americans in the 1920s. Finally, in the concluding portions of the chapter, I provide closure by discussing some of the lasting effects of these "racial" problematics.

Calvin Coolidge, Eternal "Germ Plasm," and the Immigration-Restriction Debates

Calvin Coolidge, like many other New England politicians, grew up in a cultural milieu that was obsessed with the question of how best to conserve not only America's forests and lakes, but the nation's "character" as well.[9] Between 1880 and 1920, there were countless regional and national debates about what to do with the "new immigrants" who sought "Americanization."[10] In order to avoid economic collapse and hereditary degeneration, some "native" Americans thought that they had found the best political solutions in their advocacy of "selective" immigration policies. Such strategies had been advocated since the mid-nineteenth century, based on the purported existence of at least three distinct "races." For example, William Ripley wrote a six-hundred-page study titled *The Races of Europe,* in which he claims that craniology provides an accurate picture of Western racial realities.[11] Maj. Charles Woodruff, an army surgeon who tried to extend Ripley's work, was certain that laboratory studies of many species of plants and animals showed that the races were constantly involved in the "survival of the fittest."[12] These types of arguments served as warrants for claims that Americans had both the right and the duty to protect the nation against the "flood" of indiscriminate immigrants who may or may not possess the right "germ plasm." For example, seventeen-year-old Saray Heysham, of Norristown, Pennsylvania, wrote in her prize-winning, American-Legion essay on immigration that "[W]e have a trust to preserve our Ship of State. To load aboard beyond the law of safety means the destruction of all."[13]

Selective-immigration restriction was a topic that also interested many American presidents. As early as 1903, Theodore Roosevelt told Congress that "[W]e cannot have too much immigration of the right kind, and we should have none at all of the wrong kind."[14] One university professor, Woodrow Wilson, would write the following words in his 1908 *History of the American People:* "Throughout the century [the 1800s] men of the sturdy stocks of the north of Europe had made up the main strain of foreign blood which was every year added to the vital working force of this country but now there came multitudes of men of the lower class from the south of Italy and men of the meaner sort out of Hungary and Poland—men out of the ranks where there was neither skill nor energy nor any initiative of quick intelligence—and they came in numbers which increased from year to year, as if the countries of the south of Europe were disburdening themselves of the more sordid and hapless elements of their population, men whose standards of life and work were such as American workmen had never dreamed hitherto."[15]

Several years later, state legislatures debated the topic of the health of the "feebleminded."[16] As a consequence, laws were passed that allowed for the sterilization of generations of "imbeciles."[17] American readers were bombarded with thousands of pamphlets, letters to the editor, and books that extolled the virtues of eugenic marriages, race-purity statutes, and immigration restriction.

When critics look back on the progressive era, they often associate racism with the antics of the Ku Klux Klan, but the popularity of the science of eugenics turned the conservation of the germ plasm into a national obsession. When the International Congress of Eugenics came to New York in 1921, Herbert Hoover was in attendance. The keynote speaker at that conference, Henry Osborn, extolled the importance of "barring the entrance of those who are unfit to share in the duties and responsibilities of our well-founded government."[18] In the East, organizations were formed that allowed members to trace their Puritan stock, and in the Midwest, farmers attended fairs where family members got blue ribbons that certified their genetic worth.[19]

During this time, most American presidents had vetoed various congressional attempts at immigration restriction. On at least three occasions—with Cleveland in 1897, Taft in 1913, and Wilson in 1915—the nation's chief executives found flaws in some of these regulations. Wilson, for example, justified his stance by remarking that "If the people of this country have made up their minds to limit the number of immigrants by arbitrary tests and so reverse the policy of all the generations of Americans that have gone before them, it is their right to do so. But I do not believe that they have."[20]

The exact number of legal and illegal immigrants who came into the United States before 1920 is difficult to calculate, but Alan Kraut has suggested that between 1880 and 1921, at least twenty-three million people "took advantage of America's lenient immigration policies and came to the United States."[21] Eugenists, nativists, and other concerned citizens began grumbling that the older methods of immigration control—fining the shipping lines, making hasty physical inspections for diseases, and using chalk to mark people with potential mental defects—were outmoded methods of immigration control. Higham has argued in his *Strangers in the Land* that, by 1920, the "policies of Americanization and deportation, as massive ventures, were suffering general discredit."[22]

Many members of the congressional and executive branches of government wanted stricter immigration regulations, and Pres. Warren G. Harding had no reservations about signing an "emergency" immigration measure.[23] The Emergency Quota Act that was passed in May of 1921 was based on a quota system that mandated that immigration be confined to 3 percent of the number of foreigners born of each European nationality residing in the United States in 1910.[24] As Ferrell observes, this "reduced European immigrants to a maximum of 355,000 a year—55 percent from northwestern Europe and 45 percent from southeastern."[25]

In theory, the combined limits that came from the passage of literary tests in 1917 and the new quota bill had ended the era of purported open immigration.[26] Yet many exclusionists found a plethora of problems with this emergency act. The legislation still allowed in hundreds of thousands of immigrants, and the time parameters that were included in the bill inadvertently exacerbated the problems that officials experienced in eastern harbors. The act had mandated that no more than a fifth of a nation's annual quota could be utilized in any single month and thus inaugurated a competition among steamship companies. The passage of the 1921 act ushered in a host of new public debates on the topic of permanent restrictionist legislation.

With this in mind, we turn our attention to Calvin Coolidge and his attitudes toward these particular foreign "races." In 1920, Vermont's native son had just become the vice president of the United States and a dutiful member of President Harding's cabinet. After twenty years as a major political figure in New England, Coolidge was not about to stay on the sidelines when it came to discussions of immigration restriction. The story of the groundbreaking work of Preston Hall's Immigration Restriction League is well known,[27] but there were many foot soldiers in the war against the foreign "other."

A review of Coolidge's extant press releases and speeches indicates that he often discussed the importance of balancing assimilation with restriction.

Perhaps the best example of Coolidge's views on the immigration question came in the midst of the heated ideological battles of 1921, when Americans were getting used to the idea that the days of the indiscriminate melting pot were over. In February of that year, just a month before becoming vice president, Coolidge wrote an essay titled "Whose Country Is This?" that was published in *Good Housekeeping* magazine. In that article, he defended the claim that there were "racial" considerations too grave to be brushed aside for any sentimental reasons.[28]

Coolidge's essay deserves to be analyzed at some length because it provides us with an excellent barometer of the tacit "racial" knowledge of the period and the immigration views of the future president. In the beginning of his four-page article, the vice president is careful to observe that America could always use "the right kind of inhabitants" because the country constantly needed "all the intelligence, the skill, and strength of mind and body it could get."[29] Yet for Coolidge, it was also "a self-evident truth" that "a healthy community" had no place for "the vicious, the weak of mind, the shiftless, or the improvident."[30]

These introductory words help frame an essay that shows us how conservative progressives hoped to apply these scientific truths in their advocacy of selective-immigration legislation. Coolidge argues in this composition that the "popular mind" of America needs to understand that the country can "no longer afford to remain an asylum" for those who simply prey on the property of others, and he argues that no civilization can survive if it does not possess some "active community of interest—spiritual, social, and economic."[31] The vice president was sure that such a "background" can come from either "a racial tradition" or "a national experience," but it must be consistent with "American institutions" and must be "characterized by a capacity of assimilation."[32] Although he recognizes that "any" restriction needs to be a "necessary and momentary expediency," he is sure that his readers will agree that it would be "suicidal to let down the bars for the inflowing of cheap manhood [*sic*]" that was making "our country" the "dumping ground" of the world.[33]

Throughout the rest of his article, Coolidge brings together a host of popular economic, political, and eugenic rationales that justify restrictive immigration. For example, he argues that part of the nation's problems stem from the fact that "the alien" simply does not understand that, in coming to America, a potential immigrant is taking a chance because of the shifting and "certain laws of supply and demand." Furthermore, there are potential entrants who have the "desire to teach destruction of government" and who attack "every form of religion and so basic an institution as the home." What these future immigrants need to know is that "The Nordics propagate themselves successfully. With other races, the outcome shows deterioration on both sides. Quality of mind and body suggest[s] that observance of ethnic law is as great a necessity to a nation as immigration law. From its very beginning our country has been enriched by a complex blend of varied strains in the same ethnic family. We are, in some sense, an immigrant nation, molded in the fires of common experience. . . . And it is that common experience we must hand down to our children, even as the fundamental principles of Americanism, based on righteousness, were handed down to us, in perpetuity, by the founders of our government."[34]

Such a stance was typical of the racial rhetoric of the 1920s—it appears to be an objective balance of open and closed immigration, drawing a bright line between racial difference and racial superiority. The epigraph that I have used at the beginning of this chapter shows that Coolidge was familiar with the eugenic discussions of the dangers of racial mixing and that he was sure that biological laws needed to be respected. But here we have no detailed discussion of whiteness—simply the acceptance of the view that there is an Americanization process that does not end with education or improved economics. Coolidge demanded much more—a "vital spirit" that came from the "daily exercise of the principles on which the Republic rests."[35] Some of the president's colleagues wanted the total exclusion of some "races," but Coolidge argued that some of the overseas immigration agencies needed to do a better job of screening potential immigrants. The president averred that his minimalist plan would help "put our house in order for the advancing hordes of aliens."[36]

Coolidge's *Good Housekeeping* fragment was just one of thousands of essays that were written between 1921 and 1923 on the topic of "selective" immigration, and congressional decision makers now sought permanent solutions to the immigration "problem." For example, Albert Johnson, writing in the *Nation's Business* in July,

1923, complains that his colleagues were simply not moving quickly enough to ensure that the nation's laws conformed with "biological realities."[37] This Washingtonian was sure that "We are infinitely more careful in the selection of the animals that we import for breeding purposes than we are in the selection of our incoming aliens. . . . No abnormal or diseased animal is allowed to mix its blood with that of our breeding stock. . . . An animal is an unfit animal, whether it be a man or woman, horse or sheep. Bonds are powerless to make a fit American father or mother out of a feeble-minded alien."[38] It should come as no surprise that Johnson would become an honorary member of some of America's most popular eugenic societies.

When Coolidge became president in 1923, he inherited a very messy immigration situation. An analysis of the *Calvin Coolidge Papers* reveals that for months he was bombarded with telegrams, essays, and letters written by concerned citizens who asked the chief executive to take a clearer stance on these issues.[39] The new president seemed to favor some type of restriction legislation, but he was still very vague about his level of support. In his annual message to Congress, which was delivered on December 6, 1923, Coolidge made these remarks: "America must be kept American. For this purpose, it is necessary to continue a policy of restricted immigration. It would be well to make such immigration of a selective nature with some inspection at the source, and based either on a prior census or upon the record of naturalization."[40]

It was fairly clear that the president was not going to veto all of the restrictions bills, but the legislators had better get it right. As Howard Quint and Robert Ferrell noted in 1964, this was one issue where Coolidge "did not take a stand against Congress."[41] One could add that although he occasionally quibbled with most congressional leaders about their specific proposals, the president for the most part agreed with the noble aspirations of the sponsors of what would become known as the "Johnson-Reed Bill."[42] Constituents in all parts of the country, who often sent him anecdotes of their own experiences with immigrants, worried about the possibility of another presidential veto.

Coolidge seemed to be genuinely torn. On the one hand, he believed that in some cases other nations needed to voluntarily restrict emigration, and he did not want to offend Japanese diplomats. On the other hand, there was tremendous bipartisan support for strict immigration regulation.[43]

Between November, 1923, and May, 1924, some of the members of Coolidge's cabinet became active participants in the debates over the desirability of the Johnson-Reed restrictions act. These leaders saw themselves as public servants who had been bequeathed the task of preserving the nation's natural, political, and spiritual resources. For example, James J. Davis wrote to the president on May 27, 1924, that the new statutes would represent "the longest step forward ever taken" in directing America's future generations.[44]

Things became even more complicated during the month of May because this was the time when various constituencies and their representatives sent even more mail. Most of these letters and telegrams were filled with biological, political, or economic rationales for Coolidge to veto the Johnson-Reed Immigration Act. Immigration restriction was such a popular topic that it divided not only whites but people of color as well. For example, many blacks, sure of their own patriotism and noble birth, complained about the employment of recent immigrants. "Why go to Europe," asked A. L. Jackson, "when at our very doors we have millions of the best workers in the world anxious for the opportunity to enter the lists heretofore kept open solely for the immigrant?"[45] The editor of the Pittsburgh *Courier* remarked that, "If the Negro is allowed to take the place left vacant by the excluded Southern and Eastern European; if the attitude of the Nordics toward the Negro is to improve as the country develops its Nordic family; if the family blood is made better by an increase of Nordics, and a better family blood means a better country for its citizens, then the Johnson Bill ought to mean a better opportunity for the American with the darker skin. We shall see."[46] The protean nature of these eugenic arguments meant that the opposition to such policies would be ineffectual.

Claudia Goldin, professor of economics at Harvard University, stated in 1994 that she was astonished that the "door" remained "open despite twenty-five years of assault during which 17 million immigrants from among the poorest nations in Europe found refuge in America."[47] For a long time, what kept America's gates from closing was a faith that somehow either nature or nurture would help improve the health, manners, culture, and politics of all immigrants.

These are just some of the antirestrictionist arguments that circulated in the mid-1920s. A small group of opponents of the Johnson-Reed Immigration Bill also tried to influence Coolidge's decision. For example, A. J. Sabath, a member of the House from the Fifth Congressional District in Illinois, sent a letter on May 23, 1924, that points out some of the "discriminatory provisions in the Immigration Bill."[48] This apprehensive congressional leader claimed that the use of the 1890 census prejudiced immigration from "Southern and Southeastern European nations." Sabath urged Coolidge to think about the "practical" possibility of allowing two more years for scientific study of the temporary measures before going to permanent solutions.[49] The alternative meant "branding millions of our citizens as inferior and deliberately hurting the pride of nearly all friendly nations."[50]

The president eventually decided not to veto the Reed-Johnson Immigration Bill, and for the next several months he defended his actions. During his Republican nomination address in August of 1924, Coolidge informed his listeners that "restrictive immigration is not an offense but a purely defense action" and that "we must remember that every object of our institutions of society and Government will fail unless America be kept American."[51] The presidential candidate made it clear that such policies were not "adopted in criticism of others in the slightest degree, but solely for the purposes of protecting ourselves."[52]

In sum, "Silent Cal" was not so silent when it came to discussion of the biological differences between the "races" and immigration restriction. The president's eugenic arguments were typical remarks made during a time when a host of interrelated progressive movements relied on racial differentiation. From a rhetorical perspective, Coolidge's desire to prevent the mixing of the races was a goal that was widely shared. Worries about racial "mixing," potential economic dislocation, and eugenic degeneration appeared as realistic reasons for U.S. citizens to accept the scientific limits of the "Americanization" process.[53] Did these views on "race" apply only to the foreign "others"?

Calvin Coolidge and the African American Quest for Political, Social, and Economic Equality

"Civil rights and liberties," notes Robert Ferrell, "took a backseat among social issues of the 1920s."[54] At the same time that state and local leaders tried to maintain the purity of the Anglo-Saxons by prohibiting intermarriage between "Asiatics" and "whites," they also passed domestic laws that penalized the "intermingling" of the "black" and "white" races. In Virginia, Harry Laughlin—a congressional eugenics expert—helped with the passage of racial-purity laws that made it a crime for members of different races to enter into the bonds of holy matrimony.[55] Charles Davenport, considered one of the leading biologists of his day, thought that immigration restriction did not suffice—"education, segregation, and sterilization" were needed in order to "increase the density of socially desirable traits."[56]

Such ideological positions were persuasive with audiences who were familiar with the internal logics of the "equal-but-separate" legal doctrine. Obviously, not all Americans believed in the legitimacy of these racial hierarchies. In both the North and the South, African Americans fought to avoid "wage slavery," and they watched the steady erosion of the political and civil rights that had been gained with the passage of the Thirteenth, Fourteenth, and Fifteenth post–Civil War amendments. Farmers faced peonage laws and vagrancy statutes, and urban dwellers dealt with restrictive covenants and police brutality. Wilson's Democratic administration provided little remedial help, but African Americans hoped that their patriotic efforts during World War I would translate into pragmatic changes when new leaders arrived on the scene.[57]

When Coolidge became president in August of 1923, many African Americans thought that the party of Lincoln, Stevens, and Sumner would help them make significant gains in the areas of social, political, and economic equality, but this would not be the case. John Blair has gone so far as to argue that the Coolidge administration became a "rather exclusive vehicle" that advanced the interests of "whites, Anglo-Saxons, and Protestants."[58] During Coolidge's presidential campaign against Davis, Bishop John Hurst of the Methodist Episcopal Church claimed that in spite of the faithfulness of blacks, the Republican party had broken many promises.[59] This African American leader attacked the Republicans in Congress for allowing a "handful of Southerners to filibuster the Anti-Lynching Bill to death," and he supported La Follette because "the Progressive Movement opens the door of hope to the colored Americans as at no time in a generation."[60] Bishop Hurst reported to the readers of the *New York Times* that the president had refused to denounce the Ku Klux Klan and that "The best that we have been able to get from the white public, despite repeated requests, not only by colored men of prominence but other Americans who rightfully object to the Klan on the ground of its fundamental un-Americanism, is a brief statement from the Lily-White G. Bascom Siem [*sic*], Mr. Coolidge's secretary, to the effect that Mr. Coolidge is not a Klansman. How gratifying to learn that Mr. Coolidge does not put on a night shirt and a pillow case and join the night riders after supper."[61]

Such caustic remarks did not sit well with members of the Coolidge administration, and an analysis of some of the extant texts of the times reveals that this assessment may be too harsh. There were times when Coolidge's patriotic idealism could be deployed in the defense of oppressed people and communities. For example, take the case of Charles Roberts, an African American dentist who had been designated by the Republican county committee as their candidate for New York's Twenty-first Congressional District. When one of his constituents wondered whether any black should be allowed to run for any congressional office in this "white man's country," Coolidge responded with this statement that appeared in the *New York Times* in August of 1924:[62] "I am amazed at receiving such a letter. During the war 500,000 colored men and boys were called up under the draft, not one of whom sought to evade it. They took their places wherever assigned in defense of the nation of which they are just as truly citizens as are any others. The suggestion of denying any measure of their full political rights to such a great group of our population of the colored people is one which, however it may be received in some quarters, could not possibly be permitted by one who feels a responsibility for living up to the traditions and principles of the Republican Party. Our Constitution guarantees equal rights to all citizens, without discrimination upon account of race or color."[63] At the same time, Coolidge began shying away from participating in Ku Klux Klan events, hoping that these symbolic gestures would help improve his image with African Americans.

This, however, was clearly not the only time that Coolidge came out against both racial and religious intolerance. If the president thought that particular activities violated the ideals of the nation's founders or modern views of "Americanism," then he had no hesitancy in openly espousing his views on the dangers of such Constitutional violations. For example, in October of 1925, the president spoke out at the national convention of the American Legion, which was held in Omaha, Nebraska.[64] There he gave a fiery address that attacked the "Old World" notions of "militarism" and "intolerance." He received a standing ovation when he got to the part of the presentation where he claimed that "Divine Providence has not bestowed on any race a monopoly of patriotism and character."[65] Coolidge spoke for about forty minutes, and one news reporter considered his address to be a "thoughtful resume" of "after-war conditions, governmental problems and social movements" that encouraged "young American soldiers to help eradicate the anti-racial and anti-religious movements in the United States."[66] In the Omaha address, Coolidge defended the importance of what he called "intellectual demobilization" and claimed that "No man's [sic] patriotism was impugned or service questioned because of his racial origin, his political opinion or religious convictions. Immigrants and the sons of immigrants from the Central European countries fought side by side with those who descended from the countries which were our allies; with the sons of equatorial Africa, and with the red men of our own aboriginal population, all of them equally proud of the name Americans. . . . I recognize the full and complete necessity of 100 percent Americanism, but 100 percent Americanism may be made up of various elements. . . . [W]e must all realize that there are true Americans who did not happen to be born in our section of the country, who do not attend our place of religious worship, who are not of our racial stock or who are not proficient in our language."[67] Although the president never specifically mentioned just which groups were violating the rights of some of America's citizens, one *New York Times* reporter was sure he was talking about the "Ku Klux Klan and the animosities against the German citizens bred by the World War and still smoldering in some communities."[68]

Unfortunately, these encouraging words did not mean that dramatic changes in any of the Coolidge administration's civil rights policies were going to occur. As long as racial reforms were narrowly defined as "political" rights, blacks did get some occasional help. This could be justified as part of Americanism, the continued experiment that fit within the president's nationalistic or patriotic visions. Defining the parameters of "civil" or "social" rights was considered to be either a congressional or judicial prerogative, beyond the purview of the chief executive. Sobel may be right when he indicates that Coolidge at times spoke out "for the rights" of blacks, but this stance ignores the contextualization of those rights.[69]

For example, the Coolidge administration's ideological defense of minimalist federal intervention made any massive infusion of educational funds or federal troops for the enforcement of federal law highly unlikely. The purported racial misunderstandings that had ushered in the Reconstruction years were still a part of the nation's collective memories. In many ways, Coolidge's inability to grapple with the complexities of racism during the 1920s came from his idealistic ideology that saw a clear demarcation between law and politics and between conservation of the nation's traditions and radical experimentation with social institutions. To have actively intervened with federal power in order to rectify local and state abuses would have gone against the principles of comity and respect for the social mores of the American people.

Coolidge was firmly convinced that African Americans had already "substantially solved" their economic problems and that they needed to continue "their efforts for educational progress and spiritual betterment."[70] In a highly publicized letter to Robert Moton of the National Negro Business League, the president argued that "full political rights will be won through the inevitable logic of their position and the righteousness of their claims."[71] The president's exemplar for improving race relations was not Garvey or DuBois, but rather Booker T. Washington. In a speech that he gave at Howard University, Coolidge recommended that a commission be established that would help "formulate a better policy for mutual understanding and confidence."[72]

As a result, the Coolidge administration provided very little in the way of concrete, material help for African Americans—even changes in civil-service salaries were cosmetic at best. The legality and the desirability of the "equal" but "separate" doctrines were unquestioned. As Robert Ferrell explains, "In the case of civil rights . . . the rights of black Americans had seldom concerned their white brothers and sisters. The Civil War had disposed of the issue; not until the late

1930s did civil rights come to the fore. . . . City political machines solicited black votes, but for the most part, blacks did not disturb citywide equations and had little importance in state office-holding. The wartime flux may have been the most important event for black Americans since emancipation, but in the 1920s, it had not yet acquired political importance."[73]

If there was one issue that might have galvanized interracial support for African American rights in the 1920s, it was lynching prohibitions. African Americans had been trying to change local, state, and federal laws regarding lynching for decades, but it was only after World War I that their consciousness-raising efforts came to the attention of the mass media.[74] In 1918, the National Association for the Advancement of Colored People (NAACP) gained the support of Wilson and the American Bar Association in these efforts, and these parties attacked the extrajudicial nature of mob violations of the American legal process.[75] In the spring of that same year, Attorney General A. Mitchell Palmer, Charles Evans Hughes, William Howard Taft, and the governors of eleven states attended a conference on lynching. They signed a declaration that demanded that Congress undertake "a nation-wide investigation of lynching and mob murder to the end that means may be found to end this scourge."[76]

Observers soon found that there was a great deal of difference between getting signatures on a proclamation and passing legislative enactments on that subject. In Congress, the leading proponent of antilynching laws was Rep. Leonidas C. Dyer of Missouri, who, in the fall of 1918, introduced a bill that attempted to make lynching a federal crime.[77] This very controversial document claims that blacks were entitled to "equal protection of the laws" and suggests that U.S. district attorneys be given the power to prosecute state law-enforcement officers who had been lax in their duties. Furthermore, the Dyer initiatives would have allowed these federal attorneys to bring damage suits against any county that had allowed lynchings. Four years later, a revised Dyer bill was passed by the House of Representatives, but it was buried in the Senate following the threat of a Southern filibuster.[78]

One of the key reasons for the defeat of the antilynching legislation stemmed from the alliances that had been forced between Southern and Western politicians, who had vested interests in maintaining the status quo. Many civic leaders in California, Washington, Montana, and other states wanted more restrictive foreign immigration, while some Southerners wanted to maintain racial hegemony in their region. Coolidge both privately and publicly held that lynching was a "hideous crime," but he was convinced that the Republican "Congress" was the body that needed to "exercise all of its powers of prevention and punishment."[79] As late as 1927, members of the National Negro Centre political party went to the White House and asked the president "why the Fourteenth Amendment could not be enforced for the prevention of lynching." Coolidge replied that he would "call in the Attorney General and have him see what might be done in the way of declaring martial law in a State where lynchings were rampant."[80] Decades would pass before any major federal involvement in lynching reform occurred.

Conclusion

In sum, Calvin Coolidge's views on race and civil rights are understandable, if not always agreeable. After witnessing the tragic events of World War I, many Americans were convinced that the only way to avoid a repetition of the problems of the "Old World" was to acknowledge that racial difference—and perhaps racial hierarchies—existed in politics, society, and nature. This was an incredibly cabined and domesticated view of civil rights because it helped perpetuate the view that radicals, foreigners, or militarists were the primary agents involved in racial intolerance. During the 1920s, a person who believed in the naturalness of racial differentiation or segregation was considered to be neither a racist nor an intolerant human being.

These ideological fragments would become an enduring part of our racial rhetorics. As Culpepper Clark and Raymie McKerrow note in their study of Gunnar Myrdal, pre–World War II racism was viewed as "an absolute given" and an "instinctive, visceral attitude that was beyond debate."[81] The vast majority of commentators, including some of the many critics of hard-line eugenics, took for granted the existence of immutable racial typologies.

An analysis of some of the private correspondence and public texts of the period reveals how Coolidge and many members of his cabinet still shared the excitement of the Progressive Era, with its focus on pragmatism, eugenic experimentation, and efficiency. In the area of racial and ethnic politics, this meant that the American president was supposed to keep an eye on international restriction acts and the domestic laws on racial segregation. Social actors who focused on one without the other were creating loopholes, ignoring biological imperatives, and hurting the opportunities of those who truly deserved the chance to be members of the American "race."

Calvin Coolidge and many of his contemporaries would have been shocked if they had lived to see some of the massive federal intervention that would take place in the coming generations. Such practices appeared to be blurring the lines that purportedly existed between political, social, and economic "equality." The judicial edicts that came from cases such as *Brown v. Board of Education* would also have been viewed as coercive, tyrannical, and counterproductive practices that destroyed individual initiative, hindered the gradual development of the "races," and facilitated governmental intrusion into private affairs.[82] In an interview that he gave just shortly before his death, Coolidge told Henry Stoddard that he was shocked by the "socialist notions of government" that were being introduced by Hoover's successors.[83] At one point in their conversation, the ex-president remarked that "[w]e are in a new era to which I do not belong, and it would not be possible for me to adjust myself to it."[84] He was certainly not alone.

Notes

1. In the 1920 presidential election, the Harding-Coolidge ticket received more than 16 million votes, and the Cox-Roosevelt team received 9.1 million. Robert Sobel, *Coolidge: An American Enigma* (Washington, D.C.: Regnery, 1998), p. 206.
2. Edward Robb Ellis, *A Nation in Torment: The Great American Depression, 1929–1939* (New York: Kodansha International, 1995), p. 26.
3. M. E. Hennessy, *Calvin Coolidge: From a Green Mountain Farm to the White House* (New York: G. P. Putnam's Sons, 1924), pp. vi–vii.
4. William Allen White, *A Puritan in Babylon: The Story of Calvin Coolidge* (New York: Macmillan, 1938), p. 251.
5. I share Marvin Jones's belief that "race" is an "incoherent fiction" with a great deal of "rhetorical power." D. Marvin Jones, "Darkness Made Visible: Law, Metaphor, and the Racial Self," *Georgetown Law Journal* 82 (1993): 439–40.
6. Sobel, *Coolidge*, p. 250.
7. Given space limitations, in this chapter I do not cover the Coolidge administration's handling of the political, social, and economic

rights of all of the "races" that were socially constructed at this time. As Trent observes, "[R]acist sentiment, of course, permeated American consciousness, overlapping with nativist white fears not only of blacks but also of Eastern Europeans, Mexicans and Central Americans, and East Asians." James W. Trent Jr., *Inventing the Feeble-minded: A History of Mental Retardation in the United States* (Berkeley: University of California Press, 1994), p. 139. For a brief discussion of Mexican and Filipino immigration, see Robert Ferrell, *The Presidency of Calvin Coolidge* (Lawrence: University Press of Kansas, 1998), p. 114.

8. Lothrop Stoddard, *The Rising Tide of Color against White World Supremacy* (New York: Scribner's Sons, 1920).

9. For an excellent discussion of the relationship between the "conservation of trees" and "people," see Donald K. Pickens, *Eugenics and the Progressives* (Nashville: Vanderbilt University Press, 1968), pp. 191–201.

10. See Alan M. Kraut, *The Huddled Masses: The Immigrant in American Society, 1880–1921* (Arlington Heights, Ill.: Harlan Davidson, 1982).

11. William Z. Ripley, *The Races of Europe: A Sociological Study* (New York: D. Appleton, 1899).

12. Charles E. Woodruff, *Expansion of the Races* (New York: Rebman, 1909). For a trenchant critique of Woodruff's work, see Joseph W. Bendersky, "The Disappearance of Blonds: Immigration, Race, and the Re-emergence of 'Thinking White,' " *Telos* 104 (Summer, 1995): 138.

13. "Youth Speaks to America," *American Legion Weekly* 6 (July 4, 1924): 13–14, quoted in Peter H. Wang, "The Immigration Act of 1924 and the Problem of Assimilation," *Journal of Ethnic Studies* 2 (Fall, 1974): 74.

14. Theodore Roosevelt, *Congressional Record* 38 (1903): 3, quoted in Rachel Silber, "Eugenics, Family, and Immigration Law in the 1920s," *Georgetown Immigration Law Journal* 11 (1997): 871.

15. Ibid.

16. See Trent, *Inventing*, pp. 130–70.

17. Some states passed domestic laws that were meant to address the public-health problems associated with domestic germ plasm. See Edward J. Larson, *Sex, Race, and Science: Eugenics in the Deep South* (Baltimore: Johns Hopkins University Press, 1995), p. 29.

18. Silber, "Eugenics," p. 871.

19. Ida Clyde Clarke, "Kansas Has a Big Idea," *Pictorial Review* 26 (Jan., 1925): 20.

20. Roy L. Garis, "America's Immigration Policy," *North American Review* 220 (Sept., 1924): 64.

21. Kraut, *The Huddled*, p. 2.

22. John Higham, *Strangers in the Land: Patterns of American Nativism,*

1860–1925 (New Brunswick, N.J.: Rutgers University Press, 1994 [1955]), p. 300.

23. Ibid., p. 311.

24. Robert A. Divine, *American Immigration Policy, 1924–1952* (New Haven, Conn.: Yale University Press, 1957), p. 5.

25. Ferrell, *The Presidency,* p. 113.

26. For a political breakdown of the alliances that helped pass the 1921 act, see Ferrell, *The Presidency.*

27. Matthew Frye Jacobson, *Whiteness of a Different Color* (Cambridge: Harvard University Press, 1998), pp. 69–81.

28. Coolidge, "Whose Country Is This?" p. 14.

29. Ibid., p. 13.

30. Ibid. Although Coolidge does not specifically mention any of the European nations as a source of the unfit immigrants he alludes to in this essay, the president shared the belief of "most Americans" in the 1920s that "Europe was the root of all evil." Howard H. Quint and Robert H. Ferrell, *The Talkative President* (Amherst: University of Massachusetts Press, 1964), p. 201.

31. Coolidge, "Whose Country Is This?" p. 13.

32. Ibid.

33. Ibid., p. 14.

34. Ibid., pp. 14, 106.

35. Ibid., p. 106.

36. Ibid., p. 109.

37. Albert Johnson, "Immigration: A Legislative Point of View," *Nation's Business* 11 (July, 1923): 26–28.

38. Ibid.; Bendersky, "The Disappearance," pp. 147–48.

39. For this chapter, I read all of the correspondence that Coolidge received between November, 1923, and May, 1924. *Presidential Papers Microfilm, Calvin Coolidge Papers* (Washington, D.C.: Library of Congress, 1959), no. 133, reels 78 and 79.

40. Green, *The Life,* p. 248.

41. Quint and Ferrell, *The Talkative,* p. 87.

42. Reed was the congressional sponsor of a revised bill that circulated in the Senate.

43. Sobel, *Coolidge,* p. 269.

44. James J. Davis to Calvin Coolidge, May 27, 1924, general records of the Department of Labor, record group 174, file 164/14J, National Archives, Washington, D.C., quoted in Wang, "The Immigration," p. 72.

45. See David J. Hellwig, "Black Leaders and United States Immigration Policy, 1917–1929," *Journal of Negro History* 66 (Summer, 1981): 115.

46. Ibid., p. 119.

47. Claudia Goldin, "The Political Economy of Immigration Restriction in the United States, 1890 to 1921," in *The Regulated Economy: A His-*

torical Approach to Political Economy, ed. Claudia Goldin and Gary D. Libecap (Chicago: University of Chicago Press, 1994), p. 223.

48. A. J. Sabath, letter to Calvin Coolidge, May 23, 1924, *Coolidge Papers,* reel 79.

49. Ibid.

50. Ibid.

51. "Text of Mr. Coolidge's Address Accepting Party's Nomination," *New York Times,* Aug. 15, 1924, p. 2.

52. Ibid.

53. See Paul Popenoe and Roswell Johnson, *Applied Eugenics* (New York: Macmillan, 1920), p. 304.

54. Ferrell, *The Presidency,* p. 107.

55. See Katherine M. Franke, "Becoming a Citizen: Reconstruction-Era Regulation of African American Marriages," *Yale Journal of Law and the Humanities* 11 (1999): 251–309.

56. Charles Davenport, quoted in Larson, *Sex, Race,* p. 29.

57. An assortment of commentaries on Wilson's views on race can be found in Fred Silva, *Focus on the Birth of a Nation* (Englewood Cliffs, N.J.: Prentice-Hall, 1971).

58. John L. Blair, "A Time for Parting: The Negro during the Coolidge Years," *Journal of American Studies* 3 (Dec., 1969): 177.

59. "Calls on Negroes to Back La Follette," *New York Times,* Oct. 7, 1924, p. 7.

60. Ibid.

61. Ibid.

62. Blair, "A Time," p. 190.

63. "Coolidge Defends Negro in Race for Congress, Rebukes Man Who Asked Him to Interfere," *New York Times,* Aug. 12, 1924, p. 1.

64. "Coolidge Demands Tolerance for All as Basis for Peace at Home and Abroad," *New York Times,* Oct. 7, 1925, pp. 1–2; "Text of the President's Address to the Legion in Omaha," *New York Times,* Oct. 7. 1925, p. 2.

65. "Text of the President's Address," p. 2.

66. "Coolidge Demands," p. 1.

67. "Text of the President's Address," p. 2.

68. "Coolidge Demands," p. 1.

69. Sobel, *Coolidge,* p. 249.

70. "Coolidge Pledges Rights to Negroes," *New York Times,* Aug. 22, 1924, p. 3.

71. Ibid.

72. Sobel, *Coolidge,* p. 250.

73. Ferrell, *The Presidency,* p. 107.

74. For an introduction to the literature on the antilynching efforts of African Americans during the years prior to the Coolidge administration, see Charles Flint Kellogg, *NAACP: A History of the National*

Association for the Advancement of Colored People, 1909–1920 (Baltimore: Johns Hopkins University Press, 1967).

75. William B. Hixson, "Moorfield Storey and the Defense of the Dyer Anti-Lynching Bill," *New England Review* 42 (Mar., 1969): 66.
76. Ibid.
77. Ibid.
78. Ibid., p. 67.
79. Sobel, *Coolidge,* p. 231.
80. "Report on Coolidge Visit," *New York Times,* Feb. 14. 1927, p. 10.
81. E. Culpepper Clark and Raymie E. McKerrow, "The Historiographical Dilemma in Myrdal's American Creed: Rhetoric's Role in Rescuing a Historical Moment," *Quarterly Journal of Speech* 74 (1987): 308.
82. *Brown v. Board of Education,* 347 U.S. 483 (1954).
83. Henry L. Stoddard, "Ex-President in Final Interview Declared His Time in Public Affairs Was Past," *New York Sun,* Jan. 6, 1933, p. 21.
84. Ibid.

CHAPTER 3

"We Go Ahead Together or We Go Down Together"

The Civil Rights Rhetoric of Eleanor Roosevelt

—

Diane M. Blair

Eleanor Roosevelt is perhaps best known for her central role in the crafting of the United Nations' Universal Declaration of Human Rights. That document declares that basic human rights are a world priority. ER's leadership on human rights, however, began during her years as first lady.[1] As first lady, ER was committed to a life of engaged political action that involved the most pressing and controversial questions of the twentieth century, including the issue of civil rights for black Americans. Although her civil rights arguments were not new, their significance stemmed from ER's articulation of them from the position of first lady. Never before had a woman so close to the center of presidential power publicly voiced a call for an end to racial discrimination.

Building on the work presented by Karlyn Kohrs Campbell at the very first of the Presidential Rhetoric Conferences, I argue that Eleanor Roosevelt provides us with an important case for viewing the rhetorical performances of first ladies as part of the rhetorical presidency.[2] In addition to her better-known symbolic gestures, I demonstrate that a prominent feature of ER's discourse is the articulation of *four equalities*. Not only did ER's public discourse complement and supplement her husband's rhetorical presidency, but it also enabled her to pursue a social and political agenda on behalf of civil rights that stretched above and beyond that of her husband's presidency. I make my argument by first situating her civil rights advocacy within the larger context of her rhetorical performance as first lady. Then I expound upon her rhetorical activities on behalf of civil rights, including her public examination of the nation's democracy as seen through her four equalities. I demonstrate how her focus on equality enabled her to speak out on the issue of race discrimination at the same time the radical nature of her rhetorical act was contained within a conservative framework of preserving both existing social structures and the international reputation of the nation. Such a framework formed the basis of her argument that the fate of U.S. democracy was intrinsically connected to the fate of the country's racial minorities. Finally, I suggest that this argument in turn helped establish a rhetorical foundation for presidential leadership on civil rights; at the same time, ironically, it precluded ER from attending to the country's civil rights issue as a human-rights issue.

An Outspoken First Lady

Like so many other social and political issues she addressed, ER spoke and acted publicly on the issue of racial discrimination. Her public activities and advocacy on behalf of civil rights was remarkable given the traditional confines of the first lady's role. The act of speaking publicly on *any* political issue violated the traditional gender conventions of that role. As Campbell and others have argued, the role of first lady is a difficult, almost impossible, one to play because of its ambiguous expectations and requirements.[3] As one of the most visible females in the U.S. political arena, a first lady is neither elected nor appointed, and yet she is often scrutinized as a symbol of her husband's administration; she has no official duties, and yet she serves as a representative of the nation; she is in an unpaid position, and yet the role has often been a full-time job for the women who occupy it.[4] As wives of the country's leaders, they are inevitably on the political and public stage, but as "ladies" they are expected to stay out of politics and remain in the background.[5]

Because there were no clearly defined role models for women as public figures, early first ladies adapted the roles of hostess and helpmate to national political life.[6] The role of first lady had never been used as a platform from which a woman could express bold, political ideas. Eleanor Roosevelt's performance of the role expanded its rhetorical opportunities and political possibilities. In a larger study, I argue that Eleanor Roosevelt's performance as first lady is significant for her expansion of the rhetorical opportunities for that traditionally gendered role.[7] With ER's performance, the first ladyship becomes a platform from which she and subsequent first ladies could be notable social advocates. To understand her rhetorical extension of the role of first lady, I explicate the characteristics and functions of the rhetorical resources that enabled her precedent-breaking performance. A brief overview of the rhetorical strategies she used to stretch the traditional boundaries of the role will help situate her remarkable outspokenness on civil rights.

First, it is important to understand that ER's background and experiences uniquely equipped her to assume a rhetorical role as first lady. Although her upbringing and early adulthood were quite traditional, she developed a deep sense of public duty and social commitment through her volunteer work in the settlement houses at the turn of the century and with the Red Cross during World War I. In the 1920s, ER emerged as a leading public figure in the women's reform network. Together these postsuffrage women's organizations (e.g., the Women's City Club, the National Consumers League, the League of Women Voters, the Women's Trade Union League, the Women's Division of the Democratic State Committee) sought to promote improvements in public housing, voter registration and education, pure-food-and-milk legislation, child-labor legislation, protective laws for women workers, and equal representation of women on all of the committees of the Democratic Party.[8] ER served as one of the central links among these various women's organizations. In fact, her prodigious activity in state and national politics, along with her business ventures, her teaching at the Todhunter School for girls, and her numerous public speaking and writing engagements, made her the better-known celebrity and party activist of the Roosevelt partnership prior to FDR's candidacy for the New York governorship.[9] In 1932, FDR's election to the presidency put ER in a position where her personal inclination toward social reform could respond to issues at a national level.

In addition to the extraordinary political and rhetorical experiences ER brought with her to the first ladyship, several features of her discourse enabled her precedent-breaking performance. First, ER frequently gave "time" rhetorical presence in her public discourse. She characterized the present moment as both a time of crisis and a time of possibility; she told the 1940 Democratic convention that it was "no ordinary time—no time for weighing anything except what we can best do for our country as a whole."[10] Rhetorically, her depiction of time worked with the material conditions to justify unprecedented actions by the federal government, to warrant support for bold social and political changes, and to legitimate the first lady's own public agenda. Out-of-the-ordinary times called for out-of-the-ordinary actions.[11]

Second, ER solicited, responded to, and publicly invoked the voice of the American people by incorporating their letters to her into her public speeches and essays. At the very beginning of her tenure in the White House, ER encouraged citizens to write to her about their fears, their concerns, and the adjustments they were making to "the new conditions in this amazing changing world."[12] She was soon flooded with letters, sometimes receiving up to four hundred in a single day. By ER's own estimation, she received three hundred thousand pieces of mail in one year alone.[13] ER frequently responded to these letters personally, but perhaps more interesting than her personal response is her public response. Rhetorically, she used the testimony in these letters as a form of support for her husband's New Deal programs. She also used the letters as a springboard for her own public discourse—they provided her with a way of introducing and commenting on social and political issues traditionally seen as outside the first lady's purview. In the process, she crafted an image of the American people as desiring social change, and she created a distinctive leadership role for herself as a "semiofficial intermediary" between the American people and their government. One of her columns was even titled "Ask Mrs. Roosevelt." People wrote her with questions such as "Do you think women can resist propaganda better than men?" "Do you think that the selective draft is essential to our country at this time? Won't getting prepared for war in this way lead us into war?" and "What do you consider the chief issues of this [1940] campaign?"[14]

Finally, working in concert with her depiction of time and her intermediary role, ER used rhetorical discourse to shape a vision of democracy for the country that required the active participation and inclusion of every American citizen, including those historically excluded or marginalized from the political process—it was a vision that demanded an end to racial injustice. ER's public examination of the state of the nation's democracy enabled her public critique of racism.

ER and Civil Rights

When ER entered the White House in 1933, black Americans were facing harsh social, political, and economic realities. They had long aspired to equal rights and constitutional guarantees, but a bitterly racist reaction had foreclosed many of the gains of Reconstruction. Jim Crow laws, the poll tax, lynching, and other discriminatory customs and attitudes had made racism a national phenomenon. At the initial onset of the economic depression, black laborers were relatively unorganized and the target of much discrimination and hostility. According to historian Patricia Sullivan, black laborers were "the first to absorb the economic downturn of the 1920s. The post–WWI economic slump stimulated a mass exodus of people to the cities, and as the economic squeeze tightened, white workers steadily took away what had been traditionally black jobs."[15] By 1935, 65 percent of black employees were in need of public assistance.[16] Public assistance, however, was given out on a discriminatory basis. In general, black Americans had more difficulty than their white counterparts in obtaining assistance. Even private religious and charitable organizations discriminated on the basis of skin color. When blacks did receive assistance, their relief benefits were often smaller.[17]

While FDR's New Deal brought some political hope and economic relief to the lives of black Americans, his political record reflected a reluctance to prioritize their civil rights. Like that of Lincoln before him and many presidents after him, FDR's action or inaction on behalf of civil rights was driven mostly by the interests of his broader political agenda.[18] Most historians acknowledge, and FDR himself argued, that he was constrained in his ability to address the race issue by his dependence on Southern democrats in Congress to pass his New Deal programs.[19] ER also reflected on her husband's presidential limits. In her autobiography, *This I Remember,* she wrote the following: "While I often felt strongly on various subjects, Franklin frequently refrained from supporting causes in which he believed, because of political realities. There were times when this annoyed me very much."[20] The Wagner-Costigan federal antilynching bill is a good case in point. Although FDR denounced lynching in his public addresses, he told ER that he could not push too hard for the bill because "First things come first, and I can't alienate certain votes I need for measures that would entail a fight."[21]

Unlike her husband, ER was not obligated to Congress. As first lady, she knew that her actions reflected on her husband's presidency, but the established independent nature of her activities, both prior to and during the first ladyship, enabled FDR to distance himself from her strategically. ER herself wrote of this technique: "If some idea I expressed strongly—and with which he might agree—caused a violent reaction, he could honestly say that he had no responsibility in the matter and that the thoughts were my own."[22] When ER approached FDR about advocating on behalf of rights for black Americans, he told her, "You can say anything you want. I can always say, 'Well, that is my wife; I can't do anything about her.'"[23] Thus, soon after her move to the White House, ER began expressing her own thoughts with regard to civil rights.

Blanche Wiesen Cook, one of ER's biographers, argues that the first lady's earliest significant confrontation with the subject of race discrimination came with her efforts to integrate Arthurdale, the homestead community subsidized by the federal government. Despite her personal pleas for inclusion, the residents of Scott's Run, West Virginia, worked together and picketed to keep Arthurdale a place for "whites only."[24] An examination of her public addresses suggests that she became aware of the race issue also through her interest in education. As early as March 11, 1934, ER spoke out on race discrimination at the National Conference on Fundamental Problems in the Education of Negroes. At this conference ER argued: "I feel that while we have been fortunate in this country in having many fine men and women interested in the education of the Negro race, we have also been slow, many of us who are of the white race, in realizing how important not only to your race it is, but how important to our race that you should have the best educational advantages. The menace today to a democracy is unthinking action, action which comes from people who are illiterate, who are unable to understand what is happening in the world at large, what is happening in their own country, and who therefore act without really having any knowledge of the meaning of their actions, and that is the thing that we, whatever our race is, should be guarding against today."[25] In no uncertain terms, ER told her audience that "we must learn to work together, all of us, regardless of race or creed or color; we must wipe out, wherever we find it, any feeling that grows up, of intolerance, of belief that any one group can go ahead alone. We go ahead together or we go down together."[26]

Throughout her twelve years as first lady, ER's activities on behalf of civil rights were many. Civil rights leaders often approached her as a way to get their concerns voiced to the administration.[27] She met regularly with Walter White, Mary McLeod Bethune, A. Philip Randolph, and other black leaders. She gave her support to blacks in political office. For instance, she was instrumental in getting her friend Mary McLeod Bethune named to the National Youth Administration as head of the Negro Affairs Division. She joined the NAACP's crusade to end the poll tax and to pass a federal antilynching law.[28] She spoke at assemblies of the NAACP and the National Urban League. She refused to abide by the segregationist demands of Eugene "Bull" Connor while attending the Report on the Economic Conditions of the South Conference in 1938.[29] She publicly announced her resignation from the Daughters of the American Revolution in 1939, when they refused to allow Marian Anderson to perform at Constitution Hall, and she worked behind the scenes to organize the Easter Sunday concert in front of the Lincoln Memorial, which featured Anderson.[30] She invited black entertainers to perform at the White House, and unlike previous first ladies, she allowed herself to be photographed with black Americans.[31] Her many activities took the issue of civil rights to the level of the presidency and brought national attention to the social, political, and economic discrimination black Americans faced.

In addition to these better-known and documented gestures of support for an end to segregation and racial discrimination, ER's public discourse also provides important insights into her efforts on behalf of civil rights. Continuing in the legacy of earlier civil rights advocates, such as Frederick Douglass, Mary Church Terrell, and Booker T. Washington and anticipating the civil rights rhetoric of Martin Luther King Jr., ER urged her audiences to work toward *perfecting* the democratic process instead of abandoning it. According to ER, the very future of democracy and the nation depended upon a willingness to "live up to the things that we believe in and see that justice is done to the people under the Constitution, whether they belong to minority groups or not."[32]

Articulating the "Four Equalities"

Faith in democratic principles and the earnest enactment of those principles were almost a religion to Eleanor Roosevelt, and she sought to share her commitment to democracy with the rest of the country. The turbulent times in which ER served as first lady included a constant concern that the "war to end all wars" had only led to further hostilities among nations. The depressed economic conditions around the world had given rise to fascist and totalitarian regimes. In the United States, many people expressed a belief that the great experiment of democracy failed to provide for basic human needs. ER acknowledged these doubts: "Times have been bad, many of our people still see little promise of security ahead. They are wondering if other nations have found more satisfactory solutions."[33] Just as the extraordinary times warranted bold new actions by the government, ER believed that the turbulent age also called for a reassessment of, and a recommitment to, what it meant to live in a democracy. She expressed this need in her 1940 political monograph, "The Moral Basis of Democracy": "At a time when the whole world is in a turmoil and thousands of people are homeless and hungry, it behooves all of us to reconsider our political and religious beliefs in an effort to clarify in our minds the standards by which we live."[34] Similarly, in a radio address on June 20, 1940, ER argued that "[i]n times such as this, it is necessary for every one of us to re-examine some of the fundamental concepts of Democracy."[35] In her view, democracy must be examined and perfected if the nation were going to survive the domestic and international crises challenging its security.

In addition to the critical times, the request of the American people prompted ER's assessment of the state of democracy. As mentioned earlier, ER often used letters from the public as a springboard for discussing topics that concerned her. For instance, at a Causes and Cures of War Conference in 1936, ER began her remarks by commenting on a letter she had recently received: "Just this evening as I was going through my mail, I came across a very interesting letter from a woman: 'You say that women should be interested in public affairs. I am a college woman, but for years I have not bothered to keep up with things as they were going on. Now I feel that I want to know a great many things I read about in the papers, but I don't understand the background because for years I have not paid attention to these questions. Where can I find unbiased facts? Where can I get information on international questions? Where can I get lists of books? Where can I get information about affairs in my own country?' "[36]

From this starting place, ER offered specific suggestions to her audience on how to inform themselves, and then she argued for their active participation in government. Her reflections on what it meant to live in a democracy followed this pattern. For example, in the radio address just described, ER took her cue from the letters she received when she told her radio audience that a listener wanted her to "talk about Democracy, to tell how I think everyone in this land can have a satisfying life, how people can live and not die for Democracy, how we can share the work, the joys and the sorrows in this world, so that we may all be able to enjoy life, liberty and the pursuit of happiness."[37] Throughout her public addresses and especially with the advent of World War II, ER sought to explain what she believed to be the democratic standards on which the country was founded and by which its citizens should live.

Her vision of democracy is best characterized by an articulation of four equalities that prefigured and then subsequently echoed her husband's four freedoms. While her husband emphasized freedom of expression and religion along with freedom from want and fear "everywhere in the world," ER urged her audiences to work for the four freedoms of *equality* at home.[38] ER's address to the Chicago Civil Liberties Committee in 1940, which predates her husband's famous "four freedoms" address to Congress by nine months, featured her themes of equality: "Any citizen in this country is entitled to equality before the law; to equality of education; to equality at earning a living, as far as his abilities have made it possible for him to do; to equality of participation in government so that he or she may register their opinion in just the way that any other citizens do. Now those are the basic rights, belonging to every citizen in every minority group, and we have an obligation, I think, to stand up and be counted when it comes to the question of whether any minority group does not have those rights as citizens in this country."[39]

Similarly, in a 1942 article for the *New Republic* she wrote the following: "Over and over again, I have stressed the rights of every citizen: Equality before the law. Equality of education. Equality to hold a job to his ability. Equality of participation through the ballot in the government. These are inherent rights in a democracy, and I do not see how we can fight this war and deny these rights to any citizen in our own land."[40]

Significantly, ER warranted her four equalities on the shared values she distilled from revered, national documents. She frequently linked her four equalities with the principles expressed in the Bill of Rights, the Constitution of the United States, and the Declaration of Independence. For instance, in her address to the Chicago Civil Liberties Committee, ER responded to the question, "what should be done about the social standing of the Negro race in this country?" She did not hesitate in her bold reply: "We have to make up our minds what we really believe. We have to decide whether we believe in the Bill of Rights, in the Constitution of the United States, or whether we are going to modify it because of the fears that we may have at the moment."[41] Similarly, at a celebration of the fifty-fifth anniversary of the Statue of Liberty at Orchestra Hall in Chicago on October 28, 1941, ER reminded her audience that another anniversary was not far behind: "We are coming very soon to the date when we celebrate the anniversary of the Bill of Rights. And I think that one of the valuable things that we should all do, when we come to this anniversary, is to read the Bill of Rights. . . . And as we reread it, I think we will be conscious of the fact that many of us give lip service to many of the principles laid down in the document and do not really see to it that all over this country that document is actually a reality to all the people of the United States."[42]

In an Independence Day radio address, she implored her audience to remember the following: "Upon our intelligence as a Nation to understand these words [the Declaration of Independence]; upon our willingness as a people to keep them alive, depends your future, my future, and the future of America."[43] She encouraged her audience to celebrate the sacred documents of the country by living up to the principles they expressed. These venerated documents provided a solid foundation for her argument for equality.

ER's focus on these rights as equalities is significant. Even though I am unable to claim any intentionality on the part of these two rhetors, ER's four equalities certainly share a relationship with her husband's four freedoms. While her rhetoric echoes the four freedoms her husband specified as central to establishing a safe and secure world, her own version of the four equalities was necessary for the survival of democracy domestically. From another perspective, ER's four equalities were the means to her husband's ends. Only through equality of the ballot, equality of education, equality of opportunity, and equality before the law could every citizen, regardless of race, religion, class, or gender have access to the four freedoms of democracy that FDR introduced (freedom of expression, freedom of religion, freedom from want, and freedom from fear).[44] In addition, her focus on these freedoms as equalities enabled her public critique of the nation's own racial prejudice and discrimination.[45]

Exposing Racial Injustice

Better than her husband's four freedoms, ER's four equalities as the foundation of democracy exposed the inconsistencies between stated democratic ideals and the racist social practices of the day. While ER advocated equality for many marginalized groups (e.g., women, youths, the poor), perhaps the best example of her commitment to these four equalities and her harshest critique of "democracy in practice" is represented in her rhetoric on race.

Although she argued that various types of prejudice (e.g., ethnic, religious, nationalistic) were troublesome, she claimed the treatment of black Americans took on special significance. In an article for the *New Republic* (1942) titled "Race, Religion, and Prejudice," she told her readers the following: "Perhaps because the Negroes are our largest minority, our attitude towards them will have to be faced first of all." In an address delivered at the celebration of the twenty-fifth anniversary of the National Urban League in 1936, ER professed much admiration for the black community and its leaders: "I marvel frequently at the patience with which those who work for the removal of bad conditions face their many disappointments. And I would like to pay tribute to the many leaders amongst the colored people whom I know and admire and respect."[46] In 1940 she wrote the following: "[N]o one can honestly claim that either the Indians or the Negroes of this country are free. These are obvious examples of conditions which are not compatible with the theory of Democracy. We have poverty which enslaves, and racial prejudice which does the same. There are other racial and religious groups among us who labor under certain discriminations, not quite so difficult as those we impose on the Negroes and the Indians, but still sufficient to show we do not completely practice the Democratic way of life."[47]

In a 1945 essay written for the Joint Commission on Social Reconstruction, she asserts that "Where the Negro is concerned, I think they have a legitimate complaint. We have expected them to be good citizens and yet in a large part of our country we haven't given them an opportunity to take part in our government. We have, however, made them subject to our laws and we have drafted them into our army and navy."[48] Such statements were a salient endorsement of the civil rights movement and the significant standpoint of black Americans in understanding what needed to be done to ensure a more just society. Although ER acknowledged the difficulty of forcing people to overcome their individual prejudices, she argued that "living in a Democracy, it is entirely reasonable to demand that every citizen of that Democracy enjoy the fundamental rights of a citizen."[49] Such an argument suggested a need for government intervention on behalf of civil rights.

One specific way in which ER pushed for government intervention was by calling national attention to the horrific practice of lynching and other violations of civil rights. Because the right to a fair trial and appropriate representation is fundamental to the democratic process, ER supported the NAACP's crusade to pass a federal antilynching law. Though much of her effort to pass the Wagner-Costigan bill took place behind the scenes (at FDR's request), ER spoke out on the issue.[50] In a 1936 speech before the National Urban League, she vehemently protested mob rule: "No right-thinking person in this country today who picks up a paper and reads that in some part of the country the people have not been willing to wait for the due processes of law, but have gone back to the rule of force, blind and unjust as force and fear usually are, can help but be ashamed that we have shown such a lack of faith in our own institutions."[51]

Similarly, in a 1939 article for the *Virginia Quarterly Review,* ER wrote, "It is an indisputable fact that democracy cannot survive where force and not law is the ultimate court of appeal."[52] In the same article ER responded publicly to the hysteria created over H. G. Wells's "War of the Worlds," and she claimed that it was simply the best illustration of "the state of mind in which we as a nation find ourselves today."[53] According to ER, Americans had allowed themselves to be fed on propaganda identifying various groups of people as dangerous and subversive. She often expressed exasperation over the prevalence of communist hysteria and paranoia that people used to justify their discrimination and prejudice: "If you are in the South someone tells you solemnly that all the members of the Committee of Industrial Organization are Communists, or that the Negroes are all Communist . . . and that the Jews . . . are all Communists. And so it goes, until finally you realize that people have reached a point where anything which will save them from Communism is a godsend; and if Fascism or Nazism promises more security than our own democracy we may even turn to them."[54]

Such an attitude of fear and intolerance, according to ER, always led to the use of force as a way of settling conflicts. She lamented: "We are breeding people who cannot live under a democratic form of government but must be controlled by force."[55] The appeal for change was a conservative one. Her argument crafted a motive for social change based on the preservation of an existing social structure. The horror of lynching placed the nation's justice system at risk. Similarly, ER argued that not only were the nation's social structures at risk, but the nation's international reputation was jeopardized as well. She told her audience at the National Urban League in 1936 that "the sooner we as a nation unite to stamp out any such action, the sooner and the better will we be able to face the other nations of the world and to uphold our real ideals here and abroad."[56]

Connecting the Fate of Democracy to the Fate of Minorities

Significantly, ER frequently claimed that the United States served as an example for the rest of the world. She argued that the very future of international peace depended on the enactment of democratic principles within the nation's own borders. In a radio address on July 4, 1940, ER argued that any international threat to democracy could be attended to only when citizens achieved "the farsightedness to settle their differences within their own country."[57] The preservation of democracy would succeed only "with equal justice, equal opportunity, and equal participation in the government." Only when those ideals are attained, ER argued, "can we expect to be a united country—a country that is prepared to win out in any battle, or the battle of ideas which is perhaps today the most important of all."[58]

As the foremost example of democracy, ER argued that the nation had to show the world that it could solve the race-relation issue domestically. For example, in a speech at the Causes and Cures of War Conference on January 24, 1940, ER urged her audience to "make up our minds that one of the great contributions that we can make to the peace of the world is to show that here, in a Democracy, we are able to meet our problems and to face them, and to make Democracy work."[59]

One of the most poignant arguments during World War II was that the government required black men and women to participate in the war effort and fight for democracy abroad but refused to protect their basic freedoms at home.[60] The fact that the United States was fighting on behalf of democracy around the world at the same time it neglected the democratic freedoms of some of its own citizens was an irony that was not lost on civil rights advocates, and the war years brought an acceleration of civil rights activism under the "Double V" campaign.[61] ER's rhetoric reinforced their efforts. In her article "Abolish Jim Crow!" for *New Threshold* in 1943, she argued forcefully: "If we have no hope that this [the guarantee of fundamental rights to everyone] is going to be the case, and that this is the real objective for which we fight, then I think there are many people who will feel that they cannot bear the sacrifice and the cruelty and the horror which those they love have to go through. If the future only holds a repetition of the past, if in each nation there are to be real slaves, even though they do not exist in name, then the boys who say they do not know why they fight have a right to say so."[62]

Throughout the war years, while her husband turned his attention to international affairs, ER tried to make clear the connection between her four equalities at home, her husband's four freedoms abroad, and the very future of democracy: "Now some of those things [the four equalities], in some places, are not always done. And at the present time in our country, I think it is very important that if we wish to preserve and affirm before the world that democracy does believe in civil liberties, does believe in the four freedoms which the President enunciated, that if that is so, we shall examine ourselves and make sure that we do all we possibly can to make the Bill of Rights a reality for all of our people."[63]

Arguments such as these illustrated the inconsistencies between the nation's ideals and the experiences of particular groups of citizens. They connected the fate of the nation's racial minorities to the fate of the country in general. Such arguments also laid the groundwork for government intervention on behalf of civil rights. Unfortunately, significant intercession would come not with her husband' administration but with that of her husband's successor.

A First Lady's Civil Rights Legacy

ER's civil rights activities extended beyond her husband's presidency. Her advocacy on behalf of civil rights only increased after she left the White House. In 1945, ER became a member of the NAACP's board of directors, and within months of her departure from the White House, she was asked by Pres. Harry Truman to serve as a delegate to the United Nations' Human Rights Commission. Two years later she accompanied President Truman to a session of the NAACP's annual conference. In front of the Lincoln Memorial, ER watched as President Truman committed his administration to the task of making "the Federal Government a friendly, vigilant defender of the rights and equalities of all Americans."[64] In his address, Truman praised ER's own efforts on behalf of civil rights, specifically in her role as U.S. delegate to the United Nations. In this first speech given by a president before the NAACP, Truman reiterated an extended version of ER's four equalities as the basis of his own civil rights program: "Every man should have the right to a decent home, the right to an education, the right to adequate medical care, the right to a worthwhile job, the right to an equal share in making the public decisions through the ballot, and the right to a fair trial in a fair court."[65]

Truman all but quotes ER on three of the items, and he divides economic opportunity into the basic necessities for a decent living (homes, medical care, and job opportunity). In the address, President Truman staked out an unprecedented role for the federal government in the civil rights arena.[66] He stated, "The extension of civil rights today means, not protection of the people against the Government, but protection of the people by the Government."[67] He argued that the very fate of democracy in the postwar world depended upon the United States' ability to demonstrate to the world that "we have been able to put our own house in order."[68] The argument should sound familiar.

In an insightful article, Steven Goldzwig has argued that in "Truman's inauguration of the cold war, we find one of the early rhetorical links of U.S. civil rights as central to the image and consistency of American foreign policy." Goldzwig also suggests that the argument was introduced by Truman and used as his central rationale to desegregate the military.[69] Although establishing absolute connections is always difficult, it seems reasonable to conclude that, although the Cold War offered the rhetorical exigency that finally moved Truman to action, the civil rights advocacy of former first lady Eleanor Roosevelt helped to provide some of the rhetorical foundation for his presidential civil rights program.[70]

Ironically, ER's faithful commitment to preserving U.S. democracy may have limited her willingness to respond to the country's civil rights issue as a *human-rights* issue. In the same year in which she stood in front of the Lincoln Memorial with President Truman, ER repeatedly refused to support or introduce an NAACP petition of grievances to the United Nations' Human Rights Commission. The NAACP's "Appeal to the World," prepared by W. E. B. DuBois, was an indictment of race relations in the United States and a request for international monitoring by the United Nations.[71] Reportedly, she even threatened to resign her position from the NAACP's board of directors if the organization proceeded with its complaint. Was this a sudden change of political commitments? Her biographers argue that ER worried that the petition would damage the United States' international reputation and give the Soviets a political advantage.[72] Such a perspective was already established in her earlier public addresses as first lady. ER's contention that civil rights must be guaranteed within the nation before democracy could gain world acceptance probably precluded her from bringing the issue of civil rights before the world assembly she helped to create. She may have been constrained by her own argument that only by handling the race issue within our own institutional structures would the United States be able to establish the superiority of democracy over communist dictatorships.

In spite of the limits of her appeals for civil rights, in the example of ER we have a first lady who not only complemented and supplemented her husband's rhetorical presidency but also used her White House role to advocate for a social and political agenda as no first lady had ever done before. In ER's rhetoric, the principles and ideals of democracy remained intact, but she sought to stretch its meaning to include groups of people who had historically been marginalized and excluded from the democratic process. Although hers was not a radical critique of the nation's political system, ER's vision of democracy as seen through her four equalities demanded changes in current social, economic, and political practices.

The rhetorical strength of her approach came from an argument that reaffirmed shared values, while exposing inconsistencies in the enactment of those ideals. Although some might argue that a more radical approach was needed to correct for the apparent "failing" of democracy, a radical stance was not available to ER, who was embedded and invested in established institutional structures. In true liberal democratic fashion, ER's public discourse reflected a faith in the power of both education and persuasion to accomplish necessary change. While she affirmed traditional democratic principles, she also exposed inconsistencies in the enactment of those beliefs. Thus, her dramatic call for civil rights and an expanded political constituency were contained within a conservative framework of ensuring the future of democracy and the nation. She was not calling for a radical rethinking of the nation's roots; rather, she sought a more complete fulfillment of core values as a way to envision and enact a better future.

Notes

1. In referring to Eleanor Roosevelt, I have chosen the nomenclature of "ER," even though traditional standards call for using the last name. Eleanor Roosevelt (who was a Roosevelt even before her marriage) certainly has as much claim to the name as Franklin or Theodore. At the same time, however, I feel as though part of her uniqueness and difference from her more-often-studied male counterparts is lost in the last-name reference. Using both names is plausible but somewhat cumbersome. In keeping with the convention of recent biographers and historians, I have decided to refer to her as ER. This monogram is one of her own choosing, as she often signed her letters and memos with these initials. In order to maintain consistency, I use initials to refer to Franklin Delano Roosevelt (FDR) throughout the chapter as well.
2. Karlyn Kohrs Campbell, "The Rhetorical Presidency: A Two-Person Career," in *Beyond the Rhetorical Presidency*, ed. Martin J. Medhurst (College Station: Texas A&M University Press, 1996), pp. 179–95.

For additional arguments on studying the first ladyship as an institution of the White House, see Robert P. Watson, *The Presidents'
Wives: Reassessing the Office of First Lady* (Boulder: Lynne Rienner,
2000).

3. Campbell, "Rhetorical Presidency," pp. 180–81.
4. Carl Sferrazza Anthony, *First Ladies: The Saga of the President's Wives
   and Their Power* (New York: William Morrow, 1990), 1:8; Betty
   Caroli, *First Ladies* (New York: Oxford University Press, 1987), pp.
   xvi–xvii; Ann Grimes, *Running Mates: The Making of a First Lady*
   (New York: William Morrow, 1990), p. 306.
5. Edith P. Mayo and Denise D. Meringolo, *First Ladies: Political Role and
   Public Image* (Washington, D.C.: Library of Congress, 1994), p. 8.
6. Ibid., p. 9.
7. Diane M. Blair, "Performing the First Lady: The Rhetoric of Eleanor
   Roosevelt, 1933–1945" (Ph.D. diss., University of Maryland, 2000).
8. Blanche Wiesen Cook, *Eleanor Roosevelt, 1884–1933* (New York: Penguin, 1992), pp. 339–40.
9. Allida M. Black, *Casting Her Own Shadow* (New York: Columbia University Press, 1996), p. 13.
10. Eleanor Roosevelt, address to the 1940 Democratic National Con-
    vention, sound recording, July 18, 1940, Franklin Delano Roosevelt
    Presidential Library (FDRL).
11. Diane M. Blair, "No Ordinary Time: Eleanor Roosevelt's Address to
    the 1940 Democratic National Convention," *Rhetoric and Public Af-
    fairs* 4 (2001): 203–22.
12. Eleanor Roosevelt, "I Want You to Write Me," in *What I Hope to
    Leave Behind,* ed. Allida M. Black (Brooklyn: Carlson, 1995), p. 13.
13. Eleanor Roosevelt, "Mail of a President's Wife" (1940), speech and
    article file (3039), Eleanor Roosevelt Papers, FDRL. See also Blanche
    Wiesen Cook, *Eleanor Roosevelt, 1933–1938: The Defining Years* (New
    York: Viking, 1999), p. 115.
14. Eleanor Roosevelt, "For the Digest," speech and article file (3040),
    Eleanor Roosevelt Papers, FDRL.
15. Patricia Sullivan, *Days of Hope: Race and Democracy in the New Deal
    Era* (Chapel Hill: University of North Carolina Press, 1996), p. 21.
16. "Report of the National Advisory Commission on Civil Disorders,"
    in *The Politics of Race: African Americans and the Political System,* ed.
    Theodore Rueter (Armonk, N.Y.: M. E. Sharpe, 1995), p. 36.
17. Ibid.
18. Rhoda Lois Blumberg, *Civil Rights: The 1960s' Freedom Struggle,* rev.
    ed. (New York: Twayne, 1991), p. 15.
19. Arthur M. Schlesinger Jr., *The Politics of Upheaval* (Boston: Houghton
    Mifflin, 1960), p. 434.
20. Eleanor Roosevelt, *This I Remember* (New York: Harper and Brothers,
    1949), p. 161.

21. Ibid., quoted on p. 162.
22. Ibid., p. 164.
23. Quoted in Doris Kearns Goodwin, *No Ordinary Time: Franklin and Eleanor Roosevelt: The Home Front in World War II* (New York: Touchstone, 1994), p. 164.
24. Cook, *Eleanor Roosevelt, 1933–1938,* p. 152.
25. Eleanor Roosevelt, "National Conference on Fundamental Problems in the Education of Negroes," May 11, 1934, speech and article file (3029), Eleanor Roosevelt Papers, FDRL.
26. Ibid.
27. Sullivan, *Days of Hope,* p. 62.
28. Cook, "The Crusade to End Lynching," in *Eleanor Roosevelt, 1933– 1938,* pp. 177–89; Allida Black, "A Reluctant but Persistent Warrior: Eleanor Roosevelt and the Early Civil Rights Movement," in *Multicultural Education, Transformative Knowledge, and Action: Historical and Contemporary Perspectives,* ed. James A. Banks (New York: Teachers College Press, 1996), pp. 233–47; Joanna Schneider Zangrando and Robert L. Zangrando, "ER and Black Civil Rights," in *Without Precedent: The Life and Career of Eleanor Roosevelt,* ed. Joan Hoff-Wilson and Marjorie Lightman (Bloomington: Indiana University Press, 1984), pp. 93–94.
29. Sullivan, *Days of Hope,* pp. 98–101; Zangrando and Zangrando, "ER and Black Civil Rights," p. 95.
30. Allida Black, "Championing a Champion: Eleanor Roosevelt and the Marian Anderson 'Freedom Concert,' " *Presidential Studies Quarterly* 20 (1990): 719–36; James Kearney, "Friend to a Neglected Promise," in *Anna Eleanor Roosevelt: The Evolution of a Reformer* (Boston: Houghton Mifflin, 1968), pp. 88–92; Zangrando and Zangrando, "ER and Black Civil Rights," pp. 95–96.
31. Allida Black, "Eleanor Roosevelt and the Wartime Campaign against Jim Crow," *Social Education* 60 (1996): 284–86.
32. Eleanor Roosevelt, "Civil Liberties: The Individual and the Community," Mar. 14, 1940, speech and article file (3038), Eleanor Roosevelt Papers, FDRL.
33. Eleanor Roosevelt, "For Liberty Magazine," speech and article file (3039), Eleanor Roosevelt Papers, FDRL.
34. Eleanor Roosevelt, *Moral Basis of Democracy* (New York: Howell and Soskin, 1940), p. 11.
35. Eleanor Roosevelt, "Mrs. Roosevelt's Own Radio Program," June 20, 1940, speech and article file (3038), Eleanor Roosevelt Papers, FDRL.
36. Eleanor Roosevelt, "Causes and Cures of War," Jan. 21, 1936, speech and article file (3033), Eleanor Roosevelt Papers, FDRL.
37. Eleanor Roosevelt, "Mrs. Roosevelt's Own Radio Program," June 20, 1940, speech and article file (3038), Eleanor Roosevelt Papers, FDRL.
38. FDR gave his four-freedoms speech on Jan. 6, 1941, when he ad-

dressed members of the Seventy-seventh U.S. Congress. See *The Public Papers of Franklin Delano Roosevelt* (New York: Macmillan, 1941), pp. 663–78.

39. Eleanor Roosevelt, "Civil Liberties: The Individual and the Community," Mar. 14, 1940, speech and article file (3038), Eleanor Roosevelt Papers, FDRL.

40. Eleanor Roosevelt, "Race, Religion, and Prejudice," in *What I Hope to Leave Behind,* p. 159.

41. Roosevelt, "Civil Liberties: The Individual and the Community," Mar. 14, 1940, speech and article file (3038), Eleanor Roosevelt Papers, FDRL.

42. Eleanor Roosevelt, "Civil Liberties and the Crisis," in *What I Hope to Leave Behind,* p. 102.

43. Eleanor Roosevelt, "Mrs. Roosevelt's Own Radio Program," July 4, 1940, speech and article file (3038), Eleanor Roosevelt Papers, FDRL.

44. Doris Kearns Goodwin also notes a link between ER's general "ruminations about democracy" and FDR's inspired four-freedoms speech. Although she does not focus on ER's public articulation of four equalities, she does quote ER's friend Trude Pratt Lash, who asserted that "finally [ER's] ideas took hold in the president's call for four freedoms" (201).

45. The ideograph of equality has played a significant and contested role in the history of American civil rights rhetoric and the call for an end to racial prejudice and discrimination. For an additional discussion of its rhetorical functions, see John Louis Lucaites and Celeste Condit, "Reconstructing 'Equality': Culturetypal and Counter-Cultural Rhetorics in the Martyred Black Vision," *Communication Monographs* 57 (1990): 5–24.

46. Eleanor Roosevelt, "The Negro and Social Change," in *What I Hope to Leave Behind,* pp. 145–46.

47. Eleanor Roosevelt, *The Moral Basis,* p. 48.

48. Eleanor Roosevelt, "The Minorities Question," in *What I Hope to Leave Behind,* p. 168.

49. Ibid., "Race, Religion, and Prejudice," p. 159.

50. For an interesting account of ER's activities with NAACP leaders and her behind-the-scenes efforts to get FDR to support the controversial Wagner-Costigan bill, see Cook, "The Crusade to End Lynching," in *Eleanor Roosevelt, 1933–1938,* pp. 177–89.

51. Eleanor Roosevelt, "The Negro and Social Change," in *Courage in a Dangerous World,* ed. Allida M. Black (New York: Columbia University Press, 1999), p. 36.

52. Eleanor Roosevelt, "Keepers of Democracy," in *What I Hope to Leave Behind,* p. 66.

53. Ibid., p. 65.

54. Ibid.

55. Ibid., p. 66.
56. Eleanor Roosevelt, "The Negro and Social Change," in *Courage in a Dangerous World*, p. 36.
57. Eleanor Roosevelt, "Mrs. Roosevelt's Own Radio Program," July 4, 1940, speech and article file (3038), Eleanor Roosevelt Papers, FDRL.
58. Eleanor Roosevelt, "Social Gains and Defense," in *What I Hope to Leave Behind*, p. 391.
59. Eleanor Roosevelt, "Speech at the Banquet of Causes and Cures of War Conference," speech and article file (3038), Eleanor Roosevelt Papers, FDRL.
60. Blumberg, *Civil Rights*, p. 32; Sullivan, *Days of Hope*, p. 136.
61. With the onset of war, black leaders announced that they were waging a two-front battle for democracy at home and abroad. See Sullivan, *Days of Hope*, pp. 118–19, 135–36. See also Blumberg, *Civil Rights*, p. 32.
62. Eleanor Roosevelt, "Abolish Jim Crow!" in *What I Hope to Leave Behind*, p. 162.
63. Ibid., "Civil Liberties and the Crisis," p. 102.
64. Harry Truman, "Address before the National Association for the Advancement of Colored People," June 29, 1947, in *Public Papers of the Presidents of the United States* (Washington, D.C.: Federal Register Division, National Archives and Records, 1963), p. 311.
65. Ibid., p. 312.
66. Steven R. Goldzwig, "Civil Rights and the Cold War: A Rhetorical History of the Truman Administration's Desegregation of the United States Army," in *Doing Rhetorical History: Concepts and Cases*, ed. Kathleen J. Turner (Tuscaloosa: University of Alabama Press, 1998), p. 146.
67. Truman, "Address before the National Association," p. 311.
68. Ibid., p. 312.
69. Goldzwig, "Civil Rights and the Cold War," p. 167.
70. Footnote to Black, *Casting Her Own Shadow: Eleanor Roosevelt and the Shaping of Postwar Liberalism*, p. 81.
71. Ibid., pp. 99–100, for further details on the incident; see also Zangrando and Zangrando, "ER and Black Civil Rights," p. 102.
72. Black, *Casting Her Own Shadow*, pp. 100–101; Zangrando and Zangrando, "ER and Black Civil Rights," p. 102.

CHAPTER 4

Inaugurating
the Second
Reconstruction

President Truman's Committee on Civil Rights

Steven R. Goldzwig

My dream is that . . . America will come into the full light of the day
when all shall know that she puts human rights above all other rights
and that her flag is the flag not only of America but of humanity.

—Woodrow Wilson

Immediately after World War II, the United States experienced a
heady national ferment to extend the benefits of democracy to
citizens both at home and abroad. Having fought for freedom
abroad, Americans felt renewed vigilance regarding freedom at home.
This was particularly true for the African American veterans. For the
black soldiers who returned to the South, the signs of inequality
and the continuing segregation were particularly galling, and their
persistence was simply unfathomable. Even more ominous was the
record of lynchings that continued to accrue. The vigilante violence
tore at the American promise and made a mockery of American ideals
everywhere. Freedom, equality, and justice might have been espoused
for the many, but they often escaped the experience of the few. Thus,
right after the war, minorities in the United States were particularly

susceptible to the chasm between promise and performance, and they were hard pressed to articulate, much less experience, the tangible benefits of fighting a world war.

The political climate was also changing. Establishing a vibrant peacetime economy was an enormous challenge. Pres. Harry S. Truman was vexed by inflation and shortages of goods and services. The rocky road to conversion from a wartime to a peacetime economy had spelled defeat for the Democrats in the off-year elections and did not bode well for Truman's future political viability.

For Harry Truman, the challenge was extraordinary. Absorbing all Americans into a prosperous postwar economy was a daunting task. It seemed particularly overwhelming when Truman turned his attention to the African American community, where the distorted face of ongoing violence, segregation, and discrimination was a daily image in the national mirror.

In 1943, during the FDR administration, the riots in Detroit were ominous harbingers that not all was well with race relations in the United States. Truman searched for a way to redress ongoing problems. One of the most enduring actions the president would take in his attempt to alleviate continuing tensions and abuses in civil rights was to appoint the President's Committee on Civil Rights (PCCR). The PCCR came to represent an unprecedented move by the executive branch to analyze and redress racial intolerance in the United States. Not since Reconstruction had the nation's attention been so focused on race and race relations.

Truman's convocation of the PCCR was not *primarily* a political move aimed at winning the 1948 election (although politics was never out of the equation), as is sometimes argued, but rather was convened because of a complex mix of motivations. Chief among those concerns was President Truman's sense of justice, constitutional duty, and the emerging role of civil rights in Cold War diplomacy. By convening the PCCR, supporting and employing its recommendations in proposing civil rights legislation, and speaking publicly on behalf of a new civil rights agenda, Harry S. Truman distinguished himself as a proponent of human rights both domestically and internationally. In addition, the PCCR was particularly adept at fashioning a process and a product that served as a model for an effective attack on an intractable national problem. At Truman's behest, the PCCR opened up a national dialogue on race that set a social, legal, and moral agenda for the next fifty years.

Truman's Sense of Justice and Constitutional Duty

On September 20, 1946, Harry Truman wrote Attorney General Tom Clark regarding Issac Woodard, a newly discharged African American veteran who had been blinded by an attack perpetrated by the local police. Truman wrote the following: "I have been very much alarmed at the increased racial feeling all over the country and I am wondering if it wouldn't be well to appoint a commission to analyze the situation and have a remedy to present to the next Congress—something similar to the Wickersham Commission on Prohibition. I know you have been looking into the Tennessee and Georgia lynchings, and also have been investigating the one in Louisiana, but I think it is going to take something more than the handling of each individual case after it happens—it is going to require some sort of policy to prevent such happenings."[1] Truman also sent a copy of this letter to minority affairs assistant David K. Niles. His cover memo reads as follows: "I am very much in earnest on this thing and I'd like very much to have you push it with everything you have."[2]

On December 5, 1946, President Truman issued executive order 9808, which announced his appointment of the President's Committee on Civil Rights.[3] In his informal remarks to the new committee on January 15, 1947, Truman observed, "You have a vitally important job. We are none of us entirely familiar with just how far the Federal Government under the Constitution has a right to go in these civil rights matters. I want our Bill of Rights implemented in fact. We have been trying to do this for 150 years. We are making progress, but we are not making progress fast enough." The president continued: "I am a believer in the sovereignty of the individual and the local governments. I don't think the Federal Government ought to be in a position to exercise dictatorial powers locally; but there are certain rights under the Constitution of the United States which I think the Federal Government has a right to protect. It's a big job. Go to it!"[4]

The tasks Truman had set before the committee were vast and infinitely complex. The issues were multiple: a presumed need to reorganize the Justice Department; development of codes for efficient

and effective criminal civil rights enforcement; antilynching legislation; poll-tax legislation; housing covenants; segregation in education, housing, and health care; establishment of a permanent Fair
Employment Practices Commission; minority rights of non-African
Americans—the list went on and on. The president was demanding
proposals that could be sent to Congress immediately. It was a tall
order by any standard.[5]

Committee members agreed that they would neither engage in
public statements on controversial issues nor make public appearances. This was in conformance with the president's wishes.[6] Robert L.
Carr, the executive secretary of the committee, repeatedly maintained
that the report itself would be the closest the committee would get
to real "action" on civil rights matters. It was sometimes hard for the
public and even the committee members to understand this point.
The issues were so pressing and the pain so real that a blue-ribbon
panel could seem nothing more than window dressing. Outsiders
were worried that certain issues would be neglected. There was trepi-
dation that the president's committee would simply conduct business as usual in an effort to fend off substantive progress. However,
as William E. Juhnke observes, "While political considerations were
certainly behind the PCCR project, there is no reason to believe that
the creation of an advisory committee was a cynical political maneuver designed primarily to delay or avoid action."[7] The civil rights
initiatives the committee drafted were always contemplated within a
larger context that had come to include a fierce fight for moral and
ideological superiority in the newly developed but increasingly long
tentacles of Cold War diplomacy.

Domestic Civil Rights and National Security

As the United States continued to stake its position in the newly
emerging postwar era, the cornerstone doctrines of the Cold War
were also in the making. Competition for the hearts and minds of the
world community began in earnest. The United States was determined
to cast international light on its newly defined role as a worldwide
beacon of liberty. As a signatory to the newly formed Charter of the
United Nations, the United States was hoping to attract more nations to the democratic camp. The Soviets, in due course, became the
chief rivals to the United States' vision, and the ideological warfare

soon became intense. Article 55 of the UN Charter committed the United States and other signatories to "the principle of equal rights and self-determination of peoples," and the United Nations as a body therein committed itself to higher standards of living; full employment; solutions to international economic, social, and health-related problems; and cultural and educational cooperation. Moreover, the signatories pledged "universal respect for, and observance of, human rights and fundamental freedoms for all without distinction as to race, sex, language, or religion."[8]

Just as important, "[t]he postwar decolonization movement among Third World peoples put the question of race in an entirely new light, one that many traditional Americans found unsettling. Decolonization efforts provided Afro-Americans with models of initiative that challenged existing racial assumptions and jeopardized long-standing racial arrangements that whites had taken for granted."[9] The global dimensions of the black civil rights movement had repercussions in America.

But it was Harry Truman himself who best articulated the new national importance of civil rights in his landmark address on June 29, 1947, to the NAACP: "Our immediate task is to remove the last remnants of the barriers which stand between millions of our citizens and their birthright. There is no justifiable reason for discrimination because of ancestry, or religion, or race, or color." It was now time for the federal government to "show the way," and the president was emphatic in detailing the grave problem that domestic civil rights abuses posed for foreign policy. It was necessary to best our enemies by a clear demonstration of our commitment to freedom: "Our case for democracy should be as strong as we can make it. It should rest on practical evidence that we have been able to put our own house in order. . . . We can no longer afford a leisurely attack upon prejudice and discrimination."[10]

The need to "put our own house in order" did not escape the attention of the State Department. As a July, 1947, State Department memorandum suggests,

By seizing upon and exaggerating in every way possible such defects as exist in the observance of human rights in the United States, the effort is made to destroy the idea of the United States as the land of freedom. . . . [Moreover,] [s]ince the moral position of the United States in the world is based on respect for human rights, and since the continued existence of totalitarian regimes depends upon the suppression of human rights, this may be said to be the central issue of present-day world politics. The United States should not, therefore, take a passive attitude toward its problems in the field of civil liberties. Even without aggressive use, this issue forms perhaps the greatest natural weapon in the contest and should be recognized and used wherever the opportunity avails. Similarly, the free institutions of the United States should be improved and strengthened in every way possible.[11]

With civil rights abuses in the United States now characterized as *the central issue* in world politics, civil rights and Cold War diplomacy were now inextricably intertwined, and their tangled relationship was increasingly looked upon as a serious matter. Thus the Cold War propaganda of the early postwar years recognized the pivotal role of civil rights in the United States as an important rhetorical platform in defining the struggle between East and West and between democratic and totalitarian states. The iconic role of the United States as a beacon of liberty was jeopardized by any report to the contrary, and it was the multiple contrary reports stemming from reported abuses in civil rights, especially those emanating from the South, that both fascinated and soured the foreign presses from various world capitals. The United States was smarting under a tarnished image, and it was most desirous of immediate, long-term image repair. As Mary Dudziak observes, "President Truman and his aides sought change in the domestic policies and practices that fueled international outrage."[12]

Ironically, the negative foreign press helped the administration take special cognizance of the problem of "freedom at home." Attending to civil rights at home for eyes abroad would soon become the "greatest natural weapon" in the U.S. propaganda arsenal. In short, the United States could not be the "leader of the free world" and fix its guiding star while simultaneously trampling the human rights of her own citizens. To the extent that this occurred, it was a blemish on the national reputation; at the time, this concern seemed to eclipse even matters of national conscience. By directing "moral action" in the civil rights arena as a necessary corollary to "winning" the Cold War, the president, the committee, and the State Department fashioned an argument and forged a commitment that would have complex repercussions for decades to come.[13]

"To Secure These Rights"

In his introduction to the final report, Charles E. Wilson states that "Civil rights is a national problem. The world is today confused by differing and often contradictory uses of the language in which free men express their ideals. It is our hope that our Report will help in the continuing rededication of our people to the historic principles which have made us great. We also hope that it will help other nations to judge our capacity for vigorous self-criticism and improvement through the normal processes of democracy."[14]

Ideological Rationale

The request for action was premised on fundamental moral, economic, and international convictions. Morally, the committee reasoned, "We need no further justification for a broad and immediate program than the need to reaffirm our faith in the traditional American morality. The pervasive gap between our aims and what we actually do is creating a kind of moral dry rot which eats away at the emotional and rational bases of democratic beliefs." Economically, there was a need for "maximum production and continued prosperity." Indeed, "A sort of vicious circle is produced. Discrimination depresses the wages and income of minority groups. As a result, their purchasing power is curtailed and markets are reduced. Reduced markets result in reduced production. This cuts down employment, which of course means lower wages and still fewer job opportunities. Rising fear, prejudice, and insecurity aggravate the very discrimination in employment which sets the vicious circle in motion." The "separate-but-equal" policy is cited as a cause of "the wasteful duplication of many facilities and services." Internationally, "domestic civil rights shortcomings" were perceived as an "obstacle" to "mak[ing] the United States an enormous, positive influence for peace and progress throughout the world." Moreover, the negative propaganda stemming from civil rights violations and abuses was a primary impetus to the committee's rationale for action: "We cannot escape the fact that our civil rights record has been an issue in world politics. The world's press and radio are full of it. The Committee has seen a multitude of samples. We and our friends have been, and are, stressing our achievement. Those with competing philosophies have stressed—and are shamelessly distorting—our shortcomings. They have not only tried to create hostility toward us among specific nations, races and religious groups. They have tried to prove our democracy an empty fraud, and our nation a consistent oppressor of underprivileged people. This may seem ludicrous to Americans, but it is sufficiently important to worry our friends." The rationale concludes: "The United States is not so strong, the final triumph of the democratic ideal is not so inevitable that we can ignore what the world thinks of us or our record."[15] With this rationale securely in place, the committee could advance its recommendations.

Recommendations

The final report submitted to the president recommends presidential, congressional, state, and educational remedies and action. Recommended executive actions include enlargement of the civil rights section of the Department of Justice, establishment of a special investigative unit in the FBI specifically for civil rights, establishment of a permanent commission on civil rights, review of the wartime evacuation of Japanese American citizens, administrative action to eliminate all vestiges of discrimination in the armed services, clarification of loyalty obligations of civil servants, issuance of a presidential mandate against discrimination in federal employment, Department of Justice court intervention on restrictive housing covenants, and an executive order directing the Federal Bureau of the Budget to review all governmental programs for nondiscrimination policies and actions. This last point reflects the closely contested sanctions discussion in areas such as education. Twenty-one items were earmarked for *congressional action*. Among the most important were an increase in funding for the Justice Department's civil rights section; new legislation to supplement Sections 51 and 52, which increased fines and penalties for civil rights violations, and Sections 443 and 444, which covered involuntary servitude under Title 18 of the United States Code; a call for an antilynching act; an end to poll taxes; legislation for ensuring voting rights; legislation on the aforementioned Japanese American evacuees; local self-government for the District of Columbia; the elimination of segregated housing through restrictive covenants; modification of laws for naturalized citizens; legislation to end segregation in the Panama Canal Zone; legislation to end discrimination in the military; sanctions on federal grant-in-aid programs for noncompliance with civil rights law; a disclosure law covering all groups who sought to influence public opinion; and the enactment of a Fair Employment Practices Act. Recommendations for state action followed similar directives and were to be employed at the local level. Action on education included a call for a public-education campaign on civil rights and one specifically targeted at governmental employees and the military services.[16]

President's Statement upon Receiving the Report

Almost one month after the official due date, on October 29, 1947, the president received the committee's report. He said:

> I am going to read this report with great care and I recommend to all my countrymen that they do the same thing. I created this Committee with a feeling of urgency. No sooner were we finished with the war than racial and religious intolerance began to appear and threaten the very things we had just fought for.
>
> I notice that the title of this report ["To Secure These Rights"] is taken from the Declaration of Independence. I hope this Committee has given us as broad a document as that—an American charter of human freedom in our time. The need for such a charter was never greater than at this moment. Men of goodwill everywhere are striving, under great difficulties, to create a world-wide moral order, firmly established in the life of nations. For us, here in America, a new charter of human freedom will be a guide for action; and in the eyes of the world, it will be a declaration of our renewed faith in the American goal—the integrity of the individual human being, sustained by the moral consensus of the whole nation, protected by a government based on equal freedom under just laws. The members of this Committee are busy men and women. We all owe them a debt of gratitude. I feel I am speaking for all Americans when I thank them for their unselfish, devoted service.[17]

Reaction to the report was unavoidably mixed. In the North, there was positive acceptance; in the South, predictable angst and disgust.

Harvard Law School Dean Erwin N. Griswold wrote to Robert L. Carr to laud the committee's accomplishment: "I think you have done much to educate the public, and it is, in large measure, only by education, only by bringing about a deep-seated awareness of the problem, that we can make progress in this field. The contribution of the report to that progress seems to me to be as great as any which has been made in our time."[18] Truman historian and biographer Alonzo L. Hamby credits the president with spearheading a "bold and far-reaching document." Hamby asserts, "A half-century later, with those objectives all achieved, it is hard to conceive of just how path-breaking and controversial the report was."[19]

On to Civil Rights Legislation

It had become increasingly clear that a host of minority-associated, civil rights violations and concerns in the new postwar era including lynching, violence, voting rights, and fair-employment practices was slowly filling the national cup to the point of overflow. The committee's report tends to magnify the problem in a particularly graphic way.

Truman's sense of justice, his keen recognition of his constitutional duty as president, his political instincts stemming from the stunning 1946 off-year election defeat of the Democrats, his anticipation of a tough, uphill battle for the 1948 campaign, and his desire to deflect international opprobrium by smoothing the pathways of democratic propaganda—all coalesced, if not conspired, to convince the president that civil rights legislation was the only real cure. He knew he needed the South and was fearful of the breakup of the traditional Southern Democratic coalition. He knew the Dixiecrats might threaten to break away if he moved forward with his plans. Nevertheless, he determined that he could not turn his back on civil rights; this was a significant, domestic national problem that, in the emerging Truman-doctrine-inspired era, had come to be seen as an impediment to Cold War diplomacy. A civil rights package was necessary to begin a dialogue that would help circumvent national chaos and preserve national security. Firm in the conviction that the selection of a morally righteous path in civil rights would ultimately help the United States prevail at home and abroad, the president seemed primed to trumpet his legislative goal with an unprecedented rhetorical virtuosity.

State of the Union Address

On January 6, 1948, Truman recorded the following in his diary: "Congress meets—Too bad too. They'll do nothing but wrangle, pull phony investigations and generally upset the affairs of the nation. I'm to address them soon. They won't like that address either."[20] Truman was referring to his January 7, 1948, State of the Union speech. In an election year, the State of the Union message always receives a bit more attention and perhaps more than the normal fair share of criticism. This election year was no different, except that the president's proposals seemed especially out of sync with the mood on Capitol Hill. Truman also used the occasion to announce his intentions for civil rights: "The recent report of the President's Civil Rights Committee points the way to corrective action by the Federal Government and by state and local governments. Because of the need for effective federal actions, I shall send a special message to Congress on this important subject."[21]

For Harry Truman, given his already precarious position in the public-opinion polls, the negative reaction to this address would be a clear warning of tough times ahead.[22] If many people were unimpressed, if not offended, by the president's State of the Union address, they would be even more distressed by his upcoming speech to Congress on civil rights. Truman's administrative aides began to fashion this address approximately one week after the State of the Union message.

Preparing the February 2, 1948, Civil Rights Speech

Truman's speechwriter George Elsey asked Milton D. Stewart, chief researcher and writer on the report for the PCCR and an employee at the New School for Social Research in New York, and Robert L. Carr, the PCCR's executive director and professor at Dartmouth's Department of Government, for their comments as he contemplated the president's upcoming civil rights message. Since Stewart and Carr had been the primary writers on the president's report, there was great interest in their opinion about what the president should highlight. Stewart observed that a strategy should be drawn up that was cognizant of the following context: The Republicans, he argued, have taken up the "poll-tax, anti-lynching, FEPC [Fair Employment

Practices Commission] refrain." The "Wallace crowd is planning its major appeal to the urban low-income voter. It is common gossip here that they are sold on Walter White's view that the Negro vote will spell victory or defeat in the next election—for the President, at least." Stewart continued, "There is no doubt in my mind about the strength of the president's position with minority groups. His stand on the Palestine question until now, his NAACP speech, the work of the civil rights committee—all of these add up to a solid backlog of strength. But it must be finally secured." Stewart advised that what was needed was "a clear, penetrating image of the president himself as the unquestioned leader of the nation in the civil rights field. This is an opportune moment to get it across. The essential themes are: 'Everybody else fumbles around; the President knows what to do'; 'Everybody else talks and talks; the President acts.' Decisiveness and determination should keynote the speech. If these assumptions are true, then the speech should be pointed, straightforward and very brief." Stewart also advised the president to announce some presidential action as "the clincher." His suggestions included ordering desegregation of the armed forces within a year, forming an FBI civil rights squad, ending segregation in the Panama Canal, or some other immediate executive action that would demonstrate presidential leadership. All of these recommendations were contained in some form in the PCCR's report.[23]

Carr responded as follows: "The President is confronted with something of a dilemma: it would be utterly unrealistic of him to recommend everything that is contained in the Report of the Civil Rights Committee; on the other hand, he must not disappoint those people who have had their hopes aroused by the Report. I think he can solve this dilemma by recommending a substantial, but minimum, program for immediate action and then call for further study of many additional items." Carr added the following: "I think it would be good psychology to show awareness of the fact that all of our present shortcomings are not due to the lack of legislation, and indicating that he proposes to take action himself immediately whenever that is within his power." Finally, Carr felt that the president should perhaps call for "a new statutory 'Bill of Rights'" or, failing that, at least stir "popular imagination" by announcing a "unified program, as opposed to a series of unrelated and piecemeal enactments."[24]

In preparing for the address, some of the administration's advisers were concerned that the president would be condemned not so much for what he said (although there was some fear there as well) as for what was left unsaid. Items that the committee called for would look conspicuous in their absence from the president's speech.

February 2, 1948, Address to a Joint Session of Congresson Civil Rights

On February 2, 1948, Harry S. Truman made the following entry into his diary: " I sent the Congress a Civil Rights message. They no doubt will receive it as coldly as they did my State of the Union message. But it needs to be said."[25] Indeed, President Truman had consciously and irretrievably delivered a strong civil rights message to friends and foes alike. Striking a "dignified and responsible" tone redolent of his historic NAACP speech, Truman invoked foundational principles he believed crucial to the American heritage.[26] His litany included equality; equal justice under the law; equal opportunity for jobs, homes, health, and education; voice in government; and government protection of the rights of the citizenry. Such ideals, he argued, had inspired people to come from all over the world to escape tyranny and join in the blessings of democracy conferred by the United States. He told Congress, "Unfortunately, there still are examples—flagrant examples—of discrimination which are utterly contrary to our ideals. Not all groups in our population are free from the fear of violence. Not all groups are free to live and work where they please or to improve their conditions of life by their own efforts. Not all groups enjoy the full privileges of citizenship and participation in the government under which they live." The president referred directly to the committee's findings, which had uncovered "a serious gap between our ideals and some of those practices. This gap must be closed." Truman argued assiduously that the protection of civil rights was a duty that obtains for every government "that derives its power from the consent of the people." Therefore, "[t]he Federal Government has a clear duty to see that Constitutional guarantees of individual liberties and of equal protection under the laws are not denied or abridged anywhere in our Union. That duty is shared by all three branches of the Government, but it can be fulfilled only if the Congress enacts modern, comprehensive civil rights laws, adequate to the needs of the day, and demonstrating our continuing faith in the free way of life." Truman then introduced a ten-point legislative plan that included proposals for the following items: (1) a permanent commission on civil rights; (2) the strengthening of existing civil rights statutes; (3) antilynching legislation; (4) the strengthening of voting rights by elimination of the poll tax; (5) establishment of a permanent FEPC; (6) prohibitions against discrimination in interstate-transportation facilities; (7) home-rule suffrage for residents of Washington, D.C.; (8) statehood for Hawaii and Alaska; (9) equal opportunity for naturalized citizens; and (10) settlement of the evacuation claims of Japanese Americans.

Truman had made his list shorter than his committee's list, but this was a practical and a political necessity. The president framed his legislation as "a minimum program if the Federal Government is to fulfill its obligation of insuring the Constitutional guarantees of individual liberties and equal protection under the law." He also mentioned the executive actions he was undertaking that would put his own house in order by bringing consistency to nondiscrimination policy in the federal civil service and the armed forces.

Finally, Truman, true to earlier form, linked both his present legislative proposals and his own ongoing efforts on behalf of civil rights through executive action to what he described as the unique "position of the United States in the world today," which made adoption of these measures "especially urgent." It was important to build "a world family of nations," and he referred to the UN Commission on Human Rights, which was at that very hour preparing an international bill of human rights. The president told the American people that the United States had played a leading role in that endeavor. "To be effective in these efforts," Truman argued, "we must protect our civil rights so that . . . we shall be a stronger nation—stronger in our leadership, stronger in our moral position, stronger in the deeper satisfactions of a united citizenry." He concluded on a plaintive note, summoning the mantra of an increasingly familiar, new Cold War rationale for addressing civil rights: "If we wish to inspire the peoples of the world whose freedom is in jeopardy, if we wish to restore hope to those who have already lost their civil liberties, if we wish to fulfill the promise that is ours, we must correct the remaining imperfections in our practice of democracy. We know the way. We need only the will."[27] Truman's speech was audacious and unprecedented. Never before in the history of the United States had any president delivered a special message to Congress devoted entirely to civil rights.

While Truman set his compass on restoring the moral order in his defense of civil rights and his call for legislation, not everyone was pleased with his efforts. Some were puzzled, and others were openly disdainful. An editorial in *The Christian Century* offers the following assessment: "It is hard to know how to treat President Truman's message to Congress on the protection of civil rights. Considered simply as a presidential utterance, it is one of the finest in many years. The President nobly reaffirms the principles of the Declaration of Independence and the Constitution. In striking contrast to the usual drabness of his literary style, there are several passages in this document which student orators should be quoting for years to come. Most of the proposals, also, are just and progressive. However, it is unhappily probable that by lumping all ten together—making them, as it were, part of one package—the President has adopted a legislative strategy which will result in the defeat of all."[28]

The South was threatened by the president's message as well as his civil rights package. In particular, there was fierce anger over Truman's attempt to overturn the doctrine of white supremacy in the South by calling for equality in civil rights, jobs, and education. Whites in the South were reportedly "bitterly opposed" to the president's call for a Fair Employment Practices Commission. As Truman's blatant attempt to overturn segregation and undermine discrimination was greeted with contempt, some even called for a Dixiecrat revolt. It was suggested that the Southern governors should mount a march on Washington. In addition, there was immediate talk of holding a separate convention to elect a Southern presidential candidate.[29] The president, however, had his defenders. For example, Walter White and PCCR member Channing Tobias were eloquent and forceful apologists for the president's cause.[30]

The president had raised the ante on civil rights; this divisive issue posed personal political danger to him and threatened to widen as much as to narrow the social fissures. As Alonzo L. Hamby observes, "the political consequences of presidential support for civil rights were as likely to be negative as positive. In moving as he did Truman followed his best instincts."[31] Nonetheless, many at the time and since then felt those instincts were overly political and perhaps largely insincere.

Regardless of the debate over Truman's political motivation, the combination of the distribution of "To Secure These Rights" and the president's proposed legislation, while certainly controversial, led to a new dialogue on race in the United States. As David K. Niles reported to the president, "Since the publication of the Committee's report, daily press coverage has never ceased entirely; but for eight consecutive days following the Message to Congress, the program was on the front page, top center, in news, features, editorials, and cartoons. The minority press has given the Message extensive, favorable coverage and comment. . . . The program as a whole was hailed as the strongest civil rights program ever put forth by any President. The message was referred to as the greatest freedom document since the Emancipation Proclamation. The language of the message was described as 'Lincolnesque.'" Niles reported that every major radio network was developing some kind of program highlighting civil rights issues, that the Voice of America gave the message full coverage, and that a host of state and local activities were in the planning to solve the civil rights dilemma. One development that had not been anticipated by the president's committee was the evolution of municipalities that were beginning to conduct civil rights audits as a result of the president's counsel. A series of promotional advertising spots was also developed by the Advertising Council, which had as its theme "Group Prejudice Is a Postwar Menace." Finally, Niles told the president that more than 1 million people had already visited the Freedom Train, which celebrated the American heritage at a number of whistle-stops across the nation, and that 3–3.5 million people were expected to visit the train before its run was finished. Before the Freedom Train's arrival in each town, the municipality would hold a Rededication Week, which fostered support for national pride and the celebration of civil liberties. The educational mission that was presumed as primary by many of the architects of the president's program got a substantial boost from reports like the one Niles passed to the president.[32]

Truman's Commitment to Civil Rights: Doing What Is Right

President Truman demonstrated presidential character and leadership in commissioning the report, following it up with a direct call for congressional legislation, and continuing to press for his civil rights program both substantively and symbolically throughout the 1948 campaign and beyond. In all three efforts he maintained consistency and steadfast resolve. Although some have questioned Harry Truman's commitment to civil rights legislation, I submit that his commitment to civil rights was sincere and unequivocal.[33] While the arguments presented thus far give evidence for this point of view, I employ this final section of the chapter to reinforce a point I believe has been a bit overlooked, that is, the *intensity* of Truman's resolve. Such intensity may be somewhat surprising coming from a man whose grandmother considered herself an unreconstructed Southerner, whose home state had decidedly Southern sympathies, and whose own language sometimes contained racist epithets. Harry Truman, like John F. Kennedy, who would follow him in the lineage of Democrats who occupied the Oval Office, grew on the job. Both his constitutional duty and his personal sense of justice seemed to be at play here.

Before turning to the episodes that speak powerfully to Truman's resolve, however, I would like to point out that his sincerity in the area of civil rights can also be deduced by an interesting chronological fact. On July 26, 1948, Truman issued executive orders 9980 and 9981. The former prohibited discrimination in federal employment, and the latter called for the desegregation of the armed forces. These orders were signed immediately following the divisive 1948 Democratic convention and slightly more than three months prior to the national election. This action led Ronald Sylvia to conclude that the president "reacted to events based on his personal belief in basic fairness and equality" rather than on political expediency.[34]

Other significant episodes also reveal evidence of Truman's intense feelings on civil rights. When an old friend wrote Truman to encourage him to "go slow" on civil rights, Truman replied, "I am going to send you a copy of the report of my Commission [*sic*] on Civil Rights and then if you still have that antebellum proslavery outlook, I'll be thoroughly disappointed in you." The president offered a few personal examples to reinforce the kinds of injustice he felt his committee was trying to alleviate. The following example is representative: "On the Louisiana and Arkansas Railway when coal burning locomotives were used, the [N]egro firemen were the thing because it was a backbreaking job and a dirty one. As soon as they turned to oil as a fuel it became customary for people to take shots at the [N]egro firemen and a number were murdered because it was thought that this was now a white-collar job and should go to a white man. I can't approve of such goings on and I shall never approve it, as long as I am here, as I told you before. I am going to try to remedy it and if that ends up in my failure to be reelected, that failure will be in a good cause."[35]

Robert Ferrell notes that Truman promised to make a public statement on the abuse of civil rights in the South and that he kept his word by broaching the subject with an integrated audience in Dallas, Texas, at Rebel Stadium and by shaking hands with an African American woman in Waco, Texas, whereupon Truman was summarily booed for this gesture by the local citizenry. In arguing for equal rights in the South, Truman stepped forward boldly and courageously.[36] This was an early precursor to Lyndon Johnson's advice to John Kennedy to talk about civil rights to Southerners in their own territory, with the rationale that even if they did not agree with him, at least he could garner their respect for a brave and forthright stand.

Harry Truman's attempt to pass civil rights legislation was tempered not only by Republican and conservative Democratic members of Congress but also by Truman's legitimate concerns regarding foreign policy and political timing. In April of 1949, Eben A. Ayers recorded the following in his diary: "At our staff meeting this morning Clark Clifford brought up the matter of civil rights legislation to be introduced to the Congress, particularly the timing. The president said that we could not let anything interfere with U.S. foreign policy now before Congress—the appropriation of the European Recovery Program, the Atlantic Pact or treaty, and the reciprocal trade agreement legislation. If civil rights is introduced—and there are four separate measures contemplated—it will plunge the Congress into protracted debate and possible filibuster in the Senate by Southerners who may imperil foreign policy legislation. The president expressed the belief that [this was] about all that will be accomplished along the civil rights program this session, but that some of it will be lined up and some progress will be made."[37] What some may have interpreted as a sure sign of "going slow" on civil rights may have been interpreted by others as an act of prudence at a critical juncture. At the least, a careful balance of foreign and domestic policy had to be entertained.

In June of 1952, toward the end of his presidency, Harry Truman delivered a commencement address at Howard University. He reflected on his civil rights initiatives: "Back in 1947, a good many people advised me not to raise this whole question of civil rights. They said it would only make things worse. But you can't cure a moral problem, or a social problem, by ignoring it. . . . It is no service to the country to turn away from the hard problems—to ignore injustice and human suffering. It is simply not the American way of doing things. Of course, there are always a lot of people whose motto is 'Don't rock the boat.' They are so afraid of rocking the boat, that they stop rowing. We can never get ahead that way. . . . If something is wrong, the thing to do is to dig it out, find out why it is wrong, and take sensible steps to put it right. We are all Americans together, and we can solve our hard problems together, including the problem of race relations."[38]

Truman's finely honed sense of right and wrong, his innate pragmatism, and his ability to rhetorically impart a principled vision of a just democratic society can certainly be adduced in these remarks. His resolve in the civil rights arena has had lasting implications.

Conclusion

Some people have argued that Harry S. Truman's civil rights program was merely a ploy to win the 1948 election.[39] Others have vigorously maintained that Truman truly felt his constitutional duty to protect and defend the rights of minority citizens.[40] Still others have come to the conclusion that Truman had mixed personal and public motives in this area and that those motives might never be plumbed fully or satisfactorily.[41] I contend that Truman's intentions were clear from the outset and that he never wavered. Those motives were precipitated by his personal outrage at mob violence and his sense of constitutional duty. Those aims were instantiated in the committee's work, and they were productive of a most remarkable outcome.

Certainly the pressures on Truman to turn his attention to civil rights were many, and a number of them were political, including, but not limited to, restoration of a thriving postwar economy, the revamping of a sagging defense establishment, and restoration of military preparedness in a post–World War II, postdraft era; victory in the 1948 campaign; compliance with ongoing, international human-rights agreements such as the UN Charter; and an early Cold War philosophy. These were perhaps best articulated in the emerging Truman doctrine, which, not without some hubris, demanded that the United States—as the designated leader of the free world—undertake an unprecedented, global, democratic experiment, thus launching what would become known as the American Century.

Perhaps the greatest, tangible civil rights achievement of the Truman administration can be found in President Truman's desegregation of the armed forces.[42] Clearly, Truman was unable to usher his civil rights legislation to fruition.[43] The president also weakened his case for civil rights with his government-imposed, civil-service loyalty program. Nonetheless, I maintain that we must not overlook the evidence presented here of Truman's own deep commitment to civil rights and the effectiveness of the PCCR report in sustaining that commitment. This certainly must temper our evaluations of Harry S. Truman.

Whatever suspicions we might have of the president's "true" motives, the evidence amassed here underscores Alonzo Hamby's modest claim that Truman's "civil rights program was a noble resolution of contradictory impulses," which certainly included a host of concerns, including those with personal, constitutional, political, economic, military, and international dimensions.[44] David McCullough evaluates Harry Truman's accomplishments in civil rights with the following observation: "He had achieved less in civil rights than he had hoped, but he had created the epoch-making Commission on Civil Rights, ordered the desegregation of the armed services and Federal Civil Service, done more than any president since Lincoln to awaken the American conscience to the issues of civil rights."[45]

Truman's character and leadership set the standard and the tone for the PCCR. He was responsible for picking the membership, and he was responsible for their charge. He was responsible, then, for the committee's success or failure. Although he may have given short shrift to some of its recommendations and ignored others, I find the mere existence of the PCCR a most tangible achievement—one all the more remarkable for its scope and boldness in its time. Moreover, "To Secure These Rights" still stands as a major document in the annals of human rights. It was and remains a model of principle and action in public service, and it would later be emulated by Lyndon Johnson when he commissioned the Kerner Commission Report.[46] For it was Truman's direct charge to his committee and the committee's progressive, far-sighted response that became the impetus for the most indelible series of advances in human rights in the twentieth century. Long before *Brown vs. Board of Education* or the boycott in Montgomery and the modern inauguration of the civil rights move-ment in the United States represented by Martin Luther King Jr., the committee's work was a touchstone in setting off a climate for social, legal, and moral revolution.

In short, the committee's report set a tone and fostered a climate that spurred both words and deeds on race not heard since the nineteenth century. It spun a chrysalis of dialogue and action in the United States that not only made government and people vital but also engaged actors in a national effort to frame fuller, more humane lives. It was Harry Truman who reintroduced the nation to the problem of race, not merely as a divisive civic problem fraught with tension, animosity, and political peril or as a vexing Cold War menace that had created propaganda disaster, but also (and, I believe, more importantly) as a test of high moral character—one that would ultimately define the American character. It was Harry Truman who invited both citizens and government to begin a long, arduous, but necessary process of educating each other and themselves about the stakes involved in difference, about the meaning of identity, about how to put a human face on an institution or a society—in short, about how to achieve equality and justice for all and redeem America's well-recognized but oft-broken promises. As a result of the Truman impetus, both proponents and opponents of civil rights engaged a national debate that continues today and is still shaping our tomorrows.

Carl M. Brauer credits John F. Kennedy with seeking civil rights legislation that entreated both Congress and the nation to create what Brauer calls the Second Reconstruction, which he defines as "a coher-ent effort by all three branches of the government to secure blacks their full rights."[47] According to Brauer, this process began with the famous June 11, 1963, address. Kennedy did not introduce all of his legislative proposals on June 11, but he mentioned a few items as he carefully prepared the common ground on which all of his proposals would be based, and he promised he would send a message to Con-gress the following week. However, I submit that Kennedy's premises in that address were the same as those of Truman's committee and, by proxy, of Truman as well. The ideals and the idealism expressed in

Kennedy's address had a prior establishment. Long before the inroads paved by John F. Kennedy and the legislation that Lyndon Johnson would finally sign into law, the key principles had been fashioned. The blueprint for action was already mightily forged. It was the PCCR that inaugurated the clear moral, economic, and international principles that sustained the dialogue on and concern over improving the civil rights of minorities. Truman's efforts on civil rights not only placed emphasis on race relations in the United States but also firmly and irretrievably centered better relations as important domestic and international policy concerns. If, as Brauer argues, "Kennedy both encouraged and responded to black aspirations and led the nation into its Second Reconstruction," then it is surely President Truman's civil rights committee that was responsible for its inauguration.[48]

In sum, Truman's charge and the PCCR's execution would refocus the nation's attention on minority issues, force the majority to enlarge its vision, set the social and legislative agenda for the next half century, and ultimately, I believe, help inaugurate the celebrated "second reconstruction." We have Harry S. Truman's audacious leadership and steadfastness to thank for our national invitation to embark on that momentous journey.

Notes

1. Letter, Harry S. Truman to Tom Clark, Sept. 20, 1946, Civil Rights and Minorities, 1937–1947, Niles Papers, box 26, Harry S. Truman Library (hereafter HSTL).
2. Memo, Harry S. Truman to David K. Niles, Sept. 20, 1946, Civil Rights and Minorities, 1937–1947, Niles Papers, box 26, HSTL.
3. Press release, Dec. 5, 1946, Ayers Papers in *The Truman Administration's Civil Rights Program,* vol. 2: *The Report of the Committee on Civil Rights and President Truman's Message to Congress of February 2, 1948,* ed. Dennis Merrill (Frederick, Md.: University Publications of America, 1996), document 56, pp. 197–99.
4. Informal remarks of the president to the members of the President's Committee on Civil Rights, Jan. 15, 1947, Civil Rights and Minorities, 1937–1947, Niles Papers, box 26, HSTL; press release, Jan. 15, 1947, Ayers Papers in Merrill, *The Truman Administration's Civil Rights Program,* document 67, p. 264. The committee that Truman ultimately selected comprised two corporate heads, General Electric Chair Charles E. Wilson and Lever Brothers Pres. Charles Luckman; two labor representatives, Secretary-Treasurer of the CIO James B.

Carey and AFL economist Boris Shiskin; two college presidents, University of North Carolina's Frank P. Graham and Dartmouth's John Dickey; two African Americans, Sadie Alexander, solicitor of Philadelphia, and Channing Tobias, who served as a senior officer in the YMCA and was the director of the Phelps-Stokes Fund; two Jewish representatives, ACLU lawyer Morris L. Ernst and New York Rabbi Roland B. Gittlesohn; two Catholics, Omaha corporate lawyer Francis P. Matthews and Michigan Bishop Francis J. Hass; and two Protestants, Massachusetts Episcopal Bishop Henry Knox Sherrill and Methodist philanthropist Dorothy M. Tilly. The youngest member of the committee was Franklin Delano Roosevelt Jr., who was also a lawyer. Roosevelt missed the first eight committee meetings but was still able to play a key role. The twosomes represented seemed so pronounced that some members of the press began to call the committee "Noah's Ark." On the whole the committee was liberal, moderate, and well balanced. For an excellent history of the committee's deliberations, see William E. Juhnke, "President Truman's Committee on Civil Rights: The Intersection of Politics, Protest, and Presidential Advisory Commission," *Presidential Studies Quarterly* 19 (1989): 593–608, quotation 594.

Wilson served as chair of the committee. Roosevelt and Dickey served as members of Wilson's executive committee. All of the members were ably assisted by Robert L. Carr, the committee's executive secretary. Carr and Milton D. Stewart, the lead researcher for the committee, would ultimately be chiefly responsible for writing the final report.

The committee was subdivided into three subcommittees: (1) legislation, composed of Sherrill as chair, along with Mathews, Graham, Dickey, and Alexander; (2) broad, national social, economic, and educational aspects of promoting civil liberties, composed of Luckman as chair, along with Haas, Carey, Tobias, and Gittelsohn; and (3) the role of private organizations in fostering civil rights, with Ernst serving as chair, along with Tilly, Shiskin, and Roosevelt. See minutes of the meeting of the President's Committee on Civil Rights, Feb. 5 and 6, 1947, Niles Papers in Merrill, *The Truman Administration's Civil Rights Program,* document 70, pp. 268–71.

5. As testimony in the minutes of the Mar. 6, 1947, meeting reflects, "Everyone agrees that since this committee was set up by President Truman, in all courtesy to him the committee ought to report in time to let him do something about it [civil rights] while he is still President of the United States. Congress, as you know, operates on a two-year cycle and is now in the first session of a two-year period. Many people feel that if you really expect Congress to pass any legislation as a result of recommendations made, the Presidential message ought to go to Congress at this session. Now, that limits

the time very drastically indeed, because under the Reorganization Act, Congress is supposed to adjourn July first. That means if the President is going to send a message to Congress on the basis of your report, the report would have to go to him some time in May." Members quickly determined that this request was "impossible," but they were nevertheless struck by the enormity and urgency of their charge. Transcript of the minutes of the meeting of Mar. 6, 1947, President's Committee on Civil Rights (hereafter PCCR), reading files, box 12, HSTL.

6. See, for example, the minutes of the meeting of Apr. 3, 1947, PCCR reading file, box 12, HSTL.

7. Juhnke, "President Truman's Committee," p. 594.

8. Charter of the United Nations, June 26, 1945, Department of State Publication 2353, conference series 74, chap. 9, "International Economic and Social Cooperation," p. 19, in UN Conference on International Organizations, PCCR reference file, S-Y, box 28, HSTL. Interestingly, by 1945, Eleanor Roosevelt had become a member of the board of directors of the NAACP. She had also stood on the same platform and addressed the same audience as Truman at the Lincoln Memorial at the famous NAACP plenary session on June 29, 1947. As one who had helped craft the UN Charter, she emphasized in her NAACP address that civil rights performance in the United States was then in a global fishbowl and a flashpoint in the Cold War struggle to win hearts and minds. She declared that "We have . . . to make sure that we have civil rights in this country . . . [because] it isn't any longer a domestic question—it's an international question. It is perhaps the question which may decide whether democracy or communism wins out in the world." Joanna Schneider Zangrando and Robert L. Zangrando, "Eleanor Roosevelt and Black Civil Rights," in *Without Precedent: The Life and Career of Eleanor Roosevelt,* ed. Joan Hoff-Wilson and Marjorie Lightman (Bloomington: Indiana University Press, 1984), pp. 101–102.

NAACP Executive Director Walter White, who introduced the president to the throng at the Lincoln Memorial, also took up the cause of democracy at home and abroad. He fully subscribed to the doctrine that what was good for American democracy was good for the world: "If we Americans assure that no man is denied any right of citizenship because he is dark of skin or worships his God in a different place or was born elsewhere, then democracy can never be destroyed. But we also know that human freedom must be in the hearts of men and not solely on paper. To this high objective we rededicate our every energy. We welcome to this struggle, whose outcome will help to determine the future of mankind, every citizen who believes that the Bill of Rights means what it says." Address by Walter White, Lincoln Memorial, Washington, D.C., June 29, 1947,

Clifford Files in Merrill, *The Truman Administration's Civil Rights Program,* document 91, pp. 331–33. Indeed, African Americans, long tired of redress denied, ultimately sought to bring their case for human-rights violations against the United States to the United Nations, but their efforts were ultimately rebuffed because of opposition from the United States.

9. Zangrando and Zangrando, "Eleanor Roosevelt," p. 101.

10. Address by Pres. Harry S. Truman, Lincoln Memorial, Washington, D.C., June 29, 1947, *Public Papers of the Presidents of the United States: Harry S. Truman, 1947* (Washington, D.C.: Government Printing Office, 1963), p. 312. For an excellent interpretation of this unprecedented address see Garth E. Pauley, "Harry Truman and the NAACP: A Case Study in Presidential Persuasion on Civil Rights," *Rhetoric and Public Affairs* 2 (1999): 211–41. Pauley argues that in this remarkable address Truman labels civil rights a "crisis," thus fashioning a seminal event in the annals of the modern U.S. presidency. Certainly one part of the crisis to which Truman was referring was the fact that civil rights abuses added to international anti-U.S. propaganda. For a helpful comparative approach to presidential address on civil rights, see Garth E. Pauley, *The Modern Presidency and Civil Rights: Rhetoric on Race from Roosevelt to Nixon* (College Station: Texas A&M University Press, 2001).

After President Truman's address, the *Philadelphia Inquirer* observed: "Other peoples throughout the world are watching this country for signs of weakness in our democracy. It's the claim of our kind of system that it is best suited and best able to give every individual an equal chance, according to his ability and character. So long as whole groups are arbitrarily deprived of that chance our critics will attempt to hold us up to scorn as hypocrites. And those who have consistently championed us may turn away in discouragement." News editorial, "Against Racial Injustice," *Philadelphia Inquirer,* July 1, 1947, Truman's speeches (press clippings), Correspondence and Administrative Records, PCCR, box 4, HSTL.

As the *Detroit Free Press* summarizes the matter, "With our democracy under the world's microscope, the time has come for a determined, all-out movement to exorcize the seeds of race prejudice from our hearts and minds." A drawing accompanies the editorial that depicts Uncle Sam posing with his back to a mirror. The reader is exposed to a number of patches on the back of his jacket that read "abuse of minorities," "hate," and "race bias." The editorial cartoon is captioned as follows: "As the World Sees Us." News editorial, "Rights of All," *Detroit Free Press,* July 1, 1947, Truman's speeches (press clippings), Correspondence and Administrative Records, PCCR, box 4, HSTL.

Evidence that the foreign press was wary of U.S. claims to uphold democracy was rather easy to amass. On May 3, 1947, for example, Moscow's *Pravda* published a half-page cartoon that depicts "Churchill, DeGaulle, [and] Uncle Sam. Uncle Sam['s] . . . pockets [are] full of atom bombs strangling a chained [N]egro on whose back he rides." In February, 1947, the *National Call*, a small New Delhi newspaper, cited the lynchings in the United States as proof of the failure of America to "look at the beam in their own eyes before pointing to the mote in those of others." Memo, Ottemiller to Ksould, "Recent Foreign Comments on Civil Rights in the United States," June 19, 1947, Correspondence with Government Agencies: State Department, PCCR, box 6, HSTL.

Not surprisingly, Robert L. Carr wrote Secretary of State George C. Marshall that the president's civil rights committee was "disturbed by the oft-repeated suggestion that our country's bad record in the field of race relations is being used against us in other parts of the world." Accordingly, Carr asked Marshall whether he felt that foreign policy was being harmed by poor performance on domestic civil rights. He also requested actual data to this effect that could be reported to President Truman. Moreover, he outlined "two dangers" that had surfaced in witnesses' testimony to the committee: "One of these is the use of our bad race record against us by the Soviet Union and the Communist Parties in the Near East and in China." The other problem stemmed from potential damage "done to American interests in Latin America because of our bad civil rights record in the treatment of the Spanish-speaking minority in the United States." Letter, Robert L. Carr to George C. Marshall, May 23, 1947, PCCR reading file, box 11, HSTL.

11. Report, *Motivation of Propaganda on Civil Liberties,* July 17, 1947, Correspondence with Government Agencies: State Department, PCCR, box 6, HSTL.

12. Mary L. Dudziak, *Cold War Civil Rights: Race and the Image of Democracy* (Princeton and Oxford: Princeton University Press, 2000), p. 79.

13. I have made a similar argument elsewhere. See Steven R. Goldzwig, "Civil Rights and the Cold War: A Rhetorical History of the Truman Administration's Desegregation of the United States Army," in *Doing Rhetorical History: Concepts and Cases,* ed. Kathleen J. Turner (Tuscaloosa and London: University of Alabama Press, 1998), pp. 143–69. Here I merely observe that making civil rights "the central issue" in the ongoing trade of Cold War propaganda chips would have significant, perduring national and international repercussions—both material and psychological. With the breakdown of the Soviet Union, I suggest that the focus on civil rights has also diminished. Ironically, so-called totalitarian regimes played at least an indirect role in helping to ensure that American presidents paid attention to the health of civil rights in the United States.

Of course, upholding civil liberties was also a fundamental part of many of the United States' international agreements. Examples include (but certainly are not limited to) the following: the United States as a signatory body to the Moscow Agreement of 1945; the Charter of the United Nations (as indicated earlier); the United Nations Education, Scientific, and Cultural Organization (UNESCO); the reorganization and consolidation of the Inter-American System; the Act of Chapultepec; and a host of agreements with international labor organizations. Each of these agreements had provisions protecting human and civil rights.

14. *"To Secure These Rights"*: *The Report of the President's Committee on Civil Rights* (New York: Simon and Schuster, 1947), unnumbered.

15. Ibid., pp. 139, 141, 144, 146–48.

16. Letter, C. Girard Davidson to J. Howard McGrath, Dec. 6, 1947, McGrath Papers in Merrill, *The Truman Administration's Civil Rights Program,* document 116, pp. 610–18. For a complete account of the committee's recommended actions, see *"To Secure These Rights,"* chap. 4, "A Program of Action: The Committee's Recommendations," pp. 139–73.

17. Press release, statement by the president, Oct. 29, 1947, OF 596, box 1509, HSTL.

18. Letter, Erwin N. to Robert L. Carr, Dec. 3, 1947, in Merrill, *The Truman Administration's Civil Rights Program,* documents 117 and 118, quotation, p. 620.

19. Alonzo L. Hamby, *Man of the People: A Life of Harry S. Truman* (New York and Oxford: Oxford University Press, 1995), pp. 433–34.

20. Robert H. Ferrell, *Off the Record: The Private Papers of Harry S. Truman* (New York: Harper and Row, 1980), p. 122.

21. Harry S. Truman, annual message to the Congress on the State of the Union, in *Public Papers of the Presidents: Harry S. Truman, 1948* (Washington, D.C.: Government Printing Office, 1964), pp. 1–10, quotation 3.

22. As one *New York Times* reporter describes the reaction, "[T]he State of the Union message gained a distinctly hostile reaction from Congress. Both in their stinted applause at the time of delivery, and in their unrestrained comments in private later, a good majority of members indicated varying degrees of displeasure. Republicans almost to a man, and many conservative Democrats as well, said plainly that they would not embark on another New Deal, which they construed to be the President's intention." A *Washington Daily News* editorial derides the message bluntly: "Much of the long document is a catalog of New Deal objectives, not attained by Mr. Roosevelt and Mr. Truman in 14 years of Democratic Congresses, on which Mr. Truman asks action right now by a Republican Congress." From fair-employment practices to social security to farm

price supports, the list Truman developed was allegedly so vast that it left out "practically nothing but the Beatitudes and the Ten Commandments." The *Daily News* editorial concludes as follows: "In general, this is a message of which Mr. Truman has little reason to be proud. One of its most unfortunate aspects is the strong temptation, if not justification, it offers Republicans to retaliate by making this session of Congress a political Donnybrook Fair." Cabell Phillips, "Capital Sees 'New Deal' Trend in Truman Plan," *New York Times,* undated, and "An Unfortunate Message," editorial, *Washington Daily News,* Jan. 8, 1948, both in "State of the Union Message, 1948," Murphy Files, box 3, HSTL.

23. Letter, Milton D. Stewart to George M. Elsey, Jan. 19, 1948; civil rights message, Feb. 2, 1948, drafts and suggestions, Elsey Papers, speech files, box 20, HSTL.

24. Letter, Robert L. Carr to George M. Elsey, Jan. 16, 1948; civil rights message, Feb. 2, 1948, drafts and suggestions, Elsey Papers, speech files, box 20, HSTL. Whether based on the offered advice or not, the administration began to prepare an omnibus civil rights package.

25. Ferrell, *Off the Record,* p. 122.

26. William C. Berman, *The Politics of Civil Rights in the Truman Administration* (Columbus: Ohio State University Press, 1970), p. 83.

27. Harry S. Truman, special message to Congress on civil rights, Washington, D.C., Feb. 2, 1948, in *The Public Papers of the Presidents of the United States: Harry S. Truman, 1948* (Washington, D.C.: Government Printing Office, 1964), pp. 121–26.

28. "Civil Rights and the Election," editorial, *Christian Century* 65(7) (Feb. 18, 1948). In Feb. 2, 1948, Civil Rights, presidential speech file, Clifford Papers, box 31, HSTL.

29. See, for example, "Gauging the South's Revolt," *U.S. News and World Report,* Mar. 26, 1948, pp. 22–23; civil rights message, Feb. 2, 1948, press releases and drafts for bills; Elsey Papers, speech file, box 20, HSTL; "Says Truman 'Stabbing South in the Back,'" *Mobile Press,* Feb. 3, 1948, p. 1; "Sparks Lays Turn-about to Truman," *Montgomery Advertiser,* Feb. 4, 1948, p. 1, PPF 200, speeches, box 306, HSTL.

30. Walter White, "The President Means It," Feb. 12, 1948, in Merrill, *The Truman Administration's Civil Rights Program,* document 139, pp. 726–29; statement by Channing H. Tobias on President Truman's Message on Civil Rights, Feb. 11, 1948, Civil Rights/Negro Affairs, 1949–1952, Niles Papers, box 27.

31. Hamby, *Man of the People,* p. 434.

32. Memo, David K. Niles to Harry S. Truman, Feb. 16, 1948, Civil Rights/Negro Affairs, 1949–1952, Niles Papers, box 27, HSTL. The Freedom Train was a red, white, and blue, three-boxcar traveling museum containing 150 documents and flags representing a historical depiction of the development of liberty in the United

States. Among other items, the Mayflower Compact and Thomas Jefferson's draft of the Declaration of Independence were prominently displayed. The train, whose purpose was to conduct an educational campaign for the American people, was slated to visit every state in the union during a twelve-month period beginning in September of 1947. It was sponsored by the president and the attorney general and financed by the American Heritage Foundation. Its mission was attached to the Cold War and loosely followed the PCCR's recommendation for more public education on civil liberties and civil rights. The train actually ended up taking a thirty-six-thousand-mile, sixteen-month tour that ended in January of 1949. I would like to thank the HSTL archivists with supplying me with this information. One student of the Freedom Train effort has written the following: "With old-style partisanship in decline, the Freedom Train and the American Heritage Foundation program was a venture into the modern, ultrasymbolic, national political culture during the Cold War. In the uncertain and dangerous postwar era powerful leaders experienced for themselves and helped to create for the general public the idea that the whole foundation of America and thus the American way of life were threatened. In the process they offered participation in a democratic society which restricted rather than enlarged political discourse." See Stuart Jon Little, "The Freedom Train and the Formation of the National Political Culture, 1946–1949," master's thesis, University of Kansas, 1989, p. 149.

33. A couple of interesting examples help support this claim. Civil rights aide Philleo Nash relates the following story regarding a Truman campaign speech in Harlem in October of 1948: "I had written a speech which rather stressed unity and [Truman] took the 'unity' out and said, you know, 'It's more important to be right than it is to be united.' [He continued:] 'Unity is a weak concept. Mr. Dewey has been talking about unity. I want to do what's right even if we can't be united on it.'" Here, Truman's sense of justice and fairness seems to outweigh his political instincts. In reference to the role of civil rights and the 1948 election, Nash contends, "Civil rights was the touchstone of the Truman election in 1948. It was via the civil rights route that he first showed he was the master of his own party . . . . [I]t showed that he could get the nomination in spite of his strong stand on civil rights. . . . [Truman's] integrity had been called into question by his opponents. Does he really mean the things he says? What kind of guy is he? And everybody expected him to fold on this issue." When he stayed the course on this divisive issue, Nash argues, he demonstrated his character. To many voters, the president had displayed "good faith, strength, and courage." Philleo Nash Oral History, interviewed by Jerry Hess, Washington, D.C., Aug. 19, 1966, pp. 1:227, 335.

34. Ronald D. Sylvia, "Presidential Decision Making and Leadership in the Civil Rights Era," *Presidential Studies Quarterly* 25 (1995): 391–412. For a similar conclusion on Truman and the triumph of principle over politics in civil rights, see Michael R. Gardner, *Harry Truman and Civil Rights: Moral Courage and Political Risks* (Carbondale and Edwardsville: Southern Illinois University Press, 2002). Concrete evidence of Truman's commitment to civil rights can also be gleaned from the actions of the Supreme Court in crucial cases prior to the landmark *Brown vs. Board of Education* decision. See, for example, Dudziak, *Cold War Civil Rights,* especially pp. 90–107; Gardner, *Harry Truman,* pp. 163–97.

35. Ferrell, *Off the Record,* pp. 146–47.

36. Ibid., p. 147.

37. Robert H. Ferrell, ed., *Truman in the White House: The Diary of Eben A. Ayers* (Columbia and London: University of Missouri Press, 1991), pp. 301–302.

38. Harry S. Truman, commencement address delivered at Howard University, Washington, D.C., June 13, 1952, in *Vital Speeches of the Day,* July 1, 1952, pp. 551–53; quotation, p. 551.

39. Berman, *The Politics of Civil Rights.*

40. Donald R. McCoy and Richard T. Ruetten, *Quest and Response: Minority Rights and the Truman Administration* (Lawrence: University Press of Kansas, 1973).

41. Pauley, "Harry S. Truman and the NAACP."

42. Goldzwig, "Civil Rights and the Cold War."

43. Most of 1945 and 1946 had been taken up largely with trying to make legislative advances on a permanent Fair Employment Practices Commission, which Truman considered essential to his war-reconversion program. The permanent FEPC had foundered in the House Rules Committee and by way of Senate filibuster, where a cloture vote could not be sustained. A similar fate met a Truman-endorsed poll-tax bill. Nonetheless, Truman continued his rhetorical support for advances in civil rights. In 1947, there was relative "relaxation" on civil rights initiatives. Truman focused on executive actions, including working with the defense establishment to desegregate the military services. But it was the appointment of the PCCR and its subsequent report that set the climate and sustained the arguments for Truman's introduction of specific civil rights legislation in 1948. The Republican-controlled Eightieth Congress would yield little by way of concrete civil rights legislation. In 1949, Truman challenged the Eighty-first Congress with similar legislation without success. While Truman was criticized by some for not doing all he could to support his civil rights legislation, both parties in Congress ignored a number of the president's requests. None of this precluded very real gains at the state and local levels, which were inspired

by the president's words and actions. See, for example, McCoy and Ruetten, *Quest and Response,* especially pp. 116, 154–55, 159–70.

44. Hamby, *Man of the People,* p. 641.
45. David McCullough, *Truman* (New York: Simon and Schuster, 1992), p. 915.
46. *Report of the National Advisory Commission on Civil Disorders* (New York: Bantam, 1968).
47. Carl M. Brauer, *John F. Kennedy and the Second Reconstruction* (New York: Columbia University Press, 1977), p. 260.
48. Ibid., p. 320.

CHAPTER 5

JFK and Civil Rights

Sooner or Later

—

E. Culpepper Clark

There can be no history without the gift of knowing what to leave out: no need to bring gravitation to account for the Defenestration of Prague, of which it is nonetheless a fundamental factor. History easily survives the right kind of superficiality and does not depend on "depth" for its truth value. It is by its patterning, its composition in the strict sense, that understanding is conveyed and the master is made known.

. . . One might say that it is by its *rhetoric* that a history communicates the precise fact found by the researcher and what he wants the reader to see.

—Jacques Barzun, "History: The Muse and Her Doctors"

Actually, historians are not the worst to argue, but it is difficult to imagine a more contentious lot. The fault is not in their nature but in the materials with which they must work: facts, adverbs, and pronouns. For example, try dropping the fact that in the thirteen years between the murder of Emmett Till on August 28, 1955, and the assassination of Martin Luther King Jr. on April 4, 1968, forty people lost their lives in some way connected to the civil rights movement. That fact, because it does not square with images of the period, will set most audiences stirring. Add the adverb "only" in front of "forty lives," and a riot will ensue. Adverbs like "better or worse" and "sooner or later" only add insult to whichever side has been injured by a fact. Adverbs are just so judgmental.

And pronouns? Well, they are simply another way of personalizing the attack. I am told that the pronominal "I" did not come into autobiographical usage until St. Augustine (yet another reason to complain about the *Confessions*). Imagine a time when accounting for events depended upon the *ausflus* of a civilization or tides in the affairs of humankind, not great or evil people of whatever color, creed, polity, and so on. Of course, the gods were always available to blame, but somehow that seems better and less personal than calculating Grant's mood before Vicksburg or Kennedy's flat emotional tone before any civil rights engagement.

So here we end up with a title that begins innocently enough—"JFK and Civil Rights"—until the obligatory adverbial spillage following the colon. "Sooner or later" is but another way of saying let's fight one more time about the Kennedy legacy and civil rights. Was JFK a drum major for justice or a footdragger in the ranks?

Well, enough about words and titles. Allow me to open with two scenes from my youth.

Scene 1: In the fall of 1960, I, along with some buddies on the high-school debate team, conducted a mock election. My high school was located in deepest southwest Georgia about twelve miles from the Florida line. Kennedy won in a landslide, which gratified me in that I was already a Kennedyophile. Although my classmates likely did not share my enthusiasm, the Democratic Party was still the house of their fathers.

Three years later, in the fall of 1963, cheers erupted from schools around my home county as news of Kennedy's assassination spread.

Scene 2: On June 10, 1963, I was traveling toward Charlotte, North Carolina, for my first visit in the home of my wife-to-be. I had turned twenty only three days before. As I drove, I tuned in and listened to Kennedy's commencement address at American University. His words were the finest I had heard since his inaugural and more compelling because he talked of making the world safe from (or for) nuclear arms.

He spoke of peace "as the necessary rational end of rational men," and, in lines that seem retrospectively to have prefigured his own tragic end, he said, "For, in the final analysis, our most basic common link is that we all inhabit this small planet. We all breathe the same air. We all cherish our children's futures. And we are all mortal." Words like that took away the breath of this college sophomore.

The next day, June 11, the cameras switched to Tuscaloosa, as George Wallace made his theatrical stand in the schoolhouse door. That night Kennedy went on television with still more Kennedy-style eloquence to announce that civil rights was no longer a legal but rather a moral issue and to pledge legislation that would end the worst manifestations of segregation.

It was all so inspiring, so right, so bold, so death defying in my part of the world, where jowls shook with "no-never" declarations against integration and where Medgar Evers would be shot dead that same night.

I open with these two scenes as a reminder of how John F. Kennedy was received in his rhetorical upsurge. In the years since, his reputation has been shredded, diced, minced, and generally transmogrified. He has been revealed for all his fornicating, sexist, Irish-Catholic, family-warped, image-conscious self. Camelot, we found, was an absorbing but not liberating creation. Despite his eloquence, we learned, JFK had no real feeling for civil rights or its advocates—the emotional connection would be left to his brother Bobby—and that belatedly.

All of the tomes on civil rights and the Kennedys since the mid-seventies attempt to give credit where it is due, and that is to the movement, not to presidential intervention. In *The Kennedy Imprisonment,* Garry Wills helps develop the prevailing view when he declares, "The famous antitheses and alliterations of John Kennedy's rhetoric sound tinny now. But King's eloquence endures, drawn as it was from ancient sources."[1] And Kenneth O'Reilly, who concedes more to Kennedy's persuasion, still cannot resist the conclusion that "John and Robert Kennedy remained civil rights minimalists for the whole thousand days. . . . To the extent that the Kennedys pushed the envelope on minority hiring, voting rights, federal housing, and combating segregationist violence, they did so because the civil rights movement forced their hand."[2]

Who gets credit is part of the issue here. As the movement yielded to the persuasion of black power, so historians moved to an acknowledgement of the dominant role of African Americans, a view that still obtains. However, a significant shift has occurred over the question of who within the movement deserves the most credit. Earlier debates centered on who was closest to King and, in that respect, resembled the quarrels among Lee's lieutenants as to who his favorite was or who did the most to advance the fortunes of the Army of Northern Virginia. In this comparison (which feels invidious), Ralph Abernathy, whom I have always felt got the short end, wound up like General Longstreet, Lee's "Old Warhorse," taking considerable abuse from often younger, certainly more flamboyant, generals—and both wound up apostates in the Republican parties of their respective eras.

On the generational score, the SNCC (Student Nonviolent Coordinating Committee) faction has gained in recent years at the expense of the King-led Southern Christian Leadership Conference (SCLC). This shift owes significantly to the recent focus on Mississippi in John Dittmer's *Local People* and Charles Payne's *I've Got the Light of Freedom*.[3] These historians believe that the ordeal of organizing in the backwaters of Mississippi was ultimately more important than King's more visible, institutionally supported confrontations in Alabama. SNCC students of that era point to a future of "black power" beyond what they perceive as the SCLC's more limited aims of ending segregation. Embracing this spirit, these historians also take the SNCC organizers' dim view of white students, who, by SNCC lights, were short-time patriots in Mississippi's Freedom Summer. And they are positively incensed at the suggestion (most vividly expressed in the movie *Mississippi Burning*) that there is anything good to be said about the FBI or federal intervention generally.

Another part of this equation is the scholarly suspicion of moderate liberals and elites in general. From this perspective, the best antidote to elitist great-man thinking is to get inside the chief among them, and in this case it has been the Kennedys. Garry Wills, Kenneth O'Reilly, Thomas Reeves, and others remind me of the dictum that no man is a hero to his valet.[4] Like valets, the psychic income for historians and journalists is in knowing their subjects from the inside out, and they will refuse no leads. The more things are not as they seem, the bigger the payoff. Out of this chaotic and partial knowledge about motives, historians link thought to action (à la Collingwood) until—voilà—the mask is stripped away.

Ironically, the conservative backlash abets the trend, for they find even less to admire in the graven images of Camelot—indeed, their detestation is visceral. For eighties- and nineties-style historians and journalists (most of whom were educated in the liberal-democratic tradition), attacking Kennedy-style liberalism amounts to burnishing one's credibility badge in the new conservative order. The historical result is a schizophrenic account of the Kennedys. See, for example, O'Reilly's opening paragraphs of the chapter titled "Tough Guy" from *Nixon's Piano*. Here O'Reilly says, "He [JFK] used the moral authority of the White House to condemn racism in all its forms and the executive authority of his office to attack discrimination in voting, federal civil service, public facilities, private-sector employment, and housing. And he introduced the most important civil rights legislation in a century. By the time the assassin's bullet took this young president's life, de jure segregation was reeling under the civil rights movement's righteous force and the federal government's legal force" (189).

But, having fawned over Kennedy accomplishments in the opening, O'Reilly's conclusion is that the Kennedys were minimalists and unwilling to move until forced. The very last thing O'Reilly does in this chapter is to quote RFK's exchange with Anthony Lewis, in which Bobby says he and his brother never really discussed civil rights or its terrible impact upon southern Negroes. RFK finally says, "But when you asked me: 'Did you ever talk about it or concentrate on it?'—well, we didn't do it. And we didn't do it after he became president and I became attorney general, either." Lewis then follows, "'I didn't ask you whether you talked. I asked you whether you became aware of the rather special horror of life for the Negro in the South.' RFK: 'No.'"[5]

Enough said. Or so O'Reilly seems to think. The accomplishments are damned by insufficient motivation. This is nothing new, certainly not in the decline of this last century. From the ideological heights of consensus historiography, which prevailed at midcentury, history has been fragmented by interest groups and power relationships. And with so many claimants for historical vindication, one of the easiest ways to reduce elites, if not account for them, is to question motive—a process that old parliamentarians would consider ad hominem and thus anathema to orderly debate. Rather than "what" historical actors did or do, primacy is given to "why," which is murky terrain at best.

Now watch this! "Why do we scholars do it?" I ask (assuming, of course, that "we" all do it and that I have the answer). Here is why. Motive is ultimately a question of character, and character is something we all possess for better or worse. On a question of character, the best and the brightest are no better than the ordinary. They too lust and fornicate, shower and shave, shade the truth, feel ill of others, tell dirty jokes, and so on until in the end it is not so much the fact that we are all mortal that unites us as it is the hope that we won't get caught. (But if the other fellow gets caught, well, hey.) By explaining events through the motives of actors, "gotcha" journalism and historiography have a universal and ready audience.

It is easy to see that this writer received his education in an era before locutions were known not only to dodge reality (meaning power relationships) but also to positively mask them from speaker and listener. (Today we know better. An interlocutor, sufficiently trained in critical theory, can tease meaning out of the discourse of actors who are blind to the implications of their own speech.) But in that earlier era, the likes of Collingwood, Barzun, and Becker made sense.[6] In their world one could create from the rhetoric of *doing* history what William James calls "the sentiment of rationality" and that through the "explanatory force of common speech." Part of the trick was what Barzun calls "knowing what to leave out." Motive, if it were not left out entirely, had to be treated gingerly.

By motive, I do not mean what the actor proclaims (in the postmodern world that's too easy and inevitably misleading), but that which lies hidden, the ulterior or interior recesses of motive. At first historians moved cautiously into the world of psychology. I remember the novelty of William B. Willcox putting Sir Henry Clinton, the commanding general of British forces in North America, on the couch in order to explain his failure to reclaim the rebellious colonies. Willcox himself said, "When a historian moves from considering people's actions to considering their motives for acting, he must be even more tentative."[7] Accordingly, Willcox submitted his evidence of Clinton's psychological makeup in a famous addendum to his already compelling biographical narrative. Thus, although he did not leave the interior profile of Clinton's personality out, he carefully removed it to the land of speculation.

Such circumspection today seems overly fastidious as historians and journalists dive headlong into any realm of personal effects or affects, from the knowable to the almost knowable, to the hypothetical and conjectural. Nothing is left out that may be used by any interested party to say of the personality under investigation whatever they wish. The right to know about presidents is especially without limits of either discipline or constitutional protection. Nor should anyone dare assert that the people have a right not to know. No aspect of character is without bearing or baring.

But enough of this lament for a disciplinary restraint that may well have existed more in historians' minds than in fact. What is the Kennedy legacy with respect to civil rights, and what might possibly be contributed to this question that has not been answered a thousand times? First, the "sooner or later" question begs an answer, and the answer is "sooner," for I cannot now imagine an alternative president who would have moved more quickly or with more rhetorical force. In fact, there is only one real alternative (apart from imagining some Democrat or Republican who failed in their bids), and of course that is Richard Nixon.

Martin Luther King Jr. liked him and well into the 1960 campaign considered supporting him. After all, not only did Kennedy have to deal with southern Democrats, but he also seemed positively to like them. George Smathers was a carousing buddy and had defeated the great New Deal liberal Claude Pepper (a University of Alabama graduate, I might add) in a bruising campaign that did not bode well for liberalism. One of JFK's earliest southern supporters and friends was Gov. John Patterson (a Phi Beta Kappa graduate of the University of Alabama) but a thoroughgoing racist who at one time tried to force the university to hire a psychologist from Villanova who would buttress the scientific case for Negro inferiority. You will also recall that he is the one who "outniggered" George Wallace in the 1958 election. Bobby remembered him in 1964 as "our great pal in the South."[8] In fact, if one is to be damned by the people one "gets along with," you can throw in just about the whole gargoylish bunch including Eastland, Barnett, and Wallace.

Nixon, on the other hand, had been the Republicans' token evidence during Eisenhower's placid decade that the Grand Old Party was still the party of Lincoln. When all hell was breaking loose in Tuscaloosa during the 1956 Autherine Lucy debacle, Nixon balanced Eisenhower's inaction by saying that "a great Republican chief justice, Earl Warren, has ordered an end to racial segregation in the nation's schools."[9] That little sound bite was enough to get Nixon on the Birchers' ten-most-wanted list of communist sympathizers. Retrospectively, however, it is hard to imagine Nixon doing what Kennedy did or to imagine him surrounding himself with speechwriters and think-tankers who would have come up with the movement rhetoric Kennedy so eloquently employed—no Harris Wofford, no Louis Martin, no Burke Marshall, John Siegenthaler, John Doar, or Louis Oberdorfer, and so on.

Still, it is interesting to speculate what might have happened had Daly not stolen those ballots in Chicago. What if Nixon had had to respond to the crisis of 1963 in Birmingham and Tuscaloosa? As Schlesinger said of the Kennedys, "it took presidential politics to involve them with the movement; and then the prospect of responsibility to make them think intensely about the problem."[10] One can imagine that Nixon would have had to do much of what Kennedy did. Moreover, if, as O'Reilly and others have noted, Kennedy's hand was forced by movement activists, what's to think that Nixon would not have had to respond as well; that it would have been the Republican Party, not the Democratic, that would have been compelled by circumstance to assume the mantle (or millstone) of civil rights; and that the tentative commitments of 1957 (Civil Rights Act and Little Rock) might have prefigured Republican legislation in 1964 and 1965 on accommodations and voting? Then Republicans would have been saddled with explaining themselves as the party of the Negro. In any event, Nixon would have had to act, and in those actions we would now be measuring Republican conviction on civil rights, not Democratic.

Of course, this is idle speculation, but it underscores two points. First, it is impossible to imagine anyone else in the White House moving faster than the Kennedys, and second, the White House is its own special set of circumstances. It is as much created by what it deals with as it in fact creates. In that spirit allow me to take you to Tuscaloosa in June of 1963.

Project C in Birmingham has just ended with a major victory for the King-led SCLC. The confrontation that began with his jailing and famous letter in early April ends when Bull Connor uses his dogs and fires his water cannon to cow demonstrators. Throughout, the Kennedy administration has urged caution and conciliation. Its position is not far beyond that of the clergy, whose call for conversation, not confrontation, occasioned the "Letter from Birmingham

Jail." In fact, black and white leadership together puzzle over King's tactics, and most are appalled when children sally forth from the Sixteenth Street Baptist Church on May 2—although I hasten to add that, once things got started, black leadership did not waver, at least publicly. By May 11 and in the wake of an Al Lingo-led police riot, victory is declared when the Kennedy administration facilitates a settlement.

Attention is now shifting to Tuscaloosa. The University of Alabama and the Kennedy administration have been talking for several months, including visits from the university's president, Frank Rose, one meeting taking place in the Oval Office itself. Great events have the appearance of inevitability only after the fact. (The Berlin Wall came down in one night. A week before, many were figuring on another ten years at least.) The questions about Wallace's stand in the schoolhouse door have always centered on whether it was staged, almost to the point of making it a relevant question. This has led to the conclusion that it was mere theater, its drama robbed by an inevitable closing act.

The truth is that the Kennedy administration knew on March 19 what Wallace planned to do, for on March 18 Wallace told the university's board of trustees exactly what he planned to do. The board's enterprising executive secretary took detailed notes as fast and furiously as he could under the circumstances. The notes never appeared in the official minutes. The next day President Rose's own executive assistant filed a nearly identical report with Burke Marshall at the Justice Department, the only variation being the thought that Wallace's show would take place in Huntsville (where a branch campus was located) rather than Tuscaloosa.[11]

However, to say that the Kennedy administration knew what Wallace was going to do is like saying that Roosevelt's administration knew the Japanese were going to attack Pearl Harbor. The final court order was not handed down until May 16, and by that time all eyes were on Tuscaloosa, the inevitable, historical ground zero for the confrontation. Katzenbach was soon on the scene and filing contingency plans. By June, Creighton Abrams, who later commanded American forces in Viet Nam, was also in Tuscaloosa coordinating military preparations.

Robert Kennedy had visited Wallace in Montgomery on April 25, with less than satisfactory results, although Wallace took the occasion to put the Confederate battle flag over the capital as an act of defiance, not heritage (where it remained until by political dumb luck Alabama took it down in 1994, thereby avoiding the running controversies in neighboring states). Furthermore, JFK had come into the state in mid-May for a visit to the Tennessee Valley Authority and NASA, the last federal strongholds in Alabama. Wallace accompanied Kennedy on a short helicopter flight during the visit, but nothing of substance occurred. While all of this was going on, Gordo Cooper soared overhead, proving we had the right stuff.

As the countdown began in June, matters became ever more urgent. Both the administration and Wallace were determined that Tuscaloosa would be no Ole Miss, where a shootout had killed two and left more than twenty marshals wounded. Still, when Robert Kennedy tried to reach Wallace personally on June 8 to get assurances that Wallace would not have to be forcibly removed, Wallace refused to take his call and left his aides to brush him off. As a result, federal authorities were left to ponder what they knew. With hundreds of state troopers and more than five hundred guardsmen on the scene and under Wallace's command, everything seemed under control—but then, Gov. Ross Barnett had already attempted something like that at Ole Miss, and it had all unraveled. (Wallace had studied the Mississippi situation carefully and was determined not to repeat Barnett's mistakes.)

Having to remove the governor forcibly was the most likely worst-case scenario for the Kennedys. Tricky constitutional issues would be involved, and Wallace was not wide of the mark in saying that 250,000 Alabamians would show up for his trial. So on toward June 11 the nation moved. Never had there been such a concentration of news media for an event outside Washington. The university had set the date so as not to have two black students, Vivian Malone and James Hood, register on June 10, when most summer registrants would be in line. The timing, however, could not have been better for the president since he was scheduled to be at American University on the morning of June 10. Moreover, here was an opportunity for the Kennedy administration to confront the South's most defiant champion of segregation, eyeball to eyeball, without King as an intermediary. (Although King commented on the events in Tuscaloosa, he was never involved directly, as was the case in most school desegregation matters. That was the NAACP's court.)

We now know how it turned out. Katzenbach drove down from Birmingham with Malone and Hood in a convoy on the morning of June 11. He confronted Wallace just before noon, and Wallace refused his entreaty. Katzenbach took the students to their dorms, while President Kennedy federalized the National Guard. That afternoon, around 3:30 P.M., the commanding officer of the guard faced Wallace and proclaimed it his "sad duty" to ask the governor to step aside. After a brief statement, the governor did. An hour before, Wallace had signaled through his adjutant general that the situation would end peaceably and in that manner. All had assumed it would, but no one knew for sure. As Nicholas Katzenbach later put it, "We didn't know what to expect, but it came out exactly as we expected."[12]

The show was not over. If one is to believe the Drew documentary *Crisis* (and there is no good reason to do so, at least for detail, but on this point there is corroboration), then President Kennedy gave a signal on June 10 to have the speech ready. What he and his brother did not know at that moment was where they would be in the crisis. Would it be in progress? Would it be over? The president had been embarrassed in the Ole Miss situation by proclaiming before a national audience his optimism for a peaceful resolution even as the shootout was in progress. But with Wallace's departure from Tuscaloosa, the way was clear. Wallace had his show that afternoon. Prime time belonged to the president.

The president's tough guys, Kenny O'Donnell and Larry O'Brien, were not so sure, but Bobby believed the timing was right. The president himself called the networks and asked for fifteen minutes at 8 o'clock. Robert Kennedy and Marshall arrived at the White House about an hour before. In the Cabinet room, the president looked remarkably relaxed as Sorensen moved in and out with suggestions and revisions. The speech represented the end, not the beginning, of the president's thought on the subject. "It drew," Sorensen remembers, "on at least three years of evolution in his thinking, on at least three months of revolution in the equal rights movement, on at least three weeks of meetings in the White House, on drafts of a new message to Congress, and on his remarks to the mayors on June 9 (in Honolulu) as well as on the February Civil Rights Message."[13]

Shortly after 7 o'clock, Sorensen took notes as the president talked with his brother and Marshall. After Sorensen returned to his typewriter, the president sat alone with Bobby, turning over ideas and occasionally dictating notes to his secretary, Evelyn Lincoln. This went on for about twenty minutes. Finally, Sorensen returned with the best draft he could come up with. With six minutes to spare, a tired, unsmiling president walked into the floodlit Oval Office and seated himself at his desk, still penciling notes as the countdown began.

On cue he looked up and said, "Good evening, my fellow citizens." He opened with a brief account of the events of the afternoon that resulted in "the admission of two clearly qualified young Alabama residents who happened to have been born Negro." He called for every American to "examine his conscience about this and other re-lated incidents." He started flat, almost listlessly, but then his feeling began to show. He spoke of the nation's commitment "to world-wide struggle to promote and protect the rights of all who wish to be free" and reminded his listeners that "when Americans are sent to Viet Nam or West Berlin, we do not ask for whites only." He repeated the things that "ought to be possible" for all citizens—education, public accommodations, the ballot—"in short every American ought to have the right to be treated as he would wish to be treated, as one would wish his children to be treated. But this is not the case."

By now any awkwardness was gone, fatigue forgotten, as the president moved toward his most memorable lines, the ones contributed by Louis Martin, a black journalist who served on the Democratic National Committee and as White House liaison to the African American community. "The Negro baby born in America today, regardless of the section of the Nation in which he is born, has about one-half as much chance of completing high school as a white baby born in the same place on the same day, one-third as much chance of completing college, one-third as much chance of becoming a professional man, twice as much chance of becoming unemployed, about one-seventh as much chance of earning $10,000 a year, a life expectancy which is seven years shorter, and the prospect of earning only half as much." It was neither a sectional nor a partisan issue. "We are confronted primarily," he emphasized, "with a moral issue. It is as old as the scriptures and as clear as the American Constitution." Continuing with his litany of broken promises to black Americans and the unac-ceptable costs of continued discrimination, he asked, "who among us would be content to have the color of his skin changed and stand in his place? Who among us would then be content with the counsels of patience and delay?" Having searched the nation's soul, Kennedy outlined his legislative proposals and extemporized a conclusion.

There have been excellent rhetorical analyses of the speech.[14] It is difficult to ignore the international concern JFK expressed. Segregation was an embarrassment in a world where America's prestige and influence were challenged everywhere. RFK had pressed the same point on Wallace during their meeting on April 25. (Despite the belief that nothing was accomplished in this meeting, my own close reading of the transcript leaves me convinced of Robert Kennedy's personal conviction on and considerable knowledge of the issues as he tried to score debating points with Wallace.) It is interesting to parallel Kennedy's internationalism with that of Wallace and Malcolm X, both of whom emphasized the international dimension of race to advance their causes of racial supremacy and antipathy. But it is not the international emphasis in the "Moral Issue" speech that interests so much as the national.

In the lines written by Louis Martin, Kennedy stressed race as a national, not simply a regional, problem, which may be viewed as another way of letting Kennedy's Southern pals off the hook. In fact, it played directly into the Southern tu quoque; in other words, on racial matters the North was just as bad, if not worse, and of course Wallace was the master of that argument. Rhetorically, King made considerable mileage by localizing the evil. Birmingham was the Big Apple of segregation, America's most segregated city. Attack it there and claim victory. King intuitively understood that if everyone was to blame, then no one was likely to take responsibility for the solution. Indeed, historically, any national success in expanding civil rights has always depended on isolating the cancer of racism to the South. So while Malcolm and Wallace proclaimed about international colored majorities and Kennedy about a national problem with race, King lanced the Southern boil on the body politic and moved a nation toward healing itself.

However, the focus here is on Kennedy's speech. His words did not ring down, as did his inaugural or his Berlin speech or even his commencement address the day before, but, away from the open air, seated in the Oval Office, his speech calmly and resolutely anointed the civil rights struggle with the balm of its own rhetoric. Clearly Martin Luther King's cup overflowed. The SCLC chief had kept up his attacks on the White House even through Tuesday and wondered whether the march on Washington should be directed against the president as well as Congress. He charged Kennedy with having substituted "an inadequate approach" for Eisenhower's "miserable one." Only two weeks before, Bobby himself had taken verbal abuse from James Baldwin and friends in what he had thought was to be a social gathering in the famous writer's apartment.[15]

The speech and its purpose changed everything, however. From Atlanta, King responded instantly. "I have just listened to your speech to the nation," he wrote with more enthusiasm than care. "It was one of the most eloquent[,] profound and unequiv[oc]al pleas for Justice and Freedom of all men ever made by any president. You spoke passionately to the moral issues involved in the integration struggle."[16] At last the Kennedy administration skipped into step with a movement that itself teetered on the brink of profound change—change hastened by a flash of gunfire that very night. Medgar Evers lay dead over in Jackson, Mississippi, an object lesson for those who said the events of June 11 had been only political theater—mere politics.

Of course, there is no such thing as "mere" politics. All politics is the visceral element of society. Wallace tapped into it. Kennedy tapped it. And to have Wallace as one's political enemy spoke volumes about Kennedy. It meant among other things that no politician would or could move to the left of Kennedy on race. Republicans were condemned, predilections notwithstanding, to move toward Wallace. Wallace warned as much, saying the Democratic party would lose its Southern base, a fact that revealed itself in Wallace-Democrats becoming Reagan-Democrats by 1980. Wallace himself made four stabs at the presidency with seemingly surprising results. From the Foster Auditorium doorway at Alabama to Sanders Theater at Harvard, Wallace whipped up a populist Republican base that still surfaces in Pat Buchanan's followers.

And Democrats correspondingly lost their presidential base, the anomalies of Johnson and Carter notwithstanding. The Clinton presidency may have signaled a return of the old majority party, but he now seems more a curiosity, a transitional figure who may eventually receive some credit for "righting" the Democratic Party despite the character issue. The simple fact remains that for the remainder of the century, conservative themes, often grounded in race, dominated the debate.

In deciding whether the Kennedy administration was sooner or later, I have already resolved it by answering the question of "who sooner," but at least two questions remain. First, what role in prosecuting the cause was either possible or appropriate for the president, and second, what should or could have been the expected outcome of the movement? The latter question invites the issue of what winning means. How should we judge it? By what criteria?

The consensus is that black initiative and federal intervention together constituted the formula for advancing the movement. Because black initiative has never been questioned, that leaves federal intervention. Any failures of the movement are tagged to the Kennedy predilection for politics over passion and the notoriously inept and aloof FBI and, by extension, to RFK's Justice Department. Kenneth O'Reilly's *Racial Matters* is indictment enough of J. Edgar Hoover's department and Bobby Kennedy's acquiescence. The department's racism and indifference are palpable. Taking names and pictures offered no protection against white terrorism and more often amounted to looking the other way. The decision to go after King's sexual appetite (or aggression, depending upon one's point of view) was the ultimate betrayal, JFK's own subjection as a congressman to FBI sexual surveillance notwithstanding.

This latter indifference is the pièce de résistance in the case against the Kennedys. O'Reilly, whose work on surveillance is as definitive as it gets, concludes, rightly I think, that wire taps were de rigueur. The Kennedys' primary interest in tapping King was the promise of "a gold mine of useful political information, and 'communism' provided the most convenient excuse to place the tap." Besides, the movement and all of its leaders were already under surveillance, including taps, and Robert Kennedy never saw its extension to King personally as other than ordinary. Of course, the very ordinariness of it shocks sensibilities, but O'Reilly puts it best: "'King,' as the president noted, 'is so hot these days.' Simple as that. One taps a hot phone, not a cold one."[17]

So much of what is used to argue that the Kennedys simply didn't get it on civil rights ignores their role. In King's frustration with the administration, he urged, among other things, that the president escort Vivian Malone and James Hood to the schoolhouse door. "That is not his job—and never will be," the *Baltimore Sun* cogently replied. "On the other hand," continued the *Sun,* "he has appealed to the people of Alabama and of the whole nation—including the mayors at Honolulu; and it has been a personal appeal. He has lent himself to the movement for Negro rights not only as a president responsible to the Constitution, but as a citizen responsible to his conscience. And his record on this account is remarkable in contrast with both presidents and presidential candidates for years past."

The *Sun* published its editorial the day before Wallace's stand on June 11. Events of June 11 itself underscored the larger role of the presidency. In the streets of Saigon, a Buddhist monk cremated himself, an act of self-immolation that would make the cover of *Life* and come to symbolize the end of Pax Americana in that part of the world. In Iran, fanatical followers of the Ayatullah Rouhdolah Khomaini (as spelled then) attacked well-dressed men and unveiled women. Incensed zealots yanked one woman from her car, forced her to undress, then beat her to death. Christine Keeler told the world about her tawdry affair with Profumo. Back home, Medgar Evers was murdered from ambush, while Americans measured their level of moral commitment by debating whether the movie *Cleopatra,* starring Elizabeth Taylor and Richard Burton, or any movie was worth a cool $40 million when so much misery abounded.

Another part of the continuing problem with JFK's legacy and civil rights is the assumption that there are winners and losers and that if one only does "the right thing," then good things will happen. The accomplishments of the movement do not live up to expectations; so, who is to blame? The more pessimistic in this tradition argue that in the American Civil War, the side that lost the war won the peace. In the American civil rights movement they argue that the side that triumphed over segregation lost the hard-earned fruits of victory. For them the cost of struggle may be high, even horrific, but the difference between winning and losing seldom seems as remarkable—witness Germany and Japan in this past century. In the end, sins like lust, greed, hypocrisy, avarice, and racism are obdurate and perdurable. And though they must be fought always, the only delusion is in thinking we can make them go away, and for that result, both King, our spiritual father, and Kennedy, our earthly prince, are to blame. They raised expectations. For one shining moment, we believed that the enemy was not us but the system.

If O'Reilly seems to be my favorite target in this chapter, it is not because of who his publisher is (The Free Press) but more because his error is my own prejudice, if not my conviction, that somehow we shoulda, oughta done better. O'Reilly believes that presidents have a unique opportunity to make the difference but do not, thereby yielding his downwardly inflected conclusion: "History shows what the presidency can accomplish when the stars are properly aligned, yet all too often the choices that could have been made to improve things were not made. To write of the forty-two chief executives and their deeds and dreams on the matter of race yields few profiles in courage and a great many profiles of men who agonized and analyzed only in search of more perfect ways to protect slavery or Jim Crow or a life expectancy that in the mid-1990s is lower in Harlem than Bangladesh."[18] For O'Reilly, no president has fundamentally altered the phenomenon of white over black in America, which is another way of employing the old George Wallace adage: "There ain't a dime's worth of difference between any of 'em," a pessimism bordering on cynicism.

Conclusion

I am mindful that I have been dealing with the inside debate among historians and journalists who write books that are read by their ilk and policy junkies. As tarnished as John F. Kennedy's reputation among the chattering classes may be, his standing among the general public remains high. A February 21, 2000, Gallup poll asked Americans who they thought was the greatest president. Kennedy led with 22 percent of respondents, followed in order by Lincoln at 18, FDR at 12, Reagan at 11, and Washington at 5. (This represents something of a bump in Kennedy's popularity [he had been at 12 a year earlier] and no doubt owes to the publicity surrounding his son's tragic death and corresponding media attention. Clinton tied with Washington for greatest but joined Nixon on a separate question establishing the worst presidents.) In another Gallup survey taken late in 2003 to determine the twentieth-century's "most admired" figures, Mother Teresa led with 49 percent, Martin Luther King Jr. followed at 34, with JFK coming in third at 32, followed by Albert Einstein and Helen Keller. (Respondents could name more than one, thus the numbers.)

Still, in the spate of books and magazines on great people of the twentieth century, JFK's appearance is invariably qualified. The editors of *Time* have the following to say: "It is difficult to know whether Kennedy was a visionary or simply a rhetorician" and further that "a judgment on Kennedy's presidential performance inevitably ends in a perplexity of conditional clauses." After throwing in all the reservations about his foreign adventuring, his weak performance with Khrushchev, and what they call his "deflected" response on civil rights, the editors conclude that the assassination "more profoundly affected the course of America than anything he did while he was in the White House." In short, it saved his reputation. "History," the editors say, "remembers not so much what he did as what he was: he has become an endless flame, kept alive in a special vault of the national imagination." Nevertheless, even here they note a "dual effect: his death enacted his legislative program and at the same time seemed to let loose monsters to unhinge the nation in some deep way that sent it reeling down a road toward riots and war and assassinations and Watergate."[19] Goodness!

The assumption of these opinion leaders is that Kennedy's status will slip with time, that the hagiography following his assassination will be revealed for what it is, and that his accomplishments will be seen as mere rhetoric. If this is to be the eventual judgment, I hope that it will not be based on civil rights, where he moved faster than any politician of his generation would or could. I hope the judgment of African Americans will prevail on this count, for it is in their homes that the image of John F. Kennedy finds its place alongside Martin Luther King Jr.

Many of my generation have a special affection for our innocence, the purity of our struggle, the tears we shed at the loss of our heroes. Some of us believe that "the radiance which was once so bright" should never be taken from our sight or that of our children. How do we tell of a time when the secret lives of our heroes were unknown, when action accounted for motive? Is there any rhetoric of history that can bring back the hour? Of course not. The genie of biographical deconstruction has long been out of the bottle. So, wrapping the drapes of an acquired skepticism about ourselves, we declare that shining moment to have been a conceit and, for that, somehow worse than the reality of our imperfection—or was it?

Notes

Opening epigraph is from Jacques Barzun, "History: The Muse and Her Doctors," *American Historical Review* 77(1) (Feb., 1972): 56.

1. Garry Wills, *The Kennedy Imprisonment: A Meditation on Power* (Boston: Little, Brown, 1982), p. 301.
2. Kenneth O'Reilly, *Nixon's Piano: Presidents and Racial Politics from Washington to Clinton* (New York: Free Press, 1995), p. 236.
3. John Dittmer, *Local People: The Struggle for Civil Rights in Mississippi* (Urbana: University of Illinois Press, 1994), and Charles M. Payne, *I've Got the Light of Freedom: The Organizing Tradition and the Mississippi Freedom Struggle* (Berkeley: University of California Press, 1995).
4. Thomas C. Reeves, *A Question of Character: A Life of John F. Kennedy* (New York: Free Press, 1991). Note that the books by both Reeves and O'Reilly are published by the Free Press, whose civil rights list and political leanings moved decidedly to the right during the nineties. Between the younger generation of civil rights activists and present-day conservatives, there is a convergence of interests in debunking the accomplishments of Kennedy-style liberalism and the King-led movement.
5. O'Reilly, *Nixon's Piano*, pp. 189, 237.
6. Jacques Barzun, "History: The Muse and Her Doctors," *American Historical Review* 77 (1972): 36–64; Carl Becker, *Everyman His Own Historian: Essays on History and Politics* (New York: Crofts, 1935), and Robin G. Collingwood, *The Idea of History,* ed. T. M. Knox (Oxford: Oxford University Press, 1956).
7. William B. Willcox, "The Strange Nature of Pure Joy: The Historian's Pleasure Principle," in *The Historian as Detective: Essays on Evidence,* ed. Robin W. Winks (New York: Harper and Row, 1969), p. 509.
8. O'Reilly, *Nixon's Piano*, p. 213.
9. *Tuscaloosa News,* Feb. 15, 1956. For King's assessment of Nixon, see David J. Garrow, *Bearing the Cross: Martin Luther King Jr. and the Southern Christian Leadership Conference* (New York: William Morrow, 1986), p. 119.
10. Arthur M. Schlesinger Jr., *Robert Kennedy and His Times* (Boston: Houghton Mifflin, 1978), p. 299.
11. From handwritten notes on the University of Alabama (UA) Board of Trustees meeting, Mar. 18, 1963, in Montgomery, in the UA Systems Office at Tuscaloosa. Burke Marshall, memorandum to the file, re: University of Alabama, Mar. 19, 1963, Marshall Papers, John F. Kennedy Presidential Library.
12. Phone interview with Nicholas deB. Katzenbach by author, Sept. 13, 1989, and Oct. 7, 1991, Morristown, N.J.
13. Theodore C. Sorensen, *Kennedy* (New York: Harper and Row, 1965), p. 495.
14. See, for example, Steven R. Goldzwig and George N. Dionisopoulos, *"In a Perilous Hour": The Public Address of John F. Kennedy* (Westport, Conn.: Greenwood, 1995), pp. 68–77.
15. Edwin O. Guthman and Jeffrey Shulman, eds., *Robert Kennedy in His*

Own Words: The Unpublished Recollections of the Kennedy Years (New York: Oxford University Press, 1990), p. 148. There are numerous accounts of the encounter because Baldwin and his associates were eager to get word out about their rebuke of Kennedy. There are also numerous reports of King's remark because it was released by newswire. See *Baltimore Sun,* June 10, 1963.

16. Quoted in Taylor Branch, *Parting the Waters: America in the King Years, 1954–1963* (New York: Simon and Schuster, 1988), p. 824.
17. O'Reilly, *Nixon's Piano,* p. 232.
18. Ibid., p. 12.
19. The editors of *Time*: *Great People of the Twentieth Century* (New York: Time, 1996), p. 39.

CHAPTER 6

Calling Washington Collect

Robert Parris Moses
and the Kennedy Administration

Richard J. Jensen and John C. Hammerback

John F. Kennedy is often remembered as an activist civil rights president who articulated a vision that helped initiate and sustain the civil rights movement of the 1960s. His public address is credited with inspiring and mobilizing Americans to work for the cause of freedom.[1] And indeed, in his memorable inaugural address, he clearly encouraged civil rights activists by declaring, "Let the word go forth from this time and place, to friend and foe alike, that the torch has been passed to a new generation of Americans . . . unwilling to witness or permit the slow undoing of those human rights to which this nation has always been committed today at home and around the world."[2] Although focusing mainly on foreign policy, the speech strongly suggested that Kennedy would take the lead in extending civil rights to all Americans.

Ten days later, in his State of the Union message, Kennedy reiterated his commitment to civil rights with the following words: "[T]he denial of constitutional rights to some of our fellow Americans on account of race—at the ballot box and elsewhere—disturbs the national conscience, and subjects us to the charge of world opinion that our democracy is not equal to the high promise of our heritage." But he seemed to qualify that strong statement when he continued, "But all these problems pale when placed beside those which confront us around the globe."[3]

Goldzwig and Dionisopoulos argue that Kennedy's presidential actions did not fulfill his rhetorical promises. Fearing that a powerful Southern Republican bloc in Congress might obstruct proposals on civil rights and other legislation, Kennedy believed that he could be more effective with executive rather than legislative actions. Because he doubted that he could work with Congress on civil rights issues, he concentrated on litigation by the Justice Department, on issuing executive orders and directives, and on using his persuasive powers to negotiate difficult situations.[4]

Kennedy's actions opened him to "justified, intense criticism," particularly from grass-roots activist organizers in the South, where African Americans were restricted from voting by a series of laws, customs, and practices that limited their ability to register and, once registered, to cast their vote.[5] Those restrictions were particularly blatant in Mississippi, where activists battled enormous obstacles that blocked citizens from basic rights.

This chapter examines the public address of one prominent critic of Kennedy's civil rights actions, the voting-rights activist Robert Parris Moses, who worked in Mississippi to help local citizens in their fight to win the right to the vote. Moses and other voting-rights activists might have been encouraged when Kennedy made the following statement at a press conference on January 25, 1961: "I am extremely interested in making sure that every American is given the right to cast his vote without prejudice to his rights as a citizen. And therefore I can state that this administration will pursue the problem of providing that protection with all vigor."[6] The activists became disillusioned when Kennedy's words were not followed by action. They worked without support from Washington, D.C., and sometimes even felt that Kennedy and the members of his administration were working against them, rather than helping them achieve their goals.

While Kennedy used his rhetoric to mobilize an entire nation, the voting-rights activists worked on a local level and used different tactics, ones that involved close interaction with people in local settings. Moses was a prime example of the community-organizing tradition, a tradition in which rhetor/leaders worked directly with those they sought to help. Moses used public address to organize local African Americans so they could overcome their fear and join movements that would change conditions in the South. Once a movement begins to gain power, he explained, "people begin to merge, to feel power and to act in power and to actually play a different role than that they may have been playing."[7]

Although Kennedy and Moses professed the same goal of achieving justice in racial matters, their circumstances put them into contact with different audiences and posed different constraints. As Goldzwig and Dionisopoulos point out, "civil rights activists were operating in a fundamentally different universe than the president."[8] An examination of the respective discourse of Kennedy and Moses tells a story of how they became linked in the civil rights struggle of the early 1960s and of how their divergent rhetorical means brought them into conflict. Thus this chapter provides an unconventional view of the Kennedy legacy, one from Moses who took the high moral path—who worked in a concrete, every-day setting to implement Kennedy's eloquently articulated generalizations. With white segregationists controlling the local legal system in Mississippi and with Kennedy heeding the need for support in Congress, his words seemed empty at times in Mississippi, where the real work of carrying out his inspired vision took place.

Moses in Mississippi

In 1961, Moses left a teaching job in New York City and moved to Mississippi to organize a voter-registration drive among African Americans. The previous summer, he had traveled through the South on a fact-finding mission for the Student Nonviolent Coordinating Committee (SNCC). During that trip, he made contacts with local citizens who were interested in working on voting rights. He decided to focus his efforts in Mississippi because it "was the central place to promote the subjugation of Black people and a reign of terror on them."[9] He elaborated: "Mississippi has been called 'The Closed Society.' It is closed, locked. We think the key is in the vote. Any change, any possibility for dissidence and opposition, depends first on a political breakthrough."[10] Success in Mississippi, he forecast, would lead to changes throughout the South: "If you can do it in Mississippi, you can do it anywhere. So that if we get a real breakthrough in voting in Mississippi, we will spur Negro voting throughout the South."[11]

Moses spent the next four years as a full-time organizer, encouraging Negroes to register and vote in Mississippi. His biographer describes Moses's contribution to the civil rights movement: "Moses, perhaps more than anyone, shifted the emphasis of the movement from sit-ins, freedom rides, and other forms of direct action to voter registration."[12]

Although he was an African American and had grown up in Harlem, Moses was startled by the depth of the oppression of blacks that he witnessed in Mississippi: "I never encountered the use of the law as an instrument of outright oppression: the highway patrolmen, the county clerk, the sheriff, the voting registrar, all the people who are the arms of the state and its bureaucracy were instruments of oppression the state itself organized."[13]

In *Mississippi: The Closed Society,* James W. Silver outlines the reasons whites denied the vote to blacks: "If Negro suffrage were ever permitted to become widespread, there is little doubt that the white supremacists would be in serious trouble. It is no surprise therefore that every effort is made by the minions of the closed society . . . whatever their level of office, to keep the Negro away from the poll."[14] Two common tactics used to prevent African Americans from voting were the poll tax, "forbidden by the Twenty-fourth Amendment to the Constitution . . . but still in force in local and state-wide contests," and the requirement that "a voter applicant appear before the county Registrar." During the appearance before the registrar, the "citizen applies to vote by filling out a rather lengthy application. In one section of the application the applicant is asked to interpret in writing a section of the Mississippi constitution." The registrar, "under no legal obligation to defend, explain, or state how he has reached his decision," had virtually unlimited power to decide whether the person was qualified to vote.[15] Moses illustrated the lengths registrars would go to in order to stop citizens from registering: "In many cases he simply refused to register people. Now in Hattiesburg . . . the Justice Department has had a suit against the registrar dating back from the Eisenhower administration. It has been in for 5 years. He has refused to register anybody in all that time, so far as I know. He is now up before a charge of contempt before the fifth circuit court . . . . In the meantime no Negroes are getting registered."[16]

For most blacks in Mississippi, the appearance "before the white county voter registrar was an excruciating and humiliating experience." Beyond the obstacles the registrars themselves had erected, the psychological barriers were tremendous: Blacks had been taught to be submissive to whites, and the sheer act of trying to register was a challenge. On a larger scale, "Most blacks who had even seen the inside of the county courthouse had been there not to register, but to stand trial at the whim of what was called justice."[17]

Fear and intimidation as well as registrars and written laws prevented blacks from registering. Moses outlined how whites had learned to use different levels of violence, depending on how much control they had over blacks in a particular region. In some places "their names get published in the local papers for two weeks"—there might then be some economic reprisal but no physical reprisal. In other areas, economic reprisal was used: "Negroes who attempt to register have been put off the plantations, fired from their jobs." The most extreme cases involved physical violence where "people get shot" or shots were fired at their cars and homes.[18] Thus Moses determined that he must eradicate fear in people's hearts before he could change laws and patterns of behavior. Removing this fear, he concluded, would in turn require nothing less than a change in the self-concept or identity of blacks. What Moses also discovered in his early organizing in Mississippi and what he taught those he recruited into his movement was that the essential means to changing self-identities would be rhetorical.

Moses began his arduous campaign by recruiting volunteers, many of whom were young local blacks, to distribute materials and to canvass communities. Because of the cumbersome registration process, he started citizenship classes to promote registration. He described his approach to the classes as being "really low-key." He told members of the classes, "What we're here to do is help people register to vote. We want you to feel comfortable down there [at the courthouse] and we have the forms to practice filling them out." He discovered that "gradually, people would feel comfortable that they were ready to go down there and try" to register.[19]

As he sought to diminish the fears of potential voters, Moses frequently faced violence himself. He was physically beaten several times when he accompanied potential voters to the courthouse, and he was often threatened. Yet he never allowed those fears to curtail his activities.[20]

Seeking palpable evidence of Kennedy's inspirational claims, Moses often appealed to the federal government for help. The response rarely satisfied him and his fellow activists. His biographer describes the relationship between Moses and the federal government, specifically the Kennedy administration, as an "encounter between a demand for uncompromising purity and the political mentality that is prepared to coexist with evil for the sake of achieving partial good. It is an irresolvable encounter; neither Moses nor conventional liberalism could come to terms in the tangle of morality and practicality." On many occasions, Moses "tried to force the hand of the federal government by using political techniques. The Democratic administration and party—the embodiment of the liberalism of the 1960s—in turn rationalized that their practicality achieved some partial moral good." The clash of moralities, wrote Eric Burner, "makes the voting registration campaign in Mississippi a microcosm of much that was to happen in the sixties."[21]

Two events dramatically demonstrate the Mississippi establishment's aversion to change and illustrate the powerlessness of the federal government to affect the actions of local authorities.

On August 15, 1961, Moses accompanied three African Americans to the courthouse in Liberty, Mississippi, the county seat of Amite County. When they arrived there, the local people were afraid to speak, so Moses told the registrar that a group of people was there to register to vote. The registrar asked, "Well, who are you? What do you have to do with them? Are you here to register?" Moses explained that he was conducting a school in nearby McComb and that the people who were with him had attended the school and now wanted to register. As he waited for the potential voters to fill out forms, he noticed that "a procession of people began moving in and out of the registration office. The sheriff, a couple of his deputies, people from the tax office, people who do the drivers' license, looking in, staring, moving back, muttering. A highway patrolman finally came in and sat in the office." The registration process lasted from 10 in the morning until 4:30 in the afternoon. Moses's potential registrants that day were ultimately unsuccessful though they achieved a minor victory by being allowed to fill out the forms—previously they had been denied even that right.[22]

What happened next is hard to imagine today but was commonplace in the South in the early 1960s. As Moses and the local citizens drove home, a highway patrolman followed them for several miles and then ordered them to stop. Moses stepped out of the car and asked the trooper what the problem was because "the people in the car were very, very frightened." Moses described how the officer asked "who I was, what my business was, and told me that I was interfering in what he was doing." The officer then ordered Moses back into his car. As Moses complied with the order, he wrote down the patrolman's name. The officer became angry and told Moses to follow him to McComb, where the highway patrolman and a county attorney scrutinized law books until they located a charge on which they could arrest Moses—"interfering with an officer in the process of arresting somebody"—even though Moses was the only one arrested. When the county attorney asked him whether he was ready to stand trial, Moses asked whether he could make a phone call. The county attorney said he could. Moses recalled what happened next: "I picked up the phone and called Washington, D.C., and the Justice Department, because I had been in communication with some members of the Justice Department and particularly John Doar and had received letters delineating those sections of the Civil Rights Act of 1957 and 1960 which guaranteed protection to those people who are trying to register and anyone who is aiding people who were trying to register. And he [Doar] also indicated that if we had any trouble we were to call Washington or the nearest office of the FBI. So I called them, collect; the people in the office were rather astonished that the call went through and they began to get fidgety. . . . I explained to Mr. Doar exactly what happened in their presence and told him that I thought the people were being intimidated simply because they had gone down to register."[23]

After the call, Moses was tried, found guilty, given a suspended ninety-day sentence, and fined five dollars in court costs. He refused to pay the fine, so he spent two days in jail until he was bailed out.[24] On the night he was released from jail, a protest rally took place in McComb. At the rally Moses declared, "The law down here is law made by white people, enforced by white people, for the benefit of white people."[25]

Moses's courageous actions strongly affected local citizens. Unita Blackwell, who later became an activist and politician, states: "Bob Moses was a little bitty fella. And he stood up to this sheriff and Bob said, 'I'm from SNCC.' I had never saw that happen before. From that day on, I said, 'Well, I can stand myself.'"[26] Others became active after observing Moses challenge members of the establishment.

Indeed, Moses had invited danger from the most extreme sources. Charles Jones, a civil rights worker in McComb, reported a rumor that members of the KKK had told people that they were going to take Moses out of jail and kill him and that "Bob [had] moved up to number one on the list of the Klan to be killed."[27]

A few days later Moses, though warned of possible violence, escorted a group of citizens to the courthouse in Liberty. Returning to his car from the courthouse, he was attacked by "Billy Jack Caston and some other boys." Moses was "severely beaten" and recalled that he "did not want to go immediately back to McComb" for fear that there would be violence if people saw his bloody shirt. The seemingly fearless Moses washed his shirt and drove to McComb.[28]

Moses pressed charges against Caston, an action that shocked and angered local whites—no Mississippi blacks had the audacity to undertake such acts. Moses described Caston's trial: "[T]he trial was scheduled that day and in two hours it began and in those two hours farmers came from all parts of the county bearing their guns, sitting in the courthouse. We were advised not to sit in the courthouse except while we testified, otherwise we were in the back room. After we testified, the sheriff came back and told us he didn't think it was safe for us to remain there while the jury gave its decision. Accordingly, he escorted us to the county line. We read in the papers the next day that Billy Jack Caston had been acquitted."[29]

Moses used the Liberty incident to illustrate the government's unwillingness or inability to protect people who were working to register voters. The Justice Department, he charged, would not move against those who attacked him because "it occurred in the streets and because there was some dispute as to interpretation, that is, the local white people were going to say that I was a northern Negro and agitator and did not move out of the way of the white person as we were walking toward the courthouse, therefore they had a legitimate reason for this beating."[30] As for the assistance from the FBI agent who investigated the incident, Moses related: "The FBI agent who came around to do the investigation, although we called them that night, showed up . . . two weeks later for the first time and proceeded to try and convince me that I really hadn't been beaten but had fell. And he tried to convince me that I fell three times and that the wounds in three different places were from those three different falls. And his concern and really the concern that we've had time and time again since then from southern FBI agents was at that time to . . . color the story . . . so that the picture that went back to Washington was one that would in any case favor them."[31] After this incident Moses and other civil rights workers "really realized . . . that for the time being we were out there fighting by ourselves" and that they could expect minimal help from the federal government.[32]

The collect call to Washington illustrated the useful and long-lasting relationship that had developed between Moses, "the moral, philosophical activist"; Doar, "the legalistic representative of tempered liberalism"; and the Kennedy administration. Doar describes the government's obstacles in Mississippi this way: "I can't keep a crime from being committed. . . . We try the very best we can to eliminate the lawlessness by seeking injunctions and restraining various forms of economic retaliation. But it is very difficult to win."[33]

Yet Doar worked hard to help Moses and his supporters. On September 24, 1961, he flew to Mississippi and met with Moses. Although he had received written reports from Moses, Doar was "unprepared for the graphic intimidation" he observed in the South. Doar met with local black activists E. W. Steptoe and Herbert Lee, who detailed the problems in Mississippi and confided how they feared for their lives. Moses describes the effect of Doar's visit: "Whatever the shortcomings of the Justice Department, they certainly made a visible impact on the black population of Mississippi. People like E. W. Steptoe, down in Amite County. His face lit up when John Doar and the Justice Department came out . . . so different from when a local resident FBI agent came." Doar agrees: "These people see you and get to know you. They begin to have confidence that you mean what you say."[34]

Unfortunately, the positive effects of Doar's visit were quickly undone. On September 26, after Doar had returned to Washington, D.C., Herbert Lee was shot to death in front of several witnesses by a state representative, Gene Hurst. In congressional testimony in 1963, Moses described the incident: "[Lee] happened to be a farmer who was very active in our voter registration campaign. Now, he was not killed at the courthouse and it happened that he did not go down to try to register. So there wasn't any attempt by the Justice Department to take this case into the Federal court even though, the very day before he was killed, I and the official from the Justice Department [John Doar] were in that area, were talking to some Negroes out there and one of the things they pointed out was that three people [Lee included] were in danger of losing their lives."[35] Lee's death created a climate of fear that virtually eliminated any hope of continuing the drive. In Moses's ever-deepening analysis, "The main problem is fear, literally fear on the part of the Negroes to go down to the courthouse. They own their own land. They are small farmers. They cannot be easily intimidated economically. It is not a question that they are afraid of mobs who come out to their homes, because they are willing to protect their homes. It is a question of simply being afraid to go down to the courthouse because they are exposed at the courthouse and they are subject to violence at the courthouse."[36] Moses saw the tangible effects of fear, for after Lee's death, very few people tried to register. He said, "I think the fact is simply that the Negroes down there are just afraid and what they want is more protection."[37]

The violence surrounding the Lee incident did not end quickly. Witnesses to the murder were coerced to testify that Hurst killed Lee in self-defense. One of the witnesses, Louis Allen, told Moses that he had lied and wanted to tell the truth at the grand-jury hearing on the case. But when Moses called the Justice Department to get protection for Allen, he related, "They told us that there was no way possible to provide protection for a witness at such a hearing and that probably, in any case, it didn't matter what he testified and that Hurst would be found innocent."[38]

Allen repeated the lie by telling the grand jury that the killing was in self-defense. Several months later, Allen told the FBI that he had lied and wanted to change his testimony. Moses detailed the frightening consequences of telling the truth to the legal establishment in Mississippi: "[Allen's] jaw was broken by the deputy sheriff[,] who knew that he had told the FBI that he had been forced to tell a lie to the grand jury and to the coroner's jury, because the deputy sheriff told him exactly what he had told the FBI. It's for reasons like these that we believe the local FBI is sometimes in collusion with the local sheriffs and chiefs of police and that Negro witnesses aren't safe in telling inside information to local agents of the FBI."[39]

In January of 1964, fearing for his life, Allen decided to flee the South. Before he could escape, he was killed.

Federal Support for Voting Rights

The Kennedy administration suffered significant frustration and embarrassment in attempting to deal with events surrounding the Freedom Rides in 1961 and 1962. As an alternative to controversial actions like the Freedom Rides, the administration encouraged civil rights groups to launch a massive voter-registration drive. It was clear, Brauer points out, that "the channeling of civil rights activism into voter registration work offered a much lower risk of the kind of violence that had accompanied the Freedom Rides—violence that had almost necessitated federal military intervention."[40]

Moses was pleased that the Kennedy administration decided to back voter registration and provide money to organizers of registration drives. He and his coworkers recalled, "up to then . . . [we] were living in catch as catch can day by day in many cases off the community depending on whether we were able to find friends and people who would house and feed us."[41] The money helped fund the activities of the Council of Federated Organizations (COFO), an umbrella organization of civil rights groups in Mississippi, and Moses served as field director of COFO's voting program.[42] He had concluded that success hinged upon defeating "the political establishment in Mississippi—that the white citizens councils, the governor, the state legislature, the judiciary were all part of one monolithic system and that in order to find any kind of gaps in it we were gonna have to hit right at its heart."[43]

The year 1963 was pivotal in the civil rights movement. The events in Birmingham, Alabama, the confrontation with Gov. George Wallace over the admission of black students to the University of Alabama, and the death of Medgar Evers raised public awareness of the problems in the South. The events convinced Kennedy of the South's unwillingness to change and hardened his "public resolve to attack the race relations issue on both legal and moral grounds."[44] Throughout the first half of the year Kennedy made a number of major statements on civil rights. As Goldzwig and Dionisopoulos point out, Kennedy "lent his eloquent, and finally, clear voice to the cry for racial justice in the land."[45]

On February 28, Kennedy sent a special message to Congress on civil rights that illustrated how he had changed his approach: "[T]he president transcended all the prior appeals grounded in legal principle and clearly turned the civil rights question into a matter of morality."[46]

In the message, Kennedy mentioned that 1963 was the one-hundredth anniversary of the issuing of the Emancipation Proclamation. In concrete language, however, he emphasized that "Through these long one hundred years, while slavery has vanished, progress for the Negro has been too often blocked and delayed." He detailed the results of actions of those who denied civil rights to African Americans: "The Negro baby born in America today . . . has about one-half as much chance of completing high school as a white baby born in the same place on the same day—one-third as much chance of completing college—one-third as much chance of becoming a professional man—twice as much chance of becoming employed."[47]

On June 11, 1963, Kennedy went on national television to address the nation about the events at the University of Alabama. Brauer describes the speech and its effects: "Kennedy delivered one of the most eloquent, moving and important addresses of his Presidency. It marked the beginning of what can truly be called the Second Reconstruction, a coherent effort by all three branches of the government to secure blacks their full rights."[48] Kennedy argued that the issue of civil rights was a moral one, "as old as the scriptures and . . . as clear as the American Constitution." His speech touched the essence of the issue: "The heart of the question is whether all Americans are to be afforded equal rights and equal opportunities, whether we are going to treat our fellow Americans as we want to be treated. If an American, because his skin is dark, cannot eat lunch in a restaurant open to the public, if he cannot send his children to the best public school available, if he cannot vote for the public officials who represent him, if, in short, he cannot enjoy the full and free life which all of us want, then who among us would be content to have the color of his skin changed and stand in his place?"[49] To many, Kennedy's questions about justice in the South were dramatically answered a few hours later when Medgar Evers, the head of the NAACP in Mississippi, was murdered outside his home.

Kennedy now coupled his eloquent inspiration with legislative proposals. He faced opposition from civil rights activists as well as from the Southern conservative coalition in Congress. An example was his proposal to Congress "that set a presumed literacy level at the sixth grade, attempted to expedite litigation regarding voting rights, and abolished double standards for voter qualification."[50] In testimony before a congressional subcommittee, Moses questioned the effectiveness of the proposal: "The administration has proposed that a sixth grade education be acceptable as proof of literacy. This runs into difficulty particularly in Mississippi where many Negroes have not been allowed to go to school. I think the country has to go further than that." He elaborated by pointing out that "many illiterate white people in Mississippi do register and vote. The Justice Department has presented time and again on the stand white people who have testified that they cannot read and write and that they have gone down and registered and the circuit clerk has passed them."[51]

Although Kennedy seemed to have made a dramatic change on the issue of civil rights in 1963, Moses had reached pessimistic conclusions about the administration's civil rights programs, proposals, and proclamations. To the Justice Department's claim that it must rely on local law-enforcement agencies to ensure voting rights in the South, he replied: "It is possible for the Justice Department to station men at the circuit courthouse on given days to protect people who try to register. They have refused to do this." He explained how the process might work: "We could arrange to take a certain number of people to register on a certain day. The presence of the Justice Department would serve two purposes: one, they could observe the actual registration process; and two, they could restrain local people from intimidating and beating Negroes. The Justice Department well knows that when there are Washington lawyers in town the local whites are restrained because they know the Justice Department is on hand to investigate right away." This process, he pointed out, had become effective "in gathering data, processing it and working out suits against registrars." Consequently, the Justice Department had "been successful in gaining token registration in Mississippi." [52]

When the Justice Department was helpful, according to Moses, it was not because of Kennedy's political policies. Moses distinguished "between the people who work for the Department and the policies of the Kennedy administration. The policies are subject to political situations and not the principled issue of the right to vote. Whereas the single right to vote would demand that suits be filed immediately, somewhere along the line politics intervene."[53]

In particular, political considerations determined the makeup of the federal judiciary in the South and led Moses to make this request:

"Somebody ought to do a serious study of Kennedy's appointment of judges in the South. One district judge can do away with two years' work and can seriously delay the work of the Justice Department. So in many cases you have one branch of the government working against the other. Not only that, but judges set the tone for the whole system of law enforcement in a district. If the county prosecuting attorneys know the judge won't enforce a civil rights decision, it makes a big difference in how they act. Often, they will immediately go to the district judge for an injunction to stop the movement."[54]

Such a study, Moses concluded, would find that Kennedy had caved in to the legislative domination of powerful senators and representatives from the South. Southern Democrats, in conjunction with conservative Republicans, had blocked appointments of judges and passage of legislation they did not like.[55]

In 1963, Moses dramatized his opposition to the administration's stance on civil rights in several controversial ways. During the March on Washington in August of 1963, he did not attend the ceremony and speeches at the Lincoln Memorial but instead joined with a small group that picketed the Justice Department. Moses carried a picket sign that said, "Where There Is No Justice, What Is the State but a Robber Band Enlarged?"[56]

A more ambitious plan, Freedom Vote, was designed to illustrate how African Americans would be willing to vote if given the chance. Freedom Vote was also organized to counter claims by the press that apathy was the main reason Negroes did not vote. Moses explained as follows: "If you thought . . . that the basic problem was the apathy of the people, you were also channeling your actions in a certain way. . . . If you rejected that completely—if you didn't for a second let it cross your mind that the problem was apathy on the part of black people but lay elsewhere then you would focus your attention elsewhere."[57]

Accordingly, Freedom Vote allowed citizens the opportunity to vote in a mock election that paralleled the traditional Democratic primary election in Mississippi. People were nominated for state, county, and municipal offices, as they were by the traditional parties, and African Americans were asked to vote as in a regular election.

SNCC volunteers had discovered a law, obviously aimed at helping whites, that stated that people could cast protest ballots in the primary election.[58] Moses was able to recruit approximately eighty white students from Yale and Stanford to come to Mississippi to help encourage people to vote, adding considerable media attention to Freedom Vote.

Although the Freedom Vote was successful in demonstrating that blacks would vote if afforded the opportunity, it also illuminated the depths of the challenge in gaining the vote in regular elections. "This election also makes it clear," Moses declared, "that the Negroes of Mississippi will not get the vote until the equivalent of an army is sent here." "We don't expect to correct the evils of Mississippi by this snail's pace voter registration," he added, "but we do expect to build enough pressure to make it politically impossible for a federal government to remain so indifferent. . . . We expect our efforts to dissuade those who believe anything less than federal troops will work."[59]

Any hopes that Moses had of receiving help from the Kennedy administration ended in November of 1963 with Kennedy's death. In reaction to the death, Moses continued to focus on the larger issues in the nation that needed to be changed: "Will the country be moved to face real issues, and that which is to be done, or will it shift the blame outside of America and do nothing about the condition which fostered this act of violence?"[60]

Moses continued to focus on voting rights. The success of Freedom Vote inspired him and others to propose an even larger program—Freedom Summer. In the summer of 1964, hundreds of college students, mainly white, were brought into Mississippi to register voters and teach in Freedom Schools. Moses credited these students with bringing "the rest of the country with them. They're from good schools and their parents are influential. The interest of the country is awakened, and when that happens, the government responds to that interest."[61]

Freedom Summer's ambitious program included establishing its own registrars in all eighty-two counties in Mississippi, providing its own forms, and in sum challenging the basis of voter registration in Mississippi. Moses announced the goal of registering 300,000–400,000 blacks in the state.[62]

Students chosen for the program were trained at Western College for Women in Oxford, Ohio. On the opening night of training, Moses spoke to them. "No administration in this country is going to commit political suicide over the rights of Negroes," he warned, so "don't come to Mississippi this summer to save the Mississippi Negro. Only if you understand, really understand, that his freedom and yours are one. . . . Maybe we're not going to get very many people registered this summer. Maybe, even, we're not going to get very many people into freedom schools. Maybe all we're going to do is live through this summer. In Mississippi, that will be so much!"[63]

John Doar represented the Justice Department at the sessions. Moses cautioned the students to expect little from the Justice Department, but he credited Doar with being supportive of SNCC in the past. Doar repeated the standard statement that the government could not protect voting-rights activists from violence. When questioned by students as to why the government could not offer protection, Doar responded that maintaining law and order was a state responsibility.[64]

During the training session Moses was notified that three volunteers were missing in Mississippi. The message had a profound effect on the students and particularly on Moses. At the end of the training he expressed his "weariness . . . from constant attention to the things you are doing, the struggle of good against evil. . . . The kids are dead. . . . There may be more deaths."[65] A year later the tired leader asked pointedly, "The Neshoba County murders (of Goodman, Cheney, and Schwerner) raise the whole question . . . of what does our society do where the law doesn't function at all to protect people? And clearly breaks down. And we call ourselves a society of law and order. Where are the resources in our society for what can happen?" His answer was not encouraging: "It seems to me that the country is simply not willing to face up to that. The justice department of this administration says it can't be a police force. That you can't have a federal police force in this country. Okay. But what if the local police force is not a police force? What if it's part Ku Klux Klan and part white citizens council? And in on the planning with the terrorists? Then what does society do in that situation?"[66]

Out of Freedom Summer grew the Mississippi Freedom Democratic Party (MFDP), a group that set out to challenge the seating of the Mississippi delegation to the 1964 Democratic convention in Atlantic City. Although the MFDP was unsuccessful in its bid to replace the Mississippi delegation, it ultimately helped forced the Democratic Party to change its rules and make the convention more representative. The events at the convention left Moses so bitter and frustrated that he lost his faith in political solutions and within a year left the movement he had worked so arduously and courageously to create. His absence was complete by 1966, when he fled to Canada to avoid the draft and then to Tanzania for ten years in exile.

Conclusion

The intertwined careers of civil rights organizer Robert Parris Moses and Pres. John F. Kennedy offer insights into the interrelated rhetorical and political battles for civil rights in the 1960s and perhaps into many other rhetorical campaigns that combine presidential leadership with local activism. Crucial differences in rhetorical and material purposes and means intersected with distinctions resulting from the institutional constraints inherent in the office of the presidency and the concrete challenges facing one who labors on a local level. In important respects, the conflict mirrored the differences that Moses saw between himself and Martin Luther King Jr. Moses accused King of employing an empty eloquence that gave followers false hopes, much as Kennedy's rhetoric raised false hopes among citizens in the South.[67]

While Kennedy sought to inspire and mobilize the entire nation with his powerful speaking, Moses attempted to organize locally in Mississippi. As Kennedy acceded to legislative constraints on executive power, Moses fought a local legal apparatus squarely behind perpetuating the injustices of racial discrimination. For Kennedy to be an effective president required him, at least in his own mind, to work in relative harmony with a federal legislature that was controlled by a seniority system favoring the South and its one-party system. For Moses to succeed in registering blacks to vote and in reaching other civil rights goals, he needed to recruit young would-be leaders who were justifiably fearful of the retribution sure to visit them if they stepped forward. Without federal support, Kennedy's grand goals had little local effect—and too many local blacks remained justifiably fearful of the consequences of actively working for voting and other rights.

Although Kennedy and Moses often disagreed and seemed to work against each other, each played a vital role in the civil rights movement. Neither achieved his goal completely, but together they helped create a climate where improvements in civil rights could occur. Kennedy clearly shifted the "inertia that had generally characterized the past . . . [through] a vigorous and far reaching effort to eliminate racial justice in American life."[68] Moses called national attention to injustices in the South, organized a bold group of college students and local blacks who would labor for voting rights in the most resistant corner of racial intolerance, and developed a movement that showed that a deeply entrenched and powerful racist system could be challenged forcefully and with some success.

From a sheerly rhetorical vantage point, one appropriate for addressing the careers of two leaders who relied so heavily and consciously on discourse to achieve their ends, the rhetoric of mobilizing and organizing differ in their respective goals of inspiring and identifying—even as they differ by operating either on the broad and abstract level appropriate for national audiences or on concrete and specific issues, people, and actions necessary for local success. Perhaps it is necessary for activists and politicians to take divergent rhetorical paths before change can occur, even if at times that divergence leads to conflict and estrangement. If so, Moses's painful disillusionment with Kennedy was an inevitable part of the 1960s' struggle for civil rights.

Notes

1. In an earlier study of the civil rights movement, we outlined two of its traditions: community mobilizing and community organizing. The former is characterized by large-scale public events—such as marches or rallies—that attempt to build short-term support. We submit that any public appearance there by a president would attract such attention. Community organizing is based on long-term development of leadership in ordinary men and women. Much of the organizing by civil rights activists in the South in the 1960s fits into this tradition. For a discussion of these two approaches, see Richard J. Jensen and John C. Hammerback, "Working in 'Quiet Places': The Community-Organizing Rhetoric of Robert Parris Moses," *Howard Journal of Communication* 11 (Jan.–Mar., 2000): 1–18. This article also illustrates how Moses developed a full set of principles for the rhetorical discourse that he placed at the center of his career and that he concluded was essential for anyone to be successful in achieving racial justice in the South.
2. Quoted in Steven R. Goldzwig and George N. Dionisopoulos, *"In a Perilous Hour": The Public Address of John F. Kennedy* (Westport, Conn.: Greenwood, 1995), pp. 58–59.

3. Ibid., p. 59.
4. Ibid.
5. Ibid.
6. John F. Kennedy, "The President's News Conference of January 25, 1961," *Public Papers of the Presidents* (Washington, D.C.: Federal Register Division, National Archives and Records Service, General Services Administration, 1961), p. 10.
7. Robert Parris Moses, personal interview by Charles M. Payne, Aug., 1993. Copy in possession of the authors.
8. Goldzwig and Dionisopoulos, *"In a Perilous Hour,"* p. 66.
9. Jimmie Briggs, "Freedom Summer Guru: Bob Moses Helped Lay the Foundation for Black Voting Rights in Mississippi Long before the Three Civil Rights Workers Were Killed," *Ethnic News Watch: Emerge* (June 30, 1994): 24. Available from LexisNexis, Sept., 1995. Copy in possession of the authors.
10. Robert Moses, quoted in Sally Belfrage, "Freedom Summer," in *Black Protest,* ed. Joanne Grant (Greenwich, Conn.: Fawcett, 1968), p. 394. In *Mississippi: The Closed Society* (New York: Harcourt, Brace, and World, 1963), James W. Silver describes the characteristics of that society: "Their beliefs are sustained by the unconditional and unwavering acceptance of an interlocking sequence of discredited assumptions: a) the biological and anthropological 'proof' of Negro inferiority; b) the presumed sanction of God as extrapolated from the Bible; c) the present state of affairs as one that is desired and endorsed by Negroes and whites alike; d) the repeated assurance that only through segregation can law and order prevail; e) a view of history which declares that there has been a century of satisfactory racial experience in Mississippi; f) a constitutional interpretation which denies the validity of the Supreme Court desegregation decisions" (149–50).
11. "Voter Registration Drive Moves Painfully Forward," *New America* (Feb. 6, 1963): 5.
12. Eric R. Burner, *And Gently He Shall Lead Them* (New York: New York University Press, 1994), p. 3.
13. Briggs, "Freedom Summer Guru," p. 24.
14. Silver, *Mississippi,* p. 105.
15. Ibid.
16. Robert Moses, quoted in hearings before subcommittee no. 5 of the Committee of the Judiciary, House of Representatives, Eighty-eighth Congress, 1st sess., May 8–Aug. 2, 1963, p. 1252.
17. Burner, *And Gently He Shall Lead Them,* p. 42.
18. "Voter Registration Drive," p. 5.
19. Briggs, "Freedom Summer Guru," p. 24.
20. For a discussion of Moses and his rhetoric during this period, see Richard J. Jensen and John C. Hammerback, "'Your Tools Are Really the People': The Rhetoric of Robert Parris Moses," *Communication*

Monographs 65 (1998): 126–40; Jensen and Hammerback, "Working in 'Quiet Places'"; and Richard J. Jensen and John C. Hammerback, "Robert Parris Moses," in *African American Orators: A Biocritical Sourcebook,* ed. Richard W. Leeman (Westport, Conn.: Greenwood, 1996), pp. 261–69.

21. Burner, *And Gently He Shall Lead Them,* pp. 4–5.
22. Staughton Lynd, "Mississippi: 1961–1962," *Liberation* (Jan., 1970): 8–10.
23. Ibid., p. 10.
24. Ibid.
25. Quoted in Burner, *And Gently He Shall Lead Them,* p. 52.
26. Ibid., pp. 86–87.
27. Ibid., p. 49.
28. Lynd, "Mississippi: 1961–1962," p. 10. The story also appears in Robert Penn Warren, *Who Speaks for the Negro?* (New York: Random, 1965), pp. 93–94.
29. Ibid., p. 10.
30. Moses, quoted in hearings before subcommittee no. 5, p. 1249.
31. Moses, speech at Stanford University, Palo Alto, Apr. 24, 1964, p. 3. A cassette recording of the speech is in the Stanford Archive of Recorded Sound at Stanford University. Transcript and audio recording of speech in possession of the authors.
32. Ibid.
33. Quoted in Burner, *And Gently He Shall Lead Them,* pp. 47–48.
34. Ibid., pp. 56–57.
35. Hearings before subcommittee no. 5, p. 1250.
36. Ibid.
37. Ibid.
38. Moses, quoted in Lynd, "Mississippi: 1961–1962," p. 13.
39. Ibid.
40. Carl M. Brauer, *John F. Kennedy and the Second Reconstruction* (New York: Columbia University Press, 1977), p. 112.
41. Moses at Stanford, p. 5.
42. Moses, interview by Anne Romaine, Sept. 3, 1964, at the University of Wisconsin, pp. 2–3. Transcript is in possession of the authors.
43. Moses at Stanford, p. 5.
44. Goldzwig and Dionisopoulos, *"In a Perilous Hour,"* p. 70.
45. Ibid., p. 68.
46. Ibid., p. 69.
47. John F. Kennedy, "Special Message to the Congress on Civil Rights," *Public Papers of the Presidents,* 1963, p. 222.
48. Brauer, *John F. Kennedy,* pp. 259–60.
49. Ibid., quoted on p. 260.
50. Burner, *And Gently He Shall Lead Them,* pp. 98–99.
51. Hearings before subcommittee no. 5, p. 1256.
52. Ibid., p. 5.

53. Ibid.
54. "Voter Registration Drive," p. 5.
55. Ibid., p. 12.
56. Quoted in Burner, *And Gently He Shall Lead Them,* p. 114.
57. Moses, quoted in Joseph A. Sinsheimer, "The Freedom Vote of 1963: New Strategies of Racial Protest in Mississippi," *Journal of Southern History* (1989): 223.
58. Moses, interview by Anne Romaine, p. 13.
59. Moses, quoted in Sinsheimer, "The Freedom Vote of 1963," pp. 241–42.
60. Moses, quoted in Burner, *And Gently He Shall Lead Them,* p. 120.
61. Ibid., p. 152.
62. Moses at Stanford, p. 18.
63. Quoted in Burner, *And Gently He Shall Lead Them,* p. 155–56.
64. Ibid., 157–58.
65. Ibid., p. 158.
66. "Moses of Mississippi Raises Some Universal Questions," *Pacific Scene* (Feb., 1965): 2.
67. Jensen and Hammerback, "Working in 'Quiet Places,' " p. 4.
68. Brauer, *John F. Kennedy,* p. 320.

CHAPTER 7

The Genesis of a
Rhetorical Commitment

*Lyndon B. Johnson, Civil Rights,
and the Vice Presidency*

Garth Pauley

I n a letter to his wife, Abigail, in 1794, John Adams wrote, "[M]y
country in its wisdom has contrived for me the most insignificant
office that ever the invention of man contrived or his imagination
conceived. . . . I can do neither good nor evil."[1] Adams was the first
American vice president to complain about his office but certainly
not the last. Thomas Marshall, who served under Woodrow Wilson,
compared the vice president to "a man in a cataleptic fit; he cannot
speak; he cannot move; . . . he is conscious of all that goes on, but has
no part in it."[2] Franklin Roosevelt's first vice president, John Nance
Garner, used a more colorful comparison: The vice presidency, he
claimed, "isn't worth a pitcher of warm piss." But with the expansion of the New Deal and the growth of presidential powers in the
modern era, the vice presidency has become a more significant and
more public office. Vice presidents now commonly attend cabinet
meetings, chair presidential committees, serve as goodwill ambassadors, campaign aggressively for their chief executives, and attempt to
advance the administration's legislative agenda. The vice presidency
has grown in duty, prestige, and influence.[3] Part of the increased influence resides in public discourse. For better or worse, the development
of a rhetorical presidency has also led to an increase in speech making

by vice presidents. Vice presidents regularly address the public, and occasionally they stir its imagination.

This chapter focuses on one rhetorical episode in which a vice president did awaken the public's imagination, Lyndon B. Johnson's address at Gettysburg, Pennsylvania, on May 30, 1963. The speech is among Johnson's best. Though it is now little known, in 1963, many listeners predicted that the speech would "go down in American oratorical history."[4] My purpose is twofold: to provide an analytical account of a significant, but overlooked, civil rights speech by Lyndon Johnson and to explore the character and constraints of vice-presidential discourse. The questions motivating my inquiry include the following: What kind of role did Johnson play during his vice presidency, especially in civil rights? How did rhetoric function as part of that role? Did Johnson's public speeches reflect a change in his attitudes toward civil rights? What impact did his early civil rights discourse have on the public, politicians, and Johnson himself? Finally, how did LBJ adapt to the burden weighing on him at Gettysburg, as a Southerner speaking on hallowed Northern ground, as a sometimes rhetorical bumbler speaking on Abraham Lincoln's rhetorical territory, as a perceived foe or newcomer to civil rights speaking at a moment marked by racial concerns? Johnson's civil rights messages as vice president, especially the speech at Gettysburg, merit our attention. Although most rhetoricians point to presidential speeches when remembering LBJ's civil rights legacy, Johnson himself regularly pointed to his vice-presidential discourse. Near the end of his life, the prized speech Johnson often sent to his friends and former colleagues was his Memorial Day address at Gettysburg.[5]

Vice President Johnson's speech at Gettysburg was likely motivated in part by political concerns, yet it reflects a matured, personal commitment on civil rights and functioned as part of a sincere strategy to cultivate support for President Kennedy's civil rights bill. The speech also symbolized a transformed Lyndon Johnson to some Americans, became a benchmark by which to measure him upon Kennedy's death, and provided LBJ with a vocabulary on civil rights for his own presidential discourse. The address also reveals the possibilities and limitations of rhetorical leadership by vice presidents. To develop this thesis, I (1) explore Johnson's civil rights commitments and activities during his tenure as vice president; (2) explain the context in which Johnson spoke on May 30 and discuss the preparation of the Gettysburg speech; (3) closely analyze the speech text itself; (4) evaluate the responses to LBJ's message and gauge its impact; and (5) discuss the implications of my analysis and offer a provisional commentary on the rhetoric of the American vice presidency.

Lyndon Johnson, Civil Rights, and the Vice Presidency

During the presidential campaign of 1960, few African Americans regarded Lyndon Johnson as a friendly political figure. LBJ's congressional voting record was a dismal indicator of what he might do in the White House: He had voted against antilynching legislation in 1938 and 1940; anti–poll-tax measures in 1942, 1943, and 1945; and fair-employment-practices bills in 1946. That Johnson brokered a compromise on civil rights legislation in 1957 and 1960 did not help his image: Many blacks resented his compromises on the measures and regarded him as an opportunist who had come to the civil rights debate solely for political gain. Thus, African American leaders worked against Johnson's presidential nomination and became dismayed when John F. Kennedy named LBJ as the party's vice-presidential candidate. For instance, Congress of Racial Equality (CORE) chair James Farmer called the move "a disaster." Biographer Paul Conkin claims that African Americans had good reason to be skeptical of Johnson as JFK's running mate. He argues that by 1960, LBJ was not opposed to all civil rights measures as in the past but still needed to develop the moral passion to support Kennedy's presidential campaign promises on civil rights.[6]

Scholars and Johnson's former associates have long debated whether LBJ had a deep-seated passion for civil rights at this point in his political career. What is clear, however, is that LBJ tried to convince civil rights leaders that he had a strong commitment to their cause during the campaign, claiming, "I'll do more for you in four years than anyone else has done for you in one hundred years."[7] Johnson also supported the Democrats' strong civil rights plank in his campaign speeches across the nation, including the South. Historian Paul Henggeler notes, "Particularly impressive and important was his appearance at a 'unity meeting' of Southern Democratic governors in Nashville. At a rally there he spoken to an enthusiastic crowd of eight thousand, pledging his support for the party's civil rights plank."[8] Johnson also gave whistle-stop speeches supporting the civil rights plank from his "LBJ Victory Special" train. *Newsweek* magazine reports that in every major speech in the South, Johnson promised to "protect the constitutional rights of every living American, regardless of race."[9] At times, Johnson was surprisingly direct. During a speech in Richmond, Virginia, he claimed, "I did not come down here to promise Virginia exemption from the obligation to carry out the decision of the Supreme Court [in *Brown v. Board of Education*] but instead brought an invitation to join the nation in extending civil rights. . . . A hundred years of debate among ourselves is enough, I think, don't you?"[10] On some stops in the South, LBJ even demanded that African Americans be seated on the speaking platform.

LBJ hoped that his successful election to the vice presidency would help him cast off the regionalism he saw as the chief obstacle to advancing his political career. Involvement with racial issues would allow him to tackle a problem Johnson claimed he could not address before, given his Texas constituency, and would demonstrate further that he was not captive to a Southern political ideology. Yet such action carried risks. When President Kennedy indicated that he would issue an executive order to create the President's Committee on Equal Employment Opportunity (PCEEO) and declare the vice president its chair, Johnson balked. LBJ feared that chairing the committee, which aimed to "permanently remove from Government employment and work performed for the Government every trace of discrimination," would put him in a perilous political position.[11] He also worried that his activities would antagonize Northern liberals, who would probably claim that he did too little, and Southern conservatives, who would attack him for doing too much.[12] Kennedy persisted, rejecting counsel from some advisers to keep Johnson away from the field of civil rights. Johnson eventually yielded and drafted the executive order himself with the help of longtime friend Abe Fortas. Despite his initial reluctance to head the committee, the vice president seemed determined to make it effective.[13] And those who knew him well claim that LBJ already had a budding commitment to overcoming racial discrimination by the time he assumed the helm of the PCEEO.

Some White House officials, however, believed that the motives underlying Johnson's actions were merely political. For instance, in a memorandum to Attorney General Robert Kennedy, Ralph Horton Jr. claimed that LBJ saw the committee "as an opportunity to build his image as a liberal."[14] Arthur Schlesinger Jr. believed that Johnson aimed to secure "political advantage in proving himself where he had previously been regarded with suspicion."[15] Suspicion about Johnson's motives may have contributed to dissatisfaction within the administration about the committee's progress. President Kennedy was unimpressed with LBJ's leadership and believed that the vice president was using the PCEEO as "public relations gimmick."[16] Secretaries of Labor Arthur Goldberg and Willard Wirtz complained that LBJ managed the committee poorly. Bobby Kennedy quarreled with LBJ several times over his leadership and progress on employment discrimination, most notably during a monthly committee meeting on May 29, 1963. RFK berated the vice president, criticized his emphasis on voluntary cooperation under the "Plans for Progress," and demanded more aggressive action. Johnson complained that he "was humiliated" by the attorney general.[17] A few administration officials believed that Bobby Kennedy was excessively harsh with the vice president: For instance, legislative liaison Lee White claimed that the attorney general was "tougher with Johnson than he needed to be and should have been," and Deputy Attorney General Nicholas Katzenbach believed him to underrate Johnson's ability.[18]

Indeed, many civil rights leaders were pleased with LBJ's leadership and the overall progress made by the PCEEO. Johnson may have been cautious, but his committee made solid headway on equal-employment opportunity through voluntary cooperation. Federal jobs held by African Americans increased 17 percent in 1962 and another 22 percent in 1963. The committee also directed federal contractors to correct almost seventeen hundred complaints made by black employees.[19] Certainly the PCEEO had made greater strides than its predecessor, the Government Contracts Committee, which was established by Dwight Eisenhower in 1953 and chaired by Richard Nixon. The vice president also appointed Hobart Taylor Jr., an African American attorney from Houston, to serve as the committee's executive director. In an oral history interview, Taylor claims that Johnson's leadership was often more aggressive than that recommended by the Kennedy brothers, who occasionally advised him to ignore discrimination in states represented by an important legislator.[20] LBJ's civil rights stand was more advanced than that of the White House at other times, too. Johnson pushed for a sweeping measure to end housing discrimination while the president's hand wavered before making his "stroke of a pen" on a moderate executive order in 1962.

To some observers, Lyndon Johnson seemed to change as a consequence of his direct involvement with racial problems. NAACP executive secretary Roy Wilkins suggests that LBJ "began to emerge [on civil rights] during the Kennedy Administration wholly unexpectedly and to the delight of the civil rights forces" and developed "a very personal concern."[21] Former White House and State Department official Walt Rostow claims that, during Johnson's tenure as vice president, "nothing was more important to him than the civil rights issue," a notable departure from his earlier career.[22] LBJ's new involvement with civil rights won him the support of former antagonists James Farmer and *Chicago Defender* editor Louis Martin, who lauded Johnson's leadership of the PCEEO. Biographers have also noted LBJ's development during this period. Robert Mann claims that while chairing the committee, Johnson seemed to become an all-out, civil rights liberal.[23] Paul Conkin argues that Johnson's tendency to throw himself into a job fully and to identify with his constituents and absorb their outlook made him develop a personal commitment to civil rights.[24] Interpersonally, LBJ began to tell stories about the discrimination his black employees confronted. He was stirred by their situation and seemed determined to end senseless bigotry. Johnson's contact with blatant forms of discrimination led him to speak about civil rights in a more personal and moral way, which some former skeptics interpreted as expressive of a heartfelt commitment.[25]

In short, the vice presidency provided Johnson with new opportunities to expand his understanding of the moral and political dimensions of civil rights. Political scientist Marie Natoli observes that LBJ's vice-presidential work in the civil rights field provided valuable experience and filled gaps in his background.[26] Former Kennedy adviser Arthur Schlesinger Jr. claims that the experience as head of the PCEEO "undoubtedly enlarged Johnson's knowledge of the problem and deepened his concern."[27]

Throughout his term as vice president, but especially in 1963, Johnson made known his enlarged knowledge and deepened concern for civil rights through public speeches. Public persuasion was part of LBJ's strategy to hasten equal-employment opportunities, but his rhetoric went far beyond simple appeals to induce private firms to end discriminatory business practices. One of Vice President Johnson's earliest public speeches on civil rights was his commencement address at Howard University on June 9, 1961, delivered four years before he redefined "equal opportunity" on the same occasion and same campus. Johnson considered the occasion to demand more than a perfunctory message: In a memorandum to the vice president on June 6, State Department official Carl Rowan wrote, "I know how important you feel this speech is, and I hope that it goes exceedingly well."[28] In the address, LBJ implied that the nation's ethos was on the side of civil rights progress yet acknowledged the discrimination that African Americans faced: "You are graduating into a nation that is striving for perfection and in which the national conscience is on the side of morality, justice, and right. All of you in the course of your lifetime are going to know, if you have not already known, injustice and unfairness."[29] However, he also attempted to instill a sense of hope that the nation would overcome its racial problems and thus live up to its purpose to serve as a beacon of liberty: "Let us unite in making our country an example of freedom and an enterprise of high honor, and may our light bring hope to all who dwell in dark places."

Johnson's speech received considerable attention. ABC television taped the address and broadcast it that evening, and many radio stations also transmitted the speech. African American journalists provided extensive coverage of Johnson's address and applauded what they perceived as his "slap at the recent incidents of mob violence in Montgomery and Birmingham" and his suggestion that the national conscience was on the side of civil rights.[30] Public reaction in the form of letters to the vice president was also positive: Citizens wrote to tell LBJ that his speech was "a very profound message" and "a moving and magnificent statement of the destiny of America."[31] Yet some citizens demanded more, namely that Johnson bring his moral authority to bear on the problem. For example, Newark resident Frank Szpiech commended the address at Howard University but claimed that Johnson's stand was "far short of what I feel a Vice President of the United States' position should be on this issue. . . . I feel that you should now embark on a trip thru the South and use your moral influence to bring about a peaceful settlement of this discrimination issue."[32] Martin Benis wrote to Johnson with a similar proposition: He urged the vice president to "go one step further, making up for the deficiency of the Eisenhower administration, by bringing to bear the moral weight of your office on the problem of civil rights."[33] Interestingly, the suggestions of these two citizens parallel one made by Martin Luther King Jr. The June 10 issue of the *Amsterdam News* reports that King wanted Johnson "to make a trip into the South to lend the moral weight of the federal government that is needed in this hour."[34] Though the vice presidency is often dismissed as an insignificant office, citizens and civil rights leaders apparently believed in this instance that the vice president's public discourse mattered and that his office possessed rhetorical power that could be used to bring about a solution to a significant social problem.

Johnson delivered another significant speech on civil rights at the National Urban League's annual "Equal Opportunity Day" dinner in New York on November 19, 1962. The bulk of the address recounts the PCEEO's recent accomplishments in overcoming employment discrimination, but Johnson also promised to make further advances against racial discrimination, praised the Urban League's efforts to help the nation "move beyond the habits, customs and prejudices of the past," and urged citizens to live up to the national ideal of "equality among men" by moving toward racial unity.[35] Many black listeners responded positively to the speech and considered it a bold statement on civil rights. For instance, Urban League director Whitney Young Jr. claimed that Johnson's address "made mine sound like the moderate!"[36] The speech also represents LBJ's first rhetorical association with Abraham Lincoln. The Urban League held its annual dinner on the anniversary of Lincoln's Gettysburg address and publicized the celebration as a reminder to all Americans "to rededicate themselves to the words of Lincoln's address that 'all men are created equal.'"[37]

Johnson's early speeches on civil rights were significant but did not represent the whole of his rhetorical leadership as vice president. In August of 1961, LBJ spoke in West Berlin to help calm the situation during the building of the Berlin Wall and to reaffirm the United States' commitment. In his address to a crowd of 300,000 assembled outside City Hall, Johnson eloquently reinforced America's pledge to stand behind the people of West Berlin and thus brought tears to the eyes of many listeners.[38] The ringing speech was a rhetorical triumph. In addition to this success, LBJ provided effective rhetorical leadership of the nation's space program, helping to build a national consensus for further space exploration through his speeches across the nation. These triumphs were rare, however, and Johnson generally disliked his role as goodwill ambassador and worried that, in his spokesman's role for the space program, he was being used as a political lightning rod in case of failure. Moreover, LBJ's successful speeches related to the Cold War could not compare to his discourse on racial discrimination. As scholar Joel Goldstein observes, "On no issue were his words so eloquent and his thoughts so important as civil rights."[39] In his speeches at Howard University and the National Urban League dinner and in addresses before the Catholic Interracial Council and the American Jewish Congress, Johnson demonstrated rhetorical leadership as vice president, months or years before the civil rights crisis erupted fully in 1963.

When racial tensions reached their boiling point in 1963, Johnson did not shy away from civil rights. Indeed, during the continued integration of Southern universities and the quickening of civil rights demonstrations, Johnson spoke more frequently, his words became stronger, and his concern seemed to deepen. In 1963, the vice president delivered major civil rights speeches in Cleveland, Detroit, Boston, Washington, Philadelphia, Miami, St. Louis, Los Angeles, and Sacramento. Journalists Rowland Evans and Robert Novak claim that these speeches represented Johnson's "new, firm—almost militant—civil rights stance."[40] The vice president's speech at Wayne State University on January 6 was especially strong. Echoing the discourse of many civil rights leaders, LBJ called for immediate progress on civil rights and denounced those who emphasized patience: "The counsel of delay is not the counsel of courage. A Government conceived and dedicated to the purpose that all men are born free and equal cannot pervert its mission by rephrasing the purpose to suggest that men shall be free today, but shall be equal a little later." He also urged the nation to fully emancipate African Americans from the bonds of discrimination: "It is our responsibility and our trust in this year of our Lord 1963, to strike against the chains of bias and prejudice from minds and practices as Lincoln, a century ago, struck down slavery."[41]

On January 26, the vice president delivered another forceful civil rights message, this time before the Cleveland Urban League. In the address, Johnson argued that the nation's vitality is measured in large part by its ability to guarantee civil rights to all American citizens: "Our strength as a nation and our success as a world leader in the cause of freedom depend upon the responsibility, the diligence and speed with which we attack the problems of unequal opportunity in the practices of our economy and our society." As in his speech at Wayne State and indeed most of his civil rights speeches in 1963, LBJ appealed to the memory of Lincoln in his call to end racial discrimination: "Abraham Lincoln faced the issue of men in the bondage of chains. A century later, we who live today face the issue of men in bondage to the color of their skins. The Emancipation Proclamation freed the slaves, but it did not free America of the burdens or costs of discrimination."[42]

Johnson's address at the Capital Press Club on May 18 also invoked Lincoln's memory. In the peroration, which Johnson himself penned into the otherwise typed manuscript, the vice president claimed that "Lincoln's Emancipation Proclamation freed the slave of his chains but did not free the Negro of his barriers" and that, until discrimination is ended, "emancipation will be a proclamation, but it will not be a fact." This message is perhaps his most forceful speech on civil rights prior to the address at Gettysburg. Just a week after a settlement had been brokered in Birmingham, a time when some Americans demanded that the movement toward civil rights advance more slowly, LBJ articulated a bold call for progress. In an especially moving passage, Johnson argued that the United States must move quickly toward ending racial discrimination for historical, practical, and moral reasons: "Progress must come faster because otherwise there are millions of individuals . . . who will never receive justice even though some day justice may come to their group. Progress must come faster because otherwise the tragic headlines which speak of the breakdown of law and order will increase rather than diminish. Progress must come faster because otherwise we will not achieve the unity which we must have if freedom—freedom for all of us—is to survive. And, finally, progress must come faster simply because it is right and has been too long delayed."[43]

Johnson's forthright messages on civil rights in 1963, especially the speeches in Detroit and Cleveland, received favorable attention from many African Americans. Letters to the vice president praised his rhetorical efforts to end discrimination, especially in employment. For instance, William Black, minister of First Baptist Church in San

Antonio, wrote, "Your recent speech to the Cleveland Urban League was a significant contribution to the efforts of Negroes to achieve new job opportunities. Your view . . . provides a suitable climate for communication."[44] More important than letters, perhaps, was the acclaim granted Johnson in the African American press. In February, for example, many black newspapers carried Associated Negro Press writer Adolph Slaughter's article about LBJ. The article praises Vice President Johnson's civil rights speeches as forceful, moving, and indicative of his strong, personal commitment to ending racial discrimination: "There is an unquestioned disciple in Washington, totally committed to the principle of equal opportunity for all. He is the grandson of two confederate soldiers and the Vice President of the United States. Exuding the vigor and eloquence of a Baptist minister and the dedication of a saint, Lyndon Baines Johnson undoubtedly has become an enigma to the South and a beacon of light to America's downtrodden."[45]

Conkin suggests that Slaughter's reaction to LBJ's speeches on civil rights was widespread: "From Hobart Taylor and others who listened to his sermons came one unanimous conclusion: Vice President Johnson was passionately committed to civil rights."[46] Johnson was proud of his deepened commitment and rhetorical accomplishments; he sent copies of his speeches at Wayne State University, the Cleveland Urban League, and Capital Press Club to colleagues and citizens. But if the vice president was satisfied with the acclaim his civil rights oratory garnered overall, he resented not getting credit for his speeches from the Kennedy administration.[47] Though Johnson spoke more frequently and usually more vigorously than the president, he did not receive recognition from White House officials for serving as an effective spokesperson on civil rights. LBJ's rhetorical experience and deepened commitment to racial issues were supplanted by Bobby Kennedy's apparently maturing concern.

Lyndon Johnson's growth on civil rights came at a time of general decline in morale and political involvement for the vice president. Biographer and former White House Fellow Doris Kearns Goodwin claims that Johnson's work on civil rights "clearly occupied his energies and evinced his talent" but was the only exception to his reduced political power and role.[48] LBJ's speeches on civil rights received favorable, but not overwhelming, public attention. Many of the vice president's messages were partially overshadowed in the media by concurrent events or presidential speeches. For instance, Johnson's speech before the Cleveland Urban League came as Harvey Gantt became the first African American student admitted to Clemson University and as James Meredith returned to the University of Mississippi. LBJ's remarks at the Capital Press Club came on the same day as President Kennedy's visit to Vanderbilt University, in which he encountered Alabama Gov. George Wallace. Moreover, some Southerners virtually ignored Johnson's discourse on civil rights, assuming it was merely required oratory for a member of the New Frontier. By the spring of 1963, Johnson was often overlooked. In February, *Time* magazine claimed that the vice president "is not really heard. . . . He is free to speak up, but nobody, really, has to heed him anymore." In April, *Newsweek* proclaimed that Johnson was languishing "in the obscurity of his historically obscure office."[49]

The Gettysburg Campaign

The invitation to speak at Gettysburg provided an opportunity for Johnson to step out of the shadows, speak, and be heeded. The vice president's initial reaction, however, was to reject the invitation; he worried that his words would be compared unfavorably to Abraham Lincoln's celebrated Gettysburg address. Nevertheless, Johnson's secretary, Juanita Roberts, emphasized the public-relations prospects in a memorandum urging her boss to accept the speaking invitation: "I am excited by the political possibilities it could offer. The distinguished grandson of distinguished Confederates giving on the 100th anniversary of the Gettysburg battle a speech that could be HIS Gettysburg address—a masterpiece to be remembered by. . . . All America will be observing this day—but attention will be focused—or could be—on Gettysburg this May 30. I believe the report on your speaking there could move other stories off the front page!"[50] Vice-presidential speechwriter Horace Busby also urged acceptance, claiming that the centennial address would secure public attention that would benefit Johnson politically and "serve a highly constructive purpose this year for the nation."[51] Roberts and Busby apparently moved LBJ, who constantly sought to improve his public image. Just two days after prodding from his aides, LBJ mailed an enthusiastic acceptance letter to Chester Shriver and William Weaver, who were chairing the Gettysburg Memorial Day Committee.[52]

In addition to invigorating his public image, Johnson may have hoped the speech at Gettysburg would help relieve conditions causing some of his political anxieties. Perhaps most significantly, LBJ worried about being dumped from the 1964 presidential ticket. The vice president's suspicions (largely unwarranted) were heightened by 1963: He believed that Bobby Kennedy was attempting to engineer his removal, thus ending his political career. Perhaps Johnson believed a prominent speech on race at a moment when the White House needed such support could gain favor and quiet the attorney general's recent criticism of his leadership in civil rights. Johnson may also have believed a strong, well-publicized speech could repair his relationship with liberals and thus help secure his place within the administration. In January, the vice president had drawn fire from liberal Democrats by refusing to end a Senate rules debate that might determine the outcome of a filibuster on civil rights legislation: Americans for Democratic Action (ADA) leader Joseph Rauh accused LBJ of being loyal to Southern racists. Johnson may have thought a civil rights message more vigorous than the president's oratory could gain favor with his party's liberal wing.

Though not immediately apparent, delivering an address on racial equality at Gettysburg would also allow Johnson to serve as spokesperson for President Kennedy's intended civil rights legislation. LBJ had no plans to discuss the specifics of the administration's proposals; indeed, White House officials had excluded the vice president from most of the legislative discussions following Kennedy's May 22 announcement that he would soon introduce civil rights measures.[53] But Johnson could help prepare the way by demonstrating the executive branch's commitment to civil rights and articulating a general call to redress the nation's racial wrongs. In discussions with administration officials, LBJ expressed concern that civil rights legislation would not pass Congress because the White House had not provided ample information or attempted to build political support. He recommended delaying the introduction of legislation until the president and vice president "could explain it on a proposed barnstorming tour" that would create a climate favorable to passage.[54] Johnson still loved a legislative challenge, despite Kennedy's general unwillingness to use him as a legislative liaison, and perhaps saw the Gettysburg speech as an occasion to effect legislative change. The address came at a time when congressional discussions of civil rights measures were heating up, and Walt Rostow suggests that LBJ used the speaking opportunity to try to preclude a filibuster of the administration's upcoming public-accommodations bill.[55]

Apart from motives related to public-image concerns, political advantage, or legislative preparation stood Johnson's matured commitment to helping overcome the nation's racial crisis. LBJ had developed resolve through exposure to insolent cases of racial discrimination in his PCEEO work, through interaction with African Americans, and through uttering strong speeches that had a self-persuasive function. The vice president's speeches on civil rights were moving toward a culmination at Gettysburg. His invocation of Lincoln's memory and words keyed to the Great Emancipator's language could come together most triumphantly at the Gettysburg National Cemetery. The invitation to speak on hallowed ground on Memorial Day during the nation's centennial celebration of the Emancipation Proclamation provided LBJ a prominent opportunity to make a difference on an issue of personal and national significance. Civil rights protests across the country, especially in Birmingham, Jackson, and Tallahassee, had created national distress and attracted unfavorable global attention. In his memoir, Johnson states that he "felt the need for change" most acutely during the spring of 1963 and that the brutality of Eugene "Bull" Connor's police force against nonviolent demonstrators in Birmingham had touched his feelings and the nation's: He claims, "I reflected those feelings at Gettysburg on May 30, 1963."[56] Johnson and his aides believed that to solve the nation's racial crisis, every American must be "convinced that the government means business" and that "the day of gradualism is over."[57] For his address at Gettysburg, the vice president ultimately developed a message that would demonstrate the federal government's commitment, show the necessity of immediate racial progress, urge the nation to move forward in a spirit of cooperation, and proclaim the international implications of civil rights.

Historians and political scientists have claimed that Vice President Johnson cleared all of his addresses both at home and abroad with the White House and spoke only when directed by the administration.[58] Nevertheless, LBJ neither cleared his Gettysburg speech with the Kennedy command nor solicited input from administration officials. On earlier civil rights messages, the White House had provided the vice president with rhetorical suggestions and even speech drafts. For instance, Harris Wofford was instructed to provide a draft for Johnson's 1961 address at Howard University.[59] The Gettysburg speech, however, was unmarked by recommendations from the administration, perhaps since Kennedy and his staff were busy drafting civil rights legislation.[60]

Horace Busby claims that, as the Gettysburg ceremony drew near, LBJ directed him to come to the vice-presidential home, the Elms, to discuss the speech. Busby brought a portable tape recorder to Johnson's home and recorded their conversation. During their talk, LBJ expressed concern that he "would be compared with Lincoln" and worried that he might seem like an opportunist if he emphasized issues of race in his message. Yet he also articulated his deep concern about civil rights and his belief that the nation must move promptly toward racial justice and equality. The day after this meeting, Busby prepared the address, which he claims was essentially "a transcription of the conversation we had"—and the only speech draft.[61] Busby claims that he created only the opening few paragraphs and the final two sentences; the remainder of the speech represents his conversation with Johnson fitted to the requirements of public address. Busby sent the speech text to the vice president the day after he drafted it but did not receive feedback. Without requesting revisions or showing the speech to White House officials, Johnson delivered a copy of the text to friend and *Washington Post* publisher Philip Graham, then traveled to Pennsylvania to speak.[62]

LBJ had received no rhetorical direction from his hosts: The chairs of the local Memorial Day committee had merely invited the vice president "to honor us with your presence and to deliver the address at the Ninety-sixth Annual Memorial Day service to be held in the Gettysburg National Cemetery."[63] However, Johnson did not travel to Gettysburg without some notion of his audience's expectations; he and Horace Busby had also not prepared the speech without understanding the constraints imposed by the oratorical genre. Indeed, perhaps Johnson's hosts sent no instructions in part because the situation so clearly called for an epideictic address, for which the stock-in-trade are the concepts of virtue, courage, justice, and honor.[64]

The occasion and location also seem to yield straightforward topics for rhetorical invention: Memorial Day originated as a holiday to honor Union and Confederate soldiers who died in the Civil War, and Gettysburg is perhaps the war's best-known battle site. Nonetheless, this prominent site of memorializing brought into an unstable locus several elements of public memory: Memorial Day, Lincoln, and the Emancipation Proclamation. Even the location itself was rhetorically unstable ground whose meaning had been interpreted by politicians since Lincoln, perhaps most notably by Presidents Woodrow Wilson and Franklin Roosevelt. In his analysis of FDR's two speeches at Gettysburg, Thomas Benson suggests that, although we may bring stable and universal memories of Lincoln and Gettysburg to speeches delivered there, "both 'Lincoln' and 'Gettysburg' were and are contested, contingent rhetorical constructions."[65] As a reaffirmation of the value of the sacrifices made by American soldiers killed in battle, the holiday itself was also a contingent construction enacted in public discourse. Moreover, this Memorial Day came as the nation reinterpreted what the Emancipation Proclamation meant during the year of its one-hundredth anniversary. In short, the rhetorical configuration in which Johnson's speech participated was an unsettled mixture of people, events, ideas, and symbols.

Johnson's Gettysburg Address

Vice President Johnson's speech at Gettysburg is short; even in his slow Texas drawl, it took LBJ just eight minutes to deliver the message. The address contains six sections. First, Johnson asks his audience to participate in honoring the dead through words and deeds. Second, he urges the nation to maintain a vigil of peace and justice to honor those who died abroad and at home. Third, he reflects on the importance of time and timing in the struggle for racial justice. Fourth, LBJ implores commitment to the law by both whites and blacks and asks for perseverance. Fifth, he goads all citizens to work together for equal justice and thus to preserve the nation. Finally, the peroration urges the fulfillment of the Emancipation Proclamation and of Lincoln's stated goal to secure freedom for all Americans.

Johnson begins by reinforcing the mystique of Gettysburg: He identifies the location as "hallowed ground," where "heroic deeds were performed and eloquent words were spoken."[66] Although Lincoln modestly claimed that "the world would little note, nor long remember" what he said at Gettysburg, LBJ asks his listeners to honor both the battle and the famous address that commemorates it: "[T]he world will never forget the deeds or the words of Gettysburg." Johnson petitions "a prayer for permanent peace in the world and the fulfillment of our hopes for universal freedom and justice," a prayer he intends to honor Lincoln's words and the soldiers' actions. LBJ frames his message, the prayers of the people, and the movement for peace, freedom, and justice as an homage to a sacred place and a revered figure.

However, unlike many who spoke at Gettysburg, Johnson does not here identify himself with Lincoln or reflect explicitly on what Lincoln would counsel for a contemporary crisis. Unlike Lincoln, Johnson reflects on the importance of the words being spoken at Gettysburg on the date of his speech. Lincoln effaces the words spoken on November 19, 1863, but LBJ urges his listeners to remember the words spoken on May 30, 1963, in order to honor them, too. He casts the prayer he invites the audience to pray as a motive for action: "We are called to honor our own words of reverent prayer with resolution in the deeds we must perform." Johnson's epideictic address asks his listeners—and the nation—to enact virtue themselves by demonstrating harmony between their words and deeds.

The opening passage of the vice president's speech may seem labored or cumbersome. Rather than simply asking his audience to perform deeds that "preserve peace and the hope of freedom" to honor Lincoln and the dead, Johnson asks those gathered to pray for peace, freedom, and justice to honor the dead and Lincoln and then to honor their own prayer with resolve in their deeds. But these strained words function to create a strong sense of public and private accountability. LBJ does not begin by requesting that his listeners privately enact the deeds that will effect peace, freedom, and justice; instead, he appeals to the audience to enact a public commitment through communal prayer. Then, by asking his hearers to honor their own words of prayer with action, Johnson invites them to develop a personal commitment to their public expression and therefore to become individually committed and publicly accountable. The listeners who participate in this address are accountable not only to the dead and the past, he asserts, but also to each other, the present, and themselves. Accountability is a central theme of the entire speech, not just its opening passage. Johnson holds the nation and its citizenry answerable to all citizens, the law, the fallen, Lincoln, and the Emancipation Proclamation. Writer Kathleen Norris describes prayer as "not words but the beyond words experience of coming into the presence of something greater than oneself."[67] Johnson's prayer does not call his listeners into the presence of a deity greater than themselves but rather into the presence of deified cultural symbols greater than themselves.

LBJ continues his religious language in the second section of the address, articulating his vision of "a vigil of peace around the world" and a vigil of justice at home. Johnson indicates that the nation's prayers for peace, freedom, and justice he summons in the speech's opening are connected to covenanted, moral action—a vigil. The United States' vigil of international peace, Johnson implies, is a watch against Communism: It must be kept by checking foreign aggression, tyranny, and oppression. This vigil, he claims, is a memorial that will be maintained "to make sure that our sons who died on foreign fields shall not have died in vain." LBJ suggests that the United States has kept and is keeping the vigil of peace, thus honoring part of its prayer, but "must remember that justice is a vigil, too." He is resolute in describing the nation's purpose and goals regarding justice, but his language is not declarative: The present- and future-tense verbs that mark his discussion of peace are replaced with imperatives. Whereas he affirms that the nation "shall maintain" the vigil of peace, Johnson argues that the nation "must maintain" the vigil of justice. Further action is required for America to fully honor its bilateral prayer for peace *and* freedom and justice. At this point in the speech, LBJ is vague regarding the nature of justice and the action required to achieve it. Yet he states clearly that the vigil of justice must be maintained to memorialize the dead at Gettysburg and to ensure "that those who died here on their native soil shall not have died in vain." Johnson identifies the honored dead with two purposes: peace (for those felled abroad) and justice (for those felled at home). He fixes those purposes in a prayer and he connects that prayer with a vigil.

In memorializing the dead, Johnson interprets. Although LBJ honors Lincoln, the meaning he gathers from the battle at Gettysburg and the Civil War is different from the meaning Lincoln constructed. Johnson appropriates Lincoln's language, asking the nation to ensure that the dead "shall not have died in vain." However, he suggests that racial justice—not preservation of the nation or democratic government—is the unfinished work that must be completed to honor the dead. Johnson does not state that the soldiers died for justice, yet he calls for a vigil of justice as the fitting and proper memorial. In contrast, President Lincoln states explicitly what the soldiers died for: They "gave their lives that that nation might live." Thus, the appropriate memorial within the universe of Lincoln's rhetoric is "a new birth of freedom" and the persistence of "government of the people, by the people, for the people."

By comparison, Johnson's memorializing is sometimes vague: He does not explicate his concept of justice, define why the soldiers died, or explain the relationship between the memorial he solicits and the soldiers' deaths. Still, the speech conveys a sense of requesting more than national unity, though LBJ advocates national unity, and more than a reinvigorated commitment to freedom, though he also advocates freedom. Johnson's construed meaning of Gettysburg builds upon his listeners' prior identifications with Lincoln and the dead but suggests an interpretation of what it means to honor the dead that diverges from Lincoln's construal.

In the third section of the address, Johnson reflects on the importance of timing in the struggle for civil rights and simultaneously reinforces his suggestion that justice is a fitting memorial to the soldiers who died at Gettysburg. This section is dense and at times confusing. LBJ discusses the nation's past, present, and future as they relate to African Americans. He talks about national honor and destiny, discusses freedom and justice, and considers one of the most charged words in the American vocabulary in 1963: patience. Johnson begins his argument about time and justice with the following statement: "One hundred years ago, the slave was freed. One hundred years later, the Negro remains in bondage to the color of his skin. The Negro today asks justice. We do not answer him—we do not answer those who lie beneath this soil—when we reply to the Negro by asking, 'Patience.'"

Johnson seems to use the word "justice" here to mean merit, the enactment of freedom that African Americans deserve by virtue of the Emancipation Proclamation. In this regard, LBJ foreshadows the message of Martin Luther King Jr.'s famous "I Have a Dream" speech, delivered three months later. King claims that the Emancipation Proclamation was "a joyous daybreak to end the long night of [African Americans'] captivity," yet observes that "one hundred years later, the Negro still is not free; one hundred years later, the life of the Negro is still sadly crippled by the manacles of segregation and the chains of discrimination."[68] The justice that King and Johnson demand is the immediate granting of what is merited by Lincoln's decree. In LBJ's text, to ask African Americans to be patient is to dishonor those who died at Gettysburg by further delaying the cause of freedom for which they fought. By his use of the word "justice," however, Johnson might also mean the philosophical concept of impartiality. Thus, to ask African Americans to be patient is to dishonor those who died at Gettysburg by failing to maintain the vigil of justice. LBJ still does not explicate fully what he means by justice, and his message is ambiguous as a result. Johnson was not alone in this practice, however; much of the civil rights rhetoric of the 1960s failed to distinguish between the concepts of justice, freedom, equality, opportunity, and fairness.

Despite the ambiguity in his use of the term "justice," the vice president makes clear that justice will not come simply from waiting. LBJ invests the situation with a sense of urgency and the audience with a sense of agency: "It is empty to plead that the solution to the dilemmas of the present rests on the hands of the clock. The solution is in our hands." In addition, Johnson suggests that to wait and to demand patience of African Americans will dishonor not only the fallen soldiers but also our chosen nation. He claims that, unless Americans resolve "the challenge which confronts us *today*," the nation will yield up its "destiny of greatness among the civilizations of history." LBJ endows his call for solutions to the present crisis with a civil religious appeal, simultaneously drawing upon and reinforcing the ideology of Americans as a chosen people with a special place in history.[69] Johnson claims that the nation "found its soul in honor on these fields at Gettysburg one hundred years ago" and "must not lose that soul in dishonor" at the present moment of exigency. Like Lincoln, who, in his 1862 annual message, urges the nation to recognize its place in history and save "the last best hope of earth," Johnson urges Americans to recognize the historical gravity of their current dilemma and to live up to their chosenness. If the nation keeps the vigil of peace around the world but delays the vigil of justice, Johnson implies, it will have gained the world but lost its own soul. LBJ's message regarding time and justice is forceful: It endows the cause of civil rights with a religious purpose, asks America to enact its destiny rather than lose its soul and dishonor the martyrs of the past, and acknowledges the frustrations of freedom and justice deferred.

Johnson's objection to requests for patience may have been the most appealing part of his speech to many African Americans and civil rights advocates. Blacks had long complained that whites too often asked them to be patient, but their sense of dissatisfaction seemed to burgeon during the spring of 1963. For instance, in his "Letter from Birmingham City Jail," written just over a month before LBJ's speech, Martin Luther King Jr. expresses his frustration with those who counseled patience. Johnson acknowledges that the word "wait," which King claims "echoes in the ear of every Negro with a piercing familiarity," is an unsatisfactory response to African Americans' demands.[70] Further, Johnson's claim that civil rights solutions do not rest "on the hands of the clock" echoes the ideas of King's letter. In refuting the Alabama clergy who criticized the Birmingham protests as untimely, King claims, "All that is said here grows out of a tragic misconception of time. It is the strangely irrational notion that there is something in the very flow of time that will inevitably cure all ills."[71] In sum, Johnson's claim that to "ask for patience from the Negro is to ask him to give more of what he has already given enough" seems to repeat the claims of many African Americans and give them political legitimacy.

Johnson's initial claims about timing are advanced. Historical accounts of 1963 often make it seem that images and stories of policemen and their dogs attacking protestors in Birmingham universally raised the nation's conscience and led to a sweeping demand for civil rights measures. The cultural and political reality, however, was more complicated: Many citizens had developed an eagerness for civil rights progress, but many still demanded patience and criticized the Birmingham protests as untimely and imprudent.[72] Even Attorney General Robert Kennedy deplored the demonstrators' timing at Birmingham. In his book *The Fire Next Time,* published during the spring of 1963, James Baldwin accurately observes that people still expected African Americans "to be more patient, more forbearing, more farseeing than whites."[73] A Gallup poll taken the week before LBJ's speech suggested that many citizens believed that efforts to advance civil rights were moving too quickly.[74]

Though Johnson indicts the counsels of patience, he qualifies his claims about racial progress in the fourth section of his address. After he argues that it is wrong to ask African Americans to be patient, he claims that the nation should ask of them "perseverance within the processes of a free and responsible society" as required by "the national interest." Johnson's request for perseverance is not an appeal to "law and order." He does not criticize civil rights protests directly, and he faults whites for denying the law and for "disuse of the law." Yet LBJ claims, "Law has not failed—and is not failing. We as a nation have failed ourselves by not trusting the law and by not using the law to gain sooner the ends of justice which law alone serves." Vice President Johnson's suggestion that laws were not used to their fullest capacity to bring about racial equality was true and significant, but his claims that the law was not failing and that "the Negro may underestimate what he is doing and can do for himself with the law" seem mistaken and perhaps misguided.

That the nation's laws were not used "to gain sooner the ends of justice" was a source of frustration to many African Americans, and thus Johnson's indictment of those who denied the law may have resonated. Had laws been applied and enforced during the early 1960s, some racial equality would clearly have been gained sooner. For example, the Supreme Court's 1960 ruling in *Boynton v. Virginia* prohibited segregation in waiting rooms and restaurants serving interstate bus passengers, yet African Americans were often denied public accommodation in Southern bus terminals. Southern officials also regularly violated the Civil Rights Acts of 1957 and 1960, depriving African Americans of voting rights and violating their civil rights.

Although LBJ's claim that whites had thwarted the law is undeniable, his suggestion that blacks had underestimated the possibilities of racial progress through the legal system is troublesome. The NAACP, for instance, worked relentlessly through the courts to secure civil rights, but the South regularly refused to obey court orders. The Council of Federated Organizations (COFO) and Student Nonviolent Coordinating Committee (SNCC) filed voter-registration lawsuits to try to secure the franchise, but these legal challenges proceeded slowly and usually had no effect. In addition, the Justice Department's prosecution of voting-rights cases, which it often coordinated with civil rights organizations, was laborious and slow: Lawsuits proceeded on a county-by-county basis and were met by Southern delay and obstruction.

Moreover, Johnson's claim that "the law has not failed" is false, and he should have known it. As senate majority leader, Johnson eliminated Title III from the Civil Rights Act of 1957; thus he knew that the Justice Department had extremely limited power to initiate lawsuits for equal protection under the law. He supported the addition of the jury-trial amendment to Title IV of the 1957 act, which made it nearly impossible to convict whites who violated the law in the South. Johnson also eliminated job-discrimination provisions from the Civil Rights Act of 1960. In short, though LBJ observed correctly that the law was unrealized because many whites denied it, he overlooked the failures of the law itself, given the shortcomings of existing civil rights legislation. Johnson also neglected the fact that African American activists understood well the failures of the law and the slow pace of change through the legal system; thus his claim that blacks might underestimate what they could do for themselves with the law seems inaccurate.

Perhaps Johnson intended to reinforce African Americans' commitment to the law so that nonviolent protests did not wholly supplant legal and political efforts. If LBJ could invigorate blacks' commitment to the law, they might see as significant the White House's upcoming plan to enact new civil rights legislation and thus work diligently for its passage. Johnson's request for "perseverance together" rather than confrontation "at the barricades" at the end of the speech's fourth section may have been an appeal for a united support for the administration's new civil rights measures. His request for perseverance while indicting patience may also have been a sincere appeal designed to head off racial chaos, such as the May 11 riots following the breakdown in the Birmingham negotiations, which threatened racial progress and disrupted social order. LBJ does not condemn direct protest but expresses concern that confrontation alone will "yield us no answers."

Indeed, in the fifth section of the address, Johnson claims that both disregard for the law and disuse of the law threaten the nation's integrity: "In this hour, it is not our respective races which are at stake—it is our nation." His argument has a faint echo of Abraham Lincoln's 1838 address to the Young Men's Lyceum of Springfield, Illinois, in which Lincoln argues that regard for law is the safeguard of the perpetuity of American political institutions. Like Lincoln, Johnson urges redress through legal channels, but unlike Lincoln, Johnson does not acknowledge the existence of defective laws or "grievances

. . . for the redress of which, no legal provisions have been made." To bolster his speech at Gettysburg, Johnson could have affirmed the integrity of the law in general, acknowledged the problems of existing laws, and argued for additional laws to correct the defects in previous measures and address remaining civil rights grievances. LBJ's suggestion that confrontation and chaos threatened the nation's integrity was true, and his emphasis on the rule of law without emphasizing order is admirable. However, his suggestion that African Americans had underestimated legal redress and, by implication, had contributed to social discord is troublesome. Like many politicians of the era, Johnson struggles in this speech to affirm efforts to achieve racial justice without appearing to encourage public demonstrations or social disorder. His appeal to perseverance, not patience, perhaps is equivocal, but it supports the Kennedy administration's claim that no federal law had been broken in Birmingham and other sites of recent protest yet allows LBJ to articulate an advanced claim about the timing of civil rights efforts and to argue for national integrity and unity.

Though Johnson does not point to a specific effort around which to unite and rally his listeners in the fifth section of his speech, he urges "those who care for their country" to come forward and "lead the way through this moment of challenge and decision." Since the White House had not yet solidified its legislative strategy or preferences, LBJ could not call for unity behind federal antidiscrimination laws, "the only prospect for avoiding such chaos," which LBJ suggests would threaten the United States' integrity.[75] Instead, he calls for interracial cooperation at an abstract level. In his synthesis of two antithetical claims about the timing of racial justice, LBJ provides an atemporal suggestion for racial progress: "The Negro says, 'Now.' Others say, 'Never.' The voice of responsible Americans—the voice of those who died here and the great man who spoke here—their voices say, 'Together.'" Johnson attempts to unite whites and blacks through the memory of Lincoln and the soldiers who died at Gettysburg. Neither the soldiers' actions nor Lincoln's words have a clear meaning for interracial unity, but LBJ interprets both as justifications for a cooperative effort for racial justice.

In the peroration of his address, Johnson suggests that, if the nation avoids cooperative efforts to achieve racial justice, it will tarnish Lincoln's memory and prevent the fulfillment of his efforts to advance civil rights. Using language that by now was becoming a regular feature of his civil rights oratory, he claims that "Until justice is blind to color, until all education is unaware of race, until opportunity is unconcerned with the color of men's skins, emancipation will be a proclamation, but emancipation will not be a fact. To the extent that the proclamation of emancipation is not fulfilled in fact, to that extent we shall have fallen short of assuring freedom to the free." Johnson invokes the memory of Lincoln as the Great Emancipator, though the Emancipation Proclamation freed virtually no slaves and was a war measure that, in the words of historian Richard Hofstadter, "had all the moral grandeur of a bill of lading."[76]

LBJ uses the memory of Lincoln and the proclamation to advance things never envisioned by Lincoln, especially equality in education. Still, many Americans, especially African Americans, had high regard for Lincoln and his decree. Merrill Peterson claims that to most blacks, Lincoln was more than a memory: "[H]e was a living vital force as the colored people strived to realize the promise of emancipation." Peterson also observes that many civil rights leaders still measured racial progress "by how far it had yet to go to realize the promise of the Emancipation Proclamation."[77] Like many African Americans, Johnson defines the word "emancipation" broadly, and he appeals to a potent symbol in the American culture to support his plea for universal freedom and justice. In addition, LBJ even invokes the language of Lincoln's 1862 annual message, which claims that, in "giving freedom to the slave, we assure freedom to the free." Given its grounding in Lincoln's memory and language and its utterance as the nation celebrated the one hundredth anniversary of the Emancipation Proclamation, the vice president's appeal to make emancipation a fact is forceful, dignified, timely, and resonant.

Lyndon Johnson celebrated Memorial Day in 1963 by articulating an often nebulous yet convincing plea for racial freedom, justice, and equality. He remembered the past while assessing the present and looking toward the future. LBJ invoked the memory of Lincoln and the soldiers who died at Gettysburg and held the nation accountable to his interpretation of their lives as a sanction for a vigil of justice. Johnson criticized the counsels of patience and urged the nation to act promptly or risk yielding up its sacred destiny. He urged Americans of all colors to enact a commitment to the law, perseverance, and each other. He called for national unity and leadership and urged the fruition of the seeds of freedom that many Americans believed Lincoln had sown in 1863 by issuing the Emancipation Proclamation. Johnson's speech is sometimes confusing, moderate by contemporary standards, and, like much of the public memorializing at Gettysburg, relatively mute on the complexities of slavery and the Civil War. In general, however, he effectively manages the antecedents, listeners, and constraints encompassing his well-publicized address.

A Speech to Remember

Writer Taylor Branch claims that Johnson was pleased with the immediate reaction to his address, realizing that "his directness had touched a chord in a tough audience."[78] His Memorial Day message also reached audiences far beyond Gettysburg. The vice president's decision to give an advance copy of his speech text to publisher Philip Graham paid dividends, as the *Washington Post* printed the address on the front page of its May 31 edition. The Associated Press (AP) and United Press International (UPI) wire services also picked up LBJ's speech and distributed it to subscribed news outlets. The PCEEO prepared a press release containing the speech text for distribution to journalists, and Congressman Roman Pucinski (D-IL) introduced Johnson's address into the *Congressional Record* during the House session of May 31. In addition, radio and television journalists covered LBJ's speech, and many stations broadcast portions of the address during their newscasts.[79]

Johnson's message also received subsequent attention in print: John Macy Jr., chair of the U.S. Civil Service Commission, printed the speech in an issue of the *Civil Service Journal,* and the Center for the Study of Democratic Institutions included the address in a pamphlet titled "The Negro as American." The vice president and his staff seemed to enjoy the attention afforded the speech at Gettysburg and promoted its distribution; Johnson's assistants mailed thousands of copies to individuals and organizations. Some recipients then disbursed the speech even further. For instance, a regional director of the National Council of Christians and Jews, who praised the address's "moral insight" and "compact eloquence," mimeographed copies "for wide distribution to the business and professional leadership" in his area.[80]

Johnson's speech received significant acclaim, and many of his boosters allayed the vice president's fears that he would be compared unfavorably with Lincoln. Indeed, many listeners heralded LBJ as comparably forthright and eloquent. Illinois Representative Pucinski claimed that Johnson's speech would "stand for time immemorial as the 20th century sequel to Abraham Lincoln's immortal Gettysburg Address." Sen. Hubert Humphrey (D-MN) called the speech "eloquent and challenging" and stated that it qualified "as the second Gettysburg Address."[81] The *Dallas Express,* a small African American newspaper, also heralded LBJ's speech as the "Second Gettysburg Address," and Hobart Taylor told Johnson that many African Americans claimed that his Gettysburg speech was "the most powerful statement on the problem since Mr. Lincoln's second inaugural address."[82] The *Washington Post* and *Christian Science Monitor* also compared LBJ favorably with Lincoln: The *Post* reported that Johnson's address was "eloquently reminiscent of Abraham Lincoln's own plea for a new birth of freedom."[83] Scores of letters from citizens to the vice president also praised the speech as Lincolnian in stature. For instance, a man from San Francisco claimed that, after reading Johnson's speech, he "came away with the stirring conviction that here is Lincoln's hallowed Gettysburg Day address revitalized in a moral momentous period of our country's history." A state senator from New York wrote, "With all due deference to President Lincoln, many people join me in the opinion that your address was as good [as], if not better than[,] his."[84]

The *New York Times* and many other newspapers, especially the black press, focused instead on Johnson's plea for interracial cooperation and unity. None interrogated his request for perseverance under the law. The *Times* reported that LBJ "declared today that whites and Negroes must work together 'to lead the way through this moment and challenge of decision.'"[85] The quote from the fifth section of Johnson's speech is perhaps the most commonly excerpted section of the address. Most stories in African American newspapers included this quote and featured the vice president's plea for unity. For example, the *Norfolk Journal and Guide* emphasized Johnson's suggestion that "there is no way out of the present crisis than for both sides to work together." The *Amsterdam News* called Johnson "the most forceful speaker on the subject" of civil rights on Memorial Day and reported that he "urged both white and Negro to work together." The *Kansas City Call* also emphasized LBJ's suggestion that "both white and Negro must now work together." In addition, the *Call* reported that the speech was indicative of the White House's commitment to civil rights, as did the *Pittsburgh Courier,* which claimed that Johnson, "who has been called a 'traitor to the cause' in his Southern home-land[,] made clear the administration's deep concern over mounting racial tensions" in his speech at Gettysburg.[86]

Other newspapers also interpreted LBJ's address in relation to the White House's concern for civil rights. The *Boston Globe* reported that Johnson's speech reflected "the Kennedy administration's mounting concern over the growing Civil Rights crisis." In contrast, the *Christian Science Monitor* implicitly gave LBJ credit for prodding the administration: It reported that his "strong speech . . . calling for equal justice, education and opportunity for all Americans" set in motion "a more direct and powerful administration intervention and involvement in the mounting American race problem."[87] Syndicated newspaper columnist Drew Pearson claimed explicitly that Johnson's speech demonstrated a stand on civil rights more advanced than that of the White House; the headline he prepared for his June 9, 1963, column reads, "Vice President Steps Out Ahead of President on Race Issue." Pearson wrote the following: "The speech has now become a sort of emancipation proclamation for the Kennedy Administration, and some of the White House functionaries are irked that it was the Vice President, not the President, who made it. . . . Johnson, the Southerner, has been much more forthright on civil rights than Kennedy, the Northerner."[88] Given the positive attention afforded Johnson's speech at Gettysburg and the suggestion that Kennedy's words lagged behind his vice president's, LBJ's address might have been among the many factors that shaped the president's decision to make a strong national address on civil rights on the evening of June 11. In fact, portions of Kennedy's address echo claims from Johnson's Gettysburg message.[89]

Not everyone, though, believed that Johnson's Gettysburg speech was more advanced than the White House's stand on civil rights or even that LBJ shared Kennedy's concern. Some citizens, especially Southerners, accused Johnson of speaking as a mere puppet for the Kennedy administration, against his personal sentiments. For instance, in a letter to Johnson on June 19, a Mississippi man accused LBJ of "being a Charlie McCarthy to the Kennedy Kids" and urged Johnson to stop espousing sentiments he did not believe. Similarly, a woman from Arkansas wrote, "Your speeches sound so hollow. Oh yes, you speak good English and say forceful things, but they have such a ridiculously hollow sound, one can tell that you are only repeating the president's words and opinions. Have you sold your birthright just for the sake of being called Vice President?"[90]

However, many Southerners and other Americans, too, took the Gettysburg speech as indicative of Johnson's transformation on civil rights. For example, a Georgian wrote to the vice president, claiming "I had withheld judgment on you until I saw your picture in the Atlanta newspaper yesterday as a speaker at Gettysburg. Now you go down in my book as a despicable character from Texas who condescended to speak at Gettysburg." A man from Illinois wrote, "Reluctantly I must say that you will live to regret your Memorial Day address at Gettysburg. You joined the cynical, vote buying politicians, and the soft hearted but short sighted clergy in glorifying the Negro." A resident of Mobile, Alabama, also claimed that Johnson's speech represented a deplorable conversion on civil rights: "You are a disgrace to the South. There is nothing more contemptible than a traitor like you." Some Southerners seemed incredulous at LBJ's apparent transformation. One Atlanta man wrote, "I would like to know if you were drunk when you made your speech in Pennsylvania."[91] Regardless of whether they believed Johnson's words were heartfelt, citizens who had looked to LBJ to help halt civil rights progress just weeks earlier now criticized him contemptuously.

Some Americans, however, lauded Johnson's address at Gettysburg for articulating what they saw as his personal concern for civil rights, a stance seen as especially admirable because of his regional heritage. In a letter praising the speech, a Virginian wrote, "I admire and applaud your stand on civil rights. You have been courageous, unequivocal, and above all . . . motivated by conviction rather than political expediency." In his letter to the vice president on July 27, Richard Lykes wrote, "As a Texan myself, I am proud that you have chosen to lend your heart and influence to the proposition that 'all men are created equal,' a proposition that you so eloquently defended in Gettysburg." Several Southerners, especially Texans, expressed pride that a native son had spoken out so forcefully for civil rights. One Dallas woman wrote to Johnson, "It was with a great deal of pride that we Texans saw your picture and read your words spoken at the Memorial Day services at Gettysburg last week. . . . It is good that a

Texan should be in the forefront of the leadership of this country." Even those without strong Confederate identifications praised LBJ as a Southerner of conviction. An editorial in the *Washington Post* on June 1, 1963, observes the following: "One of the great men of the South has spoken out at last in the South's best tradition. . . . By his eloquence, by his political courage, Vice President Johnson has pointed out for the South the pathway to its future and he has summoned a bemused and lethargic Nation to face the challenge of its own high principles." A letter from a man in Pennsylvania praised Johnson as a courageous Southerner who spoke up for civil rights despite the attitudes of his regional neighbors: "Such a stand, being directly opposed to that taken by your Southern friends . . . required a barrel-ful of moxie. You've proven that you have it."[92]

Apart from the positive and negative commentary it elicited regarding racial equality, Johnson's speech helped improve his public image and abolish a humiliating question often asked inside the Beltway earlier that spring, "Whatever happened to LBJ?" An early June editorial in a Tulsa, Oklahoma, newspaper observes that "the Vice President has been making speeches on civil rights" and claims that "the civil rights crisis has made LBJ one of the most important men on the Kennedy team." An editorial in the *Boston Globe* on June 1 praises his active involvement in the government and claims, "Lyndon B. Johnson is no ordinary Vice President. He showed this at Gettysburg on Memorial Day when he urged racial cooperation." Similarly, the *Washington Post* editorializes as follows: "Vice President Lyndon Johnson has been speaking out on civil rights issues with increasing frequency, force, and clarity. He is doing a great deal to shape public opinion and alter public outlook. . . . The Presidency always has been known as a great platform from which to appeal to the mind and heart of America. The Vice Presidency is being made into a great platform by Vice President Lyndon Johnson." *Look* magazine also circulated a newsletter in June praising Johnson's "eloquent Memorial Day speech in Gettysburg" and observing that "The civil rights crisis has landed Lyndon Johnson his first significant role in the Kennedy inner council since he became Vice President."[93] Reports like these enhanced LBJ's image as an administration spokesperson.

Johnson's messages on civil rights, especially the Gettysburg speech, not only improved his image as vice president but also enhanced his credibility on civil rights when he assumed the presidency on November 22, 1963. As some Americans wondered whether LBJ would continue the fallen president's commitment to civil rights, journalists presented his words as vice president as evidence of his commitment. LBJ had delivered strong messages on civil rights after May 30, most notably at Tufts University on June 9, in St. Louis on June 26, and at the Governors' Conference in Miami on July 23, but the speech that journalists quoted to demonstrate his ability and allegiance was the address at Gettysburg. An article in the *Washington Post* two days after the assassination of John F. Kennedy claimed, "President Johnson's philosophical commitment to equality and human rights is unquestioned among civil rights leaders. As Vice President, he spoke out with increasing frequency, force, and vigor on the subject." In a column in the same issue of the *Post,* writer Roscoe Drummond has excerpted Johnson's Gettysburg speech and claims the following: "I have read every major speech Mr. Johnson has delivered in the past year. It is evident that no man in public life has done more to demonstrate to the American Negroes that the conscience of the American people and the conscience of the government are on their side in the fight for equality of opportunity and status—and to stir and strengthen that conscience." Journalists Rowland Evans and Robert Novak state that LBJ's speeches demonstrate that he was not a closet segregationist but rather a sharp advocate of civil rights who sometimes articulated "a harder position than other Administration officials." Both *Time* and *Newsweek* also quoted from Johnson's address at Gettysburg in their reporting on the new president's commitment to civil rights.[94]

Finally, Johnson's address is significant because it provides a vocabulary for his speeches on civil rights as president. In his frequent presidential speeches on race, he often invoked the ideas and phrasing of his vice-presidential speaking, especially the message at Gettysburg. For instance, Johnson regularly included variations on themes from the address, especially the peroration, during his rhetorical campaign for the Civil Rights Act of 1964. In a speech at the 1964 convention of the United Auto Workers LBJ included a variation of the peroration, claiming, "We are going to free the logjam of pent-up skills and unused opportunities, because until education is blind to color, until employment is unaware of race, emancipation may be a proclamation but it will not be a fact." Johnson used the peroration in his speech at a May, 1964, meeting of the PCEEO and also invoked his claim about Lincoln and black emancipation: "Lincoln signed the Emancipation Proclamation 100 years ago, and he freed the slaves of their chains. But he did not free the Negro of the bigotry that exists in this country." In a speech at Madison Square Garden on May 28, LBJ echoed the plea he had made nearly one year earlier to fulfill the promise of the Emancipation Proclamation: "Tonight, your Democratic administration in Washington pledges itself to carry forward the fight for civil rights until emancipation is not just a proclamation but a fact."

Johnson's deployment of themes from his Gettysburg speech did not end in 1964, however; he included variations in several later speeches. For instance, his forceful "We Shall Overcome" speech of March 15, 1965, repeated the theme that the United States had yet to fully enact the Emancipation Proclamation: "A century has passed, more than a hundred years, since equality was promised. And yet the Negro is not equal. A century has passed since the day of the promise. And the promise is unkept." Upon signing the last piece of civil rights legislation of his presidency—the Civil Rights Act of 1968—Johnson also returned to this theme of unfulfilled emancipation.[95]

Conclusion

At the Lyndon B. Johnson Museum in Austin, Texas, LBJ's speech at Gettysburg now receives at least a fraction of the historical acclaim that listeners of 1963 predicted. On the first floor of the museum, a display next to a photograph of Martin Luther King Jr. at the March on Washington contains two cards from Johnson's speaking notes and a placard commemorating the rhetorical occasion: "On the one-hundredth anniversary of the battle of Gettysburg, Vice President Johnson calls for racial equality to become a reality at last. Reaffirming his own commitment to civil rights, Johnson goes further than any other national political leader in seeking a redress of racial wrongs." As a message that stands as his finest vice-presidential address, Johnson's Gettysburg speech merits remembrance. It expresses LBJ's personal and political growth on civil rights and demonstrates that he could serve the White House and the country as a national spokesperson. As a reminder that he was neither a stranger nor a newcomer to civil rights as president, Johnson's Gettysburg speech warrants our recollection. LBJ was not a sudden convert, nor was he pursuing purely political motives, as his vice-presidential speeches on race demonstrate. As an effective, though not exceptionally eloquent, response to a difficult set of rhetorical circumstances, Johnson's Gettysburg speech deserves to live on. The address managed the needs of the particular, local memorial occasion while speaking more broadly about national needs.

Though his Gettysburg message was soon overshadowed by President Kennedy's June 11, 1963, nationally televised speech on civil rights, Johnson served a significant role in the national discourse on race. Indeed, his speeches on ceremonial occasions, especially at Gettysburg, helped hasten the political action that Kennedy proposed and Congress eventually enacted. Chaim Perelman claims that epideictic rhetoric strengthens listeners' disposition toward action by intensifying adherence to the values it honors. At Gettysburg, Johnson attempted to increase adherence to the values of freedom, justice, perseverance, and honor and thus participated in an unfolding discourse that attempted to effect racial change by reminding the nation of its historic duty, principles, and commitments. Perelman suggests that all practical philosophy arises from rhetorical efforts to "strengthen a consensus around certain values which one wants to see prevail and which should orient action in the future."[96] The nation's practical philosophy of "civil rights" in the early 1960s benefited from LBJ's vice-presidential rhetoric. His speeches are vague at times, do not propose concrete action, and thus may seem "merely rhetorical." For progress to come, however, there must be rhetorical efforts to link moral action with traditional and accepted values at those moments when citizens gather to reflect explicitly on public values. Johnson's speeches on civil rights were significant efforts.

LBJ's discourse is important also because it might help us understand the limitations and possibilities of vice-presidential rhetoric. Political scientists and historians have given more attention to the American vice presidency in recent years, yet the rhetorical role of that office has received little sustained attention. Further inquiry into specific rhetorical episodes may tell us how vice presidents can mobilize support for policy initiatives, how they can fulfill a meaningful ceremonial role, how they might help the country by taking rhetorical chances the president is unwilling to take initially, and how they can maintain their personal integrity while speaking under the constraints their office imposes. Further inquiry into vice-presidential rhetoric can also help us theorize about how best to structure and execute the rhetorical duties of the nation's second-highest elected official.

Lyndon Johnson's speaking out on civil rights suggests that the ceremonial duties often assigned or afforded vice presidents need not be enacted with grandiloquence. Rather, the vice president can use ceremonial occasions to reinforce national values that might later serve as the grounds for policy initiatives. At Gettysburg, LBJ used a ceremonial occasion to evoke the nation's historical and moral aspirations to create a shared sense of purpose that might have helped change what was possible politically. Vice presidents can enact what political scientist Erwin Hargrove calls "cultural leadership" on ceremonial occasions by using fitting cultural narratives and crafting new ones to help the nation face pressing problems.[97] Political advocacy need not be confined to ceremonial occasions, of course. Johnson's civil rights addresses on more political occasions, such as his speeches on equal employment before chapters of the National Urban League, received significant attention, too, perhaps suggesting that when promoting policy initiatives, vice presidents should deliver forthright messages to audiences perceived to be tough on those elected officials.

LBJ's addresses on civil rights also suggest that vice presidents can take rhetorical risks in order to shape the president's public stances. President Kennedy was hesitant to deliver a strong speech on civil rights in the spring of 1963; he knew that citizens were outraged by violence against African Americans yet were concerned that efforts to advance civil rights were moving too fast. In his strong messages on civil rights, Vice President Johnson argued for quick progress, demanded full emancipation, and asked the nation to live up to its heritage. The vice president can demonstrate that a message the president is reluctant to advance can be successful and beneficial to the nation. Rather than looking to polling data when making rhetorical decisions, the president can look to the vice president's discourse in order to develop creative and challenging responses to rhetorical situations.

Presidents, however, should not use their vice presidents as rhetorical lightning rods. Neither should vice presidents be reckless in their speech, obscure presidents' positions, or undermine the credibility of the executive branch. The vice president should have opportunities to put forth the White House's tepid commitment, though, and possibly move the president toward a greater national good.

Johnson's forthrightness on civil rights suggests that the vice president can maintain integrity despite the restrictions the president imposes. Kennedy usually requested that LBJ clear his speeches with the White House, often asked his aides to provide speech drafts, and directed Johnson to sustain Southern political support. Kennedy was free to ascend to the bully pulpit, but Johnson toiled under the constraints of being an assistant pastor, at best. Yet at Gettysburg and elsewhere, Johnson made a move that alienated much of the South but benefited the nation as a whole. LBJ also gathered civil rights information from his own advisers, prepared the message within his own office, and did not merely repeat the White House's statements. Vice presidents should not be rash or insubordinate, but they should have independent sources of information available and their own speechwriters to help prepare messages.

To perform their rhetorical and political duties effectively, vice presidents should be given media attention, institutional authority, and official resources appropriate to the office. Journalists should not cover the vice presidency in a way that simply expands their bias toward official sources, and political reporters should stop the common practice of giving vice presidents attention only when they leak information about the president or reveal a split with the White House's position. Journalists should provide equitable coverage to avoid enticing vice presidents to make provocative speeches for attention and to enable them to provide meaningful rhetorical leadership. Presidents should provide institutional power when they want the vice president to serve as a spokesperson. For example, LBJ's power as head of the PCEEO enabled his role as spokesperson on civil rights. The institutional power of the PCEEO also provided Johnson with information and resources to help him speak effectively about racial problems. Johnson's role on the committee provided him with political experience and rhetorical training on civil rights that served him well as president.

That the vice presidency can provide its officeholders with rhetorical training should be neither overlooked nor downplayed. Many vice presidents eventually become president, whether through succession or by using their office as a stepping-stone to the White House, and thus should have significant rhetorical experience at the national level. Lyndon Johnson's strong rhetorical leadership on civil rights as president evolved from his experiences as vice president. Rhetorical experiences such as his speeches before the National Urban League and at Howard University brought LBJ into contact with African American audiences. Rhetorical experiences such as his address at Gettysburg forced him to struggle with the complex issues surrounding civil rights and required him to make his perspective understandable to the American people. In Johnson's case, his speaking experience also gave the public an opportunity to understand the politics and personality of a man who assumed the presidency, thus helping to legitimate his ascendancy. In other cases, significant speaking experience can give the public an opportunity to evaluate the rhetorical leadership of vice presidents who may seek the presidency.

Lyndon Johnson's vice-presidential speeches on civil rights reveal his developing commitments to achieving racial justice, contributed to a national discourse on race, and provided him with a vocabulary that served him throughout his tenure in politics. Vice president Johnson's speaking reached its high point at Gettysburg, where he challenged citizens to honor heroes from the past, honor the nation's covenant, honor the law, and honor each other. His address there can inform us about LBJ himself, his historical moment, the American vice presidency, and perhaps our present state of race relations. Nearly forty years after Johnson's speech, a vigil of racial justice has not freed African Americans from the bondage of the color of their skin or fulfilled our hopes for universal freedom and equality. The nation needs rhetorical leadership to reinvigorate our aspirations, create a shared sense of purpose, and move us toward the fulfillment of our historical and philosophical commitments. At the same moment, the nation needs rhetorical leadership that will help us develop new obligations and new understandings of civil rights that will help us meet the challenges of our current social and political realities. Otherwise, we may come to understand and revere the cultural narratives of our past yet remain destined to repeat our historical shortcomings.

Notes

1. John Adams, *The Works of John Adams,* ed. C. F. Adams (Boston: Little, Brown, 1850), 1:289.
2. Sidney M. Milkis and Michael Nelson, *The American Presidency: Origins and Development, 1776–1993,* 2d ed. (Washington, D.C.: CQ Press, 1994), p. 417.
3. For a discussion of the development of the vice presidency during the twentieth century, see Joel K. Goldstein, *The Modern American Vice Presidency: The Transformation of a Political Institution* (Princeton: Princeton University Press, 1982); Marie D. Natoli, *American Prince, American Pauper: The Contemporary Vice Presidency in Perspective* (Westport, Conn.: Greenwood, 1985); and Michael Turner, *The Vice President as Policy Maker: Rockefeller in the Ford White House* (Westport, Conn.: Greenwood, 1982).
4. Sen. Wayne Morse (D-OR) offered this endorsement of Johnson's speech on the Senate floor on June 4, 1963. Sen. Alan Bible (D-NV) agreed, claiming that the address would "go down in history as one of the truly great speeches of our time." *Congressional Record,* 88th Cong., 1st sess., 1963, p. 109, pt. 8:10006.
5. Taylor Branch, *Pillar of Fire: America in the King Years, 1963–1965* (New York: Simon and Schuster, 1998), p. 92.
6. Paul K. Conkin, *Big Daddy from the Pedernales: Lyndon Baines Johnson* (Boston: Twayne, 1986), p. 143.
7. "Lyndon Johnson and the Civil Rights Revolution: A Panel Discussion," in *Lyndon Baines Johnson and the Uses of Power,* ed. Bernard J. Firestone and Robert C. Vogt (New York: Greenwood, 1988), p. 174.
8. Paul R. Henggeler, *In His Steps: Lyndon Johnson and the Kennedy Mystique* (Chicago: Ivan R. Dee, 1991), p. 51.
9. "Johnson's Trek South," *Newsweek,* Oct. 24, 1960, p. 42.
10. Leonard Baker, *The Johnson Eclipse: A President's Vice Presidency* (New York: Macmillan, 1966), p. 218.
11. John F. Kennedy, *Public Papers of the Presidents of the United States: John F. Kennedy, 1961* (Washington, D.C.: Government Printing Office, 1962), p. 256.
12. Robert Dallek, "Frustration and Pain: Lyndon B. Johnson as Vice President," in *At the President's Side: The Vice Presidency in the Twentieth Century,* ed. Timothy Walch (Columbia: University of Missouri Press, 1997), p. 96.
13. According to Deputy Attorney General Nicholas Katzenbach, the executive order that Johnson and Fortas drafted "went rather further" than the White House would accept. Nicholas Katzenbach, oral history interview, Nov. 14, 1964, Oral History Collection, John F. Kennedy Library.
14. Goldstein, *Modern American Vice Presidency,* p. 153.

15. Arthur M. Schlesinger Jr., *Robert Kennedy and His Times* (New York: Ballantine, 1978), p. 336.
16. Robert F. Kennedy, oral history interview, Dec. 4, 1964, Oral History Collection, John F. Kennedy Library.
17. Edison Dictaphone recording of a telephone conversation between Lyndon Johnson and Theodore Sorensen, June 3, 1963, Lyndon B. Johnson Library.
18. Lee White, oral history interview, Jan. 28, 1970, Oral History Collection, Lyndon B. Johnson Library; Nicholas Katzenbach, oral history interview, Oct. 8, 1969, Robert F. Kennedy Oral History Program, John F. Kennedy Library.
19. Dallek, "Frustration and Pain," p. 98.
20. Hobart Taylor Jr., oral history interview, Jan. 6, 1969, Oral History Collection, Lyndon B. Johnson Library.
21. Roy Wilkins, oral history interview, Apr. 1, 1969, Oral History Collection, Lyndon B. Johnson Library.
22. Walt W. Rostow, telephone interview by author, July 29, 1999.
23. Robert Mann, *The Walls of Jericho: Lyndon Johnson, Hubert Humphrey, Richard Russell, and the Struggle for Civil Rights* (New York: Harcourt Brace, 1996), p. 318.
24. Conkin, *Big Daddy from the Pedernales*, p. 164.
25. Burke Marshall, oral history interview, May 29, 1964, Oral History Collection, John F. Kennedy Library.
26. Natoli, *American Prince, American Pauper*, p. 149.
27. Arthur M. Schlesinger Jr., *A Thousand Days: John F. Kennedy in the White House* (New York: Fawcett, 1965), p. 852.
28. Carl Rowan to Lyndon B. Johnson, June 6, 1961, Statements of LBJ, box 55, Lyndon B. Johnson Library.
29. Lyndon B. Johnson, "Address by Vice Pres. Lyndon B. Johnson at Howard University," June 9, 1961, Statements of LBJ, box 55, Lyndon B. Johnson Library. Richard Goodwin and *Manchester Guardian* journalist Max Friedman prepared early drafts of the speech; Carl Rowan gave Johnson suggestions for the message on June 6; and George Reedy prepared the final text, using portions of the earlier drafts, a few paragraphs from Rowan's memorandum to the vice president, and his own words.
30. "Vice President Condemns Mob Action in Southland," *Norfolk Journal and Guide*, June 17, 1961, p. 1.
31. Don Ferguson, June 14, 1961; Florence Hagedorn, June 9, 1961—both to Lyndon B. Johnson, in Vice-Presidential Papers, subject file, box 113, Lyndon B. Johnson Library.
32. Frank Szpiech to Lyndon B. Johnson, June 11, 1961, Vice-Presidential Papers, subject file, box 61, Lyndon B. Johnson Library.
33. Martin Benis to Lyndon B. Johnson, June 13, 1961, Vice-Presidential Papers, subject file, box 61, Lyndon B. Johnson Library.

34. James Booker, "Asks for Second 'Emancipation Proclamation,'" *Amsterdam News,* June 10, 1961.

35. Lyndon B. Johnson, "Remarks by Vice Pres. Lyndon B. Johnson, Urban League Dinner," Nov. 19, 1962, Statements of LBJ, box 73, Lyndon B. Johnson Library.

36. Whitney Young Jr., oral history interview, June 18, 1969, Oral History Collection, Lyndon B. Johnson Library.

37. "Vice President Cites Negro Job Increases," *Amsterdam News,* Nov. 24, 1962.

38. Baker, *Johnson Eclipse,* pp. 72–73.

39. Goldstein, *Modern American Vice Presidency,* p. 192.

40. Rowland Evans and Robert Novak, *Lyndon B. Johnson: The Exercise of Power* (New York: Signet, 1966), p. 397.

41. Lyndon B. Johnson, "Remarks of Vice Pres. Lyndon B. Johnson, Wayne State University," Jan. 7, 1963, Statements of LBJ, box 74, Lyndon B. Johnson Library.

42. Lyndon B. Johnson, "Remarks by Vice Pres. Lyndon B. Johnson, Cleveland Urban League," Jan. 26, 1963, Statements of LBJ, box 75, Lyndon B. Johnson Library.

43. Ibid., "Remarks by Vice Pres. Lyndon B. Johnson, Capital Press Club," May 18, 1963, Statements of LBJ, Box 80, Lyndon B. Johnson Library.

44. C. William Black to Lyndon B. Johnson, Feb. 14, 1963, Vice-Presidential Papers, subject file, box 189, Lyndon B. Johnson Library.

45. Adolph J. Slaughter, "Says Lyndon Johnson 'Thoroughly Dedicated' in Job Rights Struggle," *Kansas City Call,* Feb. 8, 1963.

46. Conkin, *Big Daddy from the Pedernales,* p. 164.

47. Robert Dallek, *Flawed Giant: Lyndon Johnson and His Times, 1961–1973* (New York: Oxford University Press, 1998), p. 36.

48. Doris Kearns Goodwin, *Lyndon Johnson and the American Dream* (New York: Harper and Row, 1976), p. 164.

49. "The Vice Presidency: Seen, Not Heard," *Time,* Feb. 1, 1963, p. 17; "The Vice Presidency: No More, No Less," *Newsweek,* Apr. 8, 1963, p. 23. The news media were responsible, in part, for Johnson's obscurity. Veteran journalist R. W. Apple has observed that reporters want to know only two things from a vice president: (1) who is advising the president on political issues and (2) whether there is a split between the vice president's and the president's views. Johnson did not leak information and was very careful to hide any disparity between his views and President Kennedy's. As such, the media often assigned LBJ to a position of relative obscurity. Apple discusses journalists' attitudes toward the vice presidency in "Defining a Public Role for Vice Presidents: A Symposium," in *At the President's Side,* p. 212.

50. Juanita Roberts to Lyndon B. Johnson, undated, Statement of LBJ, box 80, Lyndon B. Johnson Library.

51. Horace Busby to Juanita Roberts, Mar. 7, 1963, Statements of LBJ, box 80, Lyndon B. Johnson Library.

52. Lyndon B. Johnson to Chester S. Shriver and William G. Weaver, Mar. 9, 1963, Statements of LBJ, box 80, Lyndon B. Johnson Library.

53. The administration did not fully bring Johnson into the discussion until June. During a White House meeting on June 1, the president and the attorney general asked for LBJ's input regarding the administration's proposed civil rights legislation; Johnson responded that he was "not competent" to provide counsel since he had not seen the proposals. Presidential Recordings of White House Meetings and Telephone Conversations, 1962–1963: Civil Rights, 1963, audiotape 90, item 3, John F. Kennedy Library.

54. Evans and Novak, *Lyndon B. Johnson*, p. 398.

55. Rostow, interview by author.

56. Lyndon B. Johnson, *The Vantage Point: Perspectives of the Presidency, 1961–1969* (New York: Holt, Rinehart, and Winston, 1971), p. 156.

57. George Reedy to Lyndon B. Johnson, May 24, 1963, Vice-Presidential Papers, box 190, Lyndon B. Johnson Library.

58. Donald Young, *American Roulette: The History and Dilemma of the Vice Presidency* (New York: Holt, Rinehart, and Winston, 1972), p. 303; Dallek, *Flawed Giant*, p. 45.

59. Mary Margaret Wiley to Lyndon B. Johnson, undated, Statements of LBJ, box 55, Lyndon B. Johnson Library.

60. Kennedy speechwriter Theodore Sorensen claims that he had no knowledge of LBJ's speech at Gettysburg since the timing coincided with the legislative preparations. Theodore Sorensen, letter to author, Aug. 9, 1999.

61. The archives of the Lyndon B. Johnson Library contain a separate folder for the Gettysburg speech, which has only one draft of the address.

62. Horace Busby, telephone interview by author, Oct. 19, 1999.

63. Chester S. Shriver and William G. Weaver to Lyndon B. Johnson, Feb. 11, 1963, Statements of LBJ, box 80, Lyndon B. Johnson Library.

64. Aristotle, *On Rhetoric: A Theory of Civic Discourse,* trans. George A. Kennedy (New York: Oxford University Press, 1991), pp. 78–82.

65. Thomas W. Benson, "FDR at Gettysburg: The New Deal and the Rhetoric of Public Memory," in *Rhetoric and Public Memory,* ed. Stephen H. Browne and David Henry (Thousand Oaks, Calif.: Sage, forthcoming).

66. All quotations from the speech are taken from my transcription of an audiotape of the address. Lyndon B. Johnson, "Remarks of Vice Pres. Lyndon B. Johnson, Memorial Day, Gettysburg, Pennsylvania," May 30, 1963, sound recording, Audiovisual Archives, Lyndon B. Johnson Library.

67. Kathleen Norris, *Amazing Grace: A Vocabulary of Faith* (New York: Riverhead, 1998), p. 350.

68. Martin Luther King Jr., "I Have a Dream," in *A Call to Conscience: The Landmark Speeches of Dr. Martin Luther King Jr.*, ed. Clayborne Carson and Kris Shepard (New York: Warner, 2001), p. 81.

69. According to sociologist Robert Bellah, American civil religion, the religious dimension through which the nation interprets its historical experience in light of transcendent reality, includes the belief that the United States is a chosen nation. Robert N. Bellah, *The Broken Covenant: American Civil Religion in Time of Trial*, 2d ed. (Chicago: University of Chicago Press, 1992), pp. 3, 36–60.

70. Martin Luther King Jr., "Letter from Birmingham City Jail," in *A Testament of Hope: The Essential Writings and Speeches of Martin Luther King Jr.*, ed. James M. Washington (New York: HarperCollins, 1991), p. 292.

71. Ibid., p. 296.

72. See, for example, William F. Buckley Jr., "Birmingham and After," *National Review*, May 21, 1963, p. 397.

73. James Baldwin, *The Fire Next Time* (New York: Dial, 1963), p. 73.

74. George H. Gallup, *The Gallup Poll: Public Opinion, 1935–1971* (New York: Random House, 1972), 3:1823.

75. Milton Viorst, *Fire in the Streets: America in the 1960s* (New York: Simon and Schuster, 1979), p. 221.

76. Richard Hofstadter, *The American Political Tradition and the Men Who Made It* (New York: Vintage, 1973), p. 169.

77. Merrill D. Peterson, *Lincoln in American Memory* (New York: Oxford University Press, 1994), pp. 171, 348.

78. Branch, *Pillar of Fire*, p. 92.

79. Though complete broadcast information is unavailable, many citizens who wrote to the vice president during May and June noted that they had listened to his speech on television or heard it on the radio. See, for example, Ralph E. David, June 2, 1963; Elwell Parker, May 31, 1963—both to Lyndon B. Johnson, in Vice-Presidential Papers, subject file, box 234, Lyndon B. Johnson Library.

80. Max J. Karl to Lyndon B. Johnson, July 2, 1963, Vice-Presidential Papers, subject file, box 234, Lyndon B. Johnson Library.

81. *Congressional Record*, 88th Cong., 1st sess., 1963, p. 109, pt. 8:9915 and pt. 8:10005.

82. Rhett James, "Vice President Johnson Delivers Second Gettysburg Address," *Dallas Express*, June 15, 1963; Hobart Taylor Jr. to Lyndon B. Johnson, June 5, 1963, Vice-Presidential Papers, subject file, box 234, Lyndon B. Johnson Library.

83. "Johnson Makes Plea on Rights," *Washington Post*, May 31, 1963, p. A1; William H. Stringer, "Racial Plea: Johnson Signals Drive," *Christian Science Monitor*, June 1, 1963.

84. William L. Bromley; James L. Watson—both to Lyndon B. Johnson, in Vice-Presidential Papers, subject file, box 234, Lyndon B. Johnson Library.

85. "Johnson Asks Cooperation between White and Negro," *New York Times,* May 31, 1963.

86. "LBJ on Spot in Coming Rights Fight," *Norfolk Journal and Guide,* June 8, 1963, p. 1; "Memorial Day Talks Stress Civil Rights," *Amsterdam News,* June 8, 1963; "Administration Leaders Reflect JFK's Concern in Integration Crisis," *Kansas City Call,* June 7, 1963; Phyl Garland, "Historic Thrust of Negroes Puts JFK 'On Spot,'" *Pittsburgh Courier,* June 8, 1963. Though most of the black press covered Johnson's speech, it did not receive significant editorial coverage, given the schedule of most African American newspapers' weekly publication. Most of the editorials of the time focused on the developing crisis at the University of Alabama, a recent explosive meeting between James Baldwin and Robert F. Kennedy, and the protests in Jackson, Mississippi, led by Medgar Evers.

87. "Johnson: Stop Telling Negroes 'Patience,'" *Boston Globe,* May 31, 1963; Stringer, "Racial Plea," p. 1. Some African Americans shared the *Monitor*'s opinion. The director of programming and community planning for the New York branch of CORE claimed that Johnson's speech represented "a new dimension of thinking of our country's leadership." Clarence Funnye to Lyndon B. Johnson, May 31, 1963, Vice-Presidential Papers, subject file, box 234, Lyndon B. Johnson Library.

88. Drew Pearson, column copy ("Vice President Steps Out Ahead of President on Race Issue; LBJ, a Texan, Sounds New Emancipation Proclamation"), June 9, 1963, Lyndon B. Johnson Library.

89. On June 3, Johnson advised presidential speechwriter Theodore Sorensen that JFK should "make a Gettysburg speech." Edison Dictaphone recording.

90. Wayne Pinion to Lyndon B. Johnson, June 19, 1963, Vice-Presidential Papers, subject file, box 234, Lyndon B. Johnson Library; Jettie J. Byrd to Lyndon B. Johnson, July 22, 1963, Vice-Presidential Papers, subject file, box 189, Lyndon B. Johnson Library.

91. Lonnie B. McIntyre, June 1, 1963; Horace Hacker, June 3, 1963; Harry Smith, May 31, 1963; Roger Echols, June 27, 1963—all to Lyndon B. Johnson, in Vice-Presidential Papers, subject file, box 234, Lyndon B. Johnson Library.

92. Eugene Bosch to Lyndon B. Johnson, July 26, 1963, Vice-Presidential Papers, subject file, box 234, Lyndon B. Johnson Library; Richard Lykes to Lyndon B. Johnson, July 27, 1963, Vice-Presidential Papers, subject file, box 253, Lyndon B. Johnson Library; Edyth Risley to Lyndon B. Johnson, June 5, 1963, Vice-Presidential Papers, subject file, box 198, Lyndon B. Johnson Library; "A Voice from the South," *Washington Post,* June 1, 1963, p. A10; Jack Toomey to Lyndon B. Johnson, June 10, 1963, Vice-Presidential Papers, subject file, box 234, Lyndon B. Johnson Library.

93. Newspaper clipping, Vice-Presidential Papers, subject file, box 199, Lyndon B. Johnson Library; "A Happy Vice President," *Boston Globe,* June 1, 1963; "A Powerful Advocate," *Washington Post,* July 27, 1963, p. A6; "Insider's Newsletter," June 17, 1963, Vice-Presidential Papers, subject file, box 189, Lyndon B. Johnson Library.

94. Robert E. Baker, "Johnson Has Close Ties to Rights Groups," *Washington Post,* Nov. 24, 1963, p. A6; Roscoe Drummond, "The New President: Johnson Is Eminently Qualified," *Washington Post,* Nov. 24, 1963, p. A16; Rowland Evans and Robert Novak, "Inside Report: President Johnson," *Washington Post,* Nov. 25, 1963, p. A15; "Someday You'll Be Sitting in That Chair," *Time,* Nov. 29, 1963, p. 33; "The 36th U.S. President," *Newsweek,* Dec. 2, 1963, p. 28.

95. Lyndon B. Johnson, *Public Papers of the Presidents of the United States: Lyndon B. Johnson, 1963–1964* (Washington, D.C.: Government Printing Office, 1965), pp. 410, 684, 724; Lyndon B. Johnson, *Public Papers of the Presidents of the United States: Lyndon B. Johnson, 1965* (Washington, D.C.: Government Printing Office, 1966), p. 284; Lyndon B. Johnson, *Public Papers of the Presidents of the United States: Lyndon B. Johnson, 1968–1969* (Washington, D.C.: Government Printing Office, 1969), p. 509.

96. Chaim Perelman, *The Realm of Rhetoric,* trans. William Kluback (Notre Dame, Ind.: University of Notre Dame Press, 1982), p. 20.

97. Erwin C. Hargrove, *The President as Leader: Appealing to the Better Angels of Our Nature* (Lawrence: University Press of Kansas, 1998), p. 39.

CHAPTER 8

Reagan on Civil Rights

Returning to Strict Construction of the Constitution

Craig R. Smith

n 1821, four years after his presidency, James Madison wrote that
the Constitution must be interpreted according to "its true meaning as understood by the nation at the time of its ratification."[1] On
June 12, 1823, fourteen years after his presidency, Thomas Jefferson
wrote that we ought to return "to the time when the constitution
was adopted, recollect the spirit manifested in the debates, and instead of trying what meaning may be squeezed out of the text, or
invented against it, conform to the probable one in which it was
passed."[2] Thus, the two most influential writers of our civic documents argued that they should be interpreted in light of the intent
of those who composed them. Although First Amendment scholars
often glory in this hermeneutic, those favoring gun control are less
likely to endorse it. Whereas many conservatives are comfortable
with the concept, most liberals are not, preferring a living Constitution to a static one.

There are exceptions to this rule. For example, it is profoundly
interesting that President Clinton's defenders, most of them liberal
Democrats, used the precept of original intent to read meaning
into the phrase "high crimes and misdemeanors." These are the
same liberals who condemned Edwin Meese and Ronald Reagan
for their use of original intent as a hermeneutic guide. Madison
and Jefferson believed that original intent should be a guide in our
endeavors to parse meaning from the Constitution. If that made the

Constitution improper for the times, then it was to be amended, not reinterpreted.

Original intent was a cornerstone of conservative dogma into the 1980s. However, "originalism" was replaced by "textualism" among legal and scholarly conservatives, such as Justice Antonin Scalia and Robert Bork. They realized that different Founders could accept the same constitutional language for different reasons. For example, both a deist and a Puritan might support religious freedom for very different reasons. In any case, when the Supreme Court, the Congress, or the executive branch tries to create meaning where there is none, conservatives often cry foul. It was the basis of their complaint against the Warren court, which, starting in the landmark decision of *Mapp v. Ohio* in 1961, began applying the federal rules of procedure for law-enforcement officials against the states instead of allowing the states to maintain their own methods as long as they did not violate "fundamental fairness." One of the hallmarks of the Reagan administration was its desire to return to strict construction of the Constitution and to populate the courts and the administration, particularly the Justice Department, with its adherents. One of the goals of this chapter is to assess its effectiveness in that regard.

I also argue that another tenet of the Reagan administration was to oppose discrimination. This order came from on high, for if there was anything Ronald Reagan did not want to be called, it was a bigot.[3] His hatred of prejudice evolved from his youth. As black Irish, the Reagans were looked down upon, but Reagan's father, Jack (John Edward Reagan), taught the boys that their heritage was nothing to be ashamed of. When the film *Birth of a Nation* came to town, he told them the movie "deals with the Ku Klux Klan against the colored folks and I'm damned if anyone in this family will go see it."[4] Reagan claims his father refused to stay in hotels that would not serve Jews. On top of that, Reagan was deeply wounded by the prejudice he witnessed against his alcoholic father. These events may have radicalized the young Reagan, for in 1928, as a freshman, he led a student strike at Eureka College.

His appreciation of individual differences grew with the experiences he had saving children while a lifeguard, the work he did in Hollywood among blacks, homosexuals, Native Americans, and women in leading roles as well as the fight he conducted to protect the Screen Actors Guild from witch hunts by the House Un-American

Activities Committee. In fact, Reagan helped found the California Chapter of the Americans for Democratic Action; he joined the board of the United World Federalists and the left-wing American Veterans Committee. Following his father's lead, Reagan voted for Democrats through the 1948 election.[5] He made films about prejudice, such as *Juke Girl,* the first movie to treat the plight of migrant crop workers seriously. Reagan also starred in *Storm Warning,* which condemns the Klan. In my opinion, Reagan's later self-portrayal as a Roosevelt Democrat was a liberal cover for his leftist leanings.

Even though he was a novice in films in 1938, he got elected to the board of the Screen Actors Guild, an experience that would change his life. The guild was a union, and Reagan often found himself across the table from the monied interests in Hollywood—the same kind of men who had fired his father on Christmas eve during the depression. Reagan was president of the guild from 1946 to 1952 and again in 1959.

On the other hand, Reagan was an ardent anti-Communist, particularly after they attempted to take over his union. He knew that the Communist Party was trying to infiltrate unions in general and Hollywood in particular. When it was discovered that the Soviet Union was funneling money into these operations, Reagan became a secret informant for the FBI. The Screen Actors Guild published a statement in 1946 condemning "any Fascist or Communist influence."[6] Reagan tried to protect actors that had been duped by Communist front organizations, and that was how he met Nancy Davis, his future second wife.

Though Communism moved Reagan toward the right, he retained his ardent hatred of discrimination. For example, the day after Martin Luther King Jr.'s assassination, Reagan retrieved the anti-Klan rhetoric of his past, condemning "the night rider and his more gentlemanly ally, the friendly neighborhood bigot."[7] Nonetheless, Reagan opposed the Civil Rights Acts of 1964 and 1968 on philosophical grounds after discussions with Sen. Barry Goldwater (R-AZ). He embraced the Equal Rights Amendment in 1972, but he changed his mind in 1976, during his run for the presidency. The attempt to ratify the amendment died during his first term.

My knowledge of Reagan's passion for civil rights also stems from a personal experience. In 1970, just after the killings at Kent State, Reagan shut down California's universities, and many of us did teach-ins on the war in Vietnam. I took for my topic the history of the war, starting in 1870 with French colonization and concluding with Ho Chi Minh's closing of the border and the killing of fifty thousand Catholics. The governor's staff heard about it and asked me to come to a meeting in Sacramento. Of the ten professors in the room, I was the youngest by far and the only one with a beard. As the participants went around the room giving suggestions, I realized I was trapped with a bunch of right-wing zealots, long suppressed on their campuses. One called for keeping dossiers on assistant professors since they were an inflammatory element on the campus. Another went after graduate students. By the time my turn came, I was livid. I simply said, "Governor, with all due respect, these people are not just talking about violating academic freedom, they are talking about violating people's civil rights." Without missing a beat, Reagan responded, "There will be no witch hunts while I'm governor. I've seen enough of those." He then rose and left the room. At my behest, the incident was then published in the *Los Angeles Times* by Noel Greenwood.

Finally, Reagan was a federalist. In his inaugural address, he endorsed giving as much control to the individual states as possible under the Constitution. Charles Cooper at the Office of Legislative Council was one of the early advocates of federalism in the administration, as was Rich Williamson. Cooper provided the president with a memo that traced the decline of federalism and recommended ways by which it could be refurbished. The president established a working group on federalism in April, 1981, and its first goal was to extend the deregulatory policy of the Carter administration.[8] The issue was still important in 1986, when the president articulated a set of federalist principles to his Cabinet. It concluded that, "In the absence of clear constitutional or statutory authority, the presumption of sovereignty should rest with the individual states. Uncertainties regarding the legitimate authority of the national government should be resolved against regulation at the national level."[9] These principles were then converted into an executive order in 1987.

These three tenets—original intent, antidiscrimination, and federalism—were deeply embedded in Reagan's psyche. Working out a rhetorical compromise when they clashed was important to Reagan's success in the 1980 campaign. He often said, "We must not allow the noble concept of equal opportunity to be distorted into federal guidelines or quotas which require race, ethnicity, or sex—rather than ability and qualifications—to be the principle in hiring and education."[10] Soon Reagan equated affirmative action with quotas and won support not only from conservatives but also from groups opposed to quotas in hiring, particularly unions and Jews.

This chapter proceeds in several stages. First, it examines the early achievements of the Reagan administration in civil rights. Second, it turns to the fight over the reconstitution of the Civil Rights Commission. Third, it examines the initiatives of William Bradford Reynolds to reform affirmative-action policy. Fourth, it analyzes the influence of Edwin Meese. Fifth, it looks at the reforms instituted because of the Supreme Court's ruling in the *Grove City* case. Finally, it concludes with an overall assessment of Reagan's civil rights agenda.

Early Achievements

Reagan came into office in January, 1981, with a strong mandate from the American people, who had elected the first Republican Senate since 1954. On March 30, 1981, an assassin's bullet nearly took his life. His survival and his good humor during the incident enhanced his already solid credibility. By the end of the first two years of his administration, he could also claim a fairly strong record on civil rights. The Justice Department reviewed redistricting based on the 1980 census and objected to 153 submissions under the Voting Rights Act, including redistricting plans in nine states and New York City. William French Smith, Reagan's attorney general, even vetoed the redistricting plan of Mississippi, much to the dismay of House Minority Whip Trent Lott (R-MS).[11]

The same department launched sixty investigations of claims of housing discrimination. It entered one hundred employment-discrimination suits and filed fourteen new ones. It investigated eight school districts for discrimination and filed suits against three, a more aggressive record than the Carter administration for the same time period.[12]

The Department of Education under Secretary Terrell Bell had also been fairly aggressive in pursuing violations of federal law. In fact, Bell would eventually become disaffected with the likes of Ed Meese and write a scathing memoir about the bigotry he found in the Reagan White House, though he never implicated the president in any of it.[13] Bell was replaced by William Bennett, who initiated the drive to convert federal subsidies to public schools for remediation into vouchers for parents to use in either public or private schools. Some would argue that Bennett's legislative initiative violated the establishment clause of the First Amendment under the *Lemon v. Kurtzman* test, while some would cite federal vouchers to private schools that go back to the land grants of the Northwest Ordinance. Since the vouchers were available to all on an equal basis, the government could argue it was neutral with regard to the issue of the use of vouchers for religious schools.[14] In any case, the program was effectively blocked in the Congress.

By the end of 1981, Reagan had also succeeded in appointing the first woman, Sandra Day O'Connor, to the Supreme Court. The administration had also created a high-level Coordinating Council on Women, which included Elizabeth Dole, David Gergen, Peter Teeley, Margaret Tutwiler, and other operatives in the West Wing. By December of 1982, the National Women's Political Caucus had elected Kathy Wilson, a Republican, as its chair, though the membership was only one-third Republican. Wilson met with the Coordinating Council and advised the administration to make a "bold stroke" on behalf of women.[15] She urged appointing more women to the Cabinet, supporting the Economic Equity Act, and guarding against budget cuts that hurt women. By September of 1983, the administration was in full support of the "Economic Equity Act" (S. 888).

Reagan had also appointed a black man, Clarence Thomas, to head the Equal Employment Opportunity Commission (EEOC), which held to the existing interpretation of civil rights law and supported most affirmative-action programs. Thomas had been an aide to Sen. John Danforth, a moderate Republican, and then in 1981 and 1982 had served as assistant secretary for civil rights in Bell's Education Department. Although the Civil Rights Commission was critical of the Reagan administration in many areas, it singled Thomas out for praise. In fact, Thomas's EEOC was critical of the Reagan Justice Department, deciding only after major pressure not to file amicus briefs opposing it. In 1983, the EEOC resolved more than seventy-four thousand complaints, compared with fewer than fifty-eight thousand in 1980 under Carter. Only after 1984 did Thomas openly begin to question the hiring practices of the EEOC in particular and the use of quotas in general.

President Reagan signed the Voting Rights Act of 1982 over the objections of his Justice Department and at the behest of Sen. Bob Dole (R-KS) and Rep. Henry Hyde (R-IL), who converted the president on several issues including section 5, a requirement that Southern states obtain approvals for changes in the election laws.[16]

In 1983, it became obvious to the administration that the Fair Housing Act of 1968, for which then Congressman George Bush had been a major proponent, had not gone far enough. In his State of the Union address of 1983, the president called for legislation to strengthen the hand of the Secretary of Housing and Urban Development in dealing with violations and then sent legislation to the Congress that would allow the secretary to forward to the Justice Department any cases that could not be arbitrated.

In 1984, the Reagan administration began an effort to improve the lot of Native Americans residing on reservations. This effort started with a presidential commission on Indian reservation economies that conducted sixteen hearings and extensive research. It concluded that government-to-government relations with reservations constituted an essential modus operandi, that Native Americans on reservations should be encouraged to become more entrepreneurial, and that incentives should be provided for this effort.

Despite this record, the executive-branch appointments of the administration were a disappointment to women and minorities. By April 1, 1983, the president had made 992 full-time appointments of ambassadors, judges, marshals, and federal attorneys, of which only 103 were women, 45 were African American, 38 were Hispanic, and 3 were Asian. None were Native American. The administration had also begun its campaign to reconstitute the Civil Rights Commission. That campaign would ultimately do more harm to Reagan's legacy on civil rights than any other action.

Civil Rights Commission

When Reagan was inaugurated, the U.S. Commission on Civil Rights was chaired by respected moderate Republican Arthur S. Fleming. It also included moderate Republicans Stephen Horn and Jill Ruckelshaus and liberal Democrats Mary Berry, Murray Saltzman, Louis Nuñez, and Blandina Ramirez. In September of 1981, the commission released its report on the Voting Rights Act and argued that it was an unfulfilled dream. This motivated the Justice Department to begin a close examination of violations.

In November of 1981, however, the commission's report, "Affirmative Action in the 1980s: Dismantling the Process of Discrimination," led to talk of replacing Fleming with someone more sympathetic to the Reagan administration's point of view.[17] Particularly galling to opponents of affirmative action in the administration were lines such as "Today's discriminatory processes originated in our history of inequality, which was based on philosophies of white and male supremacy."[18]

The commission's next report criticized the Reagan administration for diminishing its support for civil rights enforcement. Early in 1982, Reagan removed Fleming and his ally Steve Horn. Reagan then tried to appoint Sam Hart, a religious broadcaster, to the commission. The effort failed. He then accepted Jill Ruckelshaus's resignation, much to the surprise of the press; Ruckelshaus was a loyal Republican who had supported Reagan's election after Bush dropped out of the race. The media began to speculate that Reagan's operatives were trying to purify the commission into a right-wing conservative operation.

Reagan was able to appoint Clarence Pendleton as chair and Mary Louise Smith, a Bush ally and moderate Republican, as vice chair in March of 1982. Pendleton had been chair of the Urban League of San Diego since 1975 and had headed a number of African American entrepreneurial operations. He was the only Urban League president to endorse Reagan for president.[19] After their approval, Pendleton took the hard-line conservative approach, while Smith allied herself with Democratic holdovers, including Mary Berry, whom the administration did not intend to reappoint. Berry lashed out at the Reagan administration's record on civil rights, just as Attorney General William French Smith argued that quotas were discrimination in reverse and authorized William Bradford Reynolds, the head of the Civil Rights Division, to oppose their use. The cold, dry, and imperious Reynolds annoyed his friends and foes alike with abrasive tactics.[20] Nonetheless, he emerged as one of the administration's most influential members on the issue of civil rights.

While Reynolds carried out Smith's agenda, presidential counselor Edwin Meese proposed a reform of the Eisenhower-created commission; in April, his request was transmitted to the Senate under the president's signature. It called for a reauthorization of the commission, which was required by law, on the condition that its life be extended for twenty more years (the longest ever requested or approved by any president) and for membership to be increased to eight and their terms to be fixed and staggered. Sen. Joe Biden (D-DE) compared Reagan's "reform" to FDR's attempt to pack the Supreme Court in 1937. The House rejected this plan in August, authorizing only a five-year life for the commission but inserting a provision that appointees would serve for life.

Reagan faced the possibility that he might be the president that destroyed the Civil Rights Commission, a legacy that was unacceptable to him. Thus, in his State of the Union address of 1983, he spoke to the issue directly: "Also in the area of fairness and equity, we will ask for extension of the Civil Rights Commission, which is due to expire this year. The commission is an important part of the ongoing struggle for justice in America, and we strongly support its reauthorization. Effective enforcement of our nation's fair housing laws is also essential to ensuring equal opportunity. In the year ahead, we'll work to strengthen enforcement of fair housing laws for all Americans."[21] Later that year, Reagan attempted a compromise by nominating four very credible candidates to the commission; each opposed racial quotas and forced busing. They included the following:

Morris Abram, a New York lawyer who authored anti-Klan bills in the forties and fifties, fought and won the "one-man, one-vote" *Baker v. Carr* case in the Supreme Court, and assisted in the release of Martin Luther King Jr. from the Atlanta jail (he was a strong opponent of the "use of racial preferences as a remedy for discrimination")[22]

John Bunzel, a California civil rights advocate who had been praised by the San Francisco Board of Supervisors, perhaps the most liberal supporter in America

Roberto Destro, a law professor at Catholic University, who was a civil rights activist on religious freedom and had provided legal aid to the poor

Linda Chavez, who was nominated to be staff director (she was assistant to the president of the American Federation of Teachers and had served on the staff of the House subcommittee on civil rights and constitutional rights)

Despite their virtues, the consideration of the nominees was postponed until after the summer recess, which put them in the middle of the fight to reauthorize the six-member commission, so the matter was pushed back to November 29, 1983. In October, having had enough of the slow compromise process, Reagan fired Mary Berry, Blandina Ramirez, and Murray Saltzman, the holdover Democrats on the commission. While Berry's term had expired, Ramirez's and Saltzman's had not, so the court reinstated them. In the Senate, Arlen Specter, a moderate Republican from Pennsylvania, and Biden introduced a resolution to create the Civil Rights Commission as an agency of the legislative branch; it was endorsed by fifty-five senators. In the House, an amendment to halt funding of the executive branch's commission was passed by a vote of 235 to 170. At this juncture, Sen. Howard Baker (R-TN) went over Meese's head and appealed to the president to endorse a new compromise, which he did on November 3. A compromise was struck, and on November 30, 1983, the president signed a bill creating a new commission with eight members, four to be appointed by the president and four to be appointed by the leaders of Congress. At the signing and at Meese's behest, Reagan criticized the former commission for moving beyond its charge, that is, to focus on voting rights, education, and housing discrimination and questioned the constitutionality of the current legislation.

Then, in December of 1983, the hard-liners struck again. Mary Louise Smith was not reappointed to the commission, much to the dismay of moderate Republicans and party leaders. What is particularly interesting in this development is that an ally of Vice President Bush had been ousted. Worse yet, the commission was without a quorum. Minority Leader Bob Michel (R-IL) then named Destro to the spot allocated to the minority leader, which set off more alarm bells since Michel had indicated he would choose Jill Ruckelshaus. To get even, Senate Minority Leader Robert Byrd (D-WV) nominated Ramirez. Howard Baker, the majority leader, nominated African American Francis Guess of the Tennessee Commission on Labor.

In the meantime, Fred Fielding, the White House counsel, investigated the question of whether the commission could operate at all.[23] Pendleton wrote to the president, telling him not only to hang tough but also to follow Ed Meese's advice: "I would be remiss if I did not compliment you for the fine work and continued dedication of

Ed Meese throughout the many tulmultous [sic] months. Mr. Meese never compromised your shared philosophy. He worked diligently to ensure that the new commission would include men and women who share our conservative ideology. I look forward to my new six year term."[24] Soon the commission was reconstituted in terms of the compromise membership, which included three blacks, Pendleton, Guess, and Berry, who was reappointed by House Majority Leader Jim Wright. Destro's appointment gave the White House a majority on the commission.

Linda Chavez emerged as the most influential member since she was functioning as the staff director of the commission and, in 1984, was voted in on a permanent basis. She reorganized the staff, appointed a deputy director, monitored—if not edited—all reports, and ran the employee-review system. However, it was her policy statements that caught the attention of the media. She came under almost immediate attack by the *Washington Post* (January 13, 1984), which claimed that the commission was running interference for the administration on the rights of religious fundamentalists. Chavez led the commissioners to approve unanimously a statement that the commission was independent.[25] The Republican National Hispanic Assembly of Colorado was so upset by the political implications of the new direction the commission was taking that it alerted Republican members of Congress to the problem. Its state chair, José Nuñez, wrote: "Our concern is that the actions of the commission and the publicity it is receiving are counterproductive to the efforts of the administration and the Republican Party to attract more minorities and women. The timing is terrible! It is giving the Democrats another issue to which they can rally minorities and women."[26] Responding to mounting pressure, the administration requested more funding for civil rights enforcement in the 1984 fiscal-year budget. The administration also began rationalizing its decrease in spending in this area based on more efficient operations.[27] Chavez steered the commission's report on "comparable worth" to an examination of its impact on the economy and small businesses. At the time, female workers were earning about 60 percent of what male workers were earning when full-time salaries were compared.

The conference on "Comparable Worth Consultation" began in June of 1984, with two days of hearings over four panels. On day one, two panels were established: one on occupational segregation and the earnings gap, and the other on the implementation of the comparable-worth doctrine. Before the panels, Linda Goldin of the University of Pennsylvania presented an overview of the issues. She defined "comparable worth" as requiring equal pay for jobs that its advocates argue are comparable, based on the need for similar skills, efforts, and assumptions of similar levels of responsibility. In other words, comparable-worth theory takes a step beyond equal pay for equal work.

On panel one, Solomon Polachek of SUNY Binghamton, articulated the Chavez line with his "human capitol" theory: Unlike women, men tend to remain in the work force throughout their lives and as a result invest more time in education and job training than women. And that explains the disparity in wages.[28] Other scholars supported variations of this view, the most liberal coming from Paula England of the University of Texas in Dallas, who believed that the wage gap was the result of multiple causes, including supply-side and demand-side variables. She concluded that on the supply side, segregation is perpetuated by sex-role socialization of females from an early age. On the demand side, job segregation was perpetuated by employer discrimination in hiring, placement, and promotion. She took direct issue with Polacheck.[29]

On panel two, Herbert Northrup of the Wharton School at the University of Pennsylvania argued that comparable worth is impossible to implement. Donald Schwab of the University of Wisconsin endorsed salary-survey sampling to solve the problem. The final speaker, Alvin Bellak, a business consultant, reiterated the difficulties that implementation would face.

Day two began with an overview of implementation, then moved to a panel on legal issues, where attorney Robert Williams argued that Title VII of the 1964 Civil Rights Act did not require comparable-worth pay. On the second panel, June O'Neill, program director of the Urban Institute's program known as Policy on Women and Families, argued that "Comparable worth is a truly radical policy that is alien to the operation of the economic system as we know it."[30] Joy Ann Grune, former executive director of the National Committee on Pay Equity, believed that comparable worth "is a necessary remedy for wage discrimination."[31] The next two speakers were also divided on the issue.

As with most such hearings, one can find speakers who are willing to say almost anything. That allows the hearers in charge to interpret as they please. This rhetorical hearing allowed the commission to use economic arguments instead of moral ones to justify its conclusions.

By the end of 1984, Linda Chavez was the bane of affirmative-action advocates, particularly women's groups. Clarence Pendleton won the same honor among African Americans. These two led the commission to issue a report on *Firefighters Local Union No. 1784 v. Stotts,* a Supreme Court decision of 1984, in which the Court's conservative majority prevailed and ruled that a reparation (sometimes called "remediation") solution for past hiring violations imposed in Memphis was unconstitutional. The commission "applauded" the decision for not using race or gender to reward or penalize a worker.

In March of 1985, the commission held hearings on minority and women's business set-asides as an appropriate response to discrimination. The administration had previously debated what stand it should take on minority set-aside programs. The Justice Department sought to overturn a Miami set-aside program for minority businesses. The commission followed suit when it noted that requirements that were imposed at the federal, state, and local levels ensure the awarding of public-construction contracts on the basis of race, ethnic origin, or sex. This policy results in the denial of contracts to lower-bidding firms and increased costs for consumers. The findings and recommendations section of the report opens with the following line: "Small businesses play a vital role in the national economy."[32] The commission found that when set-aside programs were measured according to their fairness and positive impact on the "minority economy [they] did not fare well."[33] The commission requested a one-year moratorium on the funding of set-asides. Once again economic considerations were used to justify an attack on an affirmative-action program.

The Reynolds Initiative

While Reagan won the battle to reconstitute the commission, the Justice Department had a more difficult time with the agenda of William Bradford Reynolds. In March of 1984, Reynolds met with "an organization of black Republicans." A few days after that meeting, Elaine Jenkins, their chair, wrote Reynolds a revealing letter. It reads in part as follows: "Some [of us] do not think that we can turn around the exceedingly negative way in which you or your office is viewed. Some of us think that if there is a very conscious effort on your part to understand the concerns of black Americans we might help to turn the views at least away from a hue and cry to replace you. . . . In addition, some of the observations about the Justice Department include: 1) lack of black professionals appointed to the agency (attorneys or consultants). 2) No black assistant to you who has a civil rights background or expertise. We will be interested in your views on how best to correct these voids."[34] Reynolds had been denied a promotion by the Senate and now continued to pursue his own course. After the *Stott* decision, the Justice Department intervened in four employment-discrimination cases seeking to alter consent decrees that required quotas.

In the meantime, opinion leaders began to question the president's commitment to human rights in terms of his own ability to revise or issue executive orders. In June of 1985, in his weekly radio address, President Reagan clarified his policy by arguing that his aim was to "protect every American." He quoted Martin Luther King Jr. on judging "men not by the color of their skin" but by their talent. Soon executive order 11246 was targeted for rescinding because William Bradford Reynolds, among others, wanted the president to revise it. Reynolds had been in the Justice Department during the Nixon administration, where he had worked closely with Solicitor General Robert Bork. Reynolds resigned—just before Nixon did—to become a highly paid utilities lawyer.

Now in 1981, with no experience in civil rights litigation, William Bradford Reynolds became head of Reagan's four-hundred-person Civil Rights Division of the Justice Department with responsibility for civil rights acts going back to the end of the Civil War. Reynolds's chief of staff was Charles Cooper, who had clerked for Justice Rehnquist. One of the first divisions they eliminated was the Indian Rights Section, which had been created in the Carter administration.

Strict constructionist Sen. Orrin Hatch (R-UT), the new chair of the Committee on Labor and Human Resources, wrote to the White House demanding a revision of Executive Order 11246, which had been in place for twenty years and required federal contractors to establish numerical goals and timetables to ensure the hiring and promotion of women and minorities. While Reynolds hoped to do Hatch's bidding behind the scenes, word soon leaked to the press that Reynolds was attempting to remove the requirement to maintain statistical data and timetables. Many business leaders were in favor of the reform; minority and women's groups were not. Jewish leaders were divided on the issue, and some business leaders claimed they had learned to live with the system. In 1983, Reynolds wrote an article that claims, "[I]t is no great revelation that a fixed and guiding principle of this administration is that race is an impermissible basis on which to allocate resources or penalties."[35] In speeches he claims that order 11246 could be used to establish quotas.[36] Nonetheless, the Reagan administration continued to enforce the order aggressively.[37]

The issue soon divided the Cabinet with Labor Secretary William Brock, Secretary of State George Schultz, Treasury Secretary James Baker, Health and Human Services Secretary Margaret Heckler, Transportation Secretary Samuel Pierce, and Vice President Bush lined up against Meese, Education Secretary Bennett, Energy Secretary John Herrington, Interior Secretary Don Hodel, and OMB Director Jim Miller. In a particularly testy Cabinet meeting on October 22, 1985, Brock defended the Labor Department's implementation of 11246, decried interference from the Justice Department, and warned of the political consequences of reform. When a compromise between Meese and Brock could not be worked out, plans for a major television speech by the president were abandoned.[38] The president was not witness to the ensuing fight since Chief of Staff Donald Regan wanted to distance him from the issue.

While the situation boiled, Reynolds sought to help Bob Jones University regain its charitable status with the IRS. The courts ruled against him, and the move prompted a mutiny within the Civil Rights Division.[39] However, it won the hearts of the religious right within the Republican party.[40] Next Reynolds took on forced busing, arguing that voluntary desegregation would be more effective than mandatory school assignments. In late 1984, Reynolds filed an amicus brief before the Fourth Circuit Court of Appeals, arguing that when racial imbalance does not result from intentional discrimination, it is not unconstitutional. Years later, when the Supreme Court finally ruled on the case, it sided with Reynolds, grounding its decision in strict construction: "Local control over the education of children allows citizens to participate in decision making, and allows innovation so that school programs can fit local needs."[41]

On November 25, 1985, twenty-five senators, a majority of whom were Republicans, wrote Reagan, asking him to retain the original executive order 11246; the issue had yet to be resolved since Reagan exercised what became known as the "Coolidge strategy": When you a see problem coming down the road, nine times out of ten it will wind up in a ditch before it gets to you. The House, however, wanted to keep this problem in the center of the legislative highway; thus it sided with the Senate. Soon the Justice Department, led by the newly appointed attorney general, Edwin Meese, was attacked by the Labor Department, which was led by moderate Republican Bill Brock; Chief of Staff Donald Regan intervened. Meese had given his "original intent" speech in July and was determined to follow up on his philosophical position. He believed that the "goals" of 11246 were merely another name for quotas, to which he and the president were unalterably opposed. Throughout this period, Press Secretary Larry Speaks made clear that the president had not yet considered—let alone decided—what he was going to do on the matter. By December, 222 members of Congress had written the president and voiced their opposition to any changes.[42]

The issue carried over to 1986, and the infighting over it continued into the summer, when Reynolds's amicus brief was endorsed by the Supreme Court in *Wygant v. Jackson Board of Education,* which many interpreted as compelling the elimination of government-imposed employment goals and timetables. The Court argued that there had to be some prior demonstration of discrimination by the government unit in question for remedial action to be mandated. The majority traced its rationale back to the original intent of the Fourteenth Amendment and required that all governmentally imposed distinctions based on race be eliminated. It did not hurt that Justice Sandra Day O'Conner was once again on the conservative side. The decision flatly overruled the extension of preferential protection against layoffs to minority teachers: Such tactics were a violation of the Fourteenth Amendment. Nonetheless, Brock's Labor Department circumvented the ruling by arguing that the Court's ruling was ambiguous. A few months later, the Court itself seemed to backslide when it approved race-conscious remedies in the name of Title VII and equal protection.[43]

In the end, Reynolds's dream of a color-blind interpretation of the Constitution faded when, in *Richmond v. Croson,* the Supreme Court, with the support of yet another new attorney general, Richard Thornburgh, came up with a 6-to-3 compromise. While invalidating Richmond's set-aside program, the decision allowed cities to adopt racial preferences only when they are justified as remediation for past action. Justice O'Connor, writing for the majority, claimed that such schemes must be held to "strict scrutiny." The Richmond plan failed this test because it had been imposed in a 5-to-4 vote by the black majority on the Richmond city council.[44]

Things also turned against the administration at the Civil Rights Commission. Just as the conservatives on that panel seemed to have control, Clarence Pendleton was hauled before the Subcommittee on Civil and Constitutional Rights of the House Judiciary Committee to defend his actions and justify continued funding of the commission based on the General Accounting Office's report of mismanagement. In April of 1986, this scandal gave the Democrats an excuse to attack the commission in general and Pendleton in particular. It was well known that the commission had in press a report critical of school busing as a tool to end segregation. It was also preparing a report that demonstrated that civil rights leaders were gerrymandering districts with a concentration of African American voters so that they would be guaranteed representation.

The House Appropriations Committee voted 27 to 16 to fund the commission only for the purpose of closing it down on December 31, 1986. This led to a battle with the now Republican-controlled Senate. Morris Abram, disgusted by the whole process, resigned in June of 1986, though he had spoken in defense of the commission at the House subcommittee hearing. In his letter of resignation, he wrote: "It causes me sadness as I now observe that so many in the civil rights movement today have turned away from its original principled campaign for equal justice under law to engage in an open contest for social and economic benefits conferred on the basis of race or other classifications previously believed to have been invidious."[45] As the administration tried to save the commission, they heard criticism from their own ranks. Sen. Warren Rudman, a moderate Republican, was described as "very heated" in his criticism of Pendleton.[46] The battle raged on into the fall. The commission's travel budget was cut as was the number of paid days that commissioners could take off.

The commission would survive, but its credibility was damaged.

In 1987, John Bunzel resigned from the commission, complaining about the uncivilized way he had been treated by civil rights activists and members of Congress: "One notion voiced in many circles is that those who do not actively support mandatory busing, quota-ridden affirmative-action programs, or various forms of differential treatment based on race are actively against civil rights progress and the cause of minorities." However, he also decried the leadership of Clarence Pendleton, who had created a "crisis of credibility" for the commission, which "is no longer an important voice in behalf of national goals and ideals."[47] Reagan nominated William B. Allen of the Harvey Mudd Colleges to replace Bunzel. Allen was a government professor who had published books on the Founders. To the administration's liking was an article he had also written, titled "Is Affirmative Action Constitutional?"[48] In April, 1987, Allen was approved by the Republican Senate, but the commission was now viewed as a partisan tool.

The Influence of Ed Meese

Meese's influence was enhanced with his appointment as attorney general in early 1985. He had been a trusted advisor to Reagan as far back as his first days as governor. Meese dealt with the demonstrators on California campuses when things got out of hand during the war in Vietnam. He had been the deputy district attorney of Alameda County and was known as a tough prosecutor. He moved from legal affairs secretary for the governor to chief of staff. He was a major player in Reagan's run for president and became a counselor to the president. No attorney general had been as close to the president since Robert Kennedy, and, since Kennedy, none had supported a more ambitious agenda. Meese personally undertook the task of revitalizing original intent as a method of interpreting the Constitution. As his book *With Reagan* makes clear, he believed the "exclusionary rule" was unworkable and unsupportable in constitutional law.[49] Even though Meese would punish blundering law-enforcement officials, he would throw out neither real evidence nor personal admissions during depositions as long as they were not induced by torture, psychological or otherwise.

On June 8, 1985, Meese spoke before the Anti-Defamation League's national commission.[50] He stated that the "Constitution arose from the principles of the Declaration of Independence and sought to give practical effect to the tenets enshrined in the Declaration."[51] He did not explain why the Founders had not included a bill of rights, which is much closer to the Declaration. Meese quoted George Washington in support of his position that "the government . . . gives to bigotry no sanction."[52] He then explained the "legal and moral basis of what we have been doing over the past four and one-half years," referencing the "outstanding leadership of Assistant Attorney General Brad Reynolds."[53] Meese and Reynolds were close personally.[54]

The acknowledgment of Reynolds was more than a friendly gesture. It was code language that said that, if you want to know the details of my philosophy, just watch Reynolds. Meese then reviewed what the Justice Department had done about hate groups and others who advocated violence on the basis of race or creed. He called for an "immediate end to all unlawful discrimination," a restoration of people who had been damaged, and a "true affirmative-action remedy: outreach, recruitment, and training programs that will lead to full utilization of the available pool of talent without regard to race, religion, or gender."[55] Then the other shoe landed: "Hiring quotas are not a remedy, they are simply discrimination with a new set of victims."[56] He quoted from the *Bakke* case to support his position, danced out the old argument about how sports teams would not tolerate quotas, and endorsed the Reconstruction Civil Rights Acts and the Civil Rights Act of 1964 as color-blind.[57]

The speech was well received, and Meese decided to deliver another one that would lay out his philosophical grounding. Speaking before the American Bar Association in Washington, D.C., on July 9, 1985, Meese expanded his attack on the doctrine of incorporation. He began by borrowing quotations from the Founders: "The intended role of the judiciary generally and the Supreme Court in particular was to serve as the 'bulwarks of a limited constitution.' . . . As the 'faithful guardians of the Constitution,' judges were expected to resist any political effort to depart from the literal provisions of the Constitution. The text of the document and the original intention of those who framed it would be the judicial standard in giving effect to the Constitution."[58] Then Meese zeroed in on his target: "Nowhere else," he said, "has the principle of federalism been dealt so politically violent and constitutionally suspect a blow. . . . [A] jurisprudence of original intention . . . would produce defensible principles of government that would not be tainted by ideological predilection."[59] He called original intent the "only reliable guide for judgment." In the course of the address, Meese took sharp aim at those cases that he believed hampered state law enforcement, particularly *Miranda v. Arizona*. That would prove prophetic when, from 1986 through 2000, the Reagan-appointed justices began to narrow the Miranda rules.

No fewer than two justices of the Supreme Court responded to Meese's attack. On October 12, 1985, at Georgetown University Law School, Justice William Brennan, in a very unusual step, commented on Meese's position. Brennan argued that Meese's stance would undercut the living and evolving Constitution and reestablish states rights' to a level of influence that preceded the civil rights movement. He maintained that original intention was undiscoverable: "But in truth it is little more than arrogance cloaked as humility. It is arrogant to pretend that from our vantage we can gauge accurately the intent of the Framers on application of principle to specific, contemporary questions. All too often, sources of potential enlightenment such as records of the ratification debates provide sparse or ambiguous evidence of the original intention."[60] On October 23, before a luncheon of the federal bar in Chicago, Justice John Paul Stevens claimed that Meese's argument was incomplete because it overlooked the importance of Civil War amendments to the Constitution. He also claimed that Meese was doing the bidding of Justice Rehnquist, who was often a target of Stevens's rhetoric.[61]

Meese, with the aid of Reynolds and Bruce Fein, continued to argue that words matter.[62] Incorporating federal interpretations of the Bill of Rights through the Fourteenth Amendment and against the states violated the intent of those who had passed the Fourteenth Amendment and was an act of legislative activism on the part of the Court. Ironically, Meese was fond of citing John Marshall's 1803 opinion in *Marbury v. Madison* to support his position, but that decision is a prime example of the Supreme Court's interpreting the Constitution in an activist way that gave it the right to review legislation, something not explicitly stated in the Constitution and something rejected at the Constitutional Convention.[63]

Meese's themes were repeated over and over, gaining more rhetorical sharpness as they were recited. For example, on November 15,

1985, Meese spoke to the Washington, D.C., chapter of the Federalist Society Lawyers Division.[64] In this address he called for a "jurisprudence of original intention": "The *Brown* decision was correcting the damage done 50 years earlier, when in *Plessy v. Ferguson,* an earlier Supreme Court had disregarded the clear intent of the Framers of the civil war [*sic*] amendments to eliminate the legal degradation of blacks, and had contrived a theory of the Constitution to support the charade of 'separate but equal' discrimination."[65] While Meese makes room for antidiscrimination measures in this case, he does not open the door to natural law as a potential measure for the Court. Lincoln certainly argued for it in his attack on the *Dred Scott* decision, and dozens of Supreme Court justices used it on other occasions in the guise of "fundamental fairness." Meese, however, may have realized that natural law can be whimsical unless codified. Perhaps he understood that original intent and strict construction prevent one from imposing one's view of natural law on others. Thus, unless natural law was written into the Constitution, Meese would not go outside that document to find it. Ironically, his attempt to square original intent with an attack on Taney's decision in *Dred Scott* is difficult to sustain, given Article IV, section 2, paragraph 3 of the Constitution. The fact is that Taney used original intent to write his infamous decision, which led to amendments to the Constitution that corrected it. Meese would have been on stronger logical ground to argue that Taney had no choice, but we do now, thanks to the Civil War amendments. In any case, in his address on November 15, Meese was "rooted in the text of the Constitution as illuminated by those who drafted, proposed, and ratified it."[66]

Aside from the exclusionary rule, Meese sought to correct the overzealous nature of affirmative-action programs and to reverse *Roe v. Wade,* which he believed was not only a case of judicial activism but also a case of fiction writing that cobbled together past rulings such as *Griswold* and misreadings of the Fourth and Ninth amendments to develop a new theory of the right to privacy. This position, more than any other, doomed the nomination of Robert Bork to the Supreme Court and contributed to the gender gap in the voting population between Republican and Democratic candidates. When Meese came to the Justice Department, however, he made it a top priority in his capacity as chair of the administration's Domestic Counsel.[67]

The first success came in the Supreme Court when the *Roe* decision was "clarified" by the *Akron* case. Justice O'Conner, differing with Justice Lewis Powell's argument that the issue was "settled" law, argued that "the Roe framework [is] clearly on a collision [course] with itself. As the medical risks of various abortion procedures decrease, the point at which the State may regulate for reasons of maternal health is moved further forward to actual childbirth. As medical science becomes better able to provide for the separate existence of the fetus, the point of viability is moved further back toward conception."[68] Soon the states were passing legislation to test the limits of *Roe* by requiring parental consent, waiting periods, and educational programs. That led to *Thornburgh v. American College of Obstetricians and Gynecologists,* in which the Justice Department supported Governor Thornburgh and the state of Pennsylvania in their attempt to require abortion clinics to advise clients of the dangers of abortion and the alternatives available. Invoking the doctrine of original intent at Meese's behest, the government argued that "The further afield interpretation travels from its point of departure in the text, the greater the danger that constitutional adjudication will be like a picnic to which the framers bring the words and the judges the meaning."[69] The administration lost the case on a 5-to-4 ruling written by Justice Blackmun. However, Justice Berger had abandoned his support for *Roe.*[70] The administration now had a legal strategy in place and knew that, with the change of one judge, it could reverse the decision.

Meese was also the administrative leader on the obscenity front. While counselor to the president, he pushed through the Commission on Pornography, some of whose members eventually resigned when scientific data were ignored or distorted in the final report. The report's one thousand pages and ninety-two recommendations led to the creation of the Obscenity Enforcement Unit in the Criminal Division of the Justice Department, which often fought with First Amendment activists. Meese believed that pornography was linked to organized crime, drugs, and prostitution and therefore presented a clear and present danger to the republic. He drafted an executive order for the president that restricted the sale of obscene materials on federal property; this move would have affected mainly military bases. However, conservative Sen. William Armstrong (R-CO) reviewed the draft and asked that even "soft pornography" such as *Playboy* be banned. Meese's staff warned that such a broad order would violate the First Amendment, specifically citing *Southeastern Promotions Ltd. v Conrad* and other cases. Others on the staff, however, cited Justice Rehnquist's lone dissent in the case, one of many for which he had gained the appellation "the lone ranger." The entire matter was actually debated in front of the president, and lo and behold, he sided with the Constitution. Senator Armstrong was rebuffed.[71]

Although the Congress often failed to pass the legislation that Meese wanted, he was able to get the states to do it by handing them "model statutes" that would pass constitutional muster. When these laws were challenged, Reagan's Justice Department would weigh in as a friend of the court on the side of the states.

Meese's most influential role was as guide for Reagan's policy of appointments to the courts. More than any other single accomplishment, the peopling of federal courts with conservative justices advanced the Reagan civil rights agenda in terms of strict construction, strong sentencing procedure, and the undermining of affirmative-action programs. By the end of his administration, Reagan had replaced nearly half of the judges on the federal bench—371, to be precise. Three were to the Supreme Court, and 83 were to the powerful appellate courts. The three for the Supreme Court—Sandra Day O'Connor, Antonin Scalia, and William Rehnquist, as chief justice—turned the court sharply to the right. In announcing his appointments, Reagan often cited the Founders and made references to original intent.

Reagan's major defeat in this regard was the rejection of Appeals Judge Robert Bork, one of the most eminent justices to be nominated to the Court. Bork was condemned for his speculative writing and his strong advocacy of strict construction, which was taken as a signal that he would vote to reverse *Roe v. Wade*. During his hearings, he also lacked the humor of Scalia, bristling at questions and providing long, academic, and often evasive answers. The rejection of Bork politicized the appointment process more than ever and eventually led to the appointments of Anthony Kennedy, David Souter, and Clarence Thomas, who was less qualified and even more conservative than Bork.

Meese's influence over the administration was not nullified until April of 1988, when charges of impropriety surfaced. Vice President Bush and Secretary of Defense Caspar Weinberger called for Meese's resignation, which he then submitted, thus ending his influence in the administration. He was replaced by Governor Thornburgh of Pennsylvania, a moderate on most issues with the exception of abortion.

The *Grove City* Case

The issue of federal strings on education grants is an old one. This issue arose in the second year of the Reagan administration after a lawsuit was brought against Grove City College in Pennsylvania, arguing that, because the campus received Pell Grants for its students, it was required to abide by federal antidiscrimination regulations in all sectors of student activity. The private college, a coeducational, Presbyterian school, had refused to file the Department of Health, Education, and Welfare's form 639A, which provides assurance of compliance with Title IX as a matter of "conscience." The college had taken no federal aid and was endowed by the conservative Pew family. Each side stipulated that the college had not engaged in discrimination. The question was how far federal regulations extended when students on a campus took federal monies.

When the college refused to sign the compliance forms, two female and two male students lost their aid and together with the college sued the government in 1980. In 1981, a counselor to the attorney general named Kenneth Starr was asked to look into the matter. He helped Solicitor General Rex Lee craft a brief that sought a compromise. The administration argued that, if students at a college take federal funds, then the college must comply with Title IX only at the agency level of the distribution of funds.

In February of 1984, the Supreme Court ruled in *Grove City College v. Bell* that the scope of Title IX of the Education Amendments of 1972, which prohibited sex discrimination in any "education program or activity" receiving federal funds, applied only to Grove City College's financial-aid office since that was the specific office receiving federal funds. Justice Byron White wrote, "We have found no persuasive evidence suggesting that Congress intended that the Department's regulatory authority follow federally aided students from classroom to classroom, building to building, or activity to activity."[72]

Moderate Republicans immediately introduced legislation to expand the application of Title IX to athletic programs, for example, in which students receiving federal aid were involved. The Reagan administration said that it would support a broadening of the ruling not only to athletic programs but also to issues of race, age, and handicap on campuses. The Reagan position was presented by Republicans in the House with HR 1881, which required any educational institution that received federal funds to abide by Title IX, Title VI of the Civil Rights Act of 1964, Section 504 of the Rehabilitation Act of 1973, and the Age Discrimination Act of 1975. In this way, the administration claimed it was seeking a reform of the *Grove City* rule. However, the Reagan administration opposed extending such regulations beyond educational institutions. Furthermore, it began closing cases of alleged discrimination that went beyond specific programs that received federal aid. Cases were closed at the universities of Maryland, Pennsylvania State, Alabama, Auburn, Duke, Idaho State, and Washington, among others.

The Leadership Conference on Civil Rights sought to expand the *Grove City* rule beyond campuses. They were supported by Republican moderates such as Senators Bob Packwood, Lowell Weicker, and John Danforth. In 1987, S. 557/HR 1214 was introduced by Sen. Edward Kennedy and fifty-seven others, mostly Democrats, and dubbed the Civil Rights Restoration Act. On April 1, 1987, the Justice Department said the bill ignored the principles of federalism.[73] In February of 1988, Congress took up the bill and approved it, despite the administration's position that it spelled "disaster" because it extended the regulations to businesses and state and local governments receiving federal funds.[74] Grocery stores, the administration argued, would be subject to these regulations under the act unless they refused to take food stamps.[75] Any churches that used federal funds would be subject to the regulations, thereby encouraging them to refuse federal aid. Such churches might come under fire for hiring only people of their faith for such projects. The debate provided another link between conservative Republicans, small and large businesses, and the religious right.

In the face of these attacks, the liberals granted Reagan several concessions, including the exclusion of direct regulation of "ultimate beneficiaries" of federal aid, for example, crop subsidies, food stamps, Medicare, Medicaid, and Social Security. Nonetheless, the president vetoed the revised bill in mid-March, reasoning that it interfered with religious freedom. The president argued in his veto message that the

Supreme Court's decision should be reversed but that restrictions and coverage should be limited to educational institutions. He then sent an alternate bill to Congress along with his veto message. The president's proposal retained portions of S.557 that were not offensive to him but amended the legislation to provide that, if only one part of a church or synagogue received federal aid, then only that part would be subject to federal regulations. The formula would be used for businesses and state and local government. Food-stamp distributors (e.g., grocery stores) and recipients and farmers would be exempted from the legislation.

In the talking points for a meeting of senior congressional staffers, T. Kenneth Cribb Jr., who was assistant to the president for domestic affairs, wrote that "if a single program of your State, county or local government receives one cent of federal aid—and there are few local governments that don't these days—that *entire* government will be subject to massive federal regulation."[76] Cribb went on to warn that the bill was so vague that it could be extended to "your local Girl Scout troop." Taking up the "federalism" cry anew, Cribb argued that the Kennedy bill would spell the end of federalism, the Reagan administration's code word for states' rights. The same talking points were provided to the president in "recommended telephone calls" to senators to support his version of the legislation. After a call to Sen. John McCain (R-AZ), the president wrote, "He seems to be with us." After a call to Sen. Nancy Kassebaum (R- KS), he wrote, "But she's agreed to really think it over."[77]

On March 22, 1988, Reagan addressed the House Republican Conference and reiterated his position. Using show-business lingo, the president said to his supporters, "But win or lose, like Crosby and Hope, like Rogers and Astaire, like the Lone Ranger and Tonto—the House Republicans and this Republican administration have made a great team."[78] Later on, the president got around to civil rights: "I'm talking about the so-called Civil Rights Restoration Act of 1987, commonly known as the Grove City bill. Equality for the law is the American standard. We can never allow ourselves to fall short. Discrimination is an evil, pure and simple, and cannot be tolerated. There are already laws, many laws, on the books to protect our civil rights. This legislation, however, isn't a civil-right restoration bill—it's a power grab by Washington, designed to take control away from states, localities, communities, and the private sectors and give it to federal bureaucrats and judges. One dollar in federal aid, direct or indirect, would bring entire organizations under federal control—from charitable social service organizations to grocery stores to churches and synagogues."[79] The president then cited examples that included Jewish yeshiva schools and churches that provide meals on wheels.

Conservative groups, such as the U.S. Chamber of Commerce, and religious groups, such as the Moral Majority, rallied to the president's call. Black leaders and feminists supported the Kennedy legislation along with a coalition of other civil rights organizations. For example, the *New York Times* reported that Congress was being inundated by calls and letters from both sides of the issue of whether to override the president's veto.[80] Kennedy's initial bill had passed 75 to 14 in the Senate and 315 to 98 in the House. An override was quite possible.

It did not help matters that Reagan's Justice Department closed several Southern desegregation cases by claiming that they were housekeeping matters since integration had been achieved. On March 22, the Senate voted 73 to 24 to override the veto; the House followed suit with a vote of 292 to 133. In the meantime, the Justice Department's orders were challenged in court by the NAACP and others, who argued that black students were being assigned to black teachers and that integration had not been achieved, particularly in eleven districts in Georgia. The administration had lost the Grove City battle.

Conclusion

President Reagan surrounded himself with men and women who were extremely loyal and, as this chapter implies, who protected Reagan from being tarred with the brush of bigotry. Even though my research indicates that Reagan worked diligently behind the scenes to advance the causes discussed here, he did not often speak out in public against "quotas" or "affirmative action." A search of his State of the Union addresses and his inaugurals does not turn up either of those terms. Instead, Reagan followed the line of his advisors, who contended that economic opportunity is the key to ending discrimination. In his 1985 State of the Union address, for example, Reagan said that "Despite our strides in civil rights, blacks, Hispanics, and all minorities will not have full and equal power until they have full economic power."[81]

These same advisors were philosophically conservative. Of these, no one was more influential than Edwin Meese, who had won Reagan's trust years before his presidency. Meese in turn relied on conservative intellectuals and operatives who came out of new think tanks during the Reagan years. The Heritage Foundation housed conservative and right-wing thinkers. The American Enterprise Institute housed conservatives of a more moderate stripe, while the Cato Institute was the home of the libertarians. Nonprofit research organizations such as the Freedom of Expression Foundation and the Media Institute argued for deregulation in amicus briefs. Thus, Reagan and Meese often benefited from sitting atop a pyramid of analysis and research that supported their agenda. The conservatives had finally matched their liberal counterparts when it came to research, analysis, argumentation, lobbying, and court briefs. Their rhetorical force was enormous.

Nonetheless, a coalition of Republican moderates and Democratic liberals in the Congress, along with a hostile press and civil rights advocates including women's groups, hamstrung the Reagan administration's civil rights reforms. They were aided by at least two other factors: inertia in the business community and the president's desire to keep Republicans united.

In his farewell address to the nation, Reagan surprised some of his critics by singling out the freedom of speech and the freedom of religion as our most important civil rights. The speech reflects the influence of FDR, whom Reagan admired, and his appreciation for the four basic freedoms that America should guarantee around the world. Perhaps Reagan was trying to repair the damage inflicted by the press and the Democrats when it came to his own record on civil rights. He might have taken comfort in the fact that, in the political realm, battles often seem large but, when measured against reality, are more like minor skirmishes. For example, both the administration and the Congress sought to correct federal discrimination law after the *Grove City* decision; however, the administration sought to expand the application of civil rights only to campuses, whereas the Democrats wanted to extend them to all entities that received federal aid. Though the administration was on the side of civil rights, it lost the public-relations battle since it was seeking less than the liberals.

Nonetheless, the administration shifted the agenda on civil rights to examinations of the impact of quota systems and set-asides on the economy and the rights of the majority. Beyond that, the Reagan administration succeeded in raising philosophical questions that many people thought had been put to sleep by the late 1960s. The doctrine of incorporation was revisited as were original intent, states' rights, sovereign immunity, and the exclusionary rule. Although the administration may have failed in the short run, and particularly with legislative issues, it won when these matters came to the Supreme Court. They are winning in the Court to this day.

As late as 2004, the Supreme Court was modifying or reversing the liberal, activist rulings of the Warren Court.[82] In *Kimel v. Florida* (98-791), which was announced on January 11, 2000, Justice O'Connor, with Rehnquist, Scalia, Kennedy, and Thomas in tow, wrote that "Congress exceeded its authority" in 1974 on the issue of age discrimination, thereby violating the "sovereign immunity" of the states as established in the Eleventh Amendment. Professors who had sued the state of Florida for age discrimination in pay negotiations were left out in the cold. Furthermore, in 2003, the Court agreed to revisit the *Miranda* rule, which excludes testimony from arrestees who have not been read their rights. It also regularly returns to the abortion issue, ever narrowing the application of *Roe v. Wade*. In this way above all others, Reagan resuscitated philosophical conservatism, reversed the concentration of power that the federal government was accumulating, and became the turning point in the debate over how we talk about civil rights.

Notes

1. Letter to John G. Jackson, as cited in Charles A. Lofgren, "The Original Understanding of Original Intent," *Constitutional Commentary* 5 (1988): 78 (77–113).
2. Lofgren, "The Original Understanding of Original Intent," p. 78.
3. See also Nicholas Laham, *The Reagan Presidency and the Politics of Race: In Pursuit of Colorblind Justice and Limited Government* (Westport, Conn.: Praeger, 1998), p. 14.
4. Ronald Reagan with Richard G. Hubler, *Where's the Rest of Me?* (New York: Duell, Sloan, and Pearce, 1965), p. 8.
5. Ibid., p. 139.
6. Ibid., p. 158.
7. As quoted in Kurt Ritter and David Henry, *Ronald Reagan: The Great*

Communicator (Westport, Conn.: Greenwood, 1992), p. 43.

8. Under Carter, the trucking and airline industries had been deregulated.

9. As quoted in Douglas W. Kmiec, *The Attorney General's Lawyer: Inside the Meese Justice Department* (Westport, Conn.: Praeger, 1992), p. 136.

10. As quoted in Hugh David Graham, "The Politics of Clientele Capture: Civil Rights and the Reagan Administration," in *Redefining Equality,* ed. Davison Douglas and Neal Devins (New York: Oxford University Press, 1998), p. 103.

11. Smith had been Reagan's personal lawyer since the early 1960s. During his confirmation hearings, he admitted to being in private clubs that excluded certain minorities, but he refused to resign from them.

12. For a complete accounting see Marissa Martino Golden, *Bureaucratic Responses to the Administrative Presidency: The Civil Rights Division under Reagan* (Berkeley: Institute of Governmental Studies, 1991).

13. Terrell H. Bell, *The Thirteenth Man: A Reagan Cabinet Memoir* (New York: Free Press, 1988), particularly pp. 104–110, where Bell reports that Reagan staffers referred to Title IX as the "lesbian bill of rights" and to Martin Luther King Jr. as "Martin Lucifer Coon."

14. See, for example, *Allegheny County v. ACLU,* 492 U.S. 573 (1989).

15. "Minutes of Coordinating Council on Women, December 16, 1982," Reagan Library, document #FG006-01 HU016, p. 1.

16. It can be argued that the Supreme Court had eviscerated section 5 prior to this time in *City of Rome v. U.S.,* 466 U.S. 156 (1980), and *Beer v. U.S.,* 475 U.S. 130 (1976). William Bradford Reynolds, a key William French Smith subordinate, used these decisions to further erode the act.

17. Washington, D.C., Clearinghouse publication no. 70, Nov., 1981.

18. Report of the U.S. Commission on Civil Rights, "Affirmative Action in the 1980s: Dismantling the Process of Discrimination," p. 2.

19. Pendleton's connection to Edwin Meese is explored by Robert J. Thompson, "The Commission on Civil Rights," in *The Reagan Administration and Human Rights,* ed. Tinsley E. Yarbrough (New York: Praeger, 1985), pp. 188–89.

20. See Raymond Wolters, *William Bradford Reynolds, the Reagan Administration, and Black Civil Rights* (New Brunswick, N.J.: Transaction, 1996).

21. State of the Union 1983 (on line at http://odur.let.rug.nl/~usa/P/rr40/speeches/su83rwr.htm).

22. Letter from Abram to Reagan, Apr. 5, 1984, Reagan Library, document #FG093-204406ss, p. 2.

23. See memorandum from Peter J. Rusthoven to Fred F. Fielding, Dec. 12, 1983, Reagan Library, document #FG093-190923, p. 1.

24. Ibid.

25. See letter from Chavez to James Baker, Feb. 13, 1984, Reagan Library,

document #FG093-212542, p. 1.

26. Letter from José Nuñez to Congressman Ken Kramer, Jan. 31, 1984, Reagan Library, document #FG093-196959, p. 1.

27. See memorandum from Mike Horowitz to Joe Wright, Craig Fuller, and Ken Cribb, Mar. 21, 1983, Reagan Library, document #FG093-194107, p. 1.

28. See news release, June 6, 1984, U.S. Commission on Civil Rights, document #FG093-238776, p. 2.

29. Ibid., p. 3.

30. Ibid., news release, June 7, 1984.

31. Ibid., pp. 3–4.

32. *Report on Minority Set-Asides*, U.S. Commission on Civil Rights, 1985, Reagan Library, document #FG093-412334, p. 79.

33. Ibid.

34. Letter from Elaine Jenkins to William Bradford Reynolds, Mar. 26, 1984, Reagan Library, document #0H11837.

35. William Bradford Reynolds, "The Justice Department's Enforcement of Title VII," *Labor Law Journal* 34 (1983): 259.

36. See Laham, *The Reagan Presidency and the Politics of Race*, p. 47. Pat Buchanan, as White House communications director, rallied conservatives to support the revision of 11246.

37. Ibid., pp. 52–53, 129.

38. Ibid., pp. 21–28, for a full account of the plans for a campaign of persuasion.

39. Howard Ball and Kathanne Greene, "The Reagan Justice Department," in Yarbrough, *The Reagan Administration and Human Rights*, p. 24.

40. *Bob Jones University v. United States*, 461 U.S. 574 (1983).

41. *Board of Education of Oklahoma City v. Dowell*, 111 S. Ct., pp. 630, 637 (1991). See also p. 638.

42. See Robert R. Detlefsen, "Affirmative Action and Business Deregulation: On the Reagan Administration's Failure to Revise Executive Order No. 11246," *Policy Studies Journal* 21 (1993): 556–67.

43. *Local 28 Sheet Metal Workers v. EEOC*, 478 U.S. 421 (1986).

44. This "strict scrutiny" standard was reinforced in 1995 in a 5-to-4 ruling in *Adarand Constructors v. Peña*, written by Justice O'Connor.

45. Letter to Ronald Reagan, June 4, 1986, Reagan Library, document #FG093-404991, p. 2.

46. Memorandum from Will Ball to Donald Regan, Aug. 14, 1986, Reagan Library, document #FGO93-435568, p. 1.

47. Letter to Ronald Reagan, Nov. 24, 1986, Reagan Library, document #FG093-445859, p. 1.

48. *Regulation*, July–Aug., 1985.

49. Meese, *With Reagan: The Inside Story* (Washington, D.C.: Regnery Gateway, 1992), p. 305.

50. Meese makes no secret of the fact that he was beholden to the

Heritage Foundation, a conservative think tank, for background research and interpretation of the Constitution. For example, in the acknowledgements section of the memoir *With Reagan,* he says the "Heritage Foundation deserves great credit for its unique contribution to the success of the Reagan administration" (viii). During the transition period leading up to Reagan's inaugural, the Heritage Foundation provided a mandate for leadership that set out the agenda for the first one hundred days of the new administration (60).

51. Reagan Library, document #FG017-335295, p. 3.
52. Ibid., p. 4.
53. Ibid., p. 7. The Senate Judiciary Committee had rejected Reynolds's promotion to associate attorney general on June 27. Reynolds claimed to support John Kennedy's initial definition of affirmative action: All things being equal, the underrepresented minority would be hired. To ensure the presence of qualified minorities in the job-applicant pool, recruitment incentives could be provided. However, Reynolds was unalterably opposed to remediation or quota systems.
54. Kmiec, *The Attorney General's Lawyer,* p. 15.
55. Document #FG017-335295, p. 9.
56. Ibid.
57. Reynolds gave a similar speech to the seventh annual convention of the National Association of Police Organizations on Aug. 1, 1985. It is a major attack on quotas (Reagan Library, document #FG017-335990). Reynolds references Meese's speech on p. 7. Reynolds, Meese, and Reagan often used the metaphor of color blindness.
58. Speech of Attorney General Edwin Meese III before the American Bar Association on July 9, 1985, as reprinted in *The Great Debate: Interpreting Our Written Constitution* (Washington, D.C.: Federalist Society, 1986), p. 1.
59. Ibid., p. 8.
60. Ibid., p. 14, Justice William J. Brennan Jr. at Georgetown University, Oct. 12, 1985. My thoughts on this issue run counter to Brennan's position. See my *To Form a More Perfect Union* (Lanham, Md.: University Press of America, 1993), which assesses the debates over the ratification of the Constitution and the Bill of Rights.
61. Justice John Paul Stevens before the Federal Bar Association on Oct. 23, 1985, in *The Great Debate,* p. 27.
62. Fein had been an associate deputy attorney general from 1981 to 1983, serving with Rudolph Giuliani, who then moved on to the Southern District of New York and later became mayor of New York City. When Fein moved Robert Gray's conservative public-relations firm, he became a speechwriter.
63. Even Meese's lawyer admits this. Kmiec, *The Attorney General's Lawyer,* p. 20.
64. Ibid., p. 18.

65. Ibid., cited on p. 23. The notion that legislatures should not change natural law can be traced as far back as Cicero. He wrote the following: "The most foolish notion of all is the belief that everything is just which is found in the customs or laws of nations." See "Laws" in *The Great Legal Philosophers: Selected Readings in Jurisprudence,* ed. Clarence Morris (Philadelphia: University of Pennsylvania Press, 1959), p. 48. For Cicero, natural law was the highest reason "implanted in Nature, which commands what ought to be done and forbids the opposite" (44).

66. Meese, before the Washington, D.C., chapter of the Federalist Society Lawyers Division, Nov. 15, 1985, in *The Great Debate,* p. 35.

67. Kmiec, *The Attorney General's Lawyer,* p. 71.

68. 462 U.S. 416, 458 (Justice O'Connor, dissenting).

69. Brief for the United States as amicus on p. 24, *Thornburgh v. American College of Obstetricians and Gynecologists,* no. 84-495, June 11, 1986.

70. The case of *Reproductive Health Service v. Webster* came out of Missouri. The administration filed a brief drafted mainly by William Bradford Reynolds in Nov., 1988.

71. Kmiec, *The Attorney General's Lawyer,* pp. 91–92.

72. 456 U.S. 555, 561.

73. Statement of Deputy Assistant Attorney General Mark Disler, Civil Rights Division, before the Senate Committee on Labor and Human Resources, document file 16534, p. 4.

74. White House Talking Points, Feb. 26, 1988, Reagan Library, document folder 16534, p. 1.

75. Ibid., p. 3.

76. "Grove City Talking Points," Mar. 14, 1988, Reagan Library, document 16534.

77. Ibid.

78. Presidential remarks, meeting with House Republican Conference, Mar. 22, 1988, document file, 16534, p. 1.

79. Ibid., p. 4.

80. Julie Johnson, "Civil Rights Bill's Foes Mount 11th-Hour Drive," *Washington Post* (Mar. 22, 1988), p. 1.

81. State of the Union 1985 (on line at http://odur.let.rug.nl/~usa/P/rr40/speeches/su85rwr.htm).

82. In *Dickerson v. U.S.* 530 U.S. 438 (2000), the court ruled that Congress could not rewrite the *Miranda* rule in such a way that it diminished the court's constitutional finding.

CHAPTER 9

George Bush and
the Transformation of
Civil Rights Discourse, 1965–1990

David Zarefsky

The zenith of presidential leadership on the issue of civil rights came in the spring of 1965. In March, in an address to a joint session of Congress, Lyndon Johnson electrified the nation by taking the anthem of the civil rights movement, "We shall overcome," and making it his own. In June, he went even further. In the commencement address at Howard University, Johnson moved to outflank the civil rights movement by calling for "not just equality as a right and a theory, but equality as a fact and a result."[1] This speech laid the groundwork for the idea of affirmative action by suggesting that equal opportunity required special efforts to overcome the effects of unequal history. Johnson invoked the metaphor of a footrace, saying, "You do not take a person who, for years, has been hobbled by chains, liberate him, bring him to the starting line of a race, saying, 'you are free to compete with all the others,' and still justly believe you have been completely fair."[2]

Twenty-five years later, George Bush vetoed the Civil Rights Act of 1990 because he believed that it would lead employers to afford blacks preferential treatment in hiring and that—far from achieving the goals of civil rights—this sort of affirmative action was antithetical to them. He referred to the bill passed by Congress as a "quota bill" and used the symbol of quotas to counteract the positive connotations associated with civil rights. He would sign a very similar bill the following year only after arguing that it really was quite different from the one he had vetoed the year before.

The difference between the rhetorical positions of Lyndon Johnson and George Bush is an index of the transformation of the public dialogue on race between 1965 and 1990. Bush's White House counsel, C. Boyden Gray, referred to it as an inversion of the Civil Rights Act of 1964, but it was more complicated than that.[3] At first, one could easily be both for civil rights and against quotas. Over time, "quotas" became a powerful symbol to discredit measures claiming to be about civil rights. Affirmative-action programs, in particular, came under scrutiny. Sometimes they were attacked as quotas by definition; at other times, the symbol of quotas forced affirmative-action advocates to dissociate the term, distinguishing among approaches to affirmative action that did and did not constitute quotas. Usually, neither "affirmative action" nor "quotas" was defined with precision in the public forum.

The case of George Bush and the Civil Rights Act of 1990 highlights the change that took place. Bush's rhetoric, though, is not idiosyncratic; the dialectical tension between the symbols "affirmative action" and "quotas" lasted for a generation and is with us still. Although the principal focus here is on George Bush in 1990 and 1991, the analysis begins with a brief account of how the rhetorical ground shifted.

From Johnson to Reagan

When Johnson spoke at Howard University, he was not responding to any groundswell. The notion of special treatment for minorities was not embraced by the mainstream of liberal thought or, for that matter, by the civil rights movement.[4] The conventional wisdom was that the removal of officially sanctioned racial discrimination was the goal: in the schools, desegregation but not necessarily integration; in the workplace, opportunity but not guarantees. Quotas were unpopular because they were widely understood in the context of measures that had been used to limit the number of blacks and Jews in prestigious colleges and professional schools. As vice president, Johnson had opposed any idea of compensatory quota hiring based on race.[5] Southern senators baited Hubert Humphrey on this issue during debates over the Civil Rights Act of 1964, leading the bill's sponsor to declare that the act sought to end desegregation, not to mandate integration.[6]

In some quarters of the movement, though, advocates pressed beyond this mainstream understanding. In 1963, the Congress on Racial Equality (CORE) developed a demand for compensatory job quotas. This move reflected an evolving view on the political left that employment discrimination should be treated as a conclusion from statistical evidence of racial differentials, rather than only as the result of individual acts of prejudice.[7] This view was seemingly given support by the Voting Rights Act of 1965, which permitted federal courts to suspend literacy tests and other qualifying procedures if they had the effect of discriminating against blacks, regardless of whether that was their intent.[8] It was further bolstered by President Johnson's Howard University address. How, after all, would one know whether "equality as a fact and as a result" had been achieved, if not by comparing the outcomes between blacks and whites?

Johnson never followed through on the implications of the "footrace" metaphor, but he did issue executive order 11246, which required federal contractors to "take affirmative action to ensure that applicants are employed, and that employees are treated" in nondiscriminatory fashion. While this might mean deliberately widening the net of potential applicants through aggressive marketing and recruiting practices, it quickly came to be understood that the test of nondiscrimination was in the final results. Graham notes that the process of implementing the 1964 and 1965 civil rights acts actually changed the goals. He wrote that, after 1965, the civil rights era entered a new phase, one in which there was "a shift of administrative and judicial enforcement from a goal of equal treatment to one of equal results" and in which federal courts justified compensatory, preferential treatment for minorities (in order to finally produce equal results) "in fields as varying as voting, employee and union security, education, hiring and promotions, and job testing."[9] Meanwhile, this shift intensified white resistance to the pace of the civil rights movement. Even seemingly neutral measures could be criticized as preferential treatment or quotas.

The administration of Richard Nixon inherited this ambiguous situation. Nixon's record can be described only as enigmatic. He did the most to identify affirmative action with numerical quotas, and yet he also campaigned vigorously against them. As vice president, he endorsed affirmative action, yet in his 1968 acceptance address he co-opted the language of civil rights and used it for other purposes, stating that "the first civil right of every American is to be free from domestic violence."[10] In office Nixon was no more straightforward.

First, he took from the shelf a Johnson proposal and transformed it into what became known as the "Philadelphia plan." It fixed target numbers for minority hiring among construction firms doing business with the federal government. If they were not met, the burden of proof was on the employer to show that a good-faith effort had been made to achieve them.[11] The author of the plan was Assistant Secretary of Labor Arthur Fletcher, but Nixon endorsed it as well. He insisted, though, that "the Philadelphia Plan does not set quotas; it points to goals."[12] It is hard to discern the difference, except perhaps that justifiable reasons might exist for failing to reach the goals.

It is ironic indeed that the greatest step toward identifying affirmative action with statistical measures of results was taken by a conservative Republican president. Why did he do it? Some saw his move as the genuine expression of his personal commitments to civil rights. Others were more cynical, suggesting that this was a stratagem by Nixon to split the majority civil rights coalition between blacks and labor, on which the Democrats depended. In this view, the Nixon administration hoped to pick up the votes of blacks even while antagonizing blue-collar, white ethnic Democrats.[13]

It didn't work. Nixon's actions did not gain black votes. Meanwhile, in the spring of 1970, the president discovered that blue-collar workers strongly supported his Vietnam policies. According to Skrentny, Nixon found more fertile ground in efforts to alienate labor from the Democrats.[14] He could appeal to this audience by railing against quotas and portraying Democrats as supporting them. Nixon had the best of both worlds. He had put the Philadelphia Plan in place; now he could condemn quotas as the number-based policies that he had earlier championed as goals and that the courts, meanwhile, had legitimized. Quotas were bad because they judged people on grounds other than ability. To object to quotas was not racist.[15]

In his campaign against quotas, Nixon was aided by a bit of serendipity. The 1972 Democratic convention changed the delegate-selection rules in order to encourage proportional representation for women, young people, and nonwhite minorities.[16] That was a quota, Nixon insisted, and hence discriminatory. "The way to end discrimination against some," he said in his 1972 acceptance speech, "is not to begin discrimination against others. Dividing Americans into quotas is totally alien to the American tradition."[17] In fact, although the Democrats' delegate-selection rules mandated state parties to take affirmative steps to encourage minority-group representation "in reasonable relationship to the group's presence in the population of the State," they did not require or encourage quotas.[18] Making no specific reference to this document and hence not needing to confront its nuances, Nixon merely *defined* quotas as discrimination and therefore a priori unacceptable.

At the same time, Nixon again distinguished quotas from goals, even though the only practical difference is whether mandatory action is to be the means of reaching the numerical target. Perhaps sensing the thin reed on which this distinction was built, the Nixon administration abandoned the Philadelphia Plan before the 1972 elections. Moreover, an unnamed federal official was quoted as saying that no more federal action in the civil rights field was needed: "Everything that needs to be legislated already has been done—we have arrived at that point where racism no longer exists as a matter of national policy."[19]

In short, Nixon was able both to advance the implementation of affirmative action and to mount a strong campaign against quotas, assuming that they were two different things. His successors, Gerald Ford and Jimmy Carter, followed the same pattern, supporting affirmative-action programs but opposing either quotas or busing—implying that there was such a thing as an affirmative-action program that was not a quota. Their goal, in other words, was to navigate between the two prongs of Richard Nixon's approach. As Carter stated in his 1978 State of the Union message, for example, "Our efforts to eliminate discrimination and promote affirmative action programs relying on flexible goals rather than quotas will continue in full force."[20]

The next stage in the discourse came during the administration of Ronald Reagan, who essentially *defined* affirmative action as numerical quotas and preferential treatment, which he attacked as violations of American principles. Rather than attack perversions of affirmative action, he launched an attack against affirmative action itself.

Reagan saw affirmative-action programs as instruments of "big government" intruding on the individual. Referring to the failures of the past, he told a Reagan-Bush rally, "Endless tax increases, deeper dependency, planned protectionism, certain sacrifices, and veiled quotas—we don't need that kind of progress, do we?"[21] His position rested on the goal of equal opportunity as meaning color blindness, as it had been understood before 1965. Once the "clarion call of the civil rights movement," it had now "become the center-right position," according to Edsall and Edsall.[22] Reagan borrowed much of the symbolism of the early movement, portrayed affirmative action as a violation of its goals, and urged a return to the right path. (It is likely that many who supported Reagan would not have approved of the movement's goals during the 1960s but now identified with them as an effective way to block a call for more radical action.)

So, for example, when a reporter asked Reagan in January, 1981, whether there would be a "retreat . . . on the government's advocacy of affirmative action programs," the new president responded, "No, there will be no retreat. This administration is going to be dedicated to equality." But then he went on to state, "I think there are some big things, however, that may not be as useful as they once were or that may even be distorted in the practice, such as some affirmative action programs becoming quota systems. And I'm old enough to remember when quotas existed in the United States for the purpose of discrimination, and I don't want to see that happen again."[23] On several occasions Reagan associated affirmative action with quotas, which he then associated with the practices of earlier decades, whereby quotas were used to keep Jews out of certain colleges or jobs.[24] Reagan did not distinguish between quotas meant to *exclude* and those meant to *include,* implying that even an inclusive quota had the dark side of excluding white males. Moreover, he implied that there is a slippery slope: Any quota will lead to a reimposition of the quotas that had excluded Jews in the past.

Believing that quotas were wrong per se and that affirmative-action programs constituted quotas, Reagan set out to challenge affirmative-action programs. His appointees to the Civil Rights Commission, especially Clarence Pendleton but also Mary Louise Smith and Morris B. Abram, had in common their opposition to such programs.[25] Solicitor General Charles Fried and Equal Opportunity Commission chair Clarence Thomas reflected similar sentiments. Yet Reagan steadfastly maintained that his policies were not retarding but advancing the goals of civil rights. One of the ways he did so was to appropriate historical symbols, particularly the memory of Martin Luther King, as support for his position.

Reagan's most complete statement on civil rights and affirmative action came in a radio address on June 15, 1985. Acknowledging that discrimination is "not yet a thing of the past," he said that the symbol of justice is what embodies our laws as nondiscriminatory: "Equal treatment and equality before the law—these are the foundations on which a just and free society is built." But then he complained, warning about his critics, "But there are some today who, in the name of equality, would have us practice discrimination. They have turned our civil rights laws on their head, claiming they mean exactly the opposite of what they say." Reagan clearly identified himself with civil rights, and his opponents—even though they claimed they supported civil rights—were its transgressors. He went on, even more specifically, but without supporting evidence, "These people tell us that the government should enforce discrimination in favor of some groups through hiring quotas, under which people get or lose particular jobs or promotions solely because of their race or sex. Some bluntly assert that our civil rights laws only apply to special groups and were never intended to protect every American."[26] President Reagan's equations are obvious. Affirmative-action programs are means for "the Government" to "enforce discrimination in favor of some groups"; numerical targets are "hiring quotas"; and underrepresented minorities are "special groups" that stand in opposition to "every American."

To make his claim even more compelling, Reagan invoked the memory of Martin Luther King: "Twenty-two years ago Martin Luther King proclaimed his dream of a society rid of discrimination and prejudice, a society where people would be judged on the content of their character, not by the color of their skin. That's the vision our entire administration is committed to, a society that keeps faith with the promise of our Declaration of Independence."[27] Reagan had earlier aligned himself with King's memory in 1983, when he dropped his long-standing opposition to a national holiday in the slain civil rights leader's name.[28] On neither occasion did he mention that, during the 1960s, he had opposed all civil rights legislation and was not in sympathy with Martin Luther King Jr.

In time, others would follow President Reagan's lead in calling on King's memory as testimony against affirmative action. House Speaker Newt Gingrich praised him as an individualist who was opposed to "group rights." In 1996, Louisiana Gov. Mike Foster signed an executive order outlawing affirmative action and explained it "as a fulfillment of King's dream."[29] Among those who would quote King in this fashion was Pres. George Bush. Never mind that Martin Luther King Jr. started Operation Breadbasket, arguably the first successful affirmative-action program on a national scale.[30] Never mind that, especially in his later years, King called for restructuring the American economy and society. And never mind that many of those invoking King's memory had opposed him while he was alive.[31]

Reagan was frequently accused by the press and civil rights organizations of being insincere or duplicitous in his commitment to civil rights. Rather than respond directly to these criticisms, he went on the offensive by claiming that his opponents were insincere or deceptive. In a 1988 speech he denounced proposed legislation as threatening "to subject nearly every facet of American life . . . to intrusive regulation by Federal agencies and courts. Ironically it does so in the name of civil rights."[32] At a Republican Party fundraiser the same year, he warned that liberals "use our words and borrow our terms, but the song is way out of key. When they say 'equality of opportunity,' they mean straight numerical quotas." Abraham Lincoln, he added, "could have told them a thing or two about trying to fool the American people."[33]

Reagan's unyielding opposition to affirmative action was not fully shared by his vice president and successor. George Bush tried to return to an older rhetorical position that provided some space for affirmative action that did not constitute quotas. An unclear and inconsistent definition of what counted as a "quota bill," however, would significantly complicate his rhetorical situation.

George Bush in 1990

As had been the case in the 1960s, the civil rights controversy of the Bush administration arose neither from dramatic evidence of systematic denial of basic rights nor from an organized movement demanding action. President Bush opposed racial injustice. Although he campaigned against the Civil Rights Act of 1964 when running for office, still, as a congressman from Houston, he had cast one of the few Republican votes for open-housing legislation during the late 1960s. As president, he signed the Americans with Disabilities Act (ADA), which he proclaimed the greatest extension of civil rights protection since the landmark act of 1964. Rather, the controversy of 1990 and 1991 would be fought on narrower ground, yet it illuminated the ways in which public discourse on this sensitive topic had changed since the 1960s.

It began with a series of Supreme Court decisions in 1989 that concerned employment discrimination. Eighteen years earlier, in *Griggs v. Duke Power Company,* the Court had held that Title VII of the Civil Rights Act of 1964 prohibits "not only overt discrimination but also practices that are fair in form but discriminatory in practice."[34] In other words, not only intentional discrimination ("disparate treatment") but also neutral practices that had the unintended effect of limiting opportunities of protected minorities ("disparate impact") were actionable under the Civil Rights Act. *Griggs* and subsequent case law established a framework for the burden of proof in deciding such cases. Initially, the plaintiffs had to demonstrate that a seemingly neutral hiring practice effectively screened out qualified minority or women candidates. Then the burden shifted to the employer to prove that the discriminatory practices arose from business necessity. To implement the *Griggs* decision, the federal bureaucracy had developed Uniform Guidelines on Employee Selection Practices. Did these constitute quotas? White House Counsel C. Boyden Gray thought so, stating as a fact that "the Uniform Guidelines, because they made it so difficult for employers to defend so many neutral practices that had a disparate impact, created enormous pressure on employers to avoid 'bad numbers' by adopting surreptitious goals."[35]

When a finding of employment discrimination was upheld, courts could order remedial action, including compensatory-hiring policies. Rather than subject themselves to costly litigation, many employees adopted voluntary affirmative-action programs that ranged from more aggressive recruiting of minorities to preferential hiring of minority candidates. Increasingly, then, there were two different types of employment-discrimination cases: those alleging disparate impact and seeking a remedy, and those filed by workers who would be disadvantaged by the remedies, challenging their legality and alleging that they constituted reverse discrimination.

Several cases raising these issues were decided by the Supreme

Court in the spring of 1989. From the standpoint of later controversy, the most significant was *Ward's Cove v. Atonio* (490 U.S. 642), a disparate-impact case. Plaintiffs contended that the hiring and promotion practices of the defendant at an Alaskan cannery had the effect of denying higher-paying jobs to nonwhite employees. The Ninth Circuit Court of Appeals ruled that a prima facie case of disparate impact in hiring had been made when the plaintiffs demonstrated statistically that a high percentage of workers in low-paying jobs and a low percentage of workers in higher-paying jobs were nonwhite. The Supreme Court held, however, that statistical evidence of racial stratification within the company was not sufficient to prove disparate impact. The proper comparison, it determined, was "between the racial composition of the qualified persons in the labor market and the persons holding at-issue jobs."[36]

Remanding the case to lower courts, the Supreme Court also stipulated that plaintiffs must link racial imbalance to one or more specific employment practices and must show that the identified practice did not result from "business necessity." This seemed to shift the burden of proof of "business necessity" from the defendant to the plaintiff. Not so, held the Court. When earlier case law established the defendant's burden, it was referring only to the *production burden*—the burden to produce evidence so that the controversy could continue. The *persuasion burden*—the ultimate responsibility to persuade the court that discrimination existed—had always rested with the plaintiff. Hence the *Ward's Cove* plaintiffs would have to prove that racial stratification of the workforce was the result of specific hiring and promotion practices and that these practices were not a business necessity. The practical effect was to make it harder for plaintiffs to win employment-discrimination suits.

Other Court cases decided that spring had the same effect. In *Price Waterhouse v. Hopkins* (490 U.S. 228), the Supreme Court held that employment decisions partially motivated by prejudice do not violate Title VII of the Civil Rights Act of 1964 if the employer can demonstrate that the same decision would have been made without any intentional discrimination. In *Martin v. Wilks* (490 U.S. 755), the Court held that white firefighters in Birmingham, Alabama, who were not party to earlier litigation, still could challenge a consent decree that established an affirmative-action program for minority hiring. In *Lorance v. AT&T Technologies* (490 U.S. 900), the Court shortened the statute of limitations on challenges to seniority plans. And in *Patterson v. McLean Credit Union* (491 U.S. 164), the Court ruled that the Civil Rights Acts of 1866 covered racial discrimination in hiring but not on the job. The *Price Waterhouse* decision was unanimous, but all of the others, including *Ward's Cove,* were decided with five-vote majorities.

A number of civil rights organizations, whose lobbying arm was the Leadership Conference for Civil Rights, sought congressional legislation to reverse these decisions. Sen. Edward M. Kennedy (D-MA) and Rep. Augustus F. Hawkins (D-CA) sponsored such a bill. Proponents of the Kennedy-Hawkins measure claimed that they were overturning *Ward's Cove* and restoring *Griggs.* They incorporated the Uniform Guidelines, which had been developed to implement *Griggs,* but Attorney General Richard Thornburgh advised Bush that codifying these guidelines did more than restore *Griggs:* It introduced quotas by stealth.

The Bush administration, like the Democrats, believed that some of the decisions, particularly *Lorance* and *Patterson,* had gone too far; thus it was willing to consider legislative relief. The president would not accept the Kennedy-Hawkins bill, however. It was, he insisted, a "quota bill" and one that would encourage litigiousness, enriching lawyers and harming businesses without promoting the cause of civil rights. A *Washington Post* story on April 5, 1990, reports a recommendation by Attorney General Richard Thornburgh that Bush veto the Kennedy-Hawkins bill if it were to pass.[37] The article quotes Ralph Neas, executive director of the Leadership Conference for Civil Rights, as saying, "What Thornburgh is asking the president to do is be the only other president except for Andrew Johnson and Ronald Reagan to veto a civil rights bill," something that would be inconsistent with his professed commitment to oppose discrimination. However, Thornburgh had reportedly told Bush that, rather that merely returning the law to the pre-*Ward's Cove* condition, the bill would actually set new standards for businesses that would be impossible to meet and would therefore lead them to avoid lawsuits by adopting "a silent practice of quota hiring and promotion."

Bush's evolving position on these issues can be traced through a series of speeches he delivered in 1990 and 1991. First, in brief remarks in the Rose Garden commemorating the reauthorization of the Civil Rights Commission, the president professed his commitment to the same goals as those of the commission but warned against quotas. He said that "this administration is committed to action that is truly affirmative, positive action in every sense, to strike down all barriers to advancement of every kind for all people."[38] He contended that "this administration seeks equal opportunity and equal protection under the law for all Americans."[39] Moreover, he asserted that Senator Kennedy and Representative Hawkins shared these goals, but he also warned, "We must see that true affirmative action is not reduced to some empty slogan." He told his listeners, "No one here today would want me to sign a bill whose unintended consequences are quotas because quotas are wrong and they violate the most basic principles of our civil rights tradition and the most basic principles of the promise of democracy." Minority communities, he insisted, deserve better. Then, lest there be any doubt, he proclaimed, "I want to sign a civil rights bill, but I will not sign a quota bill."[40]

These brief remarks reveal the basic components of Bush's rhetorical position. He proclaimed his support for the goals of equal opportunity and asserted that they were shared. This meant that any dispute between the president and his adversaries could be reduced to one of means. He implied that there was a difference between "true" affirmative action and some other kind, which he described as "some empty slogan." This dissociation—the dividing of the concept of affirmative action into acceptable and unacceptable forms—is not fleshed out in this speech, although it would be in later remarks. It is clear, however, that quotas (a term left undefined in this speech) do not constitute true affirmative action. In fact, they are a perversion of it. They violate basic principles of the civil rights movement itself, presumably the principle that "no one in this country should be excluded from opportunity."[41] Furthermore, this is true whether quotas are explicitly provided for or are an "unintended consequence" of well-intentioned legislation. The president does not specifically say that the emerging Kennedy-Hawkins bill is a quota bill, but the speech warns Congress not to pass such a bill because he will surely veto it if they do. Optimistically predicting that his warning will be understood, he immediately followed his veto threat by predicting, "I think we can work it out."[42] He then proposed standards for a successful civil rights bill.

The second text warranting attention is also brief. It consists of remarks the president made at a brief "drop-by" at the meeting of the

National Council of La Raza in Washington, D.C., on July 18, 1990. The original draft of the speech contains no reference to quotas or to the civil rights issue at all.[43] A lengthy handwritten section was added at the request of David Demarest, assistant to the president for communications. In the insert, Bush refers to a letter he had received from Morris B. Abram, who had been active in the civil rights struggle of the 1960s, was a former president of Brandeis University, was a Reagan appointee to the Civil Rights Commission, and was currently serving as U.S. representative to the European office of the United Nations. In his letter Abram had written, "All my life, even in the darkest days of segregated Georgia, I fought against the principle of color preference, then known as 'white supremacy.' This bill institutionalizes that principle under the false flag of civil rights. It is not a civil rights bill but a quota bill because it will achieve precisely what the landmark 1964 Civil Rights Act stood foursquare against."[44] It is worth noting that Abram, whom Bush quotes approvingly, went farther than the president had gone in his May remarks. Whereas Bush had been speaking hypothetically, Abram specifically indicted the Kennedy-Hawkins bill as a quota bill and made clear that a quota bill could not possibly be a civil rights bill; indeed, it would be aligned with the discredited principle of white supremacy.

In his letter, Abram had quoted Frederick Douglass in 1871, saying that "Equality of numbers has nothing to do with equality of attainment." The president cited this statement and then elaborated on his opposition to quotas: "And we all know quotas aren't right. They are not fair. They divide society instead of bringing people together." He then referred specifically to his immediate audience, saying, "And as leaders and representatives of the Hispanic-American community, I owe it to you to see that this legislation does not say to the young kids, you only fit in if you fit into a certain numbered quota. That is not the American dream."[45]

Abram's letter included other ideas that Bush did not quote directly in this speech but that would shape his thinking and that of his advisers. First, Abram explained how the Kennedy-Hawkins bill would result in quotas: "[I]t creates a presumption of guilt so difficult to overcome and so costly to fight that employers will simply capitulate and hire by the numbers."[46] Second, he appealed to Bush to take advantage of the opportunity to "forge a new and lasting civil rights consensus. Every opinion poll confirms that the American people, including blacks, share the goals of equal opportunity and color blindness." Third, elaborating on that consensus, Abram said that Americans "will support the vision of Martin Luther King Jr., who urged that we judge ourselves not by the color of our skin but 'by the content of their character.' " Although this appropriation of a line from King's "I Have a Dream" speech had become a feature of conservative rhetoric during the 1980s, this may have been the first time that it was brought to the attention of the president's close advisors. It would be featured prominently in another speech the following year, without any reference to Abram.

The day that the president spoke to La Raza, the Senate had just passed the Kennedy-Hawkins bill by a vote of 65 to 34. During the course of the debate, Senators Edward Kennedy and Orrin Hatch had argued at length whether the bill really restored *Griggs* or did something else and whether it would result in quotas. Kennedy regarded as "spurious" the charge that the bill would lead to quotas. "Any Senator," he said, "who offers the quotas issue as a basis for voting against cloture simply does not want to end job discrimination and guarantee equal opportunity for all Americans." Hatch insisted that Kennedy's bill did not incorporate the exact language from *Griggs*—language that he said the president would accept—and even as Kennedy indicated that he was willing to use what he said was the exact language, Hatch still regarded the measure as a quota bill.[47]

President Bush was not satisfied with the Kennedy-Hawkins bill but was not willing to give up hope that changes could be made. In fact, he appealed to the leadership of La Raza for their help in inducing the House to make those changes when it took up the bill: "[L]egal changes—they're relatively small—to make the changes needed to ensure that a bill does not result in quotas that could somehow inadvertently work to the detriment of the very kids you all are trying to help, changes needed to ensure a bill that will protect the rights of all Americans and injure the rights of none."[48]

The House, however, proved as insistent on the Kennedy-Hawkins bill as the Senate was, and it passed there on August 3 by a vote of 272 to 154. The bill went to conference committee for the reconciliation of differences. In an attempt to defuse the quota issue, the resulting bill included language that denied any purpose of instituting or encouraging quotas. The revised bill passed both houses in mid-October.

On October 20, the president announced in a brief statement that he would veto the bill, and he returned it to Congress accompanied by a veto message.

The October 20 statement was simple enough. Bush declared the Civil Rights Act of 1990 to be a quota bill because "inescapably it will have the effect of forcing businesses to adopt quotas in hiring and promotions." Again he stated, "I will not sign a quota bill. Instead of solving problems, quotas foster divisiveness and litigation, set group against group, minority against minority, and in so doing, do more to promote legal fees then [sic] civil rights."[49] Nevertheless, the president repeated his support for "legislation to strengthen our employment discrimination laws" and repeated that he had signed the Americans with Disabilities Act, which he called "the most sweeping civil rights bill in 25 years."[50] As if to emphasize his bona fides, President Bush announced that when he vetoed the Kennedy-Hawkins bill, he would also send proposed language that would correct the bill, making it "a true civil rights bill that I would like to see become law."[51]

The actual veto message of October 22 contains similar arguments, but the structure and emphasis are different. Bush expresses regret at having to veto the Kennedy-Hawkins bill because there are some parts of it that he endorses. Discrimination, he insists, "is worse than wrong. It is a fundamental evil that tears at the fabric of our society, and one that all Americans should and must oppose."[52] One way to oppose it, the president points out, would be for Congress to quickly enact the alternative bill that he had just submitted. Interestingly, he claims that his measure "contains several important provisions that are similar to provisions in" the bill he had just vetoed. There follow eight bullet points listing these similarities and the assertion that "the congressional majority and I are on common ground regarding these important provisions."[53]

Given these similarities, then, why did the president have to veto the Kennedy-Hawkins bill? Because, he insisted, it was not really a civil rights bill at all. "Despite the use of the term 'civil rights' in the title," he maintained, "the bill actually employs a maze of highly legalistic language to introduce the destructive force of quotas into our Nation's employment system."[54] Without mentioning that the bill included language disclaiming quotas, Bush asserted that the bill created "powerful incentives" for employers to adopt them because of the "new and very technical rules of litigation" that it contained.

These would create burdens of proof that employers could not satisfy; so, "unable to defend legitimate practices in court, employers will be driven to adopt quotas in order to avoid liability."[55]

After identifying other defects in the bill (principally the fact that it would encourage litigation rather than alternative means of dispute resolution), Bush reaffirmed his commitment to the goals of civil rights: "Our goal and our promise has been equal opportunity and protection under the law. That is a bedrock principle from which we cannot retreat." In a revealing passage, he acknowledged that it was tempting to sign any bill with the words "civil rights" in the title, particularly since, for much of our history, presumptions had run the other way. Nevertheless, he had to resist this temptation lest he actually undercut the goal of civil rights. As he said, "when our efforts, however well-intentioned, result in quotas, equal opportunity is not advanced but thwarted. The very commitment to justice and equality that is offered as the reason why this bill should be signed requires me to veto it."[56] To uphold civil rights, Bush had to veto a bill that professed to strengthen civil rights because it actually did the opposite and undermined civil rights by introducing quotas, not in so many words but as the inescapable effect of the proof requirements it otherwise imposed on employers in discrimination cases.

Obviously the president had already decided to veto the bill before he received an October 22 memorandum from Attorney General Richard Thornburgh, but this document offers detailed analysis supporting Bush's position. Sections 3 and 4 of the bill, the Attorney General argued, "create strong incentives for employers to adopt quotas. Although putatively needed to 'restore' the law that existed before the Supreme Court's opinion in *Ward's Cove*," these portions of the law "actually engage in a sweeping rewrite of employment discrimination." They go far beyond shifting the burden of proof from plaintiff to defendant in disparate-impact cases by creating a presumption of discrimination whenever statistical disparity in the workforce could be shown and by restricting an employer's ability to prove business necessity. This was not a return to the situation before *Ward's Cove*, Thornburgh explained, because earlier cases had always focused on "the impact of *particular* hiring practices." In other words, rather than merely overturning *Ward's Cove*, the bill used new language that would weight the scales far too heavily against employers. "In combination," the attorney general concluded, "these provisions will force employers to chose between (1) lengthy litigation, under rules rigged heavily against them, or (2) adopting policies that ensure that their numbers come out 'right.' Put another way, the bill exerts strong pressure on employers to adopt surreptitious quotas."[57]

The Thornburgh memorandum also took up the proponents' claim that Bush's concerns were answered through language stating that nothing in the bill "shall be construed to require or encourage an employer to adopt hiring or promotion quotas." This language would not do the job, he insisted. The problem is not that the bill would "directly require or encourage quotas, but rather that employers will in fact choose to adopt quotas in order to avoid having to defend their hiring practices under the unreasonable litigation rules established by the bill." Employers would feel the need to establish quotas regardless of whether the bill encouraged them to do so. For these reasons, the attorney general concluded, "S.2104 would do far more to disrupt our legal system and to disappoint the legitimate expectations of our citizens for equal opportunity than it would to advance the goal, to which you and I are both committed, of strengthening the laws against employment discrimination."[58]

As the Civil Rights Act of 1990 moved from consideration to final passage, then, Bush's rhetorical position hardened. Earlier, he had said that he would not sign a quota bill. By October, he was clearly *defining* the Kennedy-Hawkins measure as a quota bill and calling it the antithesis of civil rights. He did so notwithstanding the fact that the bill itself disclaimed quotas. That was just a smokescreen, he believed, because the bill's inescapable result would be to encourage employers to adopt them. It is worth noting that this crucial link in the argument—imagining what employers would do—is based entirely on speculation. The president and his aides assume that language in the bill will be interpreted a certain way and that in consequence employers will need to adopt quotas. In none of the discourse is this argument supported historically or even by employers' statements of their likely plans. The argument is based entirely on the administration's "close textual analysis" of the bill's language. "Quotas" became a symbolic framing of the issue chosen by the administration.[59]

The transcript of Press Secretary Marlin Fitzwater's briefing on October 22 suggests that the press was skeptical about the president's position. One reporter asked whether there was any evidence that the bill would lead to quotas. Another said, "it sounds like what you're saying is there is no evidence that you can rely on that this would be a quota bill; that it is only Boyden Gray and Dick Thornburgh's opinion that it would be a quota bill." Another pointed out that the head of the Civil Rights Commission did not believe that it was a quota bill and asked "whether the president has confidence in the head of the Civil Rights Commission and, if so, why he's not listening to him on what presumably is the most important civil rights matter before him." Still another asked why the president was not willing to err on the side of civil rights advocates since if, in fact, the bill required quotas, the Supreme Court would overturn it. To this last question, Fitzwater could only reply, "Well, we think it would be better to send up a bill that's a good bill and pass it and see what happens."[60]

For this reason, it should not surprise us that Kennedy-Hawkins supporters rejected this interpretation of their handiwork. Far from defending quota bills, they bristled at the suggestion that the act Congress had passed was any such thing. Some even suggested that the Bush administration was introducing the devil term "quotas" in order to mislead the public and to conceal its true opposition to civil rights. Senate Majority Leader George Mitchell (D-ME), said on *Meet the Press,* "The president's characterization of this as a quota bill is wholly inaccurate." Ralph Neas of the Leadership Conference for Civil Rights said that Bush's proposed alternative was a "cynical" attempt to give him an excuse for vetoing the act passed by Congress. Jesse Jackson charged that the president's purpose was political and that he was playing the race card in order to appeal to right-wing extremists in the 1990 midterm elections. In a revealing allusion, Jackson went on to say, "We hope that President Bush will not Willie-Horton-ize the 1990 campaign as he did the 1988 campaign."[61] The suggested similarity was that in both cases the president invoked a seemingly race-neutral symbol in order to encourage race-conscious voting, giving racist whites a legitimate means to act on their prejudices and dividing the country while he professed to unify it. Democrats in Congress vowed to override the veto, and on October 24, the Senate came within one vote of doing so.

There is little doubt that quotas played a role in the 1990 midterm elections. In a hotly contested North Carolina Senate race, incumbent Republican Jesse Helms defeated his challenger, Charlotte's Mayor

Harvey Gantt, in a campaign that prominently featured a pair of white hands holding a rejection letter and a voice-over proclaiming that the person needed a job and was qualified but that "they" had to give it to a minority. Greene maintains that the quota issue was also instrumental in the election of Pete Wilson as governor of California and in David Duke's carrying 60 percent of the white vote in his unsuccessful bid for a Louisiana Senate seat.[62]

George Bush in 1991

In the newly elected Congress, Democrats vowed to reintroduce the vetoed legislation, giving it the symbolic designation H.R.1. This time the bill included language that not only disclaimed quotas but also outlawed them. Administration officials argued that even this was not good enough. An unsigned memorandum in Press Secretary Marlin Fitzwater's files argues, "The new 'anti-quota' amendment to H.R.1 is actually a pro-quota position." The paper suggests that this language "does *nothing* to change the provisions in H.R.1 that will drive employers to use surreptitious quotas and preferences." Moreover, the memo argues, the term "quota" was defined in H.R.1—the first time in the controversy, by the way, that it was defined at all—so as to permit what it purported to ban. A long as applicants were marginally qualified for a job, employers were permitted to fill quotas with *less qualified persons* of a particular race, sex, or religion. And, as the author of the unsigned paper claimed, "The definition of a 'quota' is cleverly worded so as to make it easy to evade. Under the definition, a quota is not a quota unless the fixed number or percentage '*must* be attained.' "[63]

President Bush also took up this theme. In remarks at the commencement ceremony at the FBI Academy in Quantico, Virginia, although speaking mainly about crime, the president complained that "congressional leaders want to pass a bill that would lead employers to adopt hiring quotas and unfair job preferences." They proposed an antiquota amendment, but, the president warned, "This shouldn't fool anyone. If you look closely at the amendment, you'll see that it endorses quotas. Even the section that supposedly outlaws quotas endorses quotas. It defines the 'Q' word . . . so narrowly that it would allow employers to establish personnel systems based on numbers, not on merit."[64] Although less explicitly, Bush made the same warning in a major policy speech he delivered at the U.S. Military Academy at West Point on June 1.

The West Point speech, though, reflected a broader strategy. While continuing to decry quotas, the president sought to redefine affirmative action and, for that matter, civil rights. Moreover, he tried to position his understanding, rather than that of the supporters of the vetoed bill, as consistent with the original and true understanding of civil rights in America. His apparent goal, in short, was to reverse positions so that he and his conservative supporters emerged as the true defenders of civil rights. Celebrating the successful integration of the military on a color-blind basis provided the backdrop against which he would set out his views of affirmative action.

The overall strategy of the speech was suggested in a May 20 memo from David Demarest to White House counsel C. Boyden Gray. Demarest urged an attack on "the politics of racial suspicion," by which he meant an emphasis on groups rather than individuals. He also suggested a focus on "equality of opportunity, versus equality of results" and the need to expand rather than merely to redistribute opportunity. As examples of expanding opportunity, he suggested other aspects of the administration's legislative proposal, such as school choice and anticrime legislation as well as the "vigorous enforcement of civil rights laws."[65] The successive drafts of the West Point speech followed this advice. As the drafting process reached its end, speechwriter Curt Smith offered a more succinct summary of the speech strategy: "You then begin a larger discussion of civil rights, stressing the importance of 'character' not 'color.' You focus on how this approach has given us an army that is not only effective, but also one of the most integrated institutions in the country. You discuss the danger of quotas and race norming, and call attention to the merits of your 1991 Civil Rights Bill. Other means of empowering the individual are highlighted as necessary to equality of opportunity."[66]

The speech follows this general plan. It celebrates the successful integration of the military, achieved despite the fact that "the Army and West Point don't recruit minorities. They recruit soldiers." It acknowledges that racism and bigotry persist but pledges that the administration will fight them, thereby reducing the issue to one of means: "The real question is not whether to fight these evils but how."[67]

For guidance as to means, the president harked back to the civil rights movement of the late 1950s and early 1960s. Bush noted that the movement "reshaped a nation by appealing to this American character" and "invited people to join hands in common cause against evil, to build a society upon common decency and respect."[68] The key appeal here, of course, is to unity of purpose. In Bush's view, the civil rights movement did not contest the American dream but accepted it—sharing dominant national values—and then challenged the country to live up to its own ideals.

Immediately after this statement, the president cited Martin Luther King's reference in "I Have a Dream" to a time when "our children would—and to quote—'not be judged by the color of their skin but by the content of their character.' "[69] The president's implication, of course, is that group-centered remedies for discrimination are at odds with this basic premise and that Martin Luther King Jr., were he still alive, would oppose them. Bush thereby participates in the practice among conservatives to recognize King's iconic stature to enlist his words in opposition to affirmative action. It is unknown whether his writers had Morris Abram's 1990 advice in mind, but they followed the same course that he had suggested.

It is interesting to trace how the reference to King evolved in the consecutive drafts of this speech. The second draft, by Curt Smith and Jennifer Grossman, contains this admonition: "Let us remember how the civil rights movement began. It began as a challenge—that all citizens cooperate as members of the human race, not compete as members of one race against another. It invoked the dream that 'one day children would not be judged by the color of their skin but by the content of their character.' "[70] Here the reference is more general, and King is not identified as the author of the statement. This may suggest that, by 1991, the phrase had become a commonplace in civil rights discourse, encapsulating the difference between a focus on individuals and one on groups. The remarks stayed in this form until the sixth draft, when another staffer (presumably Roger Porter) spotted it and noted in the margin, "Is this not a Martin Luther King quote? Attribution needed."[71] While Porter's concern was for proper acknowledgement of a source, the fact is that identifying King made the statement much more strategically useful for the president. It enabled him to set the symbol of the civil rights movement against the Civil Rights Act of 1990, implicitly suggesting that the legislation was mistitled, that it threatened rather than promoted civil rights, and that his veto was the proper course.

Later in the speech, the president again refers to the early civil rights movement to contrast it with present-day advocates of civil rights. Then, "black and white, the great civil rights leaders . . . deplored intolerance, demanded equality of opportunity and equality under the law." But now, "some talk not of opportunity but of redistributing rights. They'd pit one group against another, encourage people to think of others as competitors, not colleagues. We need to adopt a more unifying, moral, and noble approach."[72]

The president makes several moves in this passage. First, he distinguishes between the early civil rights movement and the present: Then we were united; now we are divided. A united approach is better. Second, he suggests that the early movement focused on opportunity, whereas current advocates focus on rights. Opportunity is better. Third, opportunity can be expanded so that one need not suffer when another gains. In contrast, the supply of rights is finite, so redistribution is a zero-sum game. Expanding the pie is better. Finally, by implication Bush identifies himself with the early civil rights movement, suggesting that his positions are better.

Although this paragraph may seem hard hitting, it is actually toned down from earlier drafts. The second draft brands those who differ with the president's philosophy as supporters of "an America of, by, and for the government. They would pit one group against another—fracturing America into divisive special interests." The fifth draft suggests that those who disagree with the president are "ignoring history." Referring to their alleged preference for redistributing a finite supply of rights, the draft has the president say, "I respect these views. I also reject them. For what they demand—often explicitly, more often implicitly—is the use of quotas." The ninth draft retains the reference to quotas and adds, "That approach dehumanizes each of us; demeans us."[73] The final version of the text establishes a distinction between the 1960s' and the 1990s' civil rights advocates but does not at this point refer explicitly to quotas. The president gets to it later.

Having suggested that the issue is about means and that the means championed by the early civil rights movement are better than those of today, President Bush next takes up the nature of affirmative action. He dissociates the term, distinguishing between redistributing rights and "true affirmative action." The latter consists of "good faith efforts to provide opportunity for individuals based on merit, to reach out and create truly equal opportunity for those who have been left behind, those who have been excluded." Explaining how this is to be done, the president stresses the word "affirmative." In contradistinction to "a Rubik's cube of workplace guarantees," he favors efforts to "inspire people of all races to nurture affirmative values, affirmative views of themselves, affirmative lives."[74] Affirmative action has metamorphosed into "affirmative lives," a term that was introduced in the second draft of the speech. There, however, "affirmative lives" are characterized as "something better than affirmative action."[75] In the final text they are seen as the embodiment of "true affirmative action." The difference is significant. Rather than combating affirmative action, Bush has chosen to co-opt the term by shifting its definition.

The emphasis on "affirmative lives" permits the president to characterize a large part of his legislative program, though not ostensibly about civil rights, as part of an affirmative-action program, properly understood. Following speechwriter Curt Smith's suggestions, he mentions reform of public housing, enterprise zones, anticrime legislation, and "community opportunity areas." Just as Lyndon Johnson sometimes described the whole Great Society as a civil rights program because it expanded opportunity, George Bush describes his domestic program as affirmative action. There is an obvious difference, though. Johnson sought to use government as the means to expand opportunity. Bush believed that opportunity would grow by reducing the influence of government and, as he put it, "shift power from the heavy hand of the state to the hands that run the home, raise the family. . . . These policies give power back to the people, and they move us toward achieving the goal of equal opportunity."[76] Only at this point, toward the end of the speech, does Bush introduce the concept of quotas. He defends the administration's bill as consistent with affirmative action as he has just described it. Then he says, "I know there's another so-called civil rights bill out there, but it's a quota bill, regardless of how its authors dress it up. You can't put a sign on a pig and say it's a horse."[77] This is a slightly toned-down version of the president's claim in the Quantico speech that the Democrats' 1991 bill, even though it purports to ban quotas, actually promotes them. The line about the pig and the horse, which comes closest to making the point explicitly, is not on the cards prepared for the president and presumably was added spontaneously during delivery.[78] Unlike the previous year, however, the president does not threaten to veto this bill. Instead, he ends the speech with a plea to "cast off now the politics of division," to "build a society in which people respect each other," and to "honor the true grandeur of America, the dignity of the individual."[79]

In sum, then, the West Point speech sets out President Bush's position as an opponent of racial discrimination and a supporter of civil rights who believes that the issue is not whether to fight discrimination but how. The means are to be inferred from the lessons of the early civil rights movement, which is contrasted with the current version. Rather than redistributing a fixed supply of rights, we should expand opportunities. That is the true meaning of affirmative action, and it is achieved by the program Bush supports, not by quota bills.

A significant majority of Congress, however, was not convinced. On October 30, rather than accept the administration's bill, the Senate passed the Civil Rights Act of 1991 by a vote of 93 to 5. The House had passed it early in the summer by a vote of 273 to 158. If he were to be consistent with his approach of the previous year, Bush would have vetoed this bill, particularly since he had said in Quantico and implied at West Point that it was still a quota bill, which he had defined as a priori unacceptable. However, he chose to sign it. Both John Robert Greene and Herbert Parmet suggest that he did so because the Clarence Thomas hearings and the campaign of David Duke in Louisiana had fanned the flames of racial unrest and because Bush was in need of a compromise move.[80] C. Boyden Gray ridicules these explanations and says that the key factor was Senator Kennedy's acceptance of language taken from the Americans with Disabilities Act rather than the Uniform Guidelines.[81]

Bush's earlier statements, though, created a significant rhetorical problem: How could he avoid the charges that he was waffling and that his actions reflected no commitment to principles but only the shifting winds of political expediency? The president tried to address this problem in brief remarks as he signed the Civil Rights Act on November 21. He began by reaffirming his own commitment to civil rights, telling listeners, "from day one I told the American people that I wanted a civil rights bill that advances the cause of equal opportunity" because discrimination "is worse than wrong. It's an evil that strikes at the very heart of the American ideal."[82] For these reasons, he was pleased to sign the Civil Rights Act of 1991. To achieve rhetorical consistency with his statements of 1990, he had to somehow distinguish this act from the bill that was its predecessor. He did so by contending that, unlike the bill of 1990, "a bill I was forced to veto, this bill will not encourage quotas or racial preferences because this bill will not create lawsuits on the basis of numbers alone."[83] He did not note the substitution of the ADA language for the Uniform Guidelines, and he did not show that the Uniform Guidelines would have led to quotas. In a press conference a few days later, Bush made an even starker assertion: The act he had just signed "would be a source of pride for all Americans. It does not resort to quotas and it strengthens the cause of equality in the workplace." Alluding to speculation that he had labeled the 1990 act "a quota bill" as a red herring because he did not want civil rights legislation at all, Bush said, "We have a civil rights bill; it is not a quota bill, and I couldn't be happier because I have not liked . . . these characterizations that I didn't want a civil rights bill. I've wanted it all along."[84]

This distinction allowed the president to maintain consistency of his principles. Drawing the contrast between 1990 and 1991 was the central strategy in a draft outline of his remarks, which had two main topics: "last year's bill" and "this year's bill."[85] Earlier drafts had not made clear the reason that the 1990 bill was a quota bill but the 1991 bill was not, so the "because this bill will not encourage lawsuits" clause was added later.[86] The president insisted on the distinction although he did not explain why he had called the 1991 bill a quota bill in the Quantico and West Point speeches discussed earlier. It was this shift, at least as much as the shift from 1990 to 1991, that would create credibility problems for him.

President Bush acknowledged the appeal of the phrase "civil rights." An early draft says, "No one likes to veto a civil rights bill, especially not me."[87] In the final text, this was changed to "No one likes to oppose a bill containing the words 'civil rights,' especially me."[88] The final version is a sharper statement. Rather than acknowledging that the 1990 act was really a civil rights bill, the president implies that the words "civil rights" were placed in the bill's title to appeal for public support even thought the bill is really not a civil rights bill.

If no one likes to oppose a bill containing the words "civil rights," that would be true of members of Congress as well. So President Bush praises those "who stood with us against counterproductive legislation last year . . . as well as . . . those who led the way toward the important agreement we've reached today."[89] Originally this was to be a highly partisan reference. The second draft had the president say, "We had to work hard for this agreement. But the credit goes to the dedicated Republicans in Congress . . . especially Senators Dole and Danforth—for ensuring that I had a bill I could sign."[90] The final version offers "a tip of the hat" to Kennedy and Hawkins, who "got the ball rolling," and, with reference to those who made its signing possible, he explained, "I'm talking about Democrats, I'm talking about Republicans, and those outside the Congress who played a constructive role."[91] Having lavished praise on all of those involved, he then concludes the speech, as he did at West Point, by suggesting that civil rights laws were necessary but not sufficient "to ease racial tensions in America."[92] Full achievement of the goal required many other measures as well, and, as he had done at West Point, Bush incorporated virtually all of his domestic program under the rubric of equal opportunity.

One other aspect of this speech is worthy of note. Shortly before the address was to be delivered, White House counsel C. Boyden Gray reportedly issued regulations that would have ended the government's own affirmative-action programs. In fact, as Gray subsequently explained, his regulations would have required *review,* not elimination, of government affirmative-action programs—much like the review that President Clinton later ordered.[93] But the report of language eliminating governmental affirmative-action programs created a furor: The president, while proclaiming his support for affirmative action, in reality seemed to be undermining it. The press suggested that perhaps the ending of the government's own affirmative-action programs was a quid pro quo for Bush's dropping his opposition to the draft congressional bill. In any event, to stem the furor, the administration retracted the proposed language, and the president added to his remarks a statement not found in the early drafts: "I say again today: I support affirmative action. Nothing in this bill overturns the Government's affirmative action programs."[94] Even so, however, to show his commitment to affirmative action, Bush contextualized it in his previous attempts to broaden the meaning of the term: "This administration is committed to action that is truly affirmative, positive action in every sense, to strike down all barriers to advancement of every kind for all people."[95] This, it hardly need be said, is a vaguer and looser conception of affirmative action that omits compensatory treatment to remedy past discrimination. The president also makes no explicit mention of the retraction of Gray's proposed language.

From the administration's standpoint, the 1991 bill was acceptable because—if properly interpreted—it was not a quota bill.[96] Critics were quick to note, however, that it was substantially similar to the bill that Bush had vetoed the year before. Whether it was similar or different turns on the question of whether *any* of the various linguistic formulas would have required quotas. Whereas the administration claimed that Congress had complied with its insistence that legislative language be modified, others attributed the end of the controversy to the president's capitulation—to his abandonment of the assertion that the bill would encourage racial quotas.[97] From this point of view, Bush's shift was not principled but only expedient, reflecting the need to dampen racial antagonism after the Clarence Thomas hearings and the Louisiana candidacy of David Duke. Rather than receive credit for his conversion, he was pilloried for inconsistency. Greene, for example, observes that, unlike in 1990, Bush's approval rating among nonwhites dropped when he agreed to sign the 1991 bill—to a low of 28 percent, from which it never recovered.[98] Certainly the president was sensitive to this reaction. He not only used his November 25 press conference as a forum in which to state that he had wanted a bill all along, but he also instructed his senior advisors to stress his own commitments. Noting that "the press are playing 'Bush moves right,' etc.," in a February, 1992, memo, the president admonished Bob Teeter, Sam Skinner, and Dave Demarest, "We should keep reiterating our stand against racism and bigotry—let's be sure it gets in all our major speeches. I owe this to the country and I feel it deeply."[99]

Conclusion

From this detailed examination of George Bush's major statements on civil rights and affirmative action, we can extract six recurrent features of his discourse:

1. Bush professed his agreement with the goals of civil rights advocates—in particular, the goal of ending employment discrimination—and thereby portrayed the controversy as "only" about means. This is both an appeal for good will and an attempt to minimize the issue, relegating it to matters of technical detail that did not raise questions of principle. This could be interpreted cynically as an appeal for quiescence while the lawyers "work it out" or, at the very least, as an attempt to create a space in which Bush could lodge objections that amounted to less of a frontal attack on affirmative action than that lodged by Ronald Reagan.

2. Bush defined the opposition measure as a "quota bill." He thus appealed to the devil term "quotas" in order to blunt the god term "civil rights," continuing a trend that had begun in the 1960s. But he was subtler than some of his predecessors. Rather than declare affirmative action per se to mean quotas, he made this judgment about the Democrats' bill. He thereby at least opened the door for a possible alternative that defended affirmative action without invoking quotas. Yet the president advanced no argument to support the characterization of the act as a quota bill. He never even defined the word "quota." Rather, he stipulated the connection, fastening the negatively charged symbol to the legislative act so that the stigma of the former might transfer to the latter.[100]

3. Using the opportunity he thereby gave himself, Bush dissociated affirmative action into the false and the true. True affirmative action meant removing barriers, not ensuring compensatory actions. It treated people as individuals, not as members of groups. Furthermore, by focusing on expanding freedom and limiting the government's role, it empowered people to live "affirmative lives."

4. Bush identified his broader conception of affirmative action with the trailblazing civil rights movement of the early 1960s. He did so by general reference and by specifically invoking the "color of their skin" vs. "content of their character" contrast from Martin Luther King's "I Have a Dream" speech. He thereby suggested that his views occupied the high moral ground that had inspired a national consensus and that it

was his opponents who had abandoned the earlier vision and introduced divisiveness and rancor.

5. Bush clearly distinguished between opportunity and guarantees. The latter required redistribution of a fixed supply of rights and hence was zero-sum. The former involved expanding the pie—a metaphor that implies that everyone can be a winner. This theme not only permitted him to reinstate an appeal for equal opportunity that had characterized the early civil rights movement but also enabled him to associate himself with a traditional American belief in boundless possibilities and a reluctance to accept limits.

6. Finally, as Lyndon Johnson had done from the other end of the political spectrum, Bush broadened the understanding of what counts as a civil rights measure. Not just legislation aimed at racial discrimination but also many other parts of the administration's domestic program contributed to the goal. School reform, redevelopment of the inner city, anticrime and antidrug legislation, job creation and economic growth, and community service were among the elements to which the president referred. They would all be necessary to achieve "the American dream of equal opportunity for all."[101] Conversely, of course, any progress the administration would be able to make on these fronts was not just an initiative to address its intended target; it also counted as progress toward civil rights.

Left unanswered by this analysis, ultimately, is the question of George Bush's motive. Did he genuinely support the cause of civil rights but honestly disagree about methods, or was his opposition to quotas invented in order to mask his opposition to civil rights and discarded when it became politically necessary? There is no "smoking gun" in the Bush Library that answers this question, and it is doubtful that one will be found even when the confidential communications among the president's advisors are opened to scholars in 2005.[102] Bush's unwillingness to substantiate or explain his claim that the 1990 bill was a quota bill, his failure even to precisely define "quotas" so that it would become something other than a devil term, and his seeming flip-flop on whether the 1991 act entailed quotas are troubling in what they suggest about the sincerity of his motive. On the other hand, there is no reason to doubt the president's often-expressed abhorrence of bigotry and racism or his personal and long-standing commitment to root out traces of discrimination. It may be that it was only insufficient rhetorical sophistication that put him in a difficult position.

Regardless of George Bush's motives, his statements clearly illustrate a transformation in public discourse on race over the years since 1965. Put simply, the force of the god term "civil rights" has been blunted by the devil term "quotas." Richard Nixon introduced this tension by simultaneously implementing and condemning quotalike programs. Ronald Reagan went farther, regarding affirmative-action programs as quotas by definition and therefore unacceptable. George Bush began to tease out different meanings of affirmative action. If he eased away from Reagan's more absolute stance, he also established that affirmative action was not an intrinsic good and that it could sometimes undermine rather than promote civil rights. This position rendered affirmative action something of an essentially contested concept, a status it has retained since the early 1990s. George Bush's successor was elected with strong support from African Americans and was unquestionably committed to racial justice. Yet his National Conversation on Race was devoid of measures to either resolve or transcend the deeply contested meaning of affirmative action, and President Clinton's own conclusion was that we should "mend it, not end it"—a conclusion that acknowledged that there was much about it that did not seem right. It is an interesting question whether Lyndon Johnson would have understood.

Notes

1. *Public Papers of the Presidents: Lyndon B. Johnson, 1965* (Washington, D.C.: Government Printing Office, 1966), 2:636. For an analysis of the Howard University speech, see David Zarefsky, "Lyndon Johnson Redefines 'Equal Opportunity': The Beginnings of Affirmative Action," *Central States Speech Journal* 31 (Summer, 1980): 85–94.
2. Ibid.
3. C. Boyden Gray, remarks at the sixth annual Conference on Presidential Rhetoric, Texas A&M University, College Station, Mar. 4, 2000.
4. John David Skrentny, *The Ironies of Affirmative Action: Politics, Cul-*

ture, and Justice in America (Chicago: University of Chicago Press, 1996), p. 14.

5. Hugh Davis Graham, *The Civil Rights Era: Origins and Development of National Policy, 1960–1972* (New York: Oxford University Press, 1990), p. 110.

6. *Congressional Record,* 88th Cong., 2d sess., June 15, 1964, p. 13821.

7. Graham, *The Civil Rights Era,* pp. 104, 120.

8. Ibid., p. 174.

9. Ibid., pp. 456, 461.

10. Richard M. Nixon, "Acceptance Speech," *Vital Speeches of the Day* 34 (Sept. 1, 1968): 676.

11. Skrentny, *The Ironies,* p. 195.

12. "Statement Urging Senate and House Conferees to Permit Continued Implementation of the Philadelphia Plan," *Public Papers of the Presidents: Richard Nixon, 1969* (Washington, D.C.: Government Printing Office, 1970), 2:1038.

13. For differing views of Nixon's motivation, compare Joan Hoff, *Nixon Reconsidered* (New York: Basic, 1994), p. 90; Skrentny, *The Ironies,* pp. 181, 209, 210; and Kenneth O'Reilly, *Nixon's Piano: Presidents and Racial Politics from Washington to Clinton* (New York: Free Press, 1995), p. 321.

14. Skrentny, *The Ironies,* p. 212.

15. For statements by Nixon reflecting these views, see *Public Papers of the Presidents: Richard Nixon, 1972* (Washington, D.C.: Government Printing Office, 1973), 2:852, 998.

16. Skrentny, *The Ironies,* p. 216; "Quotas: The Sleeper Issue of '72?" *Newsweek,* Sept. 18, 1972, pp. 36, 39.

17. "Remarks on Accepting the Presidential Nomination of the Republican National Convention," *Public Papers of the Presidents: Richard Nixon, 1972,* 2:788.

18. Commission on Party Structure and Delegate Selection, Democratic National Committee, *Mandate for Reform* (Washington, D.C.: Democratic National Committee, 1970), p. 40. A footnote to this guideline states specifically that "It is the understanding of the Commission that this is not to be accomplished by the mandatory imposition of quotas." I am grateful to Ken Bode, who served as director of research for the commission, for bringing this document to my attention.

19. Quoted in "Major Shift by White House on Rights and Race," *U.S. News and World Report,* Jan. 15, 1973, p. 13.

20. "The State of the Union: Annual Message to Congress," *Public Papers of the Presidents: Jimmy Carter, 1978* (Washington, D.C.: Government Printing Office, 1979), 1:111.

21. "Remarks at a Reagan-Bush Rally in Austin, Texas, July 25, 1984," *Public Papers of the Presidents: Ronald Reagan, 1984* (Washington, D.C.: Government Printing Office, 1985), 2:1085.

22. Thomas Byrne Edsall with Mary D. Edsall, "Race," *Atlantic Monthly,* May, 1991, p. 73.

23. *Public Papers of the Presidents: Ronald Reagan, 1981* (Washington, D.C.: Government Printing Office, 1982), 1:58.

24. A prominent example can be found in "Remarks at the International Convention of B'nai B'rith," *Public Papers of the Presidents: Ronald Reagan, 1984,* 2:1243.

25. O'Reilly, *Nixon's Piano,* p. 372.

26. "Radio Address to the Nation on Civil Rights, June 15, 1985," *Public Papers of the Presidents: Ronald Reagan, 1985* (Washington, D.C.: Government Printing Office, 1986), 1:773.

27. Ibid. Also see the president's remarks at a press conference on Feb. 11, 1986, in which the reference is more general: "We want what I think Martin Luther King asked for: We want a color-blind society." *Public Papers of the Presidents: Ronald Reagan, 1986* (Washington, D.C.: Government Printing Office, 1987), 1:201.

28. O'Reilly, *Nixon's Piano,* p. 361.

29. "The Right Has a Dream," *Extra!* May–June, 1996, p. 13. *Extra!* is published by an organization called Fairness and Accuracy in Reporting (FAIR).

30. Ibid.

31. See Nancy MacLean, "Conservative Attacks on Affirmative Action: The Evolution and Conventions of a Genre," paper presented at the annual meeting of the Organization of American Historians, Toronto, Apr., 1999, pp. 21–22.

32. "1988 Legislative and Administrative Message: A Union of Individuals," *Public Papers of the Presidents: Ronald Reagan, 1988–1989* (Washington, D.C.: Government Printing Office, 1989), 1:96.

33. "Remarks at a Republican Party Fundraising Dinner in Houston, Texas, September 22, 1988," *Public Papers of the Presidents: Ronald Reagan, 1988–1989,* 2:1202.

34. *Griggs v. Duke Power Company,* 401 U.S. 424 (1971).

35. C. Boyden Gray, "Disparate Impact: History and Consequence," *Louisiana Law Review* 54 (July, 1994): 1491. I am grateful to Gray for alerting me to this article. Interestingly, there is no substantiation in the article for this statement, which is offered as a fact, and there are no examples of the claimed pressure on employers. In the congressional debate over the Civil Rights Act of 1990, Sen. Edward M. Kennedy alleged, to the contrary, that the implementation of the *Griggs* decision had not resulted in any allegations that it constituted quotas. See U.S. Congress, *Congressional Record,* 101st Cong., 2d sess., July 10, 1990, p. 16707.

36. *Ward's Cove v. Atonio,* 490 U.S. 651 (1989).

37. Michael Isikoff and Ann Devroy, "Civil Rights Bill Veto Threatened," *Washington Post,* Apr. 5, 1990, p. A25.

38. "Remarks at a Meeting with the Commission on Civil Rights,

May 17, 1990," *Public Papers of the Presidents: George Bush, 1990* (Washington, D.C.: Government Printing Office, 1991), 1:677.

39. Ibid., p. 676.
40. Ibid.
41. Ibid., p. 675.
42. Ibid., p. 676.
43. The text is "Remarks to the National Council of La Raza, July 18, 1990," *Public Papers of the Presidents: George Bush, 1990* (Washington, D.C.: Government Printing Office, 1991), 2:1022–24. The original draft is in a memorandum from Edward E. McNally to the president, July 16, 1990, "Drop-by for National Council of La Raza, 7/18/90," White House Office of Speechwriting, speech file, drafts, 1989–1993, box 63, George Bush Presidential Library.
44. Letter from Morris B. Abram to the president, June 7, 1990, "National Council of La Raza 7/18/90," White House Office of Speechwriting, speech file, backup, chronological file, 1989–1993, box 69, George Bush Presidential Library.
45. "Remarks to the National Council of La Raza," p. 1023.
46. Letter from Morris B. Abram to the president, June 7, 1990, White House Office of Speechwriting, speech file, backup, chronological file, 1989–1993, box 69, George Bush Presidential Library.
47. U.S. Congress, *Congressional Record,* 101st Cong., 2d sess., July 10, 1990, pp. 16707–21; July 17, 1990, pp. 17656–61.
48. "Remarks to the National Council of La Raza," p. 1023.
49. "Statement on Civil Rights Legislation, October 20, 1990," *Public Papers of the Presidents: George Bush, 1990,* 2:1435–36.
50. Ibid., p. 1436.
51. Ibid., p. 1437.
52. "Message to the Senate Returning without Approval of the Civil Rights Act of 1990, October 22, 1990," *Public Papers of the Presidents: George Bush, 1990* (Washington, D.C.: Government Printing Office, 1991), 2:1437.
53. Ibid.
54. Ibid., p. 1438.
55. Ibid. Like both Thornburgh and Gray, the president put these statements forward as assertions without citing any precedents from prior experience with the uniform guidelines.
56. Ibid.
57. Memorandum from Dick Thornburgh to the president, Oct. 22, 1990, "Civil Rights [2]," White House Press Office, Marlin Fitzwater subject file, alpha file, 1989, box 5, George Bush Presidential Library. Copies of this memorandum have been removed from several other files (including the immediately preceding file in this box) on the grounds that it constitutes confidential communication between the president and his advisers. This copy, however, was left intact. It explains the attorney general's recommendation that President Bush veto the bill.

58. Ibid.

59. White House Counsel C. Boyden Gray strongly disagreed with this claim, suggesting to me that there was nothing "symbolic" about it at all and that the 1990 act would straightforwardly have introduced quotas. C. Boyden Gray, personal conversation, College Station, Tex., Mar. 4, 2000.

60. Press briefing by Marlin Fitzwater, Oct. 22, 1990, White House Press Office, Marlin Fitzwater guidance files, box 89, George Bush Presidential Library. The text of the briefing is also found in the White House Office of Speechwriting, Mark Davis subject file, 1989–1991, box 4, George Bush Presidential Library.

61. News summary, Oct. 22, 1990, White House Press Office, Marlin Fitzwater guidance files, box 89, George Bush Presidential Library.

62. John Robert Greene, *The Presidency of George Bush* (Lawrence: University Press of Kansas, 2000), p. 66. Greene cites O'Reilly, *Nixon's Piano,* p. 393. Greene inaccurately lists Gantt as mayor of Greensboro rather than Charlotte.

63. "The New 'Anti-Quota' Amendment to H.R. 1 Is Actually a Pro-Quota Provision," "Civil Rights [1]," White House Press Office, Marlin Fitzwater subject file, alpha file, 1989, box 5, George Bush Presidential Library.

64. "Remarks at the Federal Bureau of Investigation Academy Commencement Ceremony in Quantico, Virginia, May 30, 1991," *Public Papers of the Presidents: George Bush, 1991* (Washington, D.C.: Government Printing Office, 1992), 1:583.

65. Memorandum from David Demarest to C. Boyden Gray, May 20, 1991, "West Point Commencement, U.S. Military Academy, 6/1/91," White House Office of Records Management, subject file, speeches, box 136, George Bush Presidential Library.

66. Memorandum from Curt Smith to the president, May 30, 1991, "West Point Commencement, 6/1/91," White House Office of Speechwriting, speech file drafts, 1989–1993, box 96, George Bush Presidential Library.

67. "Remarks at the United States Military Academy Commencement Ceremony in West Point, New York, June 1, 1991," *Public Papers of the Presidents: George Bush, 1991* (Washington, D.C.: Government Printing Office, 1992), 1:591.

68. Ibid., p. 590.

69. Ibid.

70. Smith and Grossman's second draft for the West Point speech, May 16, 1991, White House Office of Speechwriting, Curt Smith chronological file, 1989–1992, box 2, George Bush Presidential Library.

71. Smith and Grossman's sixth draft of the West Point speech, May 28, 1991, "West Point Commencement, 6/1/91," White House Office of

Speechwriting, speech file drafts, 1989–1993, box 96, George Bush Presidential Library. The copy sent to Porter is also in this file with the marginal note quoted. There is no evidence that Porter was aware of the correspondence the previous year from Morris B. Abram suggesting the "content of their character" line from King's speech as a reason for President Bush to veto the 1990 version of the Civil Rights Act.

72. "Remarks at the United States Military Academy," p. 591.
73. Smith and Grossman's second draft for the West Point speech, May 16, 1991, and Smith and Grossman's fifth draft for the West Point speech, May 28, 1991, both drafts in White House Office of Speechwriting, Curt Smith chronological file, 1989–1992, box 2, George Bush Presidential Library; Smith and Grossman's ninth draft for the West Point speech, May 28, 1991, "West Point Commencement, 6/1/91," White House Office of Speechwriting, speech file drafts, 1989–1993, box 96, George Bush Presidential Library.
74. "Remarks at the United States Military Academy," p. 591.
75. Smith and Grossman's second draft for the West Point speech, May 16, 1991, White House Office of Speechwriting, Curt Smith chronological file, 1989–1992, box 2, George Bush Presidential Library.
76. "Remarks at the United States Military Academy," p. 591.
77. Ibid., pp. 591–92.
78. A copy of the cards prepared for the speech can be found in "West Point Commencement, U.S. Military Academy, 6/1/91," White House Office of Records Management, subject file, speeches, box 136, George Bush Presidential Library.
79. "Remarks at the United States Military Academy," p. 592.
80. Greene, *The Presidency of George Bush*, p. 159; Herbert S. Parmet, *George Bush: The Life of a Lone Star Yankee* (New York: Scribner, 1997), p. 499.
81. C. Boyden Gray, remarks at the sixth annual Conference on Presidential Rhetoric, Texas A&M University, College Station, Mar. 4, 2000.
82. "Remarks on Signing the Civil Rights Act of 1991," *Public Papers of the Presidents: George Bush, 1991* (Washington, D.C.: Government Printing Office, 1992), 2:1502.
83. Ibid.
84. Press conference by the president, Nov. 25, 1991, "Civil Rights [3]," White House Press Office, Marlin Fitzwater subject file, alpha file, 1989, box 5, George Bush Presidential Library.
85. "Outline for Civil Rights Bill Signing Remarks," White House Office of Speechwriting, speech file, backup, chronological file, 1989–1993, box 128, George Bush Presidential Library.
86. Grant and Aarhus, second draft, Nov. 18, 1991, "Civil Rights Bill Signing Ceremony, 11/21/91," White House Office of Speechwriting, speech file, backup, chronological file, 1989–1993, box 128, George Bush Presidential Library.

87. Ibid.
88. "Remarks on Signing the Civil Rights Act," p. 1503.
89. Ibid.
90. Grant and Aarhus, second draft, Nov. 18, 1991.
91. "Remarks on Signing the Civil Rights Act," p. 1503.
92. Ibid.
93. C. Boyden Gray, remarks at the sixth annual Conference on Presidential Rhetoric, Texas A&M University, College Station, Mar. 4, 2000.
94. "Remarks on Signing the Civil Rights Act," p. 1502. Also see an unsigned paper titled "Civil Rights" in "Civil Rights [3]," White House Press Office, Marlin Fitzwater subject file, alpha file, 1989, box 5, George Bush Presidential Library; "White House News Summary, Thursday, Nov. 21, 1991, 2:30 P.M. News Update," White House Office of Speechwriting, speech file, backup, chronological file, 1989–1993, box 128, George Bush Presidential Library.
95. "Remarks on Signing the Civil Rights Act," p. 1502.
96. Ibid., p. 1504.
97. "Civil Rights," an unsigned paper in "Civil Rights [3]," White House Press Office, Marlin Fitzwater subject file, alpha file, 1989, box 5, George Bush Presidential Library.
98. Greene, *The Presidency of George Bush*, p. 159.
99. Memorandum from George Bush to Bob Teeter, Sam Skinner, and Dave Demarest, Feb. 13, 1992, White House Office of Speechwriting, Tony Snow subject file, 1988–1993, box 5, George Bush Presidential Library. This is one of the few documents currently open to scholars that contain the president's handwritten initials. The previous month, however, a draft statement for Martin Luther King Day omitted words that had been included in the preliminary draft: "Unfortunately, we can overstate this spiritual change in our national life, as some are prone to do. Racism and bigotry, blind hatred and intolerance still exist in our land." White House Office of Records Management, subject file, speeches, box 155, George Bush Presidential Library. The passage was deleted between the third (Jan. 15, 1992) and the fourth (Jan. 16, 1992) drafts of the speech.
100. This is an example of what I have elsewhere called "argument by definition." See David Zarefsky, "Definitions," *Argument in a Time of Change: Definitions, Frameworks, and Critiques,* ed. James F. Klumpp (Annandale, Va.: National Communication Association, 1998), pp. 1–11.
101. See, for example, "Statement on Signing the Civil Rights Act of 1991," *Public Papers of the Presidents: George Bush, 1991* (Washington, D.C.: Government Printing Office, 1992), 2:1505.

102. Under the provisions of the Presidential Records Act, confidential communications between a president and the president's advisers, or among those advisers, are removed from the files available to researchers until twelve years after the end of the administration. Presidents Reagan and Bush are the first to be affected by this new legislation.

CHAPTER 10

Celebritized Justice, Civil Rights, and the Clarence Thomas Nomination

Trevor Parry-Giles

What I did is look for the best man. The fact that he is black and a minority had nothing to do with this in the sense that he is the best qualified at this time.

—Pres. George Bush,
News Conference in Kennebunkport, Maine, July 1, 1991

My earliest memories . . . are those of Pin Point, Georgia, a life far removed in space and time from this room, this day, and this moment. As kids, we caught minnows in the creeks, fiddler crabs in the marshes, we played with pluffers and skipped shells across the water. It was a world so vastly different from all this.

—Judge Clarence Thomas, Nomination of Judge Clarence Thomas to
Be Associate Justice of the Supreme Court of the United States

Thurgood Marshall, the first African American justice on the U.S. Supreme Court, announced his retirement on June 27, 1991, at the age of eighty-two. Facing significant health concerns, this pillar of civil rights, this hero of *Brown v. Board of Education*, this iconoclastic voice of liberal jurisprudence decided he could hold out no longer and would have to leave the choice of his successor in the hands of a Republican president.[1] As a symbol of the Warren Court and the embodiment of its progressive, activist role in American society, Marshall personified an approach to the law that was rapidly slipping away.

It slipped further away just four days later, when Pres. George Bush proudly strode to the podium outside his palatial Kennebunkport home on the Maine coast and introduced his nominee to replace Marshall as the 106th justice of the Supreme Court. When Bush hailed Federal Circuit Court Judge Clarence Thomas as the "best qualified" person for Thurgood Marshall's Supreme Court seat, he introduced a person who saw the law and the Supreme Court very differently from the way Justice Marshall did. The nomination of Thomas was yet another step in the Reagan-Bush attempt to remake the federal judiciary through the elevation of conservative, strict-constructionist jurists to the Supreme Court and other federal courts.[2] What's more, Bush's eagerness to nominate a member of a minority group to Marshall's seat made Thomas the ideal candidate.[3]

The nomination of Clarence Thomas to the U.S. Supreme Court became, arguably, one of the most remarkable political events of the late twentieth century. What would have been a controversial, but fairly typical, Supreme Court nomination became a full-fledged media spectacle when an unknown law professor from Oklahoma, Anita Hill, came forward to accuse the nominee of sexual harassment. Three days of salacious hearings occupied the nation in October of 1991—hearings replete with accusations of sexual misconduct, delusional lunacy, high-tech lynching, and scorned fanaticism. Even after the Senate confirmed Thomas by the slimmest of margins, the reverberations of this controversy were still felt months and even years later. Senators were defeated for reelection a year later, sexual harassment became a topic of national fascination, and Anita Hill was further vilified (and glorified) for daring to challenge the nomination.[4] The Thomas nomination was, quite simply, a profound and momentous event.

Perhaps the best indicator of the significance of this event is the vast number of treatments it has received in the popular and scholarly press. It would be fruitless to count the analyses devoted to the Thomas nomination; it is sufficient to note that myriad articles,[5] books,[6] dissertations,[7] newspaper accounts, editorials, and television commentaries have scrutinized and dissected the events of October, 1991, with a thoroughness that is virtually unmatched in Supreme Court confirmation history. Much of the commentary about this event concerns the various tensions between sex, gender, and race in the hearings, the veracity of Thomas and Hill in their individual statements, and the overall consequences of the hearings for sexual harassment and gender and race relations in America.

I take a different approach in this analysis. An incomplete picture of the events in 1991 results when the sexual-harassment aspects of this controversy are removed from the larger context of the entire Thomas-confirmation process. As such, I discuss the symbolic process whereby Clarence Thomas was celebritized and examine how the rhetorical strategies of the Bush administration, supporters of the nomination, the nominee himself, and the news media prompted a predominantly affective and epideictic response to the nomination. The celebritization of Clarence Thomas, I suggest, was an attempt to circumvent the deliberative nature of Supreme Court confirmations in the Senate and worked to divert attention away from the nominee's views of the law and society, away from his judicial character, and toward his personal narrative.

This overt celebritization of a Supreme Court nominee, and this individual nominee in particular, entailed important consequences that continue to impact American political culture. First, I suggest that Anita Hill's charges of sexual harassment were perfectly consistent within the narrative trajectory of the celebritization rhetoric offered in support of the Thomas nomination and that these charges further celebritized the process by emphasizing the personal and salacious. Moreover, because the nomination of Clarence Thomas was so thoroughly celebritized, the treatment of Hill's charges was coherent within this rhetorical framework, resulting in an unsatisfying and unresolved conclusion to the hearings. Second, Thomas's response to Hill, I maintain, expanded on the affective dimensions of this nomination and invoked racial indignation as an added aspect of the evolving portrait of Clarence Thomas, judicial celebrity. As such, the subject of civil rights is implicated in this particular celebritization process, and this episode reveals another dimension of this important ideological touchstone of American political culture and how it is understood and the power it has for the larger polity. Finally, I examine the way in which the celebritization of Clarence Thomas represents the culmination and evolution of the Supreme Court confirmation process over the course of the twentieth century, reflecting on the possible dangers of celebritizing nominees to the Court.

Celebrity Culture, Celebritized Politics

The Romans called it *fama,* or *celebritas,* and it was a decidedly indistinct term in that ancient society.[8] Though transient, the idea of "celebrity" is a cornerstone of contemporary American life, just as the Romans were "animated by the urge for fame, [where] the definition of achievement was almost entirely oriented toward public behavior." Leo Braudy notes that "Fame for public action was so important to the Romans, as it was to the Homeric Greeks, because in a religion without a developed concept of the afterlife it was the only way to live beyond death."[9]

The present-day concept of "celebrity" began in the late eighteenth century, according to Thomas Baker. Baker discovers the roots of "a self-sustaining culture of celebrity" in the period from 1790 to 1830, when "the market for access to renown . . . assumed an enhanced scope and intensity," most clearly evidenced by the popularity of autographs.[10] Hollywood and network television capitalized on an extant celebrity culture and moved the construction of celebrities to a new level.[11] These media celebrities became, in the words of Guy Debord, "spectacular representations of living human beings, distilling the essence of the spectacle's banality into images of possible roles."[12] Now, celebrities and their plentiful public discourse significantly define our culture.

The power of celebrity culture infuses all aspects of public life. There are entertainment celebrities and political celebrities. Athletic celebrities command millions of dollars in salaries and product endorsements. Oprah Winfrey need only mention an author's book on her television program, and that lucky person becomes a bona fide literary celebrity. Major universities vie for the academic celebrities with large salaries and small teaching loads because these intellectual luminaries will bring fame and glory to their campuses. Scientific celebrities emerge with new discoveries in medicine or physics, and humanitarian celebrities rush to the sites of disasters or crises followed by scores of journalists and media personalities. Even the journalists themselves have become celebrities.[13]

Celebrities are people who are given greater presence in the public sphere, can express themselves individually, are listened to by the larger community, and possesses a degree of public power. Moreover, celebrities possess public power because of the emotional response they trigger in audiences and the larger culture. Celebrities are venerated not because of the rational power of their discourse and not because of the intelligence of their arguments, but because they provoke highly affective reactions. As such, celebrity power is both strong and illusory because contemporary celebrities exist in a state of ambiguity. Celebrities rise and fall quickly, are the subject of both reverence and ridicule, and are pawns in larger social, economic, and media systems over which they may or may not possess control.

Ultimately, as P. David Marshall suggests, "the concept of celebrity is best defined as a system for valorizing meaning and communication."[14] It is the process by which such valorization occurs that is of profound significance for contemporary communication inquiry. Of more interest than what celebrities actually say is the process by which a person comes to occupy celebrity status and to command celebrity attention. In addition, as Greg Siegworth argues, contemporary celebrity culture requires celebrities to engage in their own celebritization and to authenticate such rhetorics for the larger public.[15] The critical task thus becomes discerning how celebrities are constructed and how they are involved in the process of their own celebritization. As such, I seek to explain how Clarence Thomas was constructed and also constructed himself so as to become a political celebrity as well as the consequences of these rhetorical choices on Thomas, civil rights, and the Supreme Court confirmation process.

Political Celebritization

Political leaders are constructed (and construct themselves) according to the systems of discourse commonly found in celebrity culture.[16] This is particularly true of electoral politics. Candidates hire consultants, consult polling data, and repackage themselves and their messages to appeal to voters—all because those same voters are accustomed to judging public personalities according to the dictates of celebrity culture.[17] As such, there is a considerable blurring of entertainment and political discourses, which makes distinguishing between them progressively more difficult.

Of course, the packaging of political candidates as celebrities is nothing new. American political culture has always emphasized personality and flair, charisma and dynamism in the selection of political leaders.[18] The danger comes when the celebrity dimensions of politics overwhelm other aspects of electoral campaigns—policy discourse, investigative reporting, and so on.[19] Contemporary politics, despite what naysayers and cynics may say, is fairly successful at blending the focus on biography and celebrity with other criteria for electoral decision making.[20] There are instances, however, when political leaders market themselves solely on the basis of celebrity and thus become commodities in much the same way as movie stars or teen musical groups.

When political celebritization occurs, the "symbolic content of the political leader as commodity arises primarily from the similar groundwork of common cultural sentiments."[21] That is, the process of political celebritization exploits powerful ideological systems of meaning in the construction of the celebrity as a commodity worthy of consumption. Cultural myths, legends, narratives, and tokens dominate the celebritization of the individual political leader, allowing audiences, as citizens and voters, to access familiar rhetorics in their evaluation of the proffered person.

David Lusted reveals that the dominant cultural myths at work in the construction of celebrities are grounded in competing conceptions of the person. The first myth "stresses individual achievement through personal effort and competition," while the second is a "folk myth . . . in which the individual succeeds through nature or fate, rather than effort, position, or circumstance."[22] Both of these myths are common in political rhetoric in which individual personas are constructed by and for candidates. Even the most cursory review of candidates' biographies and commercials reveals that these people have typically endured hardship, overcome obstacles, and mastered difficulty on their road to political success. Such myths are also sources of identification, as candidates construct their celebrity in ways familiar to voters and reflective of their experiences.

Regardless of the actual myth employed in the political celebritization process, its preeminent locus of motivation is affective rather than deliberative. As Marshall notes, "Affect moves the political debate from the realm of reason to the realm of feeling and sentiment." Moreover, through such affect, the political celebrity "functions as a legitimating apparatus for the symbolic representation of the people."[23] Affectivity thus becomes the measure of successful celebritization. And it is affect that is presented through this process as the preferred mode of political deliberation and decision making—the basis of political judgment becomes feeling and emotion, not rationality or reasonability.

Condemning political celebritization or rejecting such rhetoric as unworthy of consideration and analysis would be a mistake. This mode of discourse is present throughout American history, and political leaders have always used such frameworks to justify their electoral or political ascendancy. Television surely technologizes and expands celebritization, and it provides political leaders with "a site through which a politics of familiarity can be developed and constructed."[24] However, celebritization should be no more or less preferred as a means of political judgment than any other process or framework. Rather, it must be recognized for its power, judged for its consequences, and analyzed for its impact on the political culture in which it occurs.

Celebritizing Clarence Thomas

Clarence Thomas was not a typical judge. His experiences were eclectic, including service in the executive branch (in the Education Department and at the Equal Employment Opportunity Commission) as well as the judicial branch. Thomas's time on the bench was limited, and his legal background and experience were light in comparison to those of other nominees to the Supreme Court.[25] In addition, Thomas had written and spoken fairly controversial statements and was affiliated with fringe groups on the conservative right.[26] Nonetheless, to the Bush administration, Thomas "seemed in most respects an ideal candidate for striding the line between confirmability and allegiance to conservatives."[27]

Unlike the administration's previous nominee to the Court, the "stealth" David Souter, Thomas had both a political and a legal record, or paper trail, that could potentially be used in the confirmation hearings and by political opponents. In response, the Bush administration's rhetorical strategy was to divert the focus away from Thomas's record and his fairly weak legal acumen and to "sell" the nominee on the basis of his personal story. This strategy emerged gradually. At the introduction of the nominee in Kennebunkport on July 1, 1991, Bush simply presented a listing of Thomas's accomplishments, and the nominee only thanked those people in his life who had made it possible for him to achieve his goals.[28] Indeed, as Mayer and Abramson recount, the "Pin Point strategy" emerged at a White House meeting after the Fourth of July holiday weekend, when a Justice Department lobbyist named John Mackey urged the assembled officials, including the nominee, "to bury ideology and sell biography" and to "tell the Pin Point story."[29]

The administration's celebritizing rhetoric about Clarence Thomas pointedly emphasizes the affective and the emotive dimensions of the nominee's upbringing. As the story was told and retold over the duration of the confirmation process, it skillfully exploited deep-seated ideological and mythic themes embedded in the American political culture, and its affective dimensions were routinely highlighted. Clarence Thomas was someone, the narrative maintains, who rose up from poverty and despair through hard work, a dedicated family, and a personal adherence to core values. From this background, the story continues, Thomas overcame hardship and discrimination to achieve the highest pinnacles of power. The conclusion of the story is obvious: Because of his upbringing, because of his triumph over adversity, because he embodied everything good about America, and because of the way he made us feel about America, this man deserved a seat on the U.S. Supreme Court.

From the Bully Pulpit: George Bush and the Pin Point Strategy

Perhaps the most powerful spokesperson for Thomas's cause, aside from the nominee himself, was Pres. George Bush. In statement after statement, the president offered Clarence Thomas's personal biography and the powerful emotional impact of that narrative as the grounds for judgment on the nomination. Bush occasionally mentioned specific qualifications that Thomas possessed, but the primary focus of his rationalization for Thomas's elevation to the Supreme Court was the affective power of the Pin Point narrative. Throughout his discourse about Thomas, the president thus reflected the reworking of "cultural sentiments" involved in the celebritizing of political leaders, so that those sentiments could "be integrated into the constructed character" of, in this case, Clarence Thomas.[30]

Bush stressed the emotional power of Thomas's biography in a speech on July 8, a week after announcing the nomination: "Our new nominee for the Supreme Court, Judge Clarence Thomas, offers what I think is a very stirring testament to what people can do when they refuse to take no for an answer; when through sheer determination they overcome obstacles that others have placed in their way. It was very emotional for me up there at our house in Maine when we announced his appointment because he outdistanced poverty and racism; because he possessed the greatest treasures of all, the love of family, the faith of teachers—remember what he said about teachers— and then the belief in himself."[31] Later, in an August 6 address, Bush commented on Thomas's "personal story," saying, "when you meet him you can't help but be impressed—in my case, deeply moved. It [his personal story] impresses everybody, everybody that's fair and open minded."[32] A week later, to the Fraternal Order of Police, Bush justified his nomination of Thomas with this argument: "He has lived the values we hold dear: duty, decency, and personal responsibility." As if to accentuate Thomas's personal story, the president added, "I don't know how many saw the announcement I made up in Maine with Clarence by my side when I announced this appointment, but his personal story cannot help but move people, inspire them."[33] Just four days later, in a teleconference with the National Governors' Association, Bush again underscored the emotional dimensions of Thomas's nomination: "I must say I got all choked up when I heard Clarence talk about his background. And he did it from the heart; there's no phoniness there."[34]

Interestingly, the president repeatedly referenced Thomas's story as told at the announcement of his nomination and the emotional impact of the narrative at that occasion. Yet, in Kennebunkport, Thomas never really elaborated on his background—he merely thanked everyone from his past who had helped him to succeed. Bush transplanted the Pin Point narrative onto the one public occasion when most Americans first encountered Clarence Thomas, giving Thomas's story greater power and relevance. The news media, furthermore, provided the details of the Pin Point story, so it was a fairly simple rhetorical maneuver to graft the narrative and its emotional impact onto the Kennebunkport announcement ceremony, and Bush did so repeatedly.

President Bush adeptly linked Clarence Thomas and his childhood narrative to enduring cultural and ideological values that marked the nominee as a representation of American ideals. As Bush told the National Association of Towns and Townships on September 6, "Clarence Thomas embodies the virtues America and all her towns and townships hold dear."[35] That same day, in an address to the nation about the Thomas nomination, Bush noted, "Most of you have heard his story, how Clarence Thomas was raised in Pin Point, Georgia, by stern and loving grandparents, educated in parochial schools, and graduated from Holy Cross and the Yale Law School." Though deprived of material wealth, the president remarked, Thomas was "blessed with the important treasures: a loving family, sturdy values, and a chance," and he "defined opportunity through education, dedication, and just plain hard work."[36] Bush reaffirmed the emotional power of Thomas's personal narrative when he told a fund-raising dinner in Philadelphia about his reaction to watching the opening statements at the confirmation hearings: "Parenthetically, I watched the opening presentation that he [Thomas] made to this committee, and I got kind of choked up listening, as I did at Kennebunkport when I nominated him."[37]

In justifying Clarence Thomas as a nominee to the Supreme Court, George Bush used his nominee's ideologically powerful, emotionally resonant biographical narrative to package Thomas as a celebrity. His rationale for the selection was that Thomas represented enduring American values and that his personal story of hardship and success was emotionally powerful. Bush often described Thomas as a "good man," and his rhetoric about the nomination frequently accessed powerful values of self-reliance, diligence, and perseverance. What was missing from Bush's acclaim for his nominee was a justification for Thomas grounded in qualification or legal exceptionality. Thomas deserved a seat on the Supreme Court, the president maintained, because he was exceptional as a person, not as a legal scholar or practitioner. In this way, George Bush established the groundwork for the Pin Point strategy and enacted the celebritization of Clarence Thomas, setting the stage for the confirmation hearings, where the Pin Point strategy would achieve its ultimate zenith.

George Bush was correct when he said on September 6, "Most of you have heard his story." By the time the confirmation hearings commenced, the Clarence Thomas Pin Point story was a common staple of news-media coverage of the nomination. In no small part because of the president's efforts, when he was sworn at his confirmation hearings, Clarence Thomas was already an American political celebrity.

For a political leader to become a celebrity, that person must enter the televisual system so critical to contemporary celebrity creation. As P. David Marshall concludes, a leader's regular appearance on television establishes "a semblance of connection to [the] mass citizenry and . . . [a] commonsensical status of legitimacy as a public personality who represents the political sphere."[38] In the case of Clarence Thomas, that legitimacy as a public celebrity came from the repetition in the news media of the Pin Point story and the connection that it created between Clarence Thomas and the enduring ideological framework of the American polity.

Two specific themes characterized the early news-media coverage of the Thomas nomination. The first theme was his personal narrative—the Pin Point story. The second theme, not surprisingly, was the confirmability of Thomas and the likely challenges he faced from opponents, interest groups, and the Democratic-controlled U.S. Senate. Both themes operated to enhance the celebritization of Thomas. Generally, the media organized the Pin Point story around the familiar themes that made the story ideologically powerful—Thomas's resolve and strength in the face of poverty and discrimination. By then highlighting the potential difficulties facing Thomas in the upcoming confirmation struggle, the media also positioned him as a victim, as someone worthy of a Supreme Court seat but who might be denied his dream by the vagaries of partisan politics. Both discourses worked to enhance his celebrity status, promoting an emotional evaluation of this emerging public figure and highlighting aspects of his persona derived solely from status and biography, not argument or political philosophy.

In her special report about the nomination, Rita Braver of CBS News described Thomas's personal story as "the stuff of American legends," complete with "a father who abandoned him, a mother who worked as a maid struggling just to feed her children, finally at age seven sent to live with the grandparents he credits with setting him on course."[39] The report then highlighted the concerns of pro-choice groups about the nomination, emphasizing their disquiet about Thomas's nomination.

ABC News also emphasized these themes in the July 1, 1991, edition of *Nightline*. In the introductory report by Forrest Sawyer, Sen. Orrin Hatch is quoted as saying, "If anybody understands the needs and rights of minorities, if anybody has felt the sting of prejudice against him, if anybody has had to fight his or her way through society in almost every step that that person made, that has to be Clarence Thomas." The program also featured a lengthy interview with Thomas's childhood friend Georgia State Sen. Roy Allen, who testified to the nominee's commonality with other African Americans: "Thomas represented probably many of us who were trained by Catholic nuns, who grew up in the close surroundings of family, of self-help, who grew up in the kind of milieu of segregation, the Deep South, in south Georgia."[40] As with CBS, *Nightline* also discussed the politics of the Thomas confirmation at length.

CBS News again featured Thomas's Pin Point upbringing in its broadcast on July 2. Reporter Erin Hayes was dispatched to the small Georgia town, and from there she told viewers that "Thomas's house is gone now. It was tiny with no plumbing. He lived there with his mother. His father left when he was two. Clarence Thomas's grandfather became his father figure and, his mother says, kept him from being embittered by the poverty and racism of the 1960s' South." Hayes concluded her report with this observation: "[T]he confirmation hearings may be tough. But he [Thomas] grew up with tough times. Folks here are convinced he can handle them."[41] On CNN, Larry King began his broadcast concerning the Thomas nomination by retelling the Pin Point story and emphasizing the confirmation challenges that Thomas faced: "Clarence Thomas was born in rural Georgia with two strikes against him: He was black, desperately poor and, from an early age on, fatherless. Now, forty-three years later and against seemingly impossible odds, he has become America's newest Supreme Court nominee. But as a black judge with a proven conservative record he has political enemies on the left and right side and his ascension to the lofty bench promises to be a battle."[42]

The news media became the Bush administration's accomplice in their Pin Point strategy. Virtually all of the coverage of the nomination—especially that coverage immediately subsequent to its announcement—emphasized Thomas's compelling personal saga and the politics of the confirmation struggle. Of course, Thomas's story was perfect for the dominant logics of television journalism precisely because his narrative was so gripping and because it resonated emotionally and was entirely consistent with the foremost metanarratives of the American experience. Some journalists noted the irony of Bush's selection of an African American conservative with such humble roots.[43] Other media sources, however, employed the story to contextualize the growing debate within African American civil rights organizations about Thomas.[44] Regardless of how it was used, the Pin Point story, as persistently retold in news-media accounts, came to define Clarence Thomas in the early days of his confirmation process.

The second theme of the journalists' coverage—the political machinations of the confirmation process itself—was also contextualized through the lens of Pin Point; thus this new celebrity, Clarence Thomas, faced opposition or was supported as a result of his background or because of his personal narrative. In this way, Pin Point came to represent the entirety of the Thomas confirmation process. This new political celebrity was either endorsed because of his dramatic personal biography or opposed because he had neglected his roots and forgotten his struggles against discrimination. Both judgments are clearly grounded in an emotional reaction to the constructed persona of Clarence Thomas as a political celebrity. Neither judgment reflects a *deliberative* assessment of Thomas's past political or legal positions or his qualifications as a potential justice of the Supreme Court. Moreover, both judgments demonstrate the power of the administration's Pin Point strategy and its grip on the confirmation process as the hearings before the Senate Judiciary Committee commenced in September, 1991.

Taking Center Stage: The Thomas Confirmation Hearings

When the confirmation hearings started in September, the Pin Point story and the emotional reactions it elicited organized the early testimony and structured the dynamics of the hearing process. The narrative had achieved such currency and emotional power that it worked as the defining marker of Clarence Thomas. As John Thompson argues, narrativization functions as a tool of ideological legitimation; thus, "claims are embedded in stories which recount the past and treat the present as part of a timeless and cherished tradition."[45] Pin Point legitimated Clarence Thomas by spinning his personal tale firmly within the ideological terrain of American myths and values. Nowhere was this more evident than in the opening days of his confirmation hearings before the Senate Judiciary Committee.

The first day of the hearings, September 10, was filled with introductory speeches, opening remarks, and the nominee's first formal statement to the committee. The Pin Point story, with all of its power and affectivity, was prominently featured. Even those who opposed Thomas's elevation to the Court were forced to acknowledge its emotional force. In his opening statement, Sen. Edward Kennedy admitted that, "In his life and in his career, Judge Thomas has overcome large barriers of poverty and injustice, and he deserves great credit for the eminence he has attained."[46] Vermont Democrat Patrick Leahy remarked, "Judge Thomas . . . I am impressed, and I believe the country is impressed, by the less-traveled road that you have taken from Pin Point, GA, to the threshold of the Supreme Court. Your self-discipline, your diligence, and your hard work are exemplary."[47] Howard Metzenbaum of Ohio noted universal agreement regarding the fact that "Judge Thomas's life story is an uplifting tale of a youth determined to surmount the barriers of poverty, segregation, and discrimination. It was an extraordinary journey from hardscrabble Pin Point, GA, to the promise and privileges of Yale Law School." Metzenbaum expressed the confounding quality of the Pin Point strategy for opponents of the nomination when he tried to undermine it: "The question for this committee is not where does Judge Thomas come from, rather, the question for the committee is this: Where would a Justice Thomas take the Supreme Court?"[48]

Of course, Thomas's supporters also invoked the narrative as they welcomed Clarence Thomas to the hearings. Ranking Republican Strom Thurmond professed confidence in Thomas's qualifications and added, "[H]is personal struggle to overcome difficult circumstances early in his life is admirable. A review of his background shows he is a man of immense courage who has prevailed over many obstacles to attain remarkable success."[49] Defining the hearings as a "chance to become acquainted with Judge Thomas," Iowa Republican Charles Grassley noted that no one in the Senate "has had to surmount the obstacles Judge Thomas confronted" and that the nominee "grew up without material comforts and even conveniences."[50] Taking his praise of Thomas to a hyperbolic level, Utah Sen. Orrin Hatch told Thomas, "I am so doggone proud of you I can hardly stand it. I think it is a terrific thing that you are nominated to this position, and I personally will support you with every fiber of my being."[51]

Republicans and Democrats alike recognized the immense capacity of Thomas's Pin Point narrative to define the nomination and the confirmation hearings. The six senators from Georgia, Missouri, and Virginia who formally introduced Thomas to the committee all stressed this narrative and Thomas's struggles as a child and young adult. Indeed, Georgia Democrat Sam Nunn even mentioned the currency of the story as the common and circulated definition of Clarence Thomas when he said, "as most Americans now know from hearing the inspiring story of his life."[52] Nunn expressed the role of this narrative in celebritizing Thomas for the larger public, and he recognized the intensity of the story to guide the hearings and deliberations about the nomination. The Pin Point strategy was coming to fruition, as the initial focus of the nomination hearings was squarely on Thomas's persona and his personal narrative, even to the point that opponents of the nomination acknowledged Thomas's celebrity. That same power was evident when Clarence Thomas offered his opening statement to the Judiciary Committee.

Clarence Thomas skillfully defined the focus of the confirmation hearings in his opening statement, and his demarcation of the proceedings' purpose is a clear indication of the celebritization of this process and the strategic shrewdness of both the administration and this nominee in securing approval for the nomination. Thomas noted, "Much has been written about my family and me over the past 10 weeks." He then offered his interpretation of the hearing process: "I hope these hearings will help to show more clearly who this person Clarence Thomas is and what really makes me tick."[53] Thomas then provided a poignant retelling of his Pin Point story. He invoked the legacy of the civil rights movement and acknowledged that he benefited from the efforts of leaders such as Martin Luther King, Roy Wilkins, Fannie Lou Haemer, and Rosa Parks. He movingly detailed the indignities his grandparents suffered in the segregated culture in which they lived. He concluded with the pledge to protect the Constitution and to "carry with me the values of my heritage: fairness, integrity, open mindedness, honesty, and hard work." Thomas made this pledge, he concluded, "Because when all is said and done, the little guy, the average person, the people of Pin Point, the real people of America will be affected not only by what we as judges do, but by the way we do our jobs."[54]

Throughout his statement, Clarence Thomas offered nothing to explicitly establish his qualifications for the U.S. Supreme Court. That is, he did not attempt to persuade the Judiciary Committee of his legal abilities, his scholarship on legal matters, or even his "judicial temperament" or philosophy of judging. What he did offer the Judiciary Committee was a portrait of Clarence Thomas as a celebrity—a person who, because of his personal narrative and that narrative's affective expression of enduring myths, ought to be confirmed for the Supreme Court. Furthermore, the Pin Point story would often reappear as the committee questioned Thomas. When asked, for instance, about his adherence to natural-law principles as a justification for the preservation of property rights, Thomas referenced the paltry wages his grandparents earned during his childhood.[55] And when queried about issues of civil rights and discrimination, Thomas would reference his own personal experiences with racial prejudice.

Indeed, the malleability of the Pin Point narrative and its usefulness on substantive matters of constitutional law allowed Thomas and his advocates to invoke the tale to blunt criticisms of his record, particularly on civil rights. Based on his tenure at the EEOC and some of his judicial rulings and public statements, Thomas was criticized for a failure to support civil rights.[56] The Pin Point story provided the nominee cover from such attacks. Senator Hatch maintained, in his opening statement, "Judge Thomas has an excellent record on civil rights and a deep personal commitment to equal opportunity." Hatch cited a quotation from Thomas, in which the nominee said, "I am a black Southerner. I grew up under the heel of segregation, and I have always found it offensive for the Government to treat people differently from others because of the color of their skin."[57]

In what must qualify as one of the profoundest statements of the celebritization of the Thomas confirmation, Sen. John Danforth of Missouri, a Thomas confidant and sponsor, put forth his desire for the committee: "I hope that sometime in the days Judge Thomas will be before this committee, someone will ask him not about unenumerated rights or the establishment clause, but about himself, what was it like to grow up under segregation, what was it like to be there when your grandfather was humiliated before your eyes, what was it like to be laughed at by seminarians because you are black. Everyone in the Senate knows something about the legal issues before the Supreme Court. Not a single member of the Senate knows what Clarence Thomas knows about being poor and black in America."[58] Danforth explicitly called upon the Judiciary Committee to decide the nomination based on the well-worn story of Thomas's background and the emotional power of that narrative. In so doing, the Missouri senator also reinforced the view that the depths of his experience with segregation and poverty blunted questions about Thomas's civil rights record. Once again, the grounds for judgment about Thomas and the critical question of his commitment to civil rights were placed on affective grounds rather than deliberative ones.

The Pin Point strategy was supremely effective.[59] Opponents of the nominee were forced to acknowledge the power of his personal story and to temper their criticisms as a result. Thomas's champions skillfully wove the Pin Point tale into virtually every statement offered in support of the nomination. Moreover, Clarence Thomas dexterously used the Pin Point story to fend off criticisms of a lackluster record on civil rights, particularly from African American organizations, and to provide a rationale for his elevation to the Supreme Court.

The historical record and the committee testimony reflect that Clarence Thomas was a person who claimed to have *never* discussed *Roe v. Wade*, was someone who upheld the preeminent role of natural rights, was a person who advocated judicial activism to overturn wrongly decided opinions, and was someone who actively lent his name and reputation to supporters of the apartheid regime in South Africa.[60] Yet for the majority of Americans, because of the celebritizing power of the Pin Point strategy, Clarence Thomas was primarily a talented and hard-working man who had triumphed over adversity, overcome the shackles of segregation, and achieved the highest pinnacles of success in America. This was the Clarence Thomas who was constructed by the administration and offered to the Senate for confirmation to the Supreme Court. This was Clarence Thomas as revealed in his own words in testimony to the Senate Judiciary Committee. This was the Clarence Thomas who was so frequently and compellingly displayed in the news media at every stage of his confirmation process. And this was the Clarence Thomas who would soon face charges from an unknown law professor in Oklahoma that would attack the persona that had been so carefully crafted over the span of ten weeks in 1991.

The Consequences of Celebritization

As with all rhetorical choices, the decision to celebritize Clarence Thomas and to justify his nomination to the Supreme Court on the basis of his emotionally powerful personal story entailed specific consequences. The ultimate outcome, the confirmation of Clarence Thomas, was achieved. Even as that end was reached, though, the decision to celebritize this Supreme Court nominee dramatically altered his personal identity (in his response to Anita Hill), the ideological power of civil rights in the United States, and the process by which the Supreme Court is staffed.

The Flip Side of Pin Point

Anita Hill's charges were not caused by the Pin Point strategy and celebritization of Clarence Thomas. Depending on the version one believes, either they were the result of the grossly inappropriate behavior of Clarence Thomas, or they were invented in the mind of a vindictive and scornful woman seeking to inflict harm on an honorable man. Nevertheless, Anita Hill's charges and the ensuing hearings before the Judiciary Committee cannot be completely assessed without reference to the celebritization of Clarence Thomas. Hill's responses to the charges that Thomas and his partisans made were constrained by the rhetorical parameters of the confirmation process as constructed by Thomas's celebritization.

Hill's incriminations offered a portrait of Clarence Thomas that was starkly opposed to the one put forth in the Pin Point story. They depicted a person who abused his power and was lewd and lascivious in his personal conduct. But just as they opposed the persona put forth in the Pin Point story, they were also perfectly consistent with the trajectory of the nomination. That is, Anita Hill's charges called forth a judgment of Clarence Thomas that was based in an affective reaction to personal behavior and circumstance. They capitalized on the tools of celebritization to construct an alternative and dramatically converse image of Clarence Thomas. The opponents of Thomas's nomination in the civil rights community used political speeches and legal texts to oppose the nomination—and such evidence was tame and tepid when placed next to the emotionally powerful and resonant Pin Point narrative. Anita Hill's accusations were different—they constructed a separate character of Clarence Thomas, a substitute vision of this celebrity that worked in utter contrast to the hard-working, religious, indefatigable Clarence Thomas of the Pin Point narrative.

As dramatic as Hill's charges were, of greater significance for the comprehension of the power of celebritization are Thomas's responses to those charges. In his reaction to Anita Hill's accusations of sexual harassment, Thomas returned to a variant of the Pin Point story, using its racially derived foundation to his advantage as he worked mightily to preserve his nomination. A central component of the Pin Point story is its racial dimensions. The fact that Thomas was poor as a child is hardly noteworthy—the fact that he was raised in abject poverty, along with his experiences with segregation and discrimination, gives the narrative its emotional and ideological reverberation. Indeed, Senator Hatch looked rather silly when he commented on his own poor upbringing without "indoor facilities" because the identification with Thomas's story was not possible given its highly racialized origin.

In his now notorious reply to Hill's indictment, Clarence Thomas again invoked the racial dimensions of his celebrity, this time in a highly provocative manner. He told the committee, "During the past 2 weeks, I lost the belief that if I did my best all would work out. I called upon the strength that helped me get here from Pin Point, and it was all sapped out of me."[61] Thomas noted that "in my 43 years on this Earth, I have been able, with the help of others and with the help of God, to defy poverty, avoid prison, overcome segregation, bigotry, racism, and obtain one of the finest educations available in this country. But I have not been able to overcome this process."[62] He proclaimed himself a "victim" of the process, and he told the committee, "I will not provide the rope for my own lynching or for further humiliation."[63] And in what would become one of the most famous statements of the hearing, Thomas condemned the hearings and the entire confirmation process in the starkest and most racially charged way: "And from my standpoint, as a black American, as far as I am concerned, it [the confirmation process] is a high-tech lynching for uppity blacks who in any way deign to think for themselves, to do for themselves, to have different ideas, and it is a message that, unless you kowtow to an old order, this is what will happen to you,

you will be lynched, destroyed, caricatured by a committee of the U.S. Senate, rather than hung from a tree."[64]

Though he denied Anita Hill's charges, it was Thomas's condemnation of the hearings and the confirmation process that exploited his celebrity and that, once again, offered highly emotional, personally derived criteria as grounds for judgment about his suitability for the Supreme Court. Initially, the nomination was justified because he had overcome poverty and segregation. In the wake of Anita Hill, the justification shifted, and Thomas deserved his seat on the Court because of the symbolic lynching he endured in the U.S. Senate. The nomination, Hill's contentions about sexual harassment, and Thomas himself should all be judged, according to this celebritized formulation, on the basis of an affective reaction to his status as a lynched, defamed, stereotyped African American man. In this way, Thomas flipped the Pin Point story, shifting the focus away from the positive tale of perseverance to a negative one of victimization and wrongful persecution. In so doing, he became, in the words of Homi Bhabha, "the avenging angel, the avatar of 'race' memory."[65] Perhaps the poet D. L. Crockett-Smith describes Thomas's response best: "Reborn, he tries his jury./He shakes his prickly pinpoint/crown, bloody in their faces."[66]

Celebritizing Civil Rights

The layers of Clarence Thomas's celebrity status deepened with his response to Anita Hill's charges. His persona now involved both the dedicated hero of Pin Point and the angry, victimized African American man, lynched for daring to overstep his boundaries. Furthermore, his discourse reflected the increasingly celebritized nature of civil rights in America, demonstrating how this important ideological foundation of law is demarcated in American political culture.

Increasingly, the collective understanding of civil rights in the United States involves highly celebritized discourses. Contemporary battles about civil rights often devolve into struggles between celebrity figures, with the power of the celebrity overtaking the legal or political issues at stake. Whether they involve Louis Farrakhan, Khalid Mohammed, Al Sharpton, Lani Guinier, Jesse Jackson, Sister Souljah, or Coretta Scott King, discussions of civil rights frequently become clashes of personality rather than deliberations about policy.

The contemporary celebritization of civil rights may be a manifestation of the cultural tendency to celebritize the collective memory of civil rights. Civil rights struggles from the past are expressed in filmic interpretations, for instance, that tend to focus on individual characters and heroism rather than on larger social or political dynamics that would complicate the cinematic narrative. *Mississippi Burning* tells the story of heroic, white FBI agents who work mightily on the front lines of the civil rights movement. *Ghosts of Mississippi* relates Myrlie Evers's quest for justice in the assassination of her husband. Spike Lee's biopic *Malcolm X* is an attempt to resurrect the celebrity of this controversial civil rights leader. Television miniseries and movies about Thurgood Marshall, Martin Luther King, and others within the civil rights movement further celebritize the collective understanding of this movement. Even the creation of a national holiday in honor of Martin Luther King speaks to the celebritization of civil rights in that our collective celebration of the struggle for civil rights is organized and recognized by reference to one person's birthday.[67]

The two sides of Clarence Thomas that emerged from his confirmation hearings echo the celebrity portrayals of civil rights that emanate from both historical and contemporary discourses. The hard-working, diligent, religious image of Clarence Thomas that dominates the Pin Point story characterizes many of the celebrity portraits offered about civil rights leaders or people involved in the movement. This celebrity representation is perfectly consistent, for example, with our images of Rosa Parks and Martin Luther King. Conversely, the angry, resentful, proud African American man standing up to the social systems that deny him his dignity and that inflict violence on him and his family is another powerful image, most frequently represented by celebritizations of Malcolm X or Jesse Jackson.[68] Clarence Thomas and the Bush administration skillfully exploited the celebritizing tendency in American political culture, particularly regarding civil rights, and expertly used competing images to navigate the nomination of Clarence Thomas through the Senate and around the allegations of sexual harassment leveled by Anita Hill.

The consequences, though, of celebritizing civil rights are profound and potentially poisonous to the achievement of equality in the United States. If civil rights become entirely celebritized, this ideological basis for public action loses its deeper moorings in traditions or belief. The vagaries of personality and the fluidity of people may come to exclusively demarcate the validity of civil rights for the American polity. If the confirmation of Clarence Thomas teaches anything, it is that celebritizing civil rights can blind a community to what may be truly important. The depictions of Pin Point and of high-tech lynching obscured and overwhelmed critical dimensions about Clarence Thomas and his adherence to particular political views that should arguably have been more central in the consideration of his nomination, especially for the larger public audiences outside of Washington, D.C.

Celebritizing may also have an "otherizing" tendency that contributes to its adverse effect on civil rights by making it a rhetorical tool of "whiteness."[69] The fact that the Bush administration used the Pin Point strategy to secure confirmation for Clarence Thomas but selected another approach in the case of Justice Souter is instructive. Indeed, even the most cursory review of Supreme Court confirmation debates reveals that elaborate renditions of personal narratives are rare. Except when such narratives are unusual, as in the case of football hero Byron White, the only tales of upbringing or extended discussions of personal background belong to those candidates for the Court who were nonwhite males. This otherizing capacity naturalizes the presence of white males and marks nonwhite, female candidates for the Court as unusual. So, in 1981, Americans learned of the frontier upbringing of Sandra Day O'Connor, and ten years later they were treated to the humble and difficult origins of Clarence Thomas. In some cases, other life experiences are celebritized, as in the cases of Justices Marshall and Ginsburg.[70] In the case of all four justices, some measure of their confirmability came from their celebrity and not from their capabilities as jurists or legal thinkers. Moreover, I suspect that the childhood experiences and struggles of Justices Rehnquist, Kennedy, Scalia, Stevens, and Breyer would elude most observers, making their presence on the Court seem ordinary and typical and representing the disturbing capacity of the Supreme Court confirmation process to only celebritize "the other"—a dangerous phenomenon in the quest for civil rights and sociopolitical equality in America.

Celebritizing the Supreme Court

One of the strengths of the American electoral system is that campaigns are long enough, candidates have to endure enough scrutiny, and the news media are intrusive enough that it would be difficult to elect a president solely on the basis of a celebritized persona. Gone are the days of "Tippecanoe and Tyler, Too," when a catchy slogan and a party affiliation were enough to propel a candidate into the presidency. Similarly, electing a representative or senator solely on the basis of a constructed celebritization would be extremely difficult, except in rare circumstances.

However, Supreme Court confirmations are different. They are a unique and evolving aspect of American democratic governance and are more susceptible, in many ways, to celebritization than the election processes of the other branches of the federal government. Presidents may nominate people for the Court because of their celebrity, as when Bill Clinton eagerly sought to nominate Mario Cuomo for the Court.[71] Moreover, the Senate may confirm or refuse to confirm a nominee based solely on a constructed celebrity persona. For instance, the Senate confirmed Benjamin Cardozo ten seconds after his nomination was announced, while Louis Brandeis's nomination in 1916 elicited gasps of shock when announced on the floor of the Senate.[72] Though judges and legal scholars are not often well-known people, the compressed nature of the Supreme Court confirmation process invites the celebritization of nominees as a means of confirmation. As the Clarence Thomas confirmation reveals, such a celebritizing tendency may be unfortunate and may undermine the very credibility of all branches of the American government.

An opposing perspective might see the celebritization of Supreme Court confirmations as a positive development. Given the Court's propensity for secrecy and isolation, a celebritized nomination process could potentially democratize the Court, making its justices and its decisions more accessible to the larger public. Of critical importance, though, is the nature of the publicity created for the Supreme Court via a celebritized confirmation process. Ideally, celebritized nominations would yield an increased interest in the Court and would engage the public in meaningful discourse about constitutional law, the power of judicial review, and the relevance of the Court's rulings. This ideal situation would have citizens regularly tuned to c-span's *America and the Courts* series and actively following the progress of foundational cases through the appellate courts. The Supreme Court's decisions to grant cert would be the topic of dinner-table and water-cooler conversation, and Americans would recognize the Court's power in all aspects of American life. Regrettably, this jurisprudential utopia seems unlikely because the leap from the affective celebritized nomination to a sustained forensic interest in law is a large one.

The celebritization of Clarence Thomas did not end when the Senate confirmed him. In a November, 1991, issue of *People Magazine,* the newest Supreme Court justice and his wife Virginia were profiled. They were pictured in various poses around their home—reclining on the carpet, drinking coffee, and sitting on a couch reading a Bible. In addition, the PBS documentary series *Frontline* explored the nature and accuracy of the Pin Point story, revealing its fissures and fictions and furthering its resonance as the defining motif for Clarence Thomas. In 1999, Showtime presented a filmic rendition of Jane Mayer and Jill Abramson's book, *Strange Justice.* Almost a decade after the events of 1991, Showtime believed that this story still possessed the emotional power to capture and interest audiences. Even as he sits on the Supreme Court, Clarence Thomas continues to be a marker of many competing emotional reactions, largely as a result of the celebrity that he crafted, with aid from the Bush administration, to ensure his confirmation.

One of the final witnesses in the Thomas hearings was a woman named Constance Berry Newman, who testified on behalf of Judge Thomas. As she ended her testimony, Newman remarked, "I am optimistic that positive change will take place as a result of these proceedings. America has seen and understood some of the delicate issues that we must face and will appreciate the governmental process, painful though it may be."[73] Newman may be right. The Thomas hearings may have forced the American political culture to confront difficult questions of sexism, racism, and the abuse of power wherever such transgressions occur. The hearings might also have motivated Americans to take an increased interest in the women and men that presidents nominate to the Supreme Court. These momentous events, furthermore, should motivate the political culture to consider more fully the consequences of celebritizing the American government and the people who populate that government. A failure to confront and learn that lesson may erode and corrode the very essence of public virtue that makes Constance Newman and so many Americans hopefully optimistic for the future.

Notes

1. For a discussion of how Thurgood Marshall came to embody competing conceptions of "civil rights" during his 1967 confirmation, see Trevor Parry-Giles, "Character, the Constitution, and the Ideological Embodiment of 'Civil Rights' in the 1967 Nomination of Thurgood Marshall to the Supreme Court," *Quarterly Journal of Speech* 82 (1996): 364–82; 347 U.S. 483 (1954).

2. There was certainly the recognition among Republicans, especially those in the "New Right," that a place for meaningful and long-lasting impact was the federal judiciary. See Richard L. Pacelle Jr., *The Transformation of the Supreme Court's Agenda* (Boulder: Westview, 1991); David G. Savage, *Turning Right: The Making of the Rehnquist Supreme Court* (New York: John Wiley and Sons, 1992); Michael Schaller, *Reckoning with Reagan: America and Its President in the 1980s* (New York: Oxford University Press, 1992); Bernard Schwartz, *The New Right and the Constitution: Turning Back the Legal Clock* (Boston: Northeastern University Press, 1990); Tinsley E. Yarbrough, "Reagan and the Courts," in *The Reagan Presidency: An Incomplete Revolution?* ed. Dilys M. Hill, Raymond A. Moore, and Phil Williams (New York: St. Martin's, 1990), pp. 68–94. The extent to which these efforts were successful is mixed and assessed in Christopher E. Smith and Thomas R. Hensley, "Unfulfilled Aspirations: The Court-Packing Efforts of Presidents Reagan and Bush," *Albany Law Review* 57 (1994): 1111–31; and James F. Simon, *The Center Holds: The Power Struggle inside the Rehnquist Court* (New York: Simon and Schuster, 1995).

3. Timothy M. Phelps and Helen Winternitz, *Capitol Games: Clarence Thomas, Anita Hill, and the Story of a Supreme Court Nomination* (New York: Hyperion, 1992), p. 4.

4. For a discussion of the political ramifications of the Thomas nomination, see Donald Grier Stephenson Jr., *Campaigns and the Court: The U.S. Supreme Court in Presidential Elections* (New York: Columbia University Press, 1999), pp. 214–17.

5. See S. Ashley Armstrong, "Arlen Specter and the Construction of Adversarial Discourse: Selective Representation in the Clarence Thomas-Anita Hill Hearings," *Argumentation and Advocacy* 32 (1995): 75–89; Karen Baker-Fletcher, "The Difference Race Makes: Sexual Harassment and the Law in the Thomas/Hill Hearings," *Journal of Feminist Studies in Religion* 10 (1994): 7–15; Joyce A. Baugh and Christopher E. Smith, "Doubting Thomas: Confirmation Veracity Meets Performance Reality," *Seattle University Law Review* 19 (1996): 455–96; Vanessa Bowles Beasley, "The Logic of Power in the Hill-Thomas Hearings: A Rhetorical Analysis," *Political Communication* 11 (1994): 287–97; William L. Benoit and Dawn M. Nill, "A Critical Analysis of Judge Clarence Thomas's Statement before the Senate

Judiciary Committee," *Communication Studies* 49 (1998): 179–95; Margaret A. Eisenhart and Nancy R. Lawrence, "Anita Hill, Clarence Thomas, and the Culture of Romance," in *Sexual Artifice: Persons, Images, Politics*, ed. Ann Kibbey, Kayann Short, and Abouali Farman-farmaian (New York: New York University Press, 1994), pp. 94–124; Nancy Fraser, "Sex, Lies, and the Public Sphere: Some Reflections on the Confirmation of Clarence Thomas," *Critical Inquiry* 18 (1992): 595–612; Michael J. Gerhardt, "Divided Justice: A Commentary on the Nomination and Confirmation of Justice Thomas," *George Washington Law Review* 60 (1992): 969–96; Emma Coleman Jordan, "Race, Gender, and Social Class in the Thomas Sexual Harassment Hearings: The Hidden Fault Lines in Political Discourse," *Harvard Women's Law Journal* 15 (1992): 1–24; John Massaro, "President Bush's Management of the Thomas Nomination: Four Years, Several Books, Two Videos Later (and Still More to Come!)," *Presidential Studies Quarterly* 26 (1996): 816–27; Ken Masugi, "Natural Right and Oversight: The Use and Abuse of 'Natural Law' in the Clarence Thomas Hearings," *Political Communication* 9 (1992): 231–50; L. Martin Overby and Beth M. Henschen, "Race Trumps Gender? Women, African Americans, and the Senate Confirmation of Justice Clarence Thomas," *American Politics Quarterly* 22 (1994): 62–73; L. Marvin Overby, Beth M. Henschen, Michael H. Walsh, and Julie Strauss, "Courting Constituents? An Analysis of the Senate Confirmation Vote on Justice Clarence Thomas," *American Political Science Review* 86 (1992): 997–1003; Alison Regan, "Rhetoric and Political Process in the Hill-Thomas Hearings," *Political Communication* 11 (1994): 277–85; Dianne Rucinski, "Rush to Judgment? Fast Reaction Polls in the Anita Hill-Clarence Thomas Controversy," *Public Opinion Quarterly* 57 (1993): 575–92; Dan Thomas, Craig McCoy, and Allan McBride, "Deconstructing the Political Spectacle: Sex, Race, and Subjectivity in Public Response to the Clarence Thomas/Anita Hill 'Sexual Harassment' Hearings," *American Journal of Political Science* 37 (1993): 699–720; Gerald R. Webster, "Geography of a Senate Confirmation Vote," *Geographical Review* 82 (1992): 154–65.

Special issues or sections of issues devoted to the Thomas nomination appear in *The Black Scholar* (vol. 22), *PS: Political Science and Politics* (vol. 25), *Political Communication* (vol. 11), and the *Southern California Law Review* (vol. 65), among others. Symposia and seminars were devoted to the nomination, and the media coverage of it was exhaustive.

6. The book-length treatments vary considerably—from essay collections and polemics to journalistic accounts of the events surrounding the nomination. See David Brock, *The Real Anita Hill: The Untold Story* (New York: Free Press, 1993); John C. Danforth, *Resurrection: The Confirmation of Clarence Thomas* (New York: Viking, 1994); Ronald Dworkin, *Freedom's Law: The Moral Reading of the American Con-*

stitution (Cambridge: Harvard University Press, 1996); Jane Flax, *The American Dream in Black and White: The Clarence Thomas Hearings* (Ithaca, N.Y.: Cornell University Press, 1998); Scott Douglas Gerber, *First Principles: The Jurisprudence of Clarence Thomas* (New York: New York University Press, 1999); Jane Mayer and Jill Abramson, *Strange Justice: The Selling of Clarence Thomas* (Boston: Houghton Mifflin, 1994); Toni Morrison, ed., *Race-ing Justice, En-gendering Power: Essays on Anita Hill, Clarence Thomas, and the Construction of Social Reality* (New York: Pantheon, 1992); Timothy M. Phelps and Helen Winternitz, *Capitol Games: The Inside Story of Clarence Thomas, Anita Hill, and a Supreme Court Nomination* (New York: Hyperion, 1992); Sandra L. Ragan, Dianne G. Bystrom, Lynda Lee Kaid, and Christina S. Beck, eds., *The Lynching of Language: Gender, Politics, and Power in the Hill-Thomas Hearings* (Urbana: University of Illinois Press, 1996); Paul Siegel, ed., *Outsiders Looking In: A Communication Perspective on the Hill/Thomas Hearings* (Cresskill, N.J.: Hampton, 1996); Paul Simon, *Advice and Consent: Clarence Thomas, Robert Bork, and the Intriguing History of the Supreme Court's Nomination Battles* (Washington, D.C.: National Press Books, 1992); Christopher E. Smith, *Critical Judicial Nominations and Political Change: The Impact of Clarence Thomas* (Westport, Conn.: Praeger, 1993); and Geneva Smitherman, ed., *African American Women Speak Out on Anita Hill-Clarence Thomas* (Detroit: Wayne State University Press, 1995).

7. I will not list them here, but *Dissertation Abstracts* reveals that eighteen doctoral dissertations and masters theses have addressed these hearings in the years since 1991.

8. See Leo Braudy, *The Frenzy of Renown: Fame and Its History* (New York: Oxford University Press, 1986), p. 17.

9. Ibid., pp. 17, 59–60. One need only consider the deaths of Princess Diana and John F. Kennedy Jr. to see a similar celebrity afterlife at work in contemporary times.

10. Thomas N. Baker, *Sentiment and Celebrity: Nathaniel Parker Willis and the Trials of Literary Fame* (New York: Oxford University Press, 1999), p. 7. A different perspective on the history of celebrity culture argues that it is a twentieth-century phenomenon, inextricably linked to the mass-media communication forms of film and television. See Richard Schickel, *Intimate Strangers: The Culture of Celebrity* (Garden City, N.Y.: Doubleday, 1986). Neal Gabler offers another analysis of the role of celebrity in history in *Winchell: Gossip, Power, and the Culture of Celebrity* (New York: Knopf, 1994). For a discussion of the role of fame in the political life of colonial and revolutionary America, see Douglass Adair, "Fame and the Founding Fathers," in *Fame and the Founding Fathers: Essays by Douglass Adair,* ed. Trevor Colbourn (New York: W. W. Norton, 1974), pp. 3–24.

11. For a commentary on the role of celebrity in Hollywood cinema,

see Wheeler Winston Dixon, *Disaster and Memory: Celebrity Culture and the Crisis of Hollywood Cinema* (New York: Columbia University Press, 1999). A history of the Hollywood star system and the inter-action between stars and the larger American public is found in Jib Fowles, *Starstruck: Celebrity Performers and the American Public* (Washington, D.C.: Smithsonian Institution Press, 1992).

12. Guy Debord, *The Society of the Spectacle* (New York: Zone, 1994), p. 38.

13. The role of celebrity journalists is alarming to some who fear that such people lose sight of the need for objectivity and humility in reporting the news. See Richard Davis and Diana Owen, *New Media and American Politics* (New York: Oxford University Press, 1998); and James Fallows, *Breaking the News: How the Media Undermine American Democracy* (New York: Vintage Books, 1997).

14. P. David Marshall, *Celebrity and Power: Fame in Contemporary Culture* (Minneapolis: University of Minnesota Press, 1997), p. x.

15. Greg Siegworth, "The Distance between Me and You: Madonna and Celestial Navigation (or You Can Be My Lucky Star)," in *The Madonna Connection: Representational Politics, Subcultural Identities, and Cultural Theory*, ed. Cathy Schwichtenberg (Boulder: Westview, 1993), p. 307.

16. Edelman offers a foundational discussion of the symbolic construction of public leaders. See Murray Edelman, *Constructing the Political Spectacle* (Chicago: University of Chicago Press, 1988).

17. The role of consultants and polling in contemporary culture and recent political history is summarized by Edwin Diamond and Robert A. Silverman, *White House to Your House: Media and Politics in Virtual America* (Cambridge: MIT Press, 1997).

18. For discussions of the role and power of these factors in political life, see Kathleen Hall Jamieson, *Packaging the Presidency: A History and Criticism of Presidential Campaign Advertising*, 3rd ed. (New York: Oxford University Press, 1996); Michael Calvin McGee, "Not Men, but Measures": The Origins and Import of an Ideological Principle," *Quarterly Journal of Speech* 64 (1978): 141–54; John M. Murphy, "Knowing the President: The Dialogic Evolution of the Campaign History," *Quarterly Journal of Speech* 84 (1998): 23–40; and Michael Schudson, *The Good Citizen: A History of American Civic Life* (New York: Free Press, 1998).

19. James Jasinski articulates this danger differently when he discusses the competing political applications of eros and philia, as conceived by Hannah Arendt. A predominant and exclusive focus on celebrity may create, in Jasinski's terms, a culture of eros characterized by an intimacy that destroys the "in-between." It is the in-between that allows for the distance that permits moral judgment. Intimacy erodes that distance and creates a "[p]reoccupation with motivation

and authenticity." See James Jasinski, "(Re)constituting Community through Narrative Argument: Eros and Philia in *The Big Chill*," *Quarterly Journal of Speech* 79 (1993): 469. Roderick Hart also offers a critique of the political intimacy that television offers. He sees such intimacy as illusory and deceptive but nonetheless seductive for the larger public. See Roderick P. Hart, *Seducing America: How Television Charms the Modern Voter* (New York: Oxford University Press, 1994). See also Trevor Parry-Giles and Shawn J. Parry-Giles, "Political Scopophilia, Presidential Campaigning, and the Intimacy of American Politics," *Communication Studies* 47 (1996): 191–205.

20. See Trevor Parry-Giles and Shawn J. Parry-Giles, "Reassessing the State of Political Communication in the United States," *Argumentation and Advocacy* 37 (2001): 158–70.

21. Marshall, *Celebrity and Power*, p. 214.

22. David Lusted, "The Glut of Personality," in *Stardom: Industry of Desire*, ed. Christine Gledhill (London: Routledge, 1990), p. 251.

23. Marshall, *Celebrity and Power*, p. 240.

24. Ibid., p. 214.

25. African American studies professor Michael Thelwell concludes that had he been under oath, President Bush could have been charged with perjury for his statement that Thomas was the most qualified person for the nomination and that race had nothing to do with his selection. Thelwell further maintains that Thomas reinforced his general lack of qualifications for the Court during his testimony before the Judiciary Committee. See Michael Thelwell, "False, Fleeting, Perjured Clarence: Yale's Brightest and Blackest Go to Washington," in *Race-ing Justice, En-gendering Power*, ed. Morrison, p. 105.

26. Phelps and Winternitz exhaustively disclose all of Thomas's affiliations and political positions in their account of the nomination. One of the most telling examples they reveal, which was not really a part of the larger debate about the nomination, is Thomas's membership on the editorial board of the *Lincoln Review*, a quarterly "whose politics lie somewhere on the far edge of the right wing." The periodical opposed sanctions against the apartheid regime in South Africa, supported the outlawing of all abortions, and advocated the repeal of the minimum wage. Thomas's writing appeared three times in the *Lincoln Review*. See Phelps and Winternitz, *Capitol Games*, pp. 60–68, 81–86.

27. David Alistair Yalof, *Pursuit of Justices: Presidential Politics and the Selection of Supreme Court Nominees* (Chicago: University of Chicago Press, 1999), p. 193. Mark Silverstein also notes the importance of Thomas's personal story and humble origins to the Bush administration's desire for a smooth confirmation process. See Mark Silverstein, *Judicious Choices: The New Politics of Supreme Court Confirmations* (New York: W. W. Norton, 1994), p. 99.

28. Thomas remarked at Kennebunkport that, as a child, he would

never have imagined an appointment to the Supreme Court, and he thanked "all of those who have helped me along the way and who helped me to this point and this moment in my life, especially my grandparents, my mother, and the nuns, all of whom were adamant that I grow up to make something of myself." See "The President's News Conference," p. 801.

29. Mayer and Abramson, *Strange Justice,* p. 30.
30. Marshall, *Celebrity and Power,* p. 213.
31. "Remarks Announcing the New American Schools Development Corporation Board, July 8, 1991," *Public Papers of the Presidents of the United States: George Bush, 1991* (Washington, D.C.: Government Printing Office, 1992), 2:830.
32. "Remarks at a Kickoff Ceremony for the Eighth Annual National Night Out against Crime in Arlington, Virginia, August 6, 1991," *Public Papers of the Presidents of the United States: George Bush, 1991* (Washington, D.C.: Government Printing Office, 1992), 2:1027.
33. "Remarks at the Annual Convention of the National Fraternal Order of Police in Pittsburgh, Pennsylvania, August 14, 1991," *Public Papers of the Presidents of the United States: George Bush, 1991* (Washington, D.C.: Government Printing Office, 1992), 2:1041.
34. "Remarks in a Teleconference with the National Governors' Association in Seattle, Washington, August 18, 1991," *Public Papers of the Presidents of the United States: George Bush, 1991* (Washington, D.C.: Government Printing Office, 1992), 2:1052.
35. "Remarks to the National Association of Towns and Townships, September 6, 1991," *Public Papers of the Presidents of the United States: George Bush, 1991* (Washington, D.C.: Government Printing Office, 1992), 2:1118.
36. "Address to the Nation on the Supreme Court Nomination of Clarence Thomas, September 6, 1991," *Public Papers of the Presidents of the United States: George Bush, 1991* (Washington, D.C.: Government Printing Office, 1992), 2:1123.
37. "Remarks at a Fundraising Dinner for Senatorial Candidate Dick Thornburgh in Philadelphia, Pennsylvania, September 12, 1991," *Public Papers of the Presidents of the United States: George Bush, 1991* (Washington, D.C.: Government Printing Office, 1992), 2:1148.
38. Marshall, *Celebrity and Power,* p. 219.
39. "CBS News Special Report," CBS, July 1, 1991, LexisNexis, Dec. 12, 1999.
40. "Nightline," ABC, July 1, 1991, LexisNexis, Dec. 12, 1999.
41. "CBS Evening News," CBS, July 2, 1991, LexisNexis, Dec. 12, 1999.
42. "Larry King Live," CNN, July 8, 1991, LexisNexis, Dec. 13, 1999.
43. Lewis Grizzard, "Watching the Liberals Squirm," *Atlanta Journal-Constitution,* July 10, 1991, C1, LexisNexis, Dec. 13, 1999.
44. ABC News, for instance, featured an attendee at the NAACP convention, which occurred a week after the nomination, who said,

"When I look at his beginnings, his background, he fits the ticket for me." See "World News Sunday," ABC, July 7, 1991, LexisNexis, Dec. 12, 1999.

45. John Thompson, *Ideology and Modern Culture* (Stanford: Stanford University Press, 1990), p. 61.

46. *Thomas Hearings I,* p. 36.

47. Ibid., p. 53.

48. Ibid., p. 63.

49. Ibid., p. 24. The irony of segregationist and Dixiecrat Strom Thurmond praising Thomas for his ability to overcome the hardship of segregation was noted by many observers.

50. Ibid., p. 66.

51. Ibid., p. 43. Hatch sought to forge a connection with the nominee by revealing that he too grew up in a home without "indoor facilities."

52. Ibid., p. 83.

53. Ibid., p. 108.

54. Ibid., p. 110. At the conclusion of the statement, Committee Chair Joe Biden was motivated to say, "Thank you very, very much for a moving statement, Judge."

55. Ibid., p. 113.

56. These criticisms are expressed most clearly in the NAACP's report on the Thomas nomination. See *Senate Committee on the Judiciary, Nomination of Judge Clarence Thomas to Be Associate Justice of the Supreme Court of the United States,* 102nd Cong., 1st sess., Sept. 20, 1991, pp. 48–124 [hereafter, *Thomas Hearings III*]. See also the *Supreme Court Watch's* report on Thomas, *Thomas Hearings III,* pp. 394–430; and the statement by the Center for Constitutional Rights, *Thomas Hearings III,* pp. 452–65. Other elaborations are found in *Senate Committee on the Judiciary, Nomination of Judge Clarence Thomas to Be Associate Justice of the Supreme Court of the United States,* 102nd Cong., 1st sess., Sept. 17 and 19, 1991 [hereafter, *Thomas Hearings II*], including the statements by the Lawyers' Committee for Civil Rights under Law, pp. 98–232; the report of the National Women's Law Center, pp. 284–363; the report of the Women's Legal Defense Fund, pp. 381–458; and the report of the People for the American Way, pp. 808–31. Also see the statements and reports reprinted in *The Black Scholar* 22 (1991–1992): 120–54.

57. *Thomas Hearings I,* p. 41.

58. Ibid., p. 97.

59. The news media duly reported on the hearings, emphasizing the themes that characterized their prehearing coverage. Much attention was given to the opening statements of the hearing. On ABC, Cokie Roberts commented on the success of the Pin-Point strategy given the racial composition of the Judiciary Committee: "I think that it was especially effective given the nature of the Senate. There

were times when he said discrimination is not necessarily the reason that only white men are sitting on the Senate Committee, but that's the case, there are only white men sitting there, four of them millionaire white men." See "World News Tonight with Peter Jennings," ABC, Sept. 10, 1991, LexisNexis, Jan. 6, 2000. CBS's Bob Schieffer labeled the hearings "high drama" with a "very emotional moment as the son of a poor Georgia sharecropper made his way through a cluster of beaming Capitol employees who had gathered near the hearing room." See "CBS Evening News," CBS, Sept. 10, 1991, LexisNexis, Jan. 6, 2000. *The MacNeil/Lehrer NewsHour* featured extensive statements from the hearings, including lengthy passages from Thomas's opening statement. See "The MacNeil/Lehrer NewsHour," PBS, Sept. 10, 1991, LexisNexis, Jan. 6, 2000. Jeff Greenfield reported on "Nightline" that "In reality, it [the hearing] is a political passion play, a struggle to define who this nominee is and what he means to the country. To his friends and foes alike, what Thomas says to the senators is less important than what he says to the country." See "Nightline," ABC, Sept. 10, 1991, LexisNexis, Jan. 6, 2000.

60. 410 U.S. 113 (1973).

61. Senate Committee on the Judiciary, *Nomination of Judge Clarence Thomas to Be Associate Justice of the Supreme Court of the United States,* 102nd Cong., 1st sess., Oct. 11–13, 1991, p. 8 [hereafter, *Thomas Hearings IV*].

62. Ibid., p. 9.

63. Ibid., p. 10. Thomas also noted that Anita Hill's sexualized charges played into existing and powerful stereotypes of African American men. As he told Senator Hatch (who claimed not to be familiar with such stereotypes), "the language throughout the history of this country, and certainly throughout my life, language about the sexual prowess of black men, language about the sex organs of black men, and the sizes, et cetera, that kind of language has been used about black men as long as I have been on the face of this Earth. These are charges that play into racist, bigoted stereotypes, and these are the kind[s] of charges that are impossible to wash off." Also see p. 202.

64. Ibid., pp. 157–58. For powerful commentary about Thomas's use of the lynching metaphor, see Jacqueline Dowd Hall, *Revolt against Chivalry: Jessie Daniel Ames and the Women's Campaign against Lynching* (New York: Columbia University Press, 1993), and Joel Williamson, "Wounds, Not Scars: Lynching, the National Conscience, and the American Historian," *Journal of American History* 83 (1997): 1221–53.

65. Homi K. Bhabha, "A Good Judge of Character: Men, Metaphors, and the Common Culture," in *Race-ing Justice, En-gendering Power,* ed. Morrison, p. 241.

66. D. L. Crockett-Smith, "Poetic Justice Thomas," *Black Scholar* 22 (1991–1992): 156.

67. For more on the celebritization of Martin Luther King, see K. L. Smith, "The Radicalization of Martin Luther King Jr.: The Last Three Years," *Journal of Ecumenical Studies* 26 (1989): 270–88. Indeed, there is a persistent struggle under way over the collective memory of King and how his celebrity should be constructed. Witness the current reaction among civil rights leaders to Michael Eric Dyson, *I May Not Get There with You: The True Martin Luther King Jr.* (New York: Free Press, 2000).

68. The accompanying rhetoric that emanates from such celebrities reflects the competing visions that each offers of civil rights and how they are achieved. See John Louis Lucaites and Celeste Michelle Condit, "Reconstructing 'Equality': Culturetypal and Counter-Cultural Rhetorics in the Martyred Black Vision," *Communication Monographs* 57 (1990): 5–24.

69. The clearest discussion of the rhetorical dimensions of "whiteness" is offered by Thomas K. Nakayama and Robert L. Krizek, "Whiteness: A Strategic Rhetoric," *Quarterly Journal of Speech* 81 (1995): 291–310.

70. See *Senate Committee on the Judiciary, Nomination of Thurgood Marshall*, 90th Cong., 1st sess., July, 1967; and *Senate Committee on the Judiciary, Nomination of Ruth Bader Ginsburg, to Be Associate Justice of the Supreme Court of the United States*, 103rd Cong., 1st sess., July 20–23, 1993.

71. See George Stephanopoulos, *All Too Human: A Political Education* (Boston: Little, Brown, 1999), pp. 166–68, 170–74.

72. See Simon, *Advise and Consent*, pp. 254–56; and Alpheus Thomas Mason, *Brandeis: A Free Man's Life* (New York: Viking Press, 1946), p. 466.

73. *Thomas Hearings IV*, p. 592.

CHAPTER 11

The Promise and Failure of President Clinton's Race Initiative of 1997–1998

A Rhetorical Perspective

Martín Carcasson and Mitchell Rice

abeled "naive," "lackluster," "rudderless," a "sham," "blind to reality," a "dud," and "timid," President Clinton's race initiative was heavily criticized throughout its fifteen-month existence. Perhaps without actually listening to what had been said, many people dismissed the entire proposition of a national dialogue on race. Others rejected the race initiative as simply a spurious attempt by the embattled president either to deflect the multitude of charges brought against him or to grasp any issue that might assist in creating his elusive "legacy" for future generations. Still others rejected Clinton's strategy because of partisan politics: Conservatives attacked the race initiative as simply a front in the defense of affirmative action, while liberals attacked Clinton's program as timid talk when bold action was needed.[1]

This chapter examines Clinton's race initiative through a rhetorical lens with the intent to better understand both the race initiative and Clinton's perspective on the nation's racial condition. By examining a large sample of the presidential remarks connected directly or indirectly to the race initiative, we provide a focused analysis of a rhetorical performance that was distributed through a number of specific addresses, political writings, and question-and-answer sessions at various meetings. We argue that Clinton's initiative as presented in 1997 and 1998 failed due to three primary factors: the inherent constraints relevant to modern discussions of race, the degree to which the presidential scandals overwhelmed the administration's and the media's time, and the presence of flaws and inconsistencies in Clinton's arguments. The faults include the assumption that the avoidance of difficult issues would somehow alleviate their salience, the contradiction between his rhetoric and his support of affirmative action, and the reliance on unrealistic ideals. Only a few positive outcomes—such as the focus on local "promising practices" and the clear acknowledgment of some of America's past racial sins—can be identified.

In addition to providing a basis from which to understand the program's criticism and failure, this analysis also reveals important themes within Clinton's remarks that unveil his particular perspective on race in America. Specifically, Clinton's rhetoric significantly downplayed the role of past or present discrimination and racism in causing current racial inequalities and was more focused on economic and geographic factors (which followed the work of sociologist William Julius Wilson) and the need for more personal responsibility (which resembled the contemporary conservative argument). Interestingly, these perspectives clearly conflicted with the conclusions reached by Clinton's own race advisory board, which emphasized the enduring legacy of past and presently active discrimination.

We begin this analysis by exploring the background surrounding Clinton's program. Next, we analyze Clinton's racial rhetoric in depth, focusing on three aspects of Clinton's message—the strategic focus on the future, the selling of a particular ideal, and his suggestions for how to arrive at that ideal. Finally, we offer an overall critique of Clinton's strategies. We conclude with some thoughts on the future and the implications of Clinton's perspective.

Background

When President Clinton introduced his national dialogue on race on June 14, 1997, during a commencement address at the University of California–San Diego, he emphasized that the time was ripe for such a national conversation precisely because no current crisis was plaguing the nation. Unlike Presidents Lincoln, Eisenhower, Kennedy, and Johnson, Clinton sought to provoke a major change in the racial climate without an obvious national urgency. By rhetorically presenting his race initiative in this manner, Clinton was attempting to give the impression that not only was he proactively creating an exigency instead of simply reacting to one, but that he also had time to approach the problem calmly and rationally.[2]

Despite Clinton's disavowal of a crisis, the racial climate was nonetheless troubling: The administration's own statistics revealed persisting, and in some cases growing, racial disparities in income, crime, education, and unemployment.[3] Regardless, the absence of a clearly definable "present crisis" more than likely worked against Clinton. Unlike past presidents who could point to something substantial that could be achieved in a relatively short time period (such as the elimination, passage, or enforcement of a law), Clinton's program had no clear purpose and no particular end in sight.

Adding to the difficulty of the situation was the degree to which Clinton's audiences were divided. Earlier in the twentieth century, one could assume the audience for a "national dialogue on race" would consist of two primary camps: white and black. As the century came to a close, however, the audience had fragmented almost to the point of absurdity. No longer was the race debate simply about black and white but also about Hispanics (from various cultures), Asian Americans (from various cultures), and Native Americans (from various tribes). Even these broad labels have been rejected by many who do not necessarily see themselves as a coherent group. The situation is further complicated by the increasing degree of racial intermarriage that produces a large number of combinations that elude easy classification. Some scholars even reject the construct of "race" altogether.[4]

In addition, the fragmentation now extends far beyond the construct of race. For example, the five major "races" can be divided by political perspective (conservative v. liberal; Democrat v. Republican; moderate v. extremist); by class (upper class, middle class, lower class, underclass); by ethnicity or national origin (German, Irish, African, West Indian, Mexican, Argentinean, Korean, Chinese, Cherokee, Sioux, etc.); and by religious preference (Protestant, Catholic, Jewish, Muslim, Hindu, Atheist, etc.). Again, many of these labels—such as conservative v. liberal—defy definition. Americans like to categorize people, but as the United States becomes more multiethnic and multicultural, the ability to categorize becomes increasingly problematic.

Clearly the different audiences will interpret and react to different arguments in different ways. They will typically have varied beliefs about the cause of racial problems, the extent of racial disparities, and the effectiveness or even necessity of possible solutions. Perhaps most distressing is the fact that intelligent, educated, well-meaning people who truly work to solve racial problems tend to gravitate toward two incompatible ideals: a color-blind society of complete integration that ignores racial differences or a multicultural society that identifies and "celebrates" racial differences.

These differences in perspective have important consequences for any speaker addressing racial issues. For example, if one were to cite a statistic about the income gap between races, the average SAT scores of first-year college students, or levels of welfare dependency, members of different audiences would interpret those facts differently. The white supremacist might allude to biological inferiority; the conservative may cite cultural deficiencies; the economist may think in terms of class, not race; the theologian would decry the moral decline of the nation as a whole; the liberal may focus on the enduring effects of past prejudice or the harsh reality of present discrimination; and the suspicious minority extremist might blame government conspiracies.[5] Thus evidence presented to support one claim (discrimination still exists) may very well, for different audiences, support an alternative claim (cultural pathologies exist).

In summary, the primary reason that talking about race is such a difficult enterprise in the United States is the heavily fractured nature of the audience.[6] In attempting to construct a national conversation on race, Clinton was confronted with the task of somehow navigating these treacherous waters. Despite these constraints, the president of the United States is the figure who is perhaps most likely to be able to rise above the various factions concerning race in this country and to make a substantial contribution to bettering the situation. As John Hope Franklin argued four years before being appointed as the chair of Clinton's Race Initiative Advisory Board, "It is too much to claim that the president of the United States, by his words and deeds, can unilaterally determine the course of history during his administration and countless subsequent years. It is not too much to assert, however, that the president of the United States, through his utterances and the politics he pursues, can greatly influence the national climate in which people live and work as well as their attitudes regarding the direction the social order should take."[7] In order to make progress and potentially impact the "national climate," Clinton needed to overcome at least some of the differences among the audiences and achieve some sort of common ground.[8]

The Rhetoric of Clinton's Race Initiative

During the commencement address that announced the race initiative, Clinton pledged to lead "the American people in a great and unprecedented conversation on race." He appointed John Hope Franklin, a noted African American historian, to chair an advisory panel to assist him. The stated purpose of the race initiative was to "help educate Americans about the facts surrounding issues of race, to promote a dialogue in every community of the land and to confront and work through these issues, to recruit and encourage leadership at all levels to help breach racial divides, and to find, develop, and recommend how to implement concrete solutions to our problems—solutions that will involve all of us in government, business, communities, and as individual citizens." During the race initiative, Clinton participated in three highly publicized "town-hall" meetings on race, made remarks at three of his advisory board's meetings, and held an "outreach meeting" at the White House with a group of conservative critics. He also delivered several speeches in which the primary topic was race, though the addresses were not tied directly to his race initiative. On September 16, 1998, the initiative came to an end as Franklin delivered the final report to the president. Clinton was expected to deliver a national address in late 1998 as a response to the final report, but that address never occurred.[9]

Though the town-hall meetings attracted the most media attention, the race initiative actually included a variety of efforts. A "progress report" was posted on the initiative's website in June of 1998. Four major areas are profiled: policy development, the national dialogue on race, the "promising practices" of community efforts toward racial harmony, and the recruitment of leaders "to help build One America." The report describes several programs and initiatives on civil rights, education, economic opportunities, housing, crime, health, and child care that were proposed or implemented during Clinton's presidency. The president's advisory board held several meetings across the nation and examined topics such as stereotypes, crime and the administration of justice, poverty, religion, and the psychology of race. The final report includes exhaustive exhibits of the various programs that the race initiative sponsored, supported, and highlighted.[10]

Three consistent themes are evident throughout Clinton's race initiative rhetoric: his focus on the future; the tactics used to "sell" his vision of the future to the American people; and the policy actions Clinton promoted to achieve that ideal. Each of these topics reveals important details concerning Clinton's assumptions about race in America. Though this analysis focuses on Clinton's remarks that are connected directly to his race initiative, other pertinent messages are also included in order to arrive at a better overall understanding of Clinton's rhetorical approach to race. Clinton's 1996 campaign book, *Between Hope and History,* for example, is particularly relevant because many of the arguments made during the race initiative are also clearly outlined in the book.[11]

Focusing on the Future

Not surprisingly, Clinton fashioned the race initiative with a distinct focus on the future. At times he made that intent obvious with comments such as "I think it's very important that we throw this into the future now, [and] we begin to focus on it" and "I'm looking at this through the perspective of the future that I want to see our country make for itself" and when he urged his fellow Americans to be "concerned not so much with the sins of our parents as with the success of our children." The future had been an enduring thesis throughout the Clinton presidency, particularly since the 1996 campaign, which was based on the theme of a "Bridge to the Twenty-first Century." In *Between Hope and History,* Clinton clearly outlines his preference for the future, writing, "It was clear to me that if my vision of twenty-first century America was to become reality, we had to break out of yesterday's thinking and embark on a new and bold course for the future."[12]

The dichotomy between the past and the future is clearly influential in any discussion about race. By urging Americans to "break out of yesterday's thinking" and think primarily in terms of the future, Clinton reaped some distinct rhetorical advantages while also confronting some significant disadvantages. The major advantage to the future focus was simply the avoidance of many of the difficult aspects of the past and the present. Rhetorically, the past and present represented minefields of opposing perspectives that would impede fruitful discussion. *Instead of being trapped in a discussion of problems and solutions, Clinton designed his race initiative more in terms of setting a goal and then identifying the various paths to best reach that goal.* Thus the most difficult dispute among race scholars—the assignment of blame for America's current racial inequalities—was temporarily rendered immaterial.

Though focused on the future, Clinton strategically examined some aspects of the past, primarily to discuss the history of discrimination levied upon all racial and ethnic groups. For example, in the UC–San Diego speech, Clinton said:

> Consider this: We were born with a Declaration of Independence which asserted that we were all created equal and a Constitution that enshrined slavery. We fought a bloody civil war to abolish slavery and preserve the union, but we remained a house divided and unequal by law for another century. We advanced across the continent in the name of freedom, yet in so doing we pushed Native Americans off their land, often crushing their culture and their livelihood. Our Statue of Liberty welcomes poor, tired, huddled masses of immigrants to our borders, but each new wave has felt the sting of discrimination. In World War II, Japanese Americans fought valiantly for freedom in Europe, taking great casualties, while at home their families were herded into internment camps. The famed Tuskegee Airmen lost none of the bombers they guarded during the war, but their African American heritage cost them a lot of rights when they came back home in peace.

Elsewhere Clinton mentioned the forced appropriation of Mexican Americans after the war with Mexico.[13] By referring to these clear instances of sanctioned discrimination against all of the groups, Clinton was creating the impression that all minorities had suffered at the hands of white America.[14]

Admitting to these sins of the past was perhaps a significant gesture to minorities, but at the same time it placed a heavy burden on whites. One tactic Clinton used to alleviate the accusatory stance against white Americans was to construct the current race problem within a multiethnic paradigm in which each group was capable of discriminating against others, rather than in terms of black versus white or even minority versus majority. At times, this tactic was clear: "To be sure, there is old, unfinished business between black and white Americans, but the classic American dilemma has now become many dilemmas of race and ethnicity. We see it in the tension between black and Hispanic customers and their Korean or Arab grocers; in a resurgent anti-Semitism even on some college campuses; in a hostility toward new immigrants from Asia to the Middle East to the former communist countries to Latin America and the Caribbean." In addition, Clinton did not limit racism to white racism, and he made the claim, refuted by some, that blacks could also be racist.[15]

In summary, Clinton fashioned his race initiative with a focus on the future, a move that helped him avoid some of the most difficult problems of the past and the present. This future perspective allowed him to more easily move the debate to a multiethnic paradigm, which, while more complicated in some aspects, eluded the intense bipolarization that had always existed in the black-white dichotomy. Interestingly, when the past was invoked, it was used to establish the past discrimination of all of America's ethnic populations. Though such comments seemed incommensurate with Clinton's positive focus on the future, the past that Clinton revisited was always several generations removed, back to a time when white racism and discrimination were clear and undeniable. He never dealt with the current difficulty of subtle, rational discrimination.[16] More importantly, *he never linked these examples of past discrimination with current problems.*

Clinton's Vision for the Future: The Ideal

Whereas Clinton could avoid many of the difficult issues by focusing on the future, such a strategy inherently magnified the dilemma over the competing ideals of assimilation (linked with integration, color blindness, and "melting pots") and dissimilation (linked with separation, diversity, cultural pluralism or multiculturalism, and metaphors of "mosaics" and "salad bowls").[17] Clinton attempted to transcend these choices by offering a compromise based on identifying common American values while respecting valuable secondary differences. Thus the initiative praised the benefits of diversity but was titled "One America for the Twenty-first Century." He hoped for an America "at peace with itself bound together by shared values and aspirations and opportunities and real respect for our differences." He asked, "Can we be One America respecting, even celebrating, our differences, but embracing even more what we have in common? Can we define what it means to be an American, not just in terms of the hyphen showing our ethnic origin but in terms of our primary allegiance to the values America stands for and values we really live by?"[18] Clinton endorsed this somewhat contradictory vision of a unified, multicultural society through three primary rhetorical tactics: mutual prosperity, civil religion, and inevitability.

Appeal to Mutual Prosperity

Similar to a corporate CEO's justifying a company's new diversity training or affirmative-action programs, Clinton tried to sell his audience on the monetary benefits of diversity. Perhaps the most powerful tool of unification in a capitalistic society is financial success, a point that Clinton did not miss. Thus when he presented his ideal of a peaceful multiethnic, multiracial, multireligious country, Clinton often enclosed his appeal in monetary terms. At the UC–San Diego speech, Clinton explained how, "with just a twentieth of the world's population, but a fifth of the world's income, we in America simply have to sell to the other 95 percent of the world's consumers just to maintain our standard of living. Because we are drawn from every culture on Earth, we are uniquely positioned to do it." In a speech to the National Association of Black Journalists on July 17, 1997, he mentioned how our diversity was both a "huge asset" in the "global economy" and our "meal ticket to the twenty-first century" and extolled the economic opportunities in the development of South America, Africa, and Asia. The "initiative overview" at the website explains how "All Americans have reason to invest in creating One America." During the Portland State University address on June 13, 1998, which primarily discussed the contributions of immigrants, Clinton relied heavily on economic arguments. He explained how immigrants "give more to our society than they take" by paying "$1,800 more in taxes every year than they cost our system in benefits." He observed that most immigrants are young; therefore, "they will help to balance the budget when we baby boomers retire and put strains on it." Appeals to prosperity clearly resonate with most Americans and work to transcend the various disputes about past problems by keeping all Americans looking forward.[19]

In addition, Clinton worked to solidify the perceived benefits of his "diversity leads to prosperity" claim by presenting a dichotomy that contrasted his vision of prosperity and racial harmony with a future of destructive separatism and animosity. In many of his speeches directed to a predominately black audience, Clinton depicted separatism as cowardly and leading to disaster. As he argued during his address commemorating the Little Rock Nine, "the alternative to integration is not isolation or a new 'separate but equal,' it is disintegration."[20]

Appeals to American Civil Religion

Another appeal made to bolster the call for "celebrating" diversity relied on one particular component of American civil religion: the myth of America as "the chosen nation." This aspect of civil religion has often been used by American presidents, especially during the Revolution, the Civil War, and the Cold War.[21] For example, during the days of the "evil empire," the divisions in America's domestic landscape were transcended by contrasting the righteousness of democracy and the depravity of communism. Simply put, America was presented as the promised land, the "New Israel," the city on the hill, and the country ordained by "God" to lead the world to paradise. With that title came responsibilities, not the least of which was an obligation to provide a moral compass to the world, often making individual "sacrifices" to ensure the expansion of democracy. With the close of the Cold War, appeals to civil religion through anticommunism lost much of their force. The villanized common enemy, the Soviet Union, had collapsed, and the American people were no longer fearful of global annihilation.

Consequently, Clinton was faced with the need to readjust the divine quest of the chosen nation.[22] To do so, he first identified the new common enemy as the potential for ethnic and racial strife. Throughout his comments, Clinton invoked numerous fear appeals concerning the "painful lessons of the civil wars and the ethnic cleansing around the world." In practically every speech, Clinton made references to the racial problems that other countries experienced. For example, in his NAACP convention address on July 17, 1997, Clinton said, "Look at the world. You pick up the newspaper any given day and you find people killing each other halfway around the world because of their racial and ethnic and religious differences. The Hutus and Tutsis in Rwanda and Burundi, the Catholics and the Protestants in Ireland. My people still argue over what happened 600 years ago. The Muslims, the Croats, the Serbs in Bosnia. The Jews and the Arabs in the Middle East." Therefore, instead of showing the world that democracy was better than communism, America would now "stand as a shining example" of a peaceful, multiracial, multiethnic society to a world immersed in racial and ethnic conflict. The Cold War and the defeat of communism, in this sense, was thus just another step toward the fulfillment of the American destiny.

Clinton claimed that the diversity of "our citizens can help America to light the globe, showing nations deeply divided by race, religion, and tribe that there is a better way." He emphasized that "our ability to lead that kind of world to a better place rests in no small measure on our ability to be a better place here in the United States [, which] . . . can be a model for the world." In the 1997 State of the Union address, Clinton linked his fear appeals directly to civil religion, saying, "All over the world, people are being torn asunder by racial, ethnic, and religious conflicts that fuel fanaticism and terror. We are the world's most diverse democracy, and the world looks to us to show that it is possible to live and advance together across those kinds of differences." During the first town-hall meeting on September 3, 1997, Clinton described how America can serve as a "beacon of hope and freedom and opportunity" by celebrating our diversity. These appeals to civil religion, similar to the monetary appeal, were intended to unify disparate audiences in the quest to establish the ideal of "One America" and combined well with the nationalistic appeal to common *American* values.[23]

The Inevitability Appeal

The final tactic Clinton employed to support his vision of the future emphasized the inevitability of multiethnicity. He often cited the demographic figures that showed the increasing levels of minorities and pointed toward the day in the not-so-distant future when whites would no longer be a majority.[24] Time and again Clinton mentioned how some school districts included more than one hundred different racial and ethnic groups.

Whereas the extent to which this appeal was emphasized and repeated indicates that Clinton viewed the inevitability of multi-ethnicity as a persuasive argument, the strategic intent of the argument is nonetheless unclear. To the white audience, that line of reasoning may be similar to the "if you do not lift them up, they will bring you down" argument used by W. E. B. Dubois at the turn of the nineteenth century.[25] The social security of today's young white professionals will be supplied by the labor of tomorrow's multiethnic youth. The argument thus presents a sense of urgency—the inequalities cannot be ignored; they are not going away. The argument can also be interpreted as a kind of fear appeal directed to white bigots, warning them to treat minorities right while they still have the chance because they will soon be the majority. To nonwhite audiences, this "demographic reality" argument could be interpreted as a message of patience and hope, emphasizing to minorities that, as their numbers grow, so will their power. Regardless of the alternative interpretations, the inevitability argument clearly supports the need to endorse Clinton's ideal. It served to shore up his claim that the choice between cooperation and competition was obvious.

The Interaction of the Appeals

All of the various arguments were designed to unify the American audience in supporting Clinton's vision of the future. Together, the three tactics reveal extraordinary range. The appeal to mutual prosperity was based on the strategy of redirecting self-interest toward the common good, whereas the appeal to civil religion was based on the sacrifice of self-interest for the common goal. Both appeals were bolstered by the work of the advisory board, which, by its own account, devoted special attention to the "religious and corporate sectors" because of the strength of the former's "moral authority" and the latter's "power of economic motivation."[26] Finally, the inevitability argument precludes any avoidance of the issue. In addition, nothing that Clinton discussed about the ideal was divisive, a result of his relative avoidance of the difficult issues from the past and present.

Paths to the Ideal: Dialogue or Action?

Throughout Clinton's addresses, he emphasized two approaches that would be employed to achieve his ideal—honest dialogue and positive action. Dialogue was identified as an important first step in the journey to racial harmony. At the UC–San Diego speech, Clinton explained, "We must begin with a candid conversation on the state of race relations today and the implications of Americans of so many different races living and working together as we approach a new century. We must be honest with each other. We have talked at each other and about each other for a long time. It's high time we all began talking with each other. Over the coming year I want to lead the American people in a great and unprecedented conversation about race." Throughout his comments, Clinton mentioned the need for honesty, candidness, and truth. He readily admitted "the barriers to honesty," such as fear, defensiveness, and political correctness, that plagued discussions of race and hoped to work through them. The advisory board presented dialogue as "one of the best tools for finding common ground and developing new understandings among people of different races."[27]

The Role of Dialogue

A main criticism of the race initiative was the focus on dialogue. Critics rejected the notion that mere talk could solve the nation's racial problems, but they seemed to miss Clinton's point.[28] Dialogue was not advanced as the solution but only as the prerequisite to positive action. Clinton seemed to realize that he would not be able to pass his concrete proposals unless some degree of cohesion were formed. The dialogue was meant to bridge the gap between the various perceptions so that Clinton could, in turn, better justify action. This strategy revealed important assumptions about Clinton's beliefs about the nature of American racism.

As far back as 1995, Clinton professed his confidence in the value of dialogue when he said, "I am convinced, based on a rich lifetime of friendships and common endeavors with people of different races, that the American people will find out they have a lot more in common than they think they do."[29] He reiterated that thought during the first town-hall meeting in Akron, Ohio, when he explained the purpose of his race initiative by saying, "what we're trying to do here is drop a pebble in the pond and have it reverberate all across America, because I honestly believe that this is a good country full of good people." At the culminating event, Clinton argued that "We should not underestimate the power of dialogue and conversation to melt away misunderstanding and to change the human heart."[30] His optimism communicated a belief that racism was rooted primarily in ignorance and that interaction would lead to understanding.

Much of the civil rights movement was in large part based on the belief that integration would lead to understanding and subsequently racial harmony. In *Between Hope and History*, Clinton reveals his acceptance of that concept: "Martin Luther King, Jr., said that men hate each other because they fear each other. They fear each other because they don't know each other. They don't know each other because they can't communicate with each other. They can't communicate with each other because they're separated from each other."[31] Thirty years after King's assassination, the assumption that interaction leads to compatibility would increasingly be questioned as racial problems persisted. Even so, Clinton's focus on honest communication was an attempt to carry on that same optimism about interaction despite the contrary evidence of the past three decades. In essence, Clinton admitted that integration had not achieved its goal, but he blamed that failure on faulty communication, not irreconcilable differences. Thus, if integration were combined with honest dialogue, he argued, the color lines could be overcome. This optimistic assumption regarding the origin of racism and racial conflict would seem to have important implications for policy. If racism is ignorance, then interaction and education may be considered viable and comprehensive solutions. Unfortunately, many factors beyond ignorance seem operative, as the sociological and psychological research on intergroup conflict and racial identity has shown.[32]

The race initiative sparked a number of programs designed to facilitate the "broad and constructive dialogue" Clinton vowed to lead. The most visible of these programs were the three nationally televised town-hall meetings President Clinton attended. The advisory board was also very active in holding public meetings throughout the nation. April of 1998 was designated a national "Month of Dialogue," during which more than six hundred colleges and universities participated in a "Campus Week of Dialogue." The board also published a "dialogue guide," which included instructions on how to structure a local dialogue and made a distinction between debate, which concerned persuading others of one's point of view, and dialogue, which simply sought to "exchange ideas and find common ground."[33] In other words, Clinton conceived of dialogue as a tool to foster identification.

The Need for Positive Action

Though Clinton stressed the need for constructive dialogue, he readily admitted that, "If we do nothing more than talk, it will be interesting, but it won't be enough."[34] The actions Clinton supported originated from two different sources: the government and the people. In examining how Clinton balanced these two entities, we should remember that Clinton fashioned his race initiative in terms of an ideal and the path to that ideal, not problems and the solutions to those problems. Therefore, the issue was not whether the government or the people were responsible for the nation's racial problems, but rather what each entity had to do in order to ensure America's future. Though Clinton avoided discussions about the causes of the problems, his suggestions for solutions indirectly revealed his assumptions about those problems.

An important component of Clinton's philosophy on the role of government and the people was exhibited in the three "American values" he used to form the basis of *Between Hope and History:* "ensuring that all citizens have the *opportunity* to make the most of their own lives; expecting every citizen to shoulder the *responsibility* to seize that opportunity; and working together as a *community* to live up to all we can be as a nation. These three values have shaped the character of our people and ensured our success as a nation and our leadership in the world. They are the basic bargain of America."[35] Of the three values, ensuring opportunity would generally be considered a governmental obligation, while the others fall predominately on the actions of the people. The race initiative clearly grew out of the ideas presented in the book, and references to the three values of opportunity, responsibility, and community appear throughout Clinton's comments.

Any discussion of the role of government versus the role of the people inevitably links to contemporary arguments about liberalism and conservatism. In simple terms, liberals argue for the government to take an important role in developing and supporting social programs to cure society's ills, whereas conservatives typically seek less government intrusion and more private effort. Considering Clinton's status as a Democratic president, his opinion would be presumed to be more sympathetic to the liberal argument and lean toward governmental action. However, an analysis of much of Clinton's rhetoric on race reveals just the opposite: an unmistakable focus on the responsibility of the people over the obligation of the government.

Clinton never clearly defined the role of the government with regard to racial matters. Certain issues were repeated frequently, such as the need to improve education and economic opportunities. The educational proposals he cited most often included the need to replace old school buildings, get better teachers in the urban schools, and provide the Internet to lower-income areas. The economic proposals included developing more urban "empowerment zones," improving access to jobs, and continuing community development. Whereas issues such as discriminatory law enforcement and the underfunding of the EEOC were also mentioned, *most of the programs Clinton supported were not designed to combat discrimination but to overcome geographic and class constraints.*

Clinton's regard for the position of sociologist William Julius Wilson is well known, and the influence of Wilson's class-based theories is obvious throughout Clinton's comments.[36] Following Wilson, Clinton seemed to presume that a broader base of people would be more likely to accept class-based programs than race-based programs, which would in turn disproportionately elevate "racial groups that have been disproportionately depressed."[37] Clinton and Wilson took the class-based focus to another level by concentrating on specific geographic areas, especially the inner city. As far back as his 1995 affirmative-action speech at the National Archives, Clinton focused on the geographic argument, saying, "There are places in our country where the free enterprise system simply doesn't reach. It simply isn't working to provide jobs and opportunity. Disproportionately, these areas in urban and rural America are highly populated by racial minorities, but not entirely. To make this initiative work, I believe government must become a better partner for people in places in urban and rural America that are caught in a cycle of poverty."

At the UC–San Diego speech, he reiterated many of these ideas: "First, we must continue to expand opportunity. Full participation in our strong and growing economy is the best antidote to envy, despair, and racism. We must press forward to move millions more from poverty and welfare to work; to bring the spark of enterprise to inner cities; to redouble our efforts to reach those rural communities prosperity has passed by. And most important of all, we simply must give our young people the finest education in the world." This combined *class*- and *geographic*-based agenda was evident throughout his *race* initiative, a point that reveals Clinton's assumptions relating to the nation's racial problems. During the third town-hall meeting, Clinton clearly supported this concept when he argued that "the primary reason for income inequality, increasing inequality in America is that we have changed the nature of the economy." Simply put, *discrimination and bigotry were given short shrift as causes of inequality.*[38]

The one major proposal that could not be justified through class and geography was the most controversial aspect of Clinton's race initiative: the support for affirmative action. Though Clinton attempted to avoid the issue of affirmative action during the race initiative, he was evidently not successful.[39] We do not attempt a thorough review of Clinton's position on affirmative action here, but some brief observations of the role of affirmative action in his race initiative are warranted. During the UC–San Diego speech, Clinton mentioned the need to continue affirmative action, but he defended it in terms of the future benefits received—"a whole generation of professionals in fields that used to be exclusive clubs"—rather than the need to overcome past discrimination. This avoidance of the discrimination argument contrasts with Clinton's 1995 remarks defending affirmative action after the *Adarand* decision, in which he relied heavily on the continuing effect of discrimination.[40] In 1997, instead of repeating his "Mend it, don't end it" slogan, Clinton challenged opponents to "come up with an alternative." This strategy was consistent with Clinton's overall construction of the race initiative as providing the path to some future ideal: He avoided justifying affirmative action in terms of past problems by defending it solely as a necessary tool to reach the promised land.

Whereas Clinton mentioned a variety of governmental programs regarding equal opportunity through the race initiative, messages calling for personal responsibility were more prevalent. Clinton seemingly tried to limit the government's role in racial matters and at times made this point clear. For example, at the UC–San Diego speech, he emphasized that "Government must play its role, but much of the work must be done by the American people as citizen service." During the first town-hall meeting, he reiterated his appeal: "Now, we have responsibilities in Washington, too. There is an economic responsibility. There is an education responsibility . . . . Yes, there is a public responsibility here. But this country, in the end, rises or falls on the day-to-day activities of its ordinary citizens." Both of these comments hark back to the philosophy he laid out in *Between Hope and History:* "Before government responsibility, before corporate responsibility, before community responsibility, we must have individual responsibility."[41]

Responsibility was thus a very important issue for Clinton, and his comments about individual responsibility are strikingly similar to those made by conservative scholars such as Shelby Steele, Dinesh D'Souza, and Glenn Loury. A core argument made by these conservatives is that discrimination is no longer the primary force holding back America's minority groups. Instead, they differentiate between past and present discrimination and point toward the "cultural pathologies" of the various ethnic groups, such as the disintegration of the family, the existence of high levels of crime and drugs, and a mentality of victimization and entitlement.[42]

Though these arguments were often attacked by liberals as racist ideas that unfairly blamed the victim, shades of many of these same premises can be seen in Clinton's rhetoric. In *Between Hope and History,* for example, Clinton makes several comments that demonstrate such conservative principles: "Our Founders . . . understood very clearly something many Americans forget: freedom works only when it is exercised with responsibility. . . . Without responsibility, no free society can prosper. . . . In the absence of responsibility, a mentality of entitlement creates narrow interest group politics, a rhetoric of helplessness, and an inability to serve the larger public interest. . . . We all know that many of them [profound social problems] are caused by a lack of personal responsibility: the teen mother who leaves school for a life on welfare; the deadbeat dad who walks away from his duty to his children; the criminal who preys on the rest of us; the neighbors who turn their backs on the children in need."[43] Though most of these comments are not given in the context of race, the issues Clinton invokes about the lack of responsibility are the same cultural issues that conservatives emphasized when establishing the need for individual changes instead of governmental action. The call for responsibility is not remarkable in itself, but the degree to which responsibility is emphasized at the expense of discrimination is significant and surprising.

Clinton's appeal to responsibility is distinctly evident in the welfare-reform bill he signed, which was titled the Personal Responsibility and Work Opportunity Reconciliation Act of 1996. Throughout the welfare debate Clinton downplayed any linkage to race in his comments; correspondingly, he rarely mentioned welfare reform throughout the race initiative.[44] The bill Clinton signed has no references to race, though some are in place in the original Republican bill that served as the basis of the act.[45] Even so, the welfare act represents a significant departure from Clinton's attachment to the theories of William Julius Wilson, who wrote a book in 1996 that focuses on the disappearance of jobs in the inner city—and thus the futility of welfare-to-work programs that do not actually create jobs.[46] Similar to his avoidance of affirmative action, Clinton tried to compartmentalize welfare reform away from his race initiative. On one hand it was commendable—why should welfare inherently be tied to race?—but on the other, considering the data on the underclass and the welfare rolls, it likely contributed to the charges of timidity and blindness to reality.[47] It represents yet another example of Clinton's avoidance of a difficult issue that required attention in order to facilitate civility in dialogue.

The emphasis on responsibility evident within Clinton's remarks is also deeply in contrast to the conclusions that the initiative's advisory board reached. The final report delivered to Clinton on September 18, 1998, emphasizes many of the topics Clinton seemed to avoid. The report focuses primarily on the effects of past and enduring discrimination and the need to examine the connection between the past and present more systematically. It concludes that "persistent barriers" to full inclusion remain in American society and cites "clear evidence of active forms of discrimination in employment, pay, housing, and consumer and credit markets." The report also reveals a contradiction in Clinton's preoccupation with class rather than race and argues flatly that "Yes, race matters." Antithetically, the report is relatively silent on the issue of personal responsibility.[48]

In summary, a close analysis of Clinton's messages reveals important insights into both the strategy of his race initiative and his concept of race in America. Despite the criticism, dialogue was considered only the first step in the process, not an end in itself. The policies that Clinton advocated were primarily politically safe, empowerment-based policies that sought to improve opportunities without considering the extent of discrimination. In his rhetoric, he continued to exhibit an inclination toward the class- and geography-based concepts of Wilson, which downplay racial discrimination. Unlike his advisory board's conclusions, Clinton's messages focus more on private responsibility, consequently placing the primary locus of control in people rather than government. The obvious exception to these themes is the defense of race-based affirmative action.

Critique

When Clinton announced his race initiative, he promised to make it the focus of his second and final term. Unfortunately, much of Clinton's second term was dominated by the many scandals that plagued him. Due to the intense media focus on the scandals, public debate about all other issues suffered greatly, and Clinton was not able to focus on much other than the defense of his presidency. In this environment, the race initiative was relegated to the back pages of the daily papers and received little television news coverage, and the end result may very well have been the most difficult audience problem imaginable: Nobody was really listening.[49] In addition, Renée M. Smith's analysis of the race initiative shows that the media were more focused on the spectacle of the town-hall meetings and Clinton's role as media performer than on the issues themselves.[50] Due to these problems, it will never be known what could have happened if Clinton, a popular president with exceptional rhetorical skills presiding over a period of unparalleled prosperity and global tranquility, had been able to focus his presidency on the issue of race in America.

Beyond the scandals, the race initiative itself suffered from a lack of focus and solidarity from the Clinton administration. After the energetic kickoff at UC–San Diego, several months passed before any major work was begun. Despite the many attempts to fashion the race initiative as a multiethnic debate, Clinton was unable to avoid charges that the initiative was still monochromatic. The communication between the advisory board and the White House was unclear and at times confusing. At one point, false news reports were given that Clinton was considering a presidential apology for slavery.[51] The coordination between Clinton's comments and the board's actions was clearly inconsistent. Once the administration seemed to have settled on a more focused approach to the initiative, the Lewinsky matter stole center stage.

The primary rhetorical hurdle that Clinton could not overcome was the fragmentation of the audience. The debate about racial matters in the United States is divided in so many ways that no one rhetor was able to transcend these differences and present a message that was acceptable to a sustainable majority. In addition, Clinton's attempt to elevate the issue to the top of his agenda likely worked to galvanize his opponents against it.[52]

Clinton's defense of affirmative action was perhaps the most difficult aspect of the race initiative. In 1995, Clinton had defended affirmative action due to the need to overcome both past and present discrimination. During the race initiative, however, the impact of past and present discrimination was clearly de-emphasized, and Clinton unsuccessfully attempted to avoid the issue of affirmative action altogether. Considering the president's perspective on race as revealed through his various addresses, the continued defense of affirmative action must be considered an inconsistency. If the primary reasons for inequality are class and geographic restrictions, along with the lack of personal responsibility, as Clinton seemed to argued throughout his race-initiative comments, then government-preference policies do not seem the appropriate solution. The defense of affirmative action based on future effect and not past injustice or even current need was unpersuasive to its critics, who maintained that affirmative action caused more problems than it solved.[53] Yet Clinton refused to back down, seemingly aware that the defense of affirmative action was *politically* necessary for him to keep his minority support, especially considering his scandal problems. In a sense, Clinton may have assumed that his defense of affirmative action would ensure the support of the liberal end of the spectrum;

thus, his other rhetoric could cater more toward the conservative end. Unfortunately, the conservatives were never able to get past the issue of affirmative action, and the liberals thought Clinton needed to go much farther than he did in indicting white privilege and establishing the existence of discrimination.[54] In the end, the initiative received the support of neither side and stalled.

In addition to the problems of audience fragmentation, Clinton's strategy of focusing on the future in order to avoid perceptions of blame played well in theory but poorly in practice. Avoiding difficult issues did not resolve them. Simply put, Clinton should not have assumed that his audience would abandon its perceptions of blame and prejudice, especially since his own advisory board was emphasizing them. His lofty rhetoric about future ideals may have worked well to inspire but did little to overcome real, everyday difficulties. The race initiative never approached the difficult issues of the inner city and the American underclass. Problems of race are most evident among those Americans in poverty, where people of every color and creed are more concerned with personal survival than becoming a "beacon of hope" to countries around the word. They do not worry about the benefits of diversity to our international economy, and they remain indifferent to racial strife in Bosnia. A focus on the future may have been necessary to temporarily transcend the difficulties of yesterday and today, but those difficulties are not forgotten for long.

Clinton was also unable to motivate the majority of Americans who did not consider race an important issue in their lives. Clinton's advisory board concluded that their efforts were "quite successful . . . in energizing people who are already involved in activities designed to bridge racial divisions" but also realized that "even stronger efforts must be made to reach beyond the choir." Overall, Clinton's strategy was very similar to the "desire to please, rather than confront" style of issue management that Denise Bostdorff has critiqued regarding the president's 1992 stance on homosexuals in the military. Both circumstances began with optimism and high expectations but ended in disappointment and presidential retreat when opposing viewpoints could not be reconciled.[55]

Despite the fact that the race initiative has been soundly criticized throughout its existence, Clinton's program did make some contributions to the national racial debate. For example, the one aspect of the race initiative that received considerable positive notice was the emphasis on local "promising practices." Considering the difficulty of conducting a "national" debate about race, many scholars felt that real change had to occur at the local level, where the everyday American people interact. In this manner, the race initiative, primarily through its website, promoted the development of numerous local programs that fostered racial goodwill.[56]

Clinton can also be commended for attempting to make a national issue of race at a time when no true racial "crisis" was evident.[57] Perhaps his true intentions can be questioned, but surely there were more simplistic issues that Clinton could have tackled in seeking a legacy than America's "constant curse." Whereas Clinton was generally criticized throughout his presidency as governing through the opinion polls, his race initiative represents an example of Clinton's not following that pathway.[58] In addition, Clinton and his advisory board conceded white America's checkered past regarding Native Americans, Mexicans, Japanese Americans, and African Americans. Clinton openly addressed the inconsistencies of the Constitution, and his board used terms such as "white privilege," "oppression," "conquest," "racial hierarchy," and "domination" in the final report.[59] For an upper-class white male to support these arguments without coercion or crisis must be considered a significant step.

Finally, the race initiative represents another significant marker in America's racial journey. Though the final report of the race initiative was criticized when compared to the hard truths presented in the 1968 Kerner Commission report, it does follow along a well-worn presidential path of self-imposed racial inspections such as Truman's "To Secure These Rights" and Johnson's "To Fulfill These Rights."[60] Much like the present-day form, these presidential programs were overly optimistic in their hope for significant change, but they nonetheless made contributions. Clinton, in defending the race initiative during his remarks at the culminating event, admitted to the enormity of the task, saying, "no one could solve this problem in fifteen months since it has not been resolved in all of human history to anyone's complete satisfaction." If anything, one positive aspect of Clinton's efforts may be that his failures will be taken into account and perhaps even avoided by the next major effort aimed at understanding and improving racial inequality in America.

Conclusion

This chapter has focused on Clinton's discourse as delivered throughout his race initiative, which was announced on June 14, 1997, during a commencement address at the University of California–San
Diego and concluded with the presentation of a final report to the
president on September 18, 1998. In the end, the constraints that
affect all discussions about race, combined with the personal legal
problems of the president and the inconsistencies in the president's
strategies, were too much to overcome, and the initiative failed to
achieve what it had promised.

Looking beyond the race initiative, Clinton's comments perhaps
exhibit a shift in the race debate that has been developing for several years, advanced primarily by William J. Wilson. Even Clinton,
arguably one of the most racially progressive presidents in American
history, spoke of race relations in the United States from a multiethnic perspective that focused on economic class, geography, and
individual barriers rather than discrimination, racism, and conflict.
Clinton's perspective, combined with the Supreme Court's growing
impatience with affirmative action, may signal a new paradigm in
race relations, one that downplays both the existence of present racial
prejudice and the significance of past discrimination. Of course, many
scholars and activists, including those who composed Clinton's advisory board, would dispute such optimistic assumptions and would
be rather troubled by their implications for policy. In the end, the
extent to which these assumptions are based on idealistic dreams,
political opportunism, or fallible public opinion is an important
question that certainly warrants critical examination.

Notes

1. Clarence Page, "Keeping Count: Saving Clinton's Race Initiative,"
    Chicago Tribune, June 17, 1998; Howard Kurtz, "In Dallas, Meet-
    ing on Race Is All-Black and Closed to Public," *Washington Post,*
    Dec. 7, 1997, p. A01; Stephen Holmes, "Critics Say Clinton Panel
    about Race Lacks Focus," *New York Times,* Oct. 12, 1997; George
    Will, "Advisory Board on Race Relations Blind to Realities," *Houston
    Chronicle,* Sept. 28, 1998, p. 3C; Steven Waldman, "Sweating to the
    Oldies," *U.S. News and World Report* 123 (Dec. 8, 1997), p. 35; Ken-
    neth Walsh, "Hand Holding as Policy," *U.S. News and World Report*

122 (June 23, 1997), p. 20; Christopher Caldwell, "The Disgrace Commission," *Weekly Standard* (Dec. 8, 1997), p. 25; Carl T. Rowan, "Race Initiative Must Be More than Just Talk," *Houston Chronicle,* July 4, 1998, p. 16A.

2. At the University of California–San Diego speech ("Remarks by the President at University of California at San Diego Commencement," June 13, 1997; hereafter "UC Speech"), Clinton said, "That is why I have come here today to ask the American people to join me in a great national effort. . . . Now, when there is more cause for hope than fear, when we are not driven to it by some emergency or social cataclysm, now is the time we should learn together, talk together, and act together to build One America." Clinton was even clearer during the published discussion with his race board the day before the speech, saying, "I think this is the right time to do this because there is not a major crisis engulfing the nation that dominates the headlines every day, the economy is strong, crime is down, our position in the world is good." At the first town-hall meeting, Clinton reiterated the noncrisis theme, saying that the country needed to work on "things that are going to be critical to our future before the wheel runs off." Unfortunately, for Clinton and the race initiative, the national "crisis" that would soon dominate the headlines every day was one of his one making: his improper relationship with White House intern Monica Lewinsky. See "Remarks by the President in Meeting with Advisory Board to the President on Race," June 13, 1997; also, "Opening Statement of the President at 'One America: President Clinton's Initiative on Race' Town Meeting," Dec. 3, 1997; hereafter "Town Hall I"). Addresses by the president were acquired on-line through the official race-initiative website, which is now available at http://clinton2.nara.gov/Initiatives/One-America/america.html.

3. One of the major conclusions of a report from the president's Council of Economic Advisors that was released on Sept. 18, 1999, is as follows: "Over the second half of the twentieth century, black Americans have made substantial progress relative to whites in many areas. But this progress generally slowed, or even reversed, between the mid-1970s and the early 1990s. In many areas, large disparities persist." See *Changing America: Indicators of Social and Economic Well-being by Race and Hispanic Origin* (Washington, D.C.: Council of Economic Advisers for the President's Initiative on Race, 1998), p. 2. *Changing America* was released alongside the final report from Clinton's race advisory board, which was titled *One America in the Twenty-first Century: Forging a New Future* (hereafter *One America*) (Washington, D.C.: Government Printing Office, Supt. of Docs., 1998). Both documents were acquired through the initiative's website. Other useful sources for statistics on race, with differing perspectives, include the following: Andrew Hacker, *Two Nations: Black*

and White, Separate, Hostile, Unequal, 2d ed. (New York: Ballantine, 1995), and Stephan Thernstrom and Abigail M. Thernstrom, *America in Black and White: One Nation, Indivisible* (New York: Simon and Schuster, 1997).

4. The "Hispanic" label encompasses several different ethnic groups. For example, in 1992, the "Hispanic American" population was divided among Mexican (62.8 percent), Central and South American (13.8 percent), Puerto Rican (11.1 percent), Cuban (4.9 percent), and "Other" (7.5 percent). In 1991, the "Asian American" population consisted of Chinese (22.6 percent), Filipino (19.3 percent), Asian Indian (11.2 percent), Japanese (11.7 percent), Korean (11.0 percent), Vietnamese (8.4 percent), and "other Asian" (15.8 percent). Statistics from the U.S. Bureau of the Census, cited in Martin N. Merger, *Race and Ethnic Relations: American and Global Perspectives,* 3rd ed. (Belmont, Calif.: Wadsworth, 1994), pp. 290, 339. Milton J. Yinger, considering the differences between "race" and "ethnicity," writes that some scholars believe the term "race" should be dispensed with because "it has too many different meanings or is loaded with too many prejudicial connotations to be of any scientific value." See Yinger, *Ethnicity: Source of Strength? Source of Conflict?* (Albany: SUNY Press, 1994), p. 16.

5. The extreme biological-differences position can be seen at its most profound in the rhetoric of the Ku Klux Klan and Aryan Nation or in the more "mainstream" bell-curve arguments, which, while not based entirely on biology, do make value distinctions between the races. The conservative perspective can be exemplified by Dinesh D'Souza on the far right or more moderately by black conservatives such as Shelby Steele and Glenn Loury. Economic arguments are made by scholars such as Thomas Sowell and William Julius Wilson. Cornel West has a more theological-moral decay perspective, though he still maintains that "race matters." Liberal arguments are made by scholars such as Andrew Hacker, Joel Kovel, and Derrick Bell. See Dinesh D'Souza, *The End of Racism: Principles for a Multiracial Society* (New York: Free Press, 1995); Richard J. Herrnstein and Charles Murray, *The Bell Curve: Intelligence and Class Structure in American Life* (New York: Free Press, 1994); Glenn C. Loury, *One by One from the Inside Out: Essays and Reviews on Race and Responsibility in America* (New York: Free Press, 1995); Thomas Sowell, *The Economics and Politics of Race: An International Perspective* (New York: William Morrow, 1983); Thomas Sowell, *Ethnic America: A History* (New York: Basic, 1981); Shelby Steele, *The Content of Our Character: A New Vision of Race in America* (New York: HarperPerennial, 1990); William J. Wilson, *The Declining Significance of Race: Blacks and Changing American Institutions* (1978; reprint, Chicago: University of Chicago Press, 1980); Derrick Bell, *Faces at the Bottom of the Well: The Perma-*

nence of Racism (New York: Basic, 1992); Joel Kovel, *White Racism; A Psychohistory* (New York: Columbia History Press, 1984); and Hacker, *Two Nations.*

6. Clinton's advisory board described the story of race as a "story of conflicting viewpoints," in which whites and most minorities see the world "through different lenses." See *One America,* p. 44. An interesting, though unfortunately dated, work examining this perspective in greater detail is *Through Different Eyes: Black and White Perspectives on American Race Relations,* ed. Peter I. Rose, Stanley Rothman, and William J. Wilson (New York: Oxford, 1973). Also see Howard Schuman, Charlotte Steeh, and Lawrence Bobo, *Racial Attitudes in America: Trends and Interpretations* (Cambridge: Harvard University Press, 1985), and James R. Kluegal and Eliot R. Smith, *Beliefs about Inequality: Americans' Views of What Is and What Ought to Be* (New York: Aldine de Gruyter, 1986). Clarence Page, in an editorial about the race initiative, puts it well by writing, "Race is a volatile topic because each of us understands it through our experiences, and all of our experiences are different." See Clarence Page, "Keeping Count: Saving Clinton's Race Initiative," *Chicago Tribune,* June 17, 1998.

7. John Hope Franklin, *The Color Line: Legacy for the Twenty-first Century* (Columbia: University of Missouri Press, 1993), p. 12.

8. Identification as a rhetorical concept is examined extensively in Kenneth Burke, *The Rhetoric of Motives* (Berkeley: University of California Press, 1969). The term "transcendence" is used in this context as a strategy that would "psychologically move the audience away from the particulars of the charge at hand in a direction toward a more abstract, general view." See B. L. Ware and Wil Linkugel, "They Spoke in Defense of Themselves: On the Generic Criticism of Apologia," *Quarterly Journal of Speech* 59 (Oct., 1973): 280. Also see the article on which Ware and Linkugel's analysis is founded: Robert Abelson, "Modes of Resolution of Belief Dilemmas," *Journal of Conflict Resolution* 3 (Dec., 1959): 342–52.

9. Executive order no. 13050, issued June 13, 1997, created the initiative on race and authorized the establishment of the advisory board. The first town-hall meeting, on Dec. 3, 1997, was held in Akron, Ohio, and received the most publicity. The second town-hall meeting was held in Houston, Texas, was broadcast on ESPN, and dealt with race and sports. The third town-hall meeting occurred on July 8, 1998, and was broadcast on the *Jim Lehrer NewsHour* show on public television. Clinton also made remarks at the advisory-board meetings on Sept. 30, 1997; Jan. 12, 1998; and Sept. 16, 1998. He attended an outreach meeting on Dec. 19, 1997, which was also attended by conservative critics of affirmative action such as Ward Connerly and Abigail Thernstrom. Clinton also spoke to the Na-

tional Association of Black Journalists on July 17, 1997 (hereafter "Black Journalists"); at the ceremony commemorating the fortieth anniversary of the desegregation of Central High School in Arkansas on Sept. 25, 1997 (hereafter "Central High School"); at the candlelight vigil honoring the Little Rock Nine on Sept. 27, 1997 (hereafter "Little Rock Nine"); and at the White House Conference on Hate Crimes on Nov. 10, 1997. He also gave a commencement address at Portland State University on June 13, 1998, in which he made several comments about racial relations on the anniversary of the original announcement of the race initiative. Considering the president's impeachment trial, the decision to cancel or postpone his major address is understandable. All of these texts were acquired on-line through the president's virtual library, available at http://clinton6.nara.gov/.

10. The progress report was acquired on-line and is currently available at http://clinton2.nara.gov/Initiatives/OneAmerica/accompreport. html. The subjects and dates of some of the advisory board meetings are as follows: "The Value of Diversity in Higher Education," Nov. 19, 1997; "Primary and Secondary Education," Dec. 17, 1997; "American Indian Tribal Leaders and Tribal Organizations," Jan. 13, 1998; "Corporate and Labor Forum," Jan. 14, 1998; "Poverty and Race," San Jose, Calif., Feb., 11, 1998; "Community Forum," Mar. 23, 1998; "Stereotypes," Mar. 24, 1998; "Race, Crime, and the Administration of Justice," May 19, 1998; "Religious Forum," May 21, 1998; "Religious Forum," June 1, 1998; "Race and Health," July 10, 1998; and "Corporate Forum," July 23, 1998. The transcripts of these meetings are available on-line at the race initiative website, http://clinton2.nara.gov/Initiatives/OneAmerica/america.html. Interestingly, in contrast to the controversial Moynihan report, the family was never an important area of concern.

11. *Between Hope and History: Meeting America's Challenges for the Twenty-first Century* (New York: Times Books, 1996) (hereafter *BHH*). Due to space constraints, this analysis focuses primarily on comments made by President Clinton, not on the conclusions derived by the advisory panel, though some comparisons between the two are made later in the chapter.

12. Clinton, "Discussion at Race Advisory Meeting," Sept. 30, 1997; Clinton, "Remarks by President in Outreach Meeting," Dec. 19, 1997 (hereafter, "Remarks at Outreach"); Clinton, "Little Rock Nine;" Clinton, *BHH*, p. 7.

13. Clinton, "Remarks by the President to the NAACP National Convention," July 17, 1997 (hereafter "NAACP").

14. The final report by the advisory board makes this strategy clear: "Each of the minority groups discussed earlier [Latinos, African Americans, Native Americans, and Asian Americans] share in com-

mon a history of legally mandated and socially and economically imposed subordination to white European Americans and their descendants."

15. Quotation from the speech at the University of California–San Diego. The clearest examples of Clinton's perspective on white and black racism are found in his "Remarks on Race Relations at Liz Sutherland Carpenter Distinguished Lectureship in Humanities and Studies," a speech given in Austin, Tex., on Oct. 16, 1995, the same day as the Million Man March transpired in Washington, D.C. (hereafter "Million Man March"). For example, Clinton said, "America, we must clean our house of racism. To our white citizens. . . . white racism may be black people's burden, but it's white people's problem. . . . To our black citizens[,] . . . your house, too, must be cleaned of racism." During the "Little Rock Nine" speech, Clinton added, "Reconciliation is important not only for those who practice bigotry, but [also] for those whose resentment of it lingers."

16. Arguments about current racism and discrimination do not enjoy the same clarity. Concepts such as "rational discrimination," "symbolic racism," and "reverse discrimination" presently muddy the waters considerably. For discussions of rational discrimination, see D'Souza, *End of Racism;* for symbolic racism, see David O. Sears, "Symbolic Racism," in *Eliminating Racism: Profiles in Controversy,* ed. Phyllis A. Katz and Dalmas A. Taylor (New York: Plenum, 1988), pp. 53–84.

17. A tremendous literature exists about assimilation and dissimilation. This analysis was guided somewhat by Marger, *Race and Ethnic Relations,* pp. 385–90, and Yinger, *Ethnicity.*

18. Clinton quotations from the speech at the University of California–San Diego. In the final report, the advisory board defended the use of "One America" after it drew some criticism from those who believed it espoused a call for assimilation. *One America,* p. 105. The report also argues that both the "melting pot" and "mosaic" metaphors are inadequate—"the melting pot suggests a loss of identity, and mosaic suggests that people will never come together but instead will maintain rigid separation"—and call for a "new language of diversity" that would be inclusive and build trust (52).

19. Kenneth Burke analyzes the use of money as a motive and "god term" in *The Grammar of Motives* (Los Angeles: University of California Press, 1945), pp. 3, 355–56. Clinton also used monetary terms to appeal specifically to the white audience. In the speech at the University of California–San Diego, for example, Clinton said, "Let me say that I know that for many white Americans, this conversation may seem to exclude them or threaten them. That must not be so. I believe white Americans have just as much to gain as anybody else from being a part of this endeavor." Additional comments by

Clinton are found in "NAACP" ("Now, in a global economy, in a global society where we're being closer together, it is a huge asset for us that we have people from everywhere else"); "UC Speech" ("more than ever, we understand the benefits of our racial, linguistic, and cultural diversity in a global society, where networks of commerce and communications draw us closer and bring rich rewards to those who truly understand life beyond their nation's borders"); and "Town Hall III" ("I think our society has a vested interest in having people from diverse backgrounds").

20. Clinton, "Million Man March," "Little Rock Nine," and "Black Journalists." At the Portland State University speech, Clinton charged that "pride in one's ethnic and racial heritage must never become an excuse to withdraw from the larger American community. That does not honor diversity, it breeds divisiveness. And that could weaken America." See "Remarks by the President at Portland State University Commencement," June 13, 1998 (hereafter "Portland State").

21. Richard Pierard and Robert Linder identify the "chosen nation" as the first of five components of American civil religion. See Pierard and Linder, *Civil Religion and the Presidency* (Grand Rapids: Academie Books, 1988), p. 48. As a concept, "civil religion" began with Rousseau in his classic *Social Contract*. It was developed further by Robert Bellah, "Civil Religion in America," *Daedalus* 96 (Winter, 1967): 1–18. See also James David Fairbanks, "The Priestly Functions of the Presidency: A Discussion of the Literature on Civil Religion and Its Implications for the Study of Presidential Leadership," *Presidential Studies Quarterly* 11 (1981): 214–32.

22. Craig Allen Smith makes a similar argument in "'Rough Sketches and Honest Disagreements': Is Bill Clinton Redefining the Rhetorical Presidency?" in *The Clinton Presidency,* p. 229. Smith points to the "rhetorical option of polarizing Americans against the common enemies of depression, fascism, and communism" that was available to every president from Franklin D. Roosevelt to George Bush. As a post–Cold War president, Clinton did not have the same option. In the same book, David E. Procter and Kurt Ritter, following the work of John Judis, argue that Clinton faced a situation in his presidency that "with the end of the cold war, Americans' sense of their national mission must be redefined." See Procter and Ritter, "Inaugurating the Clinton Presidency: Regenerative Rhetoric and the American Community," in *The Clinton Presidency,* p. 4; and John Judis, "The Great Awakening," *New Republic* (Feb. 1, 1993): 41–48.

23. The remarks from the last two paragraphs appeared, respectively, in Clinton, "NAACP," "Little Rock Nine," "UC Speech," "Portland State," "Remarks by the President in the State of the Union Address" (Feb. 4, 1997), and "Town Hall I." The advisory board somewhat

echoed the chosen-nation theme, writing, "America has emerged as the worldwide symbol of opportunity and freedom through leadership that constantly strives to give meaning to the fundamental principles of our Constitution." *One America,* p. 9. Clinton's use of both the monetary and civil-religion appeals is curiously similar to that of John F. Kennedy during his Feb. 28, 1963, speech to the nation. Kennedy argued that racial discrimination "hampers our economic growth" and "hampers our world leadership by contradicting at home the message we preach abroad."

24. According to figures displayed on the race-initiative website, the 1997 figures for the nation were 72.7 percent white, 11 percent Hispanic, 12.1 percent black, 3.6 percent Asian/Pacific Islander, and .7 percent Native American. The projections for 2050 were 53 percent white, 25 percent Hispanic, 14 percent black, 8 percent Asian/Pacific Islander, and 1 percent Native American.

25. W. E. B. DuBois, "Talented Tenth," reprinted in *The Future of the Race,* ed. Henry Louis Gates Jr. and Cornel West (New York: Alfred A. Knopf, 1996), p. 156.

26. *One America,* p. 22.

27. Ibid., p. 16. Clinton specifically examined the dichotomy between dialogue and action during the UC–San Diego address, saying, "What do I really hope we will achieve as a country? If we do nothing more than talk, it will be interesting, but it won't be enough. If we do nothing more than propose disconnected acts of policy, it would be helpful, but it won't be enough. But if ten years from now people can look back and see that this year of honest dialogue and concerted action helped to lift the heavy burden of race from our children's future, we will have given a precious gift to America."

28. See, for example, Thomas Sowell, "Talk Is Cheap in National 'Dialogue' on Race," *Chicago Sun-Times,* Jan. 4, 1998. Clinton's townhall meetings have even been described as "presidential Oprah." See Ann Scales, "Under Fire, Clinton Seeks Political Balance: President Takes Race Initiative to Conservatives," *Boston Globe,* Dec. 19, 1997, p. A3.

29. Clinton, "Million Man March."

30. Clinton, "Remarks by the President to the Advisory Board on Race," Sept. 18, 1998.

31. Clinton, *BHH,* pp. 130–31.

32. Consider, for example, Donald M. Taylor and Fathali M. Moghaddam, *Theories of Intergroup Relations: International Social Psychological Perspectives* (Westport, Conn.: Praeger, 1994). The authors outline five prevalent theories that have been developed to explain intergroup relations, including realistic-conflict theory, social-identity theory, equity theory, relative-deprivation theory, and the five-stage model of intergroup relations. For a more psychological perspective

that focuses on black identity, see Beverly Daniel Tatum, *"Why Are All the Black Kids Sitting Together in the Cafeteria?* (New York: Basic, 1997).

33. Again, sources are available through the initiative's website. The quotation about debate and dialogue is taken from *One America*, p. 16.

34. Clinton, "UC Speech."

35. Clinton, *BHH*, pp. 7–8.

36. Wilson's three primary works on the subject are *The Declining Significance of Race: Blacks and Changing American Institutions; The Truly Disadvantaged: The Inner City, the Underclass, and Public Policy* (Chicago: University of Chicago Press, 1987); and *When Work Disappears* (New York: Alfred A. Knopf, 1996). Wilson, a social democrat, does not argue that racial discrimination is no longer a problem, only that class concerns are both more substantial and more treatable. Thomas Sowell argues many of the same concepts, though from a more conservative perspective and with even less of an emphasis on discrimination, in several books, including *Ethnic America* and *The Economics and Politics of Race: An International Perspective*. Geography is linked to class for both Wilson and Sowell. For example, Wilson argues in *The Truly Disadvantaged* that the key theoretical concept is "social isolation," not the culture of poverty (61). In *Ethnic America*, Sowell flatly argues that "Location matters" (11). The advisory board examined some of these issues and concluded that both race and class are salient issues in America. See *One America*, pp. 64–71.

37. During the third town-hall meeting, Clinton said, "I think that the point I wanted to make is to whatever extent you can have an economic approach that embraces people of all races, if it elevates disproportionately racial groups that have been disproportionately depressed, you'll help to deal with the race problem." The fact that class-based programs are more likely to be acceptable is an important consideration in Wilson's theories. In *The Truly Disadvantaged*, Wilson calls for a "hidden agenda" that will assist racial minorities without relying on controversial race-based politics (chapter 7). It should be noted, however, that the Welfare Reform Act that Clinton signed contrasts sharply with Wilson's suggested policy reforms. In addition, considering the research on "symbolic racism" by scholars such as David O. Sears, the assumption that class-based programs would garner more support than race-based programs may be premature. See Sears, "Symbolic Racism," in *Eliminating Racism: Profiles in Controversy.*

38. Clinton does at times mention the existence of bigotry and discrimination, but it is certainly not a critical issue in his initiative. For example, during the UC–San Diego speech, Clinton said, "Though minorities have more opportunities than ever today, we still see evi-

dence of bigotry." During the June 13, 1997, meeting with the advisory board, Clinton responded to a question about his thoughts on "how bad race relations are in this country today" by acknowledging discrimination but then quickly moving to the economic and geographic grounds: "I think they're much better than they used to be, but I think there is still discrimination, I think there is still both illegal discrimination and discrimination that may not rise to the level of illegality, but certainly undermines the quality of life and our ability to live and work together. And I think there is still great disparity in real opportunity, particularly for racial minorities who are physically isolated from the rest of us in low-income areas with high crime rates and low rates of economic and educational opportunity."

More than once he described the racial problems or inequalities as "lingering," such as in the speech to the National Association of Black Journalists on July 17, 1997. The advisory board, on the other hand, focused much more intently on the need to overcome racial discrimination in their final report (see chapter 5). Clinton's "lingering" is qualitatively distinct from the advisory board's "enduring," "persistent," and "active."

39. Clinton received considerable criticism for essentially silencing Abigail Thernstrom's critique of affirmative action during the first town-hall meeting. At the advisory-board meeting on higher education on Nov. 19, 1997, John Hope Franklin reportedly argued that Connerly, an opponent of affirmative action, would have nothing to add to the debate, a comment that was used by many to question the "open dialogue" that Clinton had promised. Later, in December of 1997, at a meeting with top conservative scholars, most of whom were vehemently opposed to preferential programs, Clinton started the discussion by saying, "I'd like to [start with] the question of, 'Do you believe that race still matters in America and is still a problem in some ways . . . instead of your getting into a big fight about affirmative action—although if you want to discuss it, we can." After that meeting, conservative critics continued to attack the initiative as a "liberal monologue" due to the inability of the board to cheerfully allow all perspectives. Conservative Thomas Sowell argues that the meeting, of which he was not a part, was not nationally televised in order to keep the conservative arguments away from the public while still allowing Clinton to "claim to have listened to all sides" (See Thomas Sowell, "Talk Is Cheap in National 'Dialogue' on Race," *Chicago Sun-Times*, Jan. 4, 1998).

Eventually, a group of "prominent conservative activists," some of whom met with Clinton during the "outreach meeting" in December of 1997, formed their own panel to examine American race relations. Headed by Ward Connerly, the "Citizens' Initiative on Race and Ethnicity" group planned to hold public meetings and present their own findings. See "A New Race Relations Panel," *Washington Post,* Apr. 30, 1998, p. A12. Clinton's attempts to avoid the inflammatory issue led to accusations that the race initiative was simply a veiled attempt to protect such preferential programs. Christopher Caldwell, for example, wrote that "The real purpose of the president's initiative is to assemble a bipartisan, multiracial coalition to defend affirmative action against a legal, legislative, and plebiscitary onslaught." See Caldwell, "The Disgrace Commission."

40. "Remarks by William Jefferson Clinton on Affirmative Action," July 19, 1995. Available on-line through the White House's virtual library [http://clinton6.nara.gov/]. The court case was *Adarand Constructors Inc. v. Peña,* 115 S. Ct. 2097 (1995). During that address, Clinton made the following comments: "Despite great progress, discrimination and exclusion on the basis of race and gender are still facts of life in America"; "The purpose of affirmative action is to give our nation a way to finally address the systematic exclusion of individuals of talent on the basis of their gender or race"; "The job of ending discrimination in America is not over"; and "If affirmative action has worked and if there is evidence that discrimination still exists on a wide scale in ways that are conscious and unconscious, then why should we get rid of it?" Clinton repeated the "job of ending discrimination in this country is not over," in *BHH* (131) but never in his comments during the race initiative. During the "UC Speech," Clinton introduced the topic by saying, "In our efforts to extend economic and educational opportunity to all our citizens, we must consider the role of affirmative action." Discrimination had been de-emphasized.

41. Clinton, *BHH,* p. 65.

42. See D'Souza, *The End of Racism.* For example, D'Souza argues that the "main contemporary obstacle facing African Americans is neither white racism, as many liberals claim, nor black genetic deficiency, as Charles Murray and others imply. Rather it involves destructive and pathological cultural patterns of behavior: excessive reliance on government, conspiratorial paranoia about racism, a resistance to academic achievement as 'acting white,' a celebration of the criminal and outlaw as authentically black, and the normalization of illegitimacy and dependency. These group patterns arose as a response to past oppression, but they are now dysfunctional and must be modified" (24). See also pages xiii and 497. Scholars such as Loury and Steele place more blame on past discrimination but still believe that ample opportunities exist for those who seek to take advantage of them. Incidentally, both Steele and Loury have distanced themselves from D'Souza's stance (the preface to D'Souza's second edition of *The End of Racism* examines the liberal and conservative responses to D'Souza's conclusions).

43. Clinton, *BHH,* pp. 61–62, 64, 65.

44. Clinton also avoids any mention of race throughout most of *BHH,* especially those portions dealing with the need for responsibility.

45. Jerry Watts, "The End of Work and the End of Welfare," *Contemporary Sociology* 26 (1996): 409. Watts describes how Clinton was "flanked by several black women and their children" during the signing ceremony that was "incontrovertibly associated with blacks."

46. See Wilson, *When Work Disappears.* Wilson reportedly faxed a memorandum to Clinton soon after the signing of the bill, telling the president that he was "disappointed and very upset" with the welfare bill. See Jack E. White, "Let Them Eat Birthday Cake: Clinton's Welfare Reform Dismays President's Favorite Poverty Scholar," *Time,* Sept. 2, 1996, p. 45.

47. An extensive literature exists about the underclass, but the debate about whether the underclass is multiethnic or primarily African American is summarized well by Donald Massey and Nancy A. Denton in *American Apartheid: Segregation and the Making of the Underclass* (Cambridge: Harvard University Press, 1993), p. 218: "However one defines the underclass, it is clear that African-Americans are overrepresented within in [*sic*] it." See also Christopher Jencks, "Is the American Underclass Growing?" In *The Urban Underclass,* ed. Christopher Jencks and Paul E. Peterson, pp. 28–102 (Washington, D.C.: Brookings Institution, 1991); Christopher Jencks, *Rethinking Social Policy: Race, Poverty, and the Underclass* (Cambridge: Harvard University Press, 1992); Michael B. Katz, ed., *The "Underclass" Debate: Views from History* (Princeton: Princeton University Press, 1993); Michael Kaus, *The End of Equality* (New York: Basic, 1992); Abigail Thernstrom and Stephan Thernstrom, *America in Black and White: One Nation, Indivisible* (New York: Simon and Schuster, 1997); Wilson, *The Truly Disadvantaged;* William J. Wilson, ed., *The Ghetto Underclass: Social Science Perspectives* (Newbury Park, Calif.: Sage, 1993); and Wilson, *When Work Disappears.* Unfortunately, the stereotype of the "typical" welfare recipient evokes images of primarily African American women. Under Clinton's welfare-reform program, images imitated reality as statistics indicated that the number of African Americans on welfare outnumbered whites. See Jason Deparle, "Shrinking Welfare Rolls Leave Record High Share of Minorities: Fast Exodus of Whites Alters the Racial Balance," *New York Times,* July 27, 1998, p. A1. *One America* acknowledges this trend and identifies welfare as "an issue in need of monitoring." *One America,* pp. 66–67.

48. *One America,* pp. 4, 33. The report is sympathetic to many of William J. Wilson's concepts about class discrimination but maintains that race is still an important factor.

49. A reporter for the *Los Angeles Times,* remarking on the issuance of

the final report, wrote, "Good intentions notwithstanding, the legacy of his [Clinton's] advisory board is likely to be a mere footnote in the second term of a troubled presidency." See "Race Panel's Lost Chance," *Los Angeles Times*, Sept. 21, 1998, p. B4. Also see Jonathon Tilove, "Race Initiative Overshadowed by Lewinsky Affair," *Plain Dealer*, Sept. 19, 1998, p. 2a. In Tilove's article, Clinton is quoted as dismissing the notion that the scandal had affected his race initiative.

50. Renée M. Smith, "The Public Presidency Hits the Wall: Clinton's Presidential Initiative on Race," *Presidential Studies Quarterly* 28 (Fall, 1998): 783. The media's misplaced focus on style over substance is examined further in Murray Edelman, *Constructing the Political Spectacle* (Chicago: University of Chicago Press, 1988).

51. Several instances can be cited. For example, no Native American was named to the advisory board, and no Hispanic was originally named to the panel for the town-hall meeting on sports until Felipe Lopez, a black Hispanic, was added late in the process. At the third town-hall meeting, Roberto Suro mentioned the need for the conversation to "go beyond the black-white paradigm that we've worked with for so long," and at the Dec. 19, 1997, advisory-board meeting, which Clinton attended, Chao complained that the debate had been "monochromatic." See "Remarks at Outreach." Clinton's board even admitted that despite their "best efforts," their research "seemed to veer almost inevitably to black-white issues." *One America*, p. 54. *One America* describes America as a nation undergoing a "racial transition." With regard to the lack of communication, see Richard Blow, "Race Wars at the White House," *George* 3 (Mar., 1998): 64–65; and concerning the apology, see Karen Breslau, "A Polite Kind of Race War," *Newsweek*, Jan. 26, 1998, p. 29.

52. Craig Allen Smith has written that while presidential addresses can function to crystallize public opinion, they can also "galvanize the president's opposition, leading to a hardening of the rhetorical arteries and an undermining of negotiations." Comment from "'Rough Sketches and Honest Disagreements': Is Bill Clinton Redefining the Rhetorical Presidency?" in *The Clinton Presidency*, p. 234.

53. Clinton's inconsistency on affirmative action was even more evident during the Portland State University speech, where Clinton argued that "every American should reject identity politics that seeks to separate us, not bring us together." Many opponents of affirmative action argue that it produces more harm than good. For example, D'Souza, in *End of Racism*, argues that "Far from canceling out the effects of wrongful discrimination, racial preferences appear to exacerbate them" (297). In *Content of Our Character*, Steele discusses how affirmative-action policies create a "politics of difference" that leads groups to define themselves through difference (132).

54. For the conservative response to affirmative action, refer to note 44. Examples of arguments calling for more action include Clarence Page, "Race Board Too Timid and Too Wishy-Washy," *Houston Chronicle*, Sept. 22, 1998, p. 28A; and Carl T. Rowan, "Race Initiative Must Be More than Talk," *Houston Chronicle*, July 14, 1998, p. 16A.

55. Advisory-board comments from *One America*, p. 101. Denise Bostdorff, "Clinton's Characteristic Issue Management Style: Caution, Conciliation, and Conflict Avoidance in the Case of Gays in the Military," in *The Clinton Presidency*, pp. 189–224. Bostdorff argues that Clinton's "characteristic issue-management style strives to position him as a moderate through transcendent moral appeals—attractive to all—interwoven with specific promises to specific groups," which has earned the president the reputation as a waffler (216). Much like David Zarefsky's argument about Lyndon Johnson's War on Poverty, such strategies may work well to initially mobilize support but tend to taper off considerably as the difficulty of the task is realized. Zarefsky, *The War on Poverty: Rhetoric and History* (Tuscaloosa: University of Alabama Press, 1986). The public-opinion data in Smith, "The Public Presidency Hits the Wall," also support the argument that the race initiative was unable to inspire the majority.

56. For example, Christopher Edley Jr. writes, "For my money, perhaps the greatest contribution Clinton and Co. can make is to find those promising practices around the country that may be instructive to the school superintendent, the union local official, the rabbi, and the state legislator who want to build bridges but are not sure how." See Edley, "Why Talk about Race? President Clinton's Initiative Is More than a Gabfest," *Washington Post*, Dec. 7, 1997, p. C01. Noted columnist Clarence Page also recognizes the promising practices as perhaps the most useful part of the initiative ("A Disappointing Report on Race," *Sacramento Bee*, Sept. 24, 1998, p. B7). *One America* emphasizes how "promising practices give us hope" (28). In January, 1999, the White House released *Pathways to One America in the Twenty-first Century: Promising Practices for Racial Reconciliation*, a document that reviews the various local efforts highlighted during the race initiative. This document was acquired on-line through www.whitehouse.gov/.

57. *One America* claims that the initiative "represents an example of leadership that seeks to move America toward its highest aspirations. No other president in the history of this nation has had the courage to raise the issue of race and racism in American society in such a dramatic way" (9). Raymond Winbush, director of the Race Relations Institute at Fisk University, though critical of the initiative overall, believes the effort was historically unprecedented and remarks, "To acknowledge this as a national problem and to say

we need to do something about it, no president has done that, not Lincoln, not Kennedy, not Johnson, and that's to his credit." See Tilove, "Race Initiative Overshadowed," p. 2A. Clinton is also cited as deserving some credit for "using the bully pulpit of the presidency to say, 'America, we have a race problem. Let's talk about it.'" See "Racial Harmony in America Requires Will and Work," *Houston Chronicle,* Oct. 2, 1998, p. 38A.

58. Public-opinion polls revealed that racism was not a major public concern before or during the race initiative. See Smith, "The Public Presidency Hits the Wall," p. 782.

59. For example, the advisory board wrote that "A critical component for a constructive and honest national dialogue about race and racism is a greater public awareness of the history of oppression, conquest, and private and government-sanctioned discrimination and their present-day consequences. Fundamental to this historical understanding is an appreciation of the ways in which the long history of slavery in this country has codified the system of racial hierarchy in which white privilege has been protected by custom and then by law." *One America,* pp. 35–36. Similar comments appear on pp. 37, 46, and 49.

60. The comparison to the Kerner Commission report is somewhat unfair, considering the fact that Clinton's advisory board was not an independent body, was more limited financially, and was not in response to cataclysmic events such as the urban riots of the 1960s. Nevertheless, Clinton's initiative was attacked for missing an important opportunity, and *One America* was criticized for being "more descriptive than prescriptive." See "Race Panel's Lost Chance," *Los Angeles Times,* Sept. 21, 1998, p. B4; "Clinton's Race Initiative: Report Descriptive, Not Prescriptive," *Minneapolis Star Tribune,* Sept. 24, 1998, p. 22a; and Clarence Page, "A Disappointing Report on Race."

Index

Abernathy, Ralph, 117
Abram, Morris, 214, 236, 243–44,
    250
Abramson, Jill, 275, 291
Adams, Abigail, 155
Adams, John, 155
Adarand Constructors Inc. v. Peña,
    317
Affirmative Action, 9, 10, 11, 202,
    203, 205, 210, 215, 216, 218,
    220, 224, 231–39, 240, 242,
    250, 251–54, 256, 258, 301, 319,
    321
African Americans, 3, 6, 12, 13,
    17, 19, 21–25, 28–34, 36, 42,
    49, 51–56, 62, 66, 67, 71, 72, 75,
    83, 84, 87, 116, 125, 131, 135,
    145, 147, 157, 158, 159, 161, 164,
    168, 173–77, 190, 205, 214, 260,
    280
agenda, presidential, 5, 22, 84
*Akron v. Akron Center for
    Reproductive Health*, 219
Allen, Roy, 279
Allen, William B., 215
American Bar Association, 55
Americans for Democratic Action
    (ADA), 167, 200
Americans with Disabilities Act
    (ADA), 239, 245, 254
Anderson, Marian, 68
Armstrong, William, 219
Arthur, Chester A., 25, 29

Baker, Howard, 207, 212
Baker, Thomas, 271
Baker v. Carr, 206

Baldwin, James, 175
Bartlett, Charles, 25
Barzun, Jacques, 114, 119
Becker, Carl, 119
Bell, Terrell, 202
Bellak, Alvin, 209
Bennett, Lerone, Jr., 17
Bennett, William, 203, 212
Benson, Thomas, 170
Berger, Warren, 219
Berry, Mary, 204, 205, 208
Bethune, Mary McLeod, 68
Biden, Joseph, 206, 207
Bill of Rights, 71, 75, 85
Black, Edwin, 24
Blackmun, Harry, 219
Blaine, James, 21
Blair, John, 51
Bob Jones University, 212
Bork, Robert, 199, 211, 218,
    220
Bostdorff, Denise, 322
Boynton v. Virginia, 176
Bradley, Justice Joseph, 28
Branch, Taylor, 180
Brandeis, Louis, 290
Braudy, Leo, 271
Brauer, Carl M., 103, 104, 144
Brennan, William, 217
Brock, William, 212, 213
Brown v. Board of Education, 57,
    103, 158, 218, 268
Brummett, Barry, 27
Buchanan, Patrick, 126
Bunzel, John, 206, 215
Burner, Eric, 139
Busby, Horace, 166, 169

Bush, George H. W., 204, 205, 207, 212, 220, 231–32, 238–59, 269, 274, 275–77, 279; drop-by for National Council of La Raza, 18 July 1990, 242–44; remarks at a Meeting with the Commission on Civil Rights, 17 May 1990, 241–42; remarks at the U.S. Military Academy Commencement Ceremony in West Point, New York, 1 June 1991, 250, 254, 255, 256; statements on Civil Rights Legislation, 20 October 1990, 245

Bush, George W., 12

Byrd, Robert, 207

Campbell, Karlyn Kohrs, 62, 63

Cardozo, Benjamin, 290

Carr, Robert L., 86, 92, 93, 94

Carter, James, 201, 202, 203, 235

"celebritization," 269–72, 275–78; civil rights and, 287–89; consequences of, 285–88; political, 272–82; Supreme Court and, 289–91

Chavez, Linda, 206, 208, 210

Christianity, 12, 20, 30, 208, 212, 222

civil rights, 3–6, 9, 11, 18, 20, 22, 24, 27–29, 53–55, 62, 67, 73, 74, 76–78, 84, 86, 87–89, 92, 93, 95–97, 99, 101, 121, 129, 134, 135, 144, 151, 157, 173, 177, 179, 185, 187, 202, 205, 214, 220, 223, 224, 231, 237, 239, 243, 245, 246, 248, 250, 255, 256, 259, 270, 280, 283

Civil Rights Act: of 1875, 29, 33, 216; of 1957, 176, 177; of 1960, 176, 177; of 1964, 200, 209, 216, 232, 233, 238, 239, 240, 243; of 1965, 233; of 1968, 186, 200; of 1990, 231, 232, 247, 251, 259; of 1991, 254, 257, 259

Civil Rights Cases, U.S. Supreme Court, 1883, 17, 27, 29

Civil Rights Commission. See U.S. Commission on Civil Rights

Civil Rights Division, Department of Justice, 211, 212

Civil Rights Restoration Act, 222–23

Clark, E. Culpepper, 56

Clark, Tom, 85

Cleveland, Grover, 24, 25, 30, 31, 32, 34, 35, 44

Clinton, William Jefferson, 127, 198, 256, 260, 290, 301–305; Between Hope and History, 1996, 306, 314, 315, 318; Little Rock Nine 27 September 1997 speech, 310; "Month of Dialogue," 315; NAACP 17 July 1997 speech, 311; National Association of Black Journalists 17 July 1997 speech, 309; National Conversation on Race, 12, 303, 304; Portland State University 13 June 1998 speech, 309; race initiative, 301–305, 306–13, 316; State of the Union 1997 speech, 311; UC San Diego 14 June 1997 speech, 307, 309, 313, 317, 321

Cohen, Jeffrey E., 5

Cold War, the, 7, 77, 84, 86, 88, 92, 96, 101, 103, 163, 310, 311

Collingwood, Robin G., 119

Committee on Labor and Human Relations, 211

"comparable worth," 208, 209

Consultation Conference, 208–209

Congress, U.S. See U.S. Congress

Congress on Racial Equality (CORE), 157, 233

Conkin, Paul, 160, 165

Connor, Eugene "Bull," 68, 121, 168

Constitution, U.S. See U.S.
Constitution
Cook, Blanche Wiesen, 67
Coolidge, Calvin, 41, 45, 47–57,
213
Cooper, Charles, 201, 211
Coordinating Council on Women,
203
Council of Federated
Organizations (COFO), 144, 176
Cribb, T. Kenneth, Jr., 223
Crummell, Alexander, 35
culture, 3, 17

Danforth, John, 203, 256, 283–84
Daughters of the American
Revolution (DAR), 68
Davenport, Charles, 51
Davis, David Brion, 16
Debord, Guy, 271
Declaration of Independence, 21,
71, 91, 97, 216, 237
Demarest, David, 243, 250, 257
democracy, 3, 42, 65–66, 67–78,
87–90, 102, 172, 242
desegregation, 10, 20, 21, 27, 77,
90, 94, 99, 102, 123, 212, 214,
224, 232, 233
Destro, Roberto, 206, 207, 208
Dionisopoulos, George N., 134,
136, 144
discrimination, 62, 72, 73, 89– 91,
96, 97, 99, 150, 164, 201, 205,
206, 207, 211–13, 216, 218, 221,
223, 224, 226, 232, 233, 235–
37, 239, 244–47, 255, 257, 258,
283, 308, 317
Dittmer, John, 117
Doar, John, 140, 142, 149
Doenecke, Justus, 31
Dole, Elizabeth, 203
Dole, Robert, 204, 256
Douglass, Frederick, 16, 25, 28, 29,
68, 243
Dred Scott v. Sanford, 218

Drummond, Roscoe, 185
Du Bois, W. E. B., 35, 54, 77, 312
Dudziak, Mary, 88
Duke, David, 249, 254, 257
Dyer, Rep. Leonidas C., 55

Economic Equity Act, 203
Edsall, Mary D., 236
Edsall, Thomas Byrne, 236
education, 24, 25, 35, 36, 42, 54,
67, 78, 87, 90, 92, 97, 125, 145–
46, 185, 207, 212, 221–22, 223
Eisenhower, Dwight D., 127, 137,
159, 162, 205
Ellis, Edward, 41
Elsey, George, 93
Emancipation Proclamation, 98,
144, 164, 168, 170, 171, 173,
179, 186
Emergency Quota Act of 1921, 45
England, Paula, 209
epideictic address, 169, 171, 187
Equal Employment Opportunity
Commission (EEOC), 203, 274
Equal Rights Amendment (ERA),
200
eugenics, 6–7, 44–51, 56
Evans, Rowland, 163, 185
Evers, Medgar, 116, 127, 129, 144,
145

Farmer, James, 160
Federalism, 4, 28, 201, 216, 222,
223
Fein, Bruce, 217
Ferrell, Robert, 45, 48, 50, 54, 100
Fielding, Fred, 207
*Firefighters Local Union No. 1784 v.
Stotts*, 210, 211
First Lady, U.S., 62–65, 67, 68, 69,
77
Fitzwater, Marlin, press briefing 22
October 1990, 247
Fleming, Arthur S., 204, 205
Fletcher, Arthur, 234

Ford, Gerald, 235
Foreign policy, U.S., 86, 87, 88, 94, 95, 100
Foster, Mike, 238
Founders, the, 47, 199, 216, 217, 218, 220, 318
Franklin, John Hope, 17, 304
Freedom Rides, 144
Freedom Summer, 148–49
Freedom Vote, 147–48
Fried, Charles, 236

Gallup Poll, 5, 130, 175
Gantt, Harvey, 249
Garfield, James, 21, 22, 24, 25
Garner, John Nance, 155
Garvey, Marcus, 54
Gergen, David, 203
Gingrich, Newt, 238
Goldin, Claudia, 49
Goldin, Linda, 209
Goldberg, Arthur, 159
Goldstein, Joel, 163
Goldwater, Barry, 200
Goldzwig, Steven, 77, 134, 136, 144
Goodwin, Doris Kearns, 165
Graham, Hugh Davis, 10, 233
Graham, Philip, 169
Grassley, Charles, 281
Gray, C. Boyden, 232, 239, 248, 250, 256, 257
Greene, John Robert, 249, 254, 257
Griggs v. Duke Power Company, 239, 241, 244
Griswold, Erwin N., 92
Griswold v. Connecticut, 218
Grove City College v. Bell, 221, 222, 223, 224, 225
Grossman, Jennifer, 251
Grune, Joy Ann, 209
Guess, Francis, 207, 208

Haemer, Fannie Lou, 282
Haider, Jörg, 13
Hall, Preston, 45

Hamby, Alonzo L., 92, 97, 102
Harding, Warren G., 45
Hargrove, Erwin, 188
Harrison, Benjamin, 24, 25, 27, 29, 30, 31, 32, 33
Hart, Sam, 205
Hatch, Orrin, 211, 212, 244, 278, 281, 283
Hawkins, Augustus, 241–45, 248, 256
Hayes, Rutherford B., 18, 19, 22–26, 29, 31, 35
Heckler, Margaret, 212
Helms, Jesse, 248
Henggler, Paul, 157
Hennessy, M. E., 41
Herrington, John, 212
Higham, John, 45
Hill, Anita, 269–70, 285–89
Hodel, Don, 212
Hoff, Joan, 10
"home rule," 17
Hoover, Herbert, 44, 57
Hoover, J. Edgar, 128
Horn, Steven, 204, 205
Horton, Ralph, Jr., 158
House Un-American Activities Committee (HUAC), 200
Housing and Urban Development, 204
Hughes, Charles Evans, 55
Humphrey, Hubert, 181, 232
Hurst, John, Bishop, 51–52

ideology, 4, 6, 8, 17, 20–22, 25, 26, 28, 34, 42, 46, 54, 86, 89, 118, 174, 208, 217, 270, 275 276
immigrants, 43, 44, 46, 49
immigration, 43–50
Immigration Restriction League, 45
industrial revolution, 19, 25, 34
Ingersoll, Robert G., 28
integration, 22, 212, 224, 232, 233
International Congress of Eugenics, 44

Jackson, Jesse, 248
James, William, 119
Jefferson, Thomas, 198
Jenkins, Elaine, 211
Jim Crow, 11, 17, 66, 75, 130
Johnson, Albert, 47
Johnson, Andrew, 241
Johnson, Lyndon B., 100, 102, 104,
    157–68, 177, 179, 181, 231, 232,
    253, 259, 260, 323; Cleveland
    Urban League 26 January 1963
    speech, 163, 165; Gettysburg
    30 May 1963 speech, 156, 166–
    90; Howard University 9 June
    1961 speech, 161, 169, 190, 231,
    232, 233; United Auto Workers
    Convention 1964 speech,
    185; Urban League Equal
    Opportunity Day 19 November
    1962 speech, 162, 190; Wayne
    State University 6 January 1963
    speech, 163, 164, 165
Johnson-Reed Bill, 48, 49, 50
Juhnke, William E., 86
justice, 3, 69, 74, 83, 84, 92, 138,
    145, 147, 161, 170–76, 178–79,
    182, 187

Kaczorowski, Robert J., 31
Kassebaum, Nancy, 223
Katzenbach, Nicholas deB., 122,
    124, 159
Kennedy, Anthony, 220, 226
Kennedy, Edward M., 222–23, 224,
    241–45, 248, 254, 256, 281
Kennedy, John F., 99, 100, 103–
    104, 115–16, 118–19, 120, 121,
    122, 124, 129, 130, 131, 134,
    135–36, 138–39, 142, 144, 146,
    147, 150, 151, 157, 158, 178,
    182, 187; inaugural address,
    134; State of the Union
    address, 134
Kennedy, Robert F., 116, 118, 120,
    122–23, 124, 125, 129, 158, 159,
    165, 167, 175

Kernell, Samuel, 4
Kimel v. Florida, 226
King, Martin Luther, Jr., 68, 103,
    116, 122, 123, 126, 127, 128,
    131, 150, 162, 200, 206, 211,
    237–38, 250, 258, 282; "Letter
    from Birmingham City Jail,"
    121–22, 175; "I Have a Dream,"
    173, 211, 237, 244, 251, 258
Kirkwood, Samuel J., 29
Kraut, Alan, 44
Krushchev, Nikita, 131
Ku Klux Klan, 42, 44, 51, 52, 53,
    141, 149, 199, 200

Lamar, Lucius Q.C., 19, 21, 22
Laracy, Melvin C., 4
Laughlin, Harry, 51
Le Pen, Jacques, 13
Leahy, Patrick, 281
Lee, Rex, 221
Lemon v. Kurtzman, 203
Lewis, Anthony, 118
Lincoln, Abraham, 162, 163, 164,
    169, 170, 171, 172, 173, 174,
    179, 181, 186, 238; Gettysburg
    Address, 162, 166, 170, 171,
    181; Young Men's Lyceum
    of Springfield, Illinois 1838
    speech, 177
Lodge, Henry Cabot, 33
Lorance v. AT&T Technologies, 240,
    241
Lott, Trent, 202
Lusted, David, 273
lynching, 17, 29, 30, 31, 32, 52,
    55–56, 66, 67, 73, 74, 83, 85,
    86, 90, 92, 93, 96, 157, 286

McCain, John, 223
McCullough, David, 102
McKerrow, Raymie, 56
Mackey, John, 275
McKinley, William, 25, 30, 31, 32,
    34, 35
Macy, John, Jr., 180

Madison, James, 198
Mann, Robert, 160
Mapp v. Ohio, 199
Marbury v. Madison, 217
Marshall, John, 217
Marshall, P. David, 272, 273, 278
Marshall, Thomas, 155
Marshall, Thurgood, 268–69
Martin, Louis, 125, 160
Martin v. Wilks, 240
Marx, Anthony, 34
Marxian analysis, 6
Matthews, Stanley, 18
Mayer, Jane, 275, 291
Meese, Edwin, 198, 202, 205,
    207, 208, 212, 213, 215–20,
    225; American Bar Association
    9 July 1985 speech, 216;
    Federalist Society Lawyers
    Division, Washington, D.C., 15
    November 1985 speech, 218;
    National Commission of the
    Anti-Defamation League 8 June
    1985 speech, 216
Metzenbaum, Howard, 281
Mexican Americans, 307
Michel, Robert, 207
Michener, Louis T., 29
Miller, Jim, 212
Miranda v. Arizona, 217, 226
Mississippi Freedom Democratic
    Party, 149
Mitchell, George, 248
Moses, Robert Parris, 135–51
Moynihan, Daniel Patrick, 11
Myrdal, Gunnar, 12, 56
myth, 273, 280, 283

National Association for the
    Advancement of Colored
    People (NAACP), 55, 68, 73,
    76, 77, 87, 94, 95, 123, 145, 176,
    224
National Committee on Pay
    Equity, 209

National Conference on
    Fundamental Problems in the
    Education of Negroes, 67
National Women's Political
    Caucus, 203
Native Americans, 72, 73, 204,
    303, 323
Natoli, Marie, 160
Neas, Ralph, 241, 248
New Deal, The, 66
Newman, Constance Berry, 291
Niles, David K., 85, 98
Nixon, Richard, 10–11, 120, 121,
    159, 211, 233–35
Norris, Kathleen, 171
North American Review, 21
Northrup, Herbert, 209
Novak, Robert, 163, 185
Nuñez, José, 208
Nuñez, Louis, 204
Nunn, Sam, 282

obscenity, 219
Obscenity Enforcement Unit,
    Criminal Division, Department
    of Justice, 219
O'Connor, Sandra Day, 203, 213,
    214, 220, 289
O'Neill, June, 209
O'Reilly, Kenneth, 24, 25, 116,
    118, 121, 128, 129
Office of Legislative Council, 201
Osborn, Henry, 44

Palmer, Gen. A. Mitchell, 55
Parks, Rosa, 282
Parmet, Herbert, 254
Patterson, John, 120
Patterson v. McLean Credit Union,
    241
Payne, Charles, 117
Pendleton, Clarence, 205, 207,
    208, 209, 214, 215, 236
Perelman, Chaim, 187
performance, 3, 4, 6, 7, 63

Peterson, Merrill, 179
Phillips, Wendell, 21
Pierce, Samuel, 212
place, 24, 25, 28, 35, 36, 170;
    significance of, 19–20; "politics
    of," 17, 21, 22, 25, 26, 28, 29,
    32, 33, 34, 36
Playboy, 219
Plessy v. Ferguson, 29, 218
Polachek, Solomon, 209
political science, 4
pornography, 219
President's Committee on Civil
    Rights (PCCR), 7, 84, 85, 86,
    89–90, 91–93, 94, 102, 103,
    104; report of, 1948, 90–92, 93,
    94, 98, 99, 102
President's Committee on Equal
    Employment Opportunity
    (PCEEO), 158–59, 160, 162,
    168, 180, 185, 189
Price Waterhouse v. Hopkins, 240,
    241
Prohibition, 42, 85
pronouncement, presidential, 5
public affairs, 3
public assistance, 66
Pucinski, Roman, 180

Quint, Howard, 48
quotas, 214, 224, 231, 232, 234–
    36, 238, 239, 241–49, 252, 253,
    257, 258, 260; immigration, 45;
    employment, gender, 211–12,
    237; employment, racial, 9,
    202, 203, 205, 206, 211, 212,
    213, 214, 215, 216, 233, 237

Ramirez, Blandina, 204, 207
Randolph, A. Philip, 68
Rauh, Joseph, 167
Reagan, Ronald, 198–14, 215, 220–
    25, 235–38, 241, 258; Radio
    Address to the Nation on Civil
    Rights 15 June 1985, 237; State

of the Union 1983 address, 204,
    206; State of the Union 1985
    address, 224
Reconstruction, 17, 18, 21, 24, 25,
    28, 30, 32, 34, 51, 54, 66, 84
Redeemers, Southern, 17, 32
Reed, Adolph Jr., 12
Regan, Donald, 212, 213
Rehnquist, William, 211, 217, 220,
    226
Republicanism, 4
Reeves, Thomas, 117
*Regents of the University of
    California v. Bakke*, 216
Reynolds, William Bradford, 202,
    205, 210–14, 216, 217
rhetoric, 3, 4, 18, 20, 24, 27, 47, 72,
    77, 88, 92, 114, 121, 150, 151,
    156, 160, 164, 168, 169, 173,
    174, 187, 189–90, 210, 217, 225,
    232, 247, 270, 274, 289, 301,
    304
rhetorical construction, 170
rhetorical presidency, 4, 5, 155
Richmond v. Croson, 214
Riley, Russell, 5
Ripley, William, 43
Roberts, Charles, 52
Roberts, Juanita, 166
Roe v. Wade, 218, 219, 220, 226,
    284
Roosevelt, Eleanor, 62; rhetorical
    strategies, 64–65, 67, 68, 69, 72,
    76; civil rights activity, 66, 68
Roosevelt, Franklin Delano, 66,
    72, 75, 76, 84, 155, 170
Roosevelt, Theodore, 35, 41, 43
Rostow, Walt, 160, 168
Rowen, Carl, 161
Ruckelshaus, Jill, 204, 205, 207
Rudman, Warren, 214

Sabath, A. J., 50
Saltzman, Murray, 204, 207
Scalia, Antonin, 199, 220, 226

Schlesinger, Arthur M., 121, 160
Schultz, George, 212
Schwab, Donald, 209
Scott, Robert, 27
"Second Reconstruction," 103, 104
segregation, 11, 17, 31, 34, 56–57, 68, 83, 84, 90, 91, 97, 117, 118, 120, 123, 126, 129, 174, 176, 279, 283, 285; gender, 209; occupation, 208, 209
"separate but equal," 89, 218, 310
Sherman, Sen. John, 29
Shull, Steven, 5
Siegworth, Greg, 272
silence, rhetoric of, 27
Silver, James W., 137
Sinkler, George, 24, 25
Skinner, Sam, 257
Skrentny, John David, 234
Slaughter, Adolph, 165
Slaughter-House Cases, 28
slavery, 6, 16, 20, 23, 27, 28–29, 32, 99, 130, 163, 173, 179, 180
Smith, Curt, 250, 251, 253
Smith, Mary Louise, 205, 207, 236
Smith, Renée M., 320
Smith, William French, 202, 205
Sobel, Robert, 42, 54
Sorensen, Theodore C., 124, 125
Souter, David, 220, 274
Southeastern Promotions Ltd. v. Conrad, 220
Southern Christian Leadership Conference (SCLC), 117, 121
Speaks, Larry, 213
Specter, Arlen, 207
Starr, Kenneth, 221
Stephens, Alexander, 19, 20, 21
Stevens, John Paul, 217
Stewart, Milton D., 93, 94
Stoddard, Henry, 57
Student Nonviolent Coordinating Committee (SNCC), 117, 136, 140, 147, 149, 176
Sullivan, Patricia, 66

Supreme Court, U.S. See U.S. Supreme Court
Sylvia, Ronald, 99

Taft, William Howard, 44, 55
Taylor, Hobart, 181
Taylor, Hobart, Jr., 159, 165
Teeley, Peter, 203
Teeter, Robert, 257
television, 274, 288
Terrell, Mary Church, 35, 68
Thomas, Clarence, 203, 220, 226, 236, 254, 257, 269–70, 274–84, 285–91; confirmation hearings, 280–90; "high tech lynching," 286, 289; "Pin Point" strategy, 275–84, 288, 291; response to Hill, 285–87
Thompson, John, 280
Thornburgh v. American College of Obstetricians and Gynecologists, 219
Thornburgh, Richard, 221, 241, 246, 248
Memorandum to the President 22 October 1990, 246
Thurmond, Strom, 281
Tilden, Samuel, 18
Till, Emmett, 114
time, as rhetorical topic, 65, 69, 170, 175, 178, 190
Tobias, Channing, 97
Truman, Harry S., 76, 77, 84, 91, 323; Civil Rights 2 February 1948 speech, 93, 96–97, 98; State of the Union 1948 speech, 93
Tulis, Jeffrey, 4
Turner, Henry McNeal, Bishop, 35
Tushnet, Mark, 11
Tutwiler, Margaret, 203

United Nations, 86–87
U.S. Commission on Civil Rights, 202–208, 210, 214–15, 236, 243, 248

U.S. Congress, 17, 18, 25, 28, 29, 30, 32, 33, 47, 48, 55, 66, 95, 135, 142

U.S. Constitution, 4, 5, 17, 21–25, 27, 28, 30–32, 51, 52, 56, 69, 71, 75, 84, 85, 92, 95–97, 125, 129, 137, 145, 198, 207, 210, 213–15, 217, 218. 220, 282; First Amendment, 198, 220; original intent, 198, 199, 215, 216–17, 218, 219, 226; strict construction, 199, 212, 220, 269

U.S. Supreme Court, 11, 17, 18, 25, 27–29, 31–33, 158, 176, 199, 203, 206, 210, 213, 214, 240, 269–70, 280, 282, 284, 289–91

vice presidency, U.S., 155–56, 160, 161, 162, 165–66, 167, 182–83, 184, 187–90

Vietnam, 122, 125, 129, 201, 215, 234

voting, 12, 21, 23, 33, 64, 71, 72, 90, 92, 96, 118, 135, 136, 137–38, 142, 146, 147–50, 176, 207

Voting Rights Act: of 1965, 233; of 1982, 202, 204

Wagner-Costigan Bill, 67, 73

Wallace, George, 94, 116, 122–23, 126, 127, 129, 130, 144

Wander, Philip, 12

Ward's Cove v. Atonio, 240, 241, 246

Washington, Booker T., 26, 35, 36, 54

Washington, George, 216

Weinberger, Caspar, 220

Wells-Barnett, Ida, 30

West, Cornel, 12

White, James Boyd, 3

White, Walter, 68, 94, 97

White, William Allen, 42

Wilkins, Roy, 160, 282

Williams, Robert, 209

Williamson, Joel, 20, 29–30

Wills, Gary, 116

Wilson, Charles E., 89

Wilson, Kathy, 203

Wilson, Pete, 249

Wilson, William Julius, 12, 302, 319, 320, 324

Wilson, Woodrow, 30, 43, 44, 51, 55, 83, 155, 170

Winfrey, Oprah, 271

Wirtz, Willard, 159

Woodruff, Charles, Major, 43

Woodward, C. Vann, 17, 22, 33–34, 36

Wright, James, 208

Wygant v. Jackson Board of Education, 213

X, Malcolm, 126